The Sociolinguistic Economy of Berlin

Language and Social Life

Editors
David Britain
Crispin Thurlow

Volume 17

The Sociolinguistic Economy of Berlin

Cosmopolitan Perspectives on Language, Diversity and Social Space

Edited by
Theresa Heyd
Ferdinand von Mengden
Britta Schneider

DE GRUYTER
MOUTON

ISBN 978-1-5015-1656-6
e-ISBN (PDF) 978-1-5015-0810-3
e-ISBN (EPUB) 978-1-5015-0803-5
ISSN 2364-4303

Library of Congress Control Number: 2019939358

Bibliographic information published by the Deutsche Nationalbibliothek
The Deutsche Nationalbibliothek lists this publication in the Deutsche Nationalbibliografie; detailed bibliographic data are available on the Internet at http://dnb.dnb.de.

Typesetting: Integra Software Services Pvt. Ltd.
Printing and binding: CPI books GmbH, Leck

www.degruyter.com

Contents

Section 3: **Commodification**

Section 4: **Localities**

Britta Schneider, Theresa Heyd and Ferdinand von Mengden

1 The sociolinguistic economy of Berlin: cosmopolitan perspectives on language, diversity and social space

The city as a culturally and linguistically diverse place has inspired public imagination and social scientific inquiry for over a century (see e.g. Simmel 1903, Park, Burgess et al. 1925). In sociolinguistics, since the inception of the discipline, it was language variation in urban places that attracted attention, probably most famously in Labov's department-store study (Labov 1972). In an age of globalisation, language practices of urban areas, involving multilingualism, language contact and hybrid forms of language use, form a central focus of contemporary linguistic research. There is a high number of publications and events that discuss, in one way or another, language in the city and regard this as central for understanding multilingualism, the emergence of new and diverse kinds of language phenomena and for the general theorising of language and language use (see e.g. Maher 2005, Creese and Blackledge 2010, Pennycook and Otsuji 2015). This volume on *The Sociolinguistic Economy of Berlin* is part of this heightened interest in urban language phenomena. In taking one city as the starting point, rather than one variety spoken in the city, we hope to open new perspectives on the role of language in social life. The book is a collection of diverse studies on language and linguistic diversity, all conducted in the context of the city of Berlin, Germany. In this introduction, we present a conceptualisation of the study of language in urban social worlds and the theoretical grounding of this book. This is followed by a brief visit to the linguistic and historical particularities of the city of Berlin and an outline of the contributions to the volume.

1 "The city" – new framings of the social to overcome methodological nationalism in linguistics

In sociolinguistics, the city is a fashionable and glimmering buzzword. And yet, despite its popularity in contemporary language research, the city has hardly been

Britta Schneider, Europa-Universität Viadrina
Theresa Heyd, Universität Greifswald
Ferdinand von Mengden, Freie Universität Berlin

https://doi.org/10.1515/9781501508103-001

theoretically conceptualised as a unit of linguistic inquiry. Older publications tend to present cities as given social units that host many different, countable languages (see e.g. Baker and Eversley 2000, Fürstenau, Gogolin et al. 2003). In more contemporary publications, new varieties in cities, their fusions and social meanings become a focus (see section above); we find studies on the particularities of urban visual semiotic practices (e.g. in studies on linguistics landscapes, see e.g. Shohamy, Eliezer Ben-Rafael et al. 2010); on the relationships of time and space (e.g. in accounts of the rhythms in cities, see Penny-cook and Otsuji 2015: ch. 3) or on human-nonhuman networks within cities (e.g. ibid. ch. 7). Cities, in their entirety, as concept and socio-spatial category, however, so far have received little attention and there is negligible thought on what actually constitutes a city. Given that this question has not even been answered in disciplines whose core interest it is (such as social geography, see e.g. Brenner and Schmid 2014), it is maybe unsurprising that we still have no concluding definition of what differentiates an urban from a non-urban linguistic setting (see below in this section for sociological, political and anthropological approaches to the question).

The recently developed *metrolingual* view on language, which eponymizes the metropolis as a term for the city,[1] places central emphasis on language in urban spatial context (see Pennycook and Otsuji 2015). It is here understood that "multilingualism is not merely a plurality of languages but rather a creative space of language making, where rules and boundaries are crossed and changed" (16). The concept suggests to make "central the relations between language practices and the city" (ibid.: 4) and aims to grasp the interaction between people, resources and material conditions in places with high demographic density. Yet, it still remains unclear what the city is and why it is necessarily different from non-urban dwellings. Besides the problem of a lacking definition, within sociolinguistics, there is scant debate on how the different kinds of language practices and language ideologies within cities potentially interrelate – from local dialectal diversity, migrant multilingualism, "foreign" language education to cosmopolitan uses of language, from purist standard language discourse to ideologies on diversity and language acquisition. Additionally, the existence of urban linguistic diversity is rarely discussed in connection to global, national and local social, political and economic conditions (on cities in a global economy, see Sassen 1994), and we observe limited regard to the social and sociolinguistic function of cities in globally connected cultures, economies and language hierarchies.

1 Note that the problematic colonial associations with the term *metropolis*, and its continuing meaning of 'the mother country' in postcolonial countries remain uncommented in the approach.

Methodological nationalism – the "assumption that the nation/state/society is the natural social and political form of the modern world" (Wimmer and Schiller 2002:301), has shaped linguistic epistemologies where languages, broadly speaking, have been operationalized as existing in monocultural social entities like ethnic groups or nation-states (for an early critique, see e.g. Hymes 1968[2]; for examples in the discipline of linguistics, see Schneider 2018). Languages, as bounded entities of culturally distinct groups, have – more often than not – been taken as given and as base for structural linguistic or sociolinguistic inquiry. This epistemological framework has had an impact on the study of urban multilingualism. Even though it has become common to conceive of languages as discursive constructs (see e.g. Makoni and Pennycook 2005), the study of languages of minority groups in urban settings, for example, often does not question the reproduction of ethnic and linguistic boundaries, which may have as well to do with values of cultural heritage as with local politics in the urban area in question. Studying language practices of urban minorities in isolation may give crucial insight into the linguistic practices of social cohorts of people who are understood as socially belonging to each other. It runs, however, the danger of tacitly reproducing methodological nationalism on a smaller scale. The framing of languages as intrinsically belonging to groups that are envisioned as culturally homogenous has had an impact not only on theory but also on language practice and therefore cannot be ignored in linguistic research. In this book, by presenting a collection of diverse studies on the many different linguistic realities in one city and their complex historical and contemporary ties, we aim to slightly change the direction of our way of looking at language in society by conceiving of cities as focal points in globally connected societies.

Society, if we do not assume nations to be unquestioned givens, may be described as involving rhizomatic social ties (Deleuze and Guattari 1977: 11, Deleuze and Guattari 1992), that is, complex relationships and networks that may be of global, national or local character. Networks may be of greater or smaller density, where cities (or typically: particular parts of cities) are places of greater density, as many different kinds of ties meet (see Milroy 1987 on local social networks, see Castells 2010 on the role of electronic information processing in contemporary social networks). Rather than presupposing national, cultural or ethnic boundaries when framing the world, we take the local diversity

2 We hereby want to remind of the potentially unknown contributors to these seminal ideas who may have remained invisible in a work environment that was overshadowed by accusations of sexist discrimination and sexual molestation on sides of Dell Hymes in his function as Dean of the Graduate School of Education (see Elegant 2018, O'Donnell 1988).

of a city as point of departure for linguistic analysis. Thus, by recognising that "the dualities of the global and the local, the national and the international, us and them, have dissolved and merged together in new forms that require conceptual and empirical analysis" (Beck and Sznaider 2006: 3) we want to "make the empirical investigation of border crossings and other transnational phenomena possible" (ibid.: 3). Looking at a city as a knot in a global social context is one way to approach this. Figure 1 below illustrates the world if we do not visualize it according to a national 'container model' of culture (Pries 2008) but according to a global network that typically constitutes focal points where cities are located.

Figure 1: Visualisation of global networks, here the case of scientific collaboration. Beauchesne & SCImage Lab 2014.

The linguistic conditions of a city are shaped by the manifold translocal connections that the inhabitants of cities bring along or activate. Therefore, the study of the linguistic repertoires of a city, where we understand these as embedded in complex transnational, national and local discursive contexts, means to develop research perspectives on language beyond methodological nationalism – that is: beyond essentialist concepts of languages as bounded entities. If we want to understand languages in a globally connected world that cannot be conceived as consisting of social units that are "normally" homogenous, it makes sense to consider research settings other than nations or ethnic groups for sociolinguistic inquiry. This does not mean to ignore that nationality and ethnicity continue to be central in language practice and affiliation. Some studies in this book thus do take ethnic or national background as reference point. However, these individual approaches reveal fine-grained insight about how ethnic practices interact in a city, and acquire new and sometimes unexpected social meanings. Thus an in fact heterogeneous concept like Arabic, widely considered as "one language" and as such stigmatized in the local language ideologies of Berlin, can act as an indicator of upward mobility under specific conditions (see Stock). Vietnamese traders in Berlin-Lichtenberg are shown to have translocal ties with many other ethnic communities (see Hüwelmeier). We see how the local social meaning of "being Italian" changes over the years, relating to processes of social change in Italy and Berlin alike, which is indicated by semiotic practices in Italian restaurant names (see Pichler).

It is vital to note that these translocal practices take place against the background of historical linguistic change of the locally dominant German variety (see Auer), the continuing use of the local dialect *Berlinisch* (see Schlobinski) and national language policies that foster ideologies of monolingualism and monoculturalism (see Tanager). These more traditional practices and ideological framings contrast with language use that is not straightforwardly tied to ethnic belonging as in the local multi-ethnic vernacular *Kiezdeutsch* (see Jannedy, Mendoza-Denton and Weirich and Bunk and Pohle), or in uses of English in elite contexts like the Berlin artist community (see Farrell). We get insight into the multiple indexical functions of fused resources of English-German bilinguals from a school in the wealthy district of Steglitz-Zehlendorf (see Schulte), and into the commodified perspectives on the acquisition of Spanish in the Berlin education sector and hotel business (see Krämer). A closer look at material linguistic and semiotic practices in central parts of the city reveals the public presence of resources that are traditionally associated with "other" places in the local linguistic landscape (see Fuller and Özcan) and a glimpse into the linguistic reality of the inhabitants of one *Mietshaus* (pre-WWII residential building) shows that we find linguistic diversity and chronotopic complexity (Blommaert 2015) even on a scale as small as a house or at an individual level (see Stevenson).

In this sense, the city-centric perspective that we propose here reveals diversity, translocal ties and inter-ethnic relationships that go well beyond established categories of diasporic pockets or ethnic speech communities. The role of contemporary discourses on the instrumental or social value of languages also comes to the fore. We see that the way linguistic resources can be commodified – or not – impacts on their possibility to become visible and on the way their presence is discursively negotiated. Thus, Heller's and Duchêne's work, showing that value is no longer only attributed to languages on grounds of expressing national/ethnic pride and solidarity but can be based on their potential to gain economic profit (Heller 2003, Heller and Duchêne 2012a) is relevant to interpret the translocal indexical meanings of languages in Berlin. This is very obvious in the discourses attached to the acquisition of Spanish in the local hotel industry (Krämer) and in the way English is celebrated (see Farrell and Schulte) but has to be considered also in the discourses around the local multi-ethnic vernacular Kiezdeutsch (Bunk and Pohle, Jannedy, Weinrich and Mendoza-Denton), which works like an antithesis to neoliberal discourses on languages as an economic asset. As a whole, our collection attempts to move towards an empirical understanding of the sociolinguistic complexity of the socio-spatial category of "city". We understand the city to be characterised by its multiple internal and external interrelationships, where local diversity is embedded in contemporary and historical discourses from different places that operate on different scales (Blommaert 2015). The value of the same linguistic resource therefore depends on simultaneously existing discourses and can be multiple as well – from valuable marker of solidarity to a threat to national unity, from mobile chic to precarious lack of competence.

2 Language, cities and economies

Along these lines, the study of a city as a place of different types of linguistic diversity, allowing insights into simultaneously existing chronotopes – the different time-spatial arrangements attached to different linguistic resources (see Blommaert 2015 on chronotopes) – in one territorial place, creates an understanding of language in a social world that is globally connected and locally diverse. And regardless to what extent diversity has reached new dimensions – popularly put forward in the postulation of contemporary *superdiversity* (Vertovec 2007, Blommaert and Rampton 2011) – we believe trans-local connections and local diversities to be phenomena as old as humankind. Cities are social spaces that have always been multilingual and diverse, as markets and trade relations have been central for the development of towns since ancient times (Clark 2016).[3] The question of how constructions and practices of homogeneity, national standard languages in particular, became stable and frequent and of the future of these discourses and practices of stability in the face of contemporary complexity, becomes at least as urgent as the study of diversity. In any case, economic relations seem to play a crucial role in the formation of

3 See https://worldmap.harvard.edu/maps/europeoutlinemap on the link of trade routes and cities from the Roman Empire to the Middle Ages in Europe, which illustrates the interrelations of trade and the development of urbanity.

cities as well as in the formation of linguistic diversity (on the role of economic practices in linguistic homogeneity, see Schneider 2017).

Given the lack of answers to the question of what actually is a city in the context of sociolinguistic and linguistic anthropological research, we turn to theoretical approaches on the urban condition in sociology, human geography and cultural anthropology, which conceive of the city as a discursive and socio-spatial entity that is dialectically related to global economic forces (Urry and Gregory 1985, Sennett 2005). Cities have a central role in the global economy (Sassen 1994) and economic practices are and always have been crucial for the emergence of demographically dense spaces in which people of diverse social, cultural and linguistic backgrounds intermingle. Besides leading to demographic density and cultural diversity, economic discourses and practices co-produce social value and affect what is considered prestige (as has been discussed in analyses on the commodification of language, see Heller 2003, Heller and Duchêne 2012b). Clothes, lifestyles and ways of talking of New York, Berlin or Lagos typically function as model, those from provincial villages not so much. Many standard languages are based on varieties spoken in urban capitals. Urban ways of living thus have an effect on social relations and are therefore also relevant for language as a social practice, for language diversity and homogeneity, and for the conceptualisation of sociolinguistic relationships and hierarchies.

The distinct symbolic and practical values that languages, varieties and their speakers represent in particular contexts is what Blommaert and others have referred to as *sociolinguistic economy* (Blommaert, Collins et al. 2005: 201). The term economy – similarly to its etymological history, where it at one point meant household management (*oĩkos* 'house', *nómos* 'law, manage', see New Oxford American Dictionary 2009) – here not only relates to monetary or financial aspects of social life but also extends to Bourdieu's concept of the different kinds of *capital* (financial, social, cultural, see e.g. Bourdieu 1992), which in combination constitute the status of an individual in society. We use the concept of the sociolinguistic economy in this holistic sense, as encompassing the different kinds of value that are interrelated to and co-produced by language, where financial economies ("economy" in today's everyday meaning) are linked to the symbolic values that linguistic repertoires may have, but where, simultaneously, the different repertoires of a city engage in a symbolic economic relationship, or rather, their speakers do. As the particular sociolinguistic economy of a place shapes the framing and ideological meaning of language in specific ways, we can observe that "multilingualism is not what individuals have and don't have, but what the environment, as structured determinations and interactional emergence, enables and disables." (Blommaert,

Collins et al. 2005: 197). The "environment", in the case of a city, needs to be understood as encompassing the actual spatial materialities (as focused on in accounts of linguistic landscapes but also in metrolingualism, see Pennycook and Otsuji 2015) and the complex ties to other places, near and far, old and new.

At the same time, cities do form part of very concrete financial economic orders, like, for example, the global real estate market, which interacts with the commodification of linguistic and other cultural resources and in some (typically more expensive) parts of cities, with an emerging tacit norm of standardised elite multilingualism. The different socio-economic and cultural conditions under which different linguistic repertoires exist and emerge are crucial aspects for understanding the social functions of language in a globally stratified economy. The sociolinguistic economy of a city furthermore involves specific features of urban geography, such as high density or the emergence of and potential interaction between close-knit communities such as "Little Istanbuls" or "Chinatowns". In addition, it can be posited that the organization of public space and structures of a city can have an impact on its linguistic constitution: thus we may think of the presence and absence of public spaces like parks and places, enabling or disabling communicative events, to the importance of public transport routes and routines, to physically limiting artefacts such as the Wall in the history of Berlin. Besides, it is non-territorial economic and neoliberal discourses that may impact on the contribution of value or on the devaluing of speech practices, among them modernist ideologies of purism and regularity, neoliberal discourses that regard language primarily in an instrumentalist manner (see e.g. Heller and Duchêne 2012b) and the manifold practices of digital communication, social media and the representation of language and culture in online space that may contribute to discourses that value creativity and hybridity.

3 Methodological cosmopolitanism

An outlook on language as essentially interwoven with social space, where social space is not understood as materialising in different cultural categories, imagined as internally homogenous, but as being constituted by globally interwoven relationships, corresponds to the notion of "methodological cosmopolitanism" (Beck and Sznaider 2006: 3). Cosmopolitanism is another buzzword of our times and, very roughly speaking, simply means "including people from many different countries and cultures" (New Oxford American Dictionary 2009). Oftentimes, cosmopolitanism is understood as having a normative dimension, particularly in philosophical debate, where an attitude of "world citizenship", above cultural, religious or ethnic affiliation, is regarded as an ideal (on the ethics of cosmopolitanism, see e.g. Appiah 2006). This understanding of cosmopolitanism displays similarities to the everyday conceptualisation of the term, which tends to refer to practices and identities that associate with mobile social elites. Cultural anthropologists in the 1990s also regarded cosmopolitanism to be found primarily in the upper social strata (see e.g. Hannerz 1996). Cosmopolitanism, in these earlier texts, was defined as "first of all an orientation, a willingness to engage with the Other." (Hannerz 1996: 103). This engagement results in a changed relationship to the culture of origin as contact and cultural competence in a different culture imply "personal autonomy vis-á-vis the culture where he [sic.] originated." (ibid.: 104). Thus, the cosmopolitan develops cultural meta-knowledge, which enables her or him to understand systems of meaning of origin as non-natural. Cosmopolitanism is thus understood as leading to the development of cultural meta-knowledge and to the ability to construct a non-naturalised relationship to the culture of origin, in other words, a reflexive awareness regarding cultural categories like "nation" or "culture" in general. Based on this particular understanding, "methodological cosmopolitanism" is an epistemological framework that considers cultural (and in our case: linguistic) categories not as natural givens but as, discursively constructed realities that need to be understood from a wider meta-perspective. It "does not mean, of course, that a cosmopolitan social science can and should ignore different national traditions of law, history, politics and memory. These traditions exist and become part of our cosmopolitan methodology." (Beck and Sznaider 2006: 3). The same is true, of course, for national traditions of linguistics.

In the context of these discussions, there is a call to treat cosmopolitanism as existing "on the ground" and as part of very real and not necessarily elite or ideal social conditions (see e.g. Römhild 2007). These accounts of "grassroots" cosmopolitanism argue that we can discover cosmopolitan developments in a large number of everyday social practices and relationships, such as, for example, multilingual families, cross-national consumption, work-life interaction, or transnational companies and institutional structures like NGOs. Such views on the cosmopolitan condition assume that there is an on-going process of *cosmopolitanization*, which "happens "from within" and which, therefore, "dissolves the 'onion model' of the world, where the local and the national form the core and inner layer and the international and the global form the outer layers" (Beck and Sznaider 2006: 6). This concept of cosmopolitanization fits well with the approach taken in this volume, which studies the presence, function and status of the different languages and language ideologies on the scale of a city in order to understand "really-existing relations of interdependence" (ibid.) in a framing of the social that is essentially global.[4]

It needs to be emphasised that cosmopolitanization "from within" does not primarily mean the fragmentation of social life. The traditional social units of nation or ethnicity may no longer be as dominant in defining legitimate and preeminent forms of linguistic or cultural practice in specific territories. Migrants for example, may not integrate (assimilate?) into dominant linguistic practices in the way it is desired by dominant public discourses. And yet, most people do become affiliated with at least some social contexts that exist in their local territorially close realms. These are often contexts that are transnational in nature (if they consider one place to be their common origin, they are also referred to as diaspora, see Clifford 1994). We thus do find manifold ways of "integrating" into local social life – albeit maybe not or not only or not primarily into those social units that have been the target of official integration policies, i.e. majority groups. Consider, for example, the case of the communication network of a Cameroonian student in Ghent that Brandehof introduces (Brandehof 2014, quoted in Blommaert 2018: 75). The student interacts on a regular basis with people in Ghent, Cameroon, and, for private and job-related reasons, in other African and European countries, making use of diverse media, among them face-to-face talk, telephone, instant messaging, VoIP, and other forms of digital linguistic practice. He uses a variety of different languages, from Fulbe, Pidgin and Vengo to English and Pidgin (the local Dutch is not part of his daily repertoire). He is thus embedded in different social networks that spread globally and his linguistic resources are adapted to these specific communicative needs. Studying the social functions of languages in cities, we can observe how particular linguistic resources serve to socially integrate into transnational, often, but not necessarily, ethnic kinds of communities that interact with other forms of local, national and transnational social organization (e.g. other minority groups, the majority society, job-related networks, local political initiatives, religious or educational institutions, ethnically shaped economic enterprises, sports associations, . . .). Based on the observation that individuals such as the Cameroonian student in Ghent thus do not lead an isolated, lonely life among culturally alien Belgians but are part of very lively translocal contexts, we see that "emotional engagement and social integration and not only fragmentation [are] part of the cosmopolitan world" (Beck and Sznaider 2006: 8). It is, at the same time,

4 It needs to be noted that the sociological use of "cosmopolitanism" is specific and so far rather limited to the debates mentioned. In everyday communication, it continues to refer to practices and identity constructions of mobile social elites, an understanding of the term to which we return in a later part of this text.

important to ask what these individualised networks imply for communication and for the reproduction of shared rules of linguistic behaviour.

Considering the complex communicative and mediated processes involved in the formation of local linguistic diversity that do include the discourses of the nation-state but are not confined to them, we can define *methodological cosmopolitanism* as entailing "the systematic breaking up of the process through which the national perspective of politics and society, as well as the methodological nationalism of political science, sociology, history and law, confirm and strengthen each other in their definition of reality." (Beck and Sznaider 2006: 3). Given the complexity of the social field that thus appears in front of us, we do not limit our examinations to one perspective or methodological approach in this volume. The inclusion of multiple views on multiple languages (understood as discursive but empirically efficacious constructs) is part of the concept of our endeavour, assuming that we "can and must observe and investigate the boundary-transcending and boundary-effacing multi-perspectivalism of social and political agents through very different 'lenses' (ibid.). Accordingly, we do not believe that it is possible to give a comprehensive account of the entire range of linguistic repertoires; nor do we attempt to give a systematic account of how such repertoires relate to each other. Rather, the collection of articles, understood as a whole, gives access to the multiple experiences and perspectives of speakers and communities affiliated by language in a social space conceptualized as one city, on sociolinguistic hierarchical and historically developing configurations, on language ideological discourses and practices, and on the theoretical implications of this multiplicity. *The Sociolinguistic Economy of Berlin* is in this sense an attempt to accomplish the demand of "multi-perspectivalism" and to implement methodological cosmopolitanism in the study of language in society.

What unites the different perspectives and approaches in this book is the core question of what happens to our view on language when we take a city – Berlin – rather than "a language" as the social unit on which we base our linguistic inquiry.

4 The case of Berlin

Berlin as a city to study language diversity offers particularly compelling conditions. Besides its traditional diversities and its current popularity as a global city of fashion, media and youth culture, its special history as a divided place sheds light on the role of the political-economic system in shaping linguistic diversity. There are still-felt effects of the Berlin Wall, such as slightly different indexical meanings of local repertoires of "Berlinisch" in eastern and western parts of the city, ranging from "locally authentic" or "non-gentrified" to "working-class". The specific formations of ethnic patterning in Berlin are different in the west and in the east, where the east, due to its socio-political history, still has more intense links with former socialist states, while the 1950s to 1970s *Gastarbeiter* schemes have had strong effects on the ethnic composition of West Berlin. For example, in 2016, the district with the largest percentage of inhabitants of Turkish descent (who typically came to West-Berlin as *Gastarbeiter*) was the western neighbourhood of Neukölln with 11.4% (36,313 individuals).[5] This contrasts with the eastern district of Marzahn-Hellersdorf, which was part of the Russian occupation zone, where only 0.4% of the residents have a Turkish background (1,082). At the same time, 7% (17,817) of the residents of Marzahn-Hellersdorf have a Russian (or other former USSR) background, while it is only 1.6% (5,283) in Neukölln. Despite the Wall having come down more than 25 years ago, and despite the fact that the city has changed rather dramatically since then, the history of Berlin makes apparent that diversity is no natural effect of a city, but is caused by market conditions and socio-political systems. Currently, economic market conditions are often discussed as having an effect predominantly on demographic shifts and on an increase of diversity. Yet, considering that "eastern" and "western" histories continue to have specific local consequences in Berlin, the example shows that we can also observe the historical permanence of some social discourses.

Berlin hosts a wide range of languages and varieties that have different histories in the local context of the city. They include German dialect variation, urban vernaculars such as Kiezdeutsch, the use of English among mobile elites, and the many established and more recent linguistic practices associated with immigrants and their communities – from Turkish and Russian to Portuguese, from Italian to Vietnamese. Furthermore, we find locally-based language ideologies perspectives and policies that are influenced by policies from the federal governmental and local educational realm and by national public discourse. For example, the tendency to conceive of homogeneity as positive is traditionally pronounced in German discourses (see e.g Koopmans 2001, on language policy, migration and citizenship in Germany, see Stevenson and Schanze 2009), particularly in the educational sector, and cultural homogeneity seems indeed more prevalent in parts of the city with high real estate prices. In the case of Berlin,

5 See https://www.statistik-berlin-brandenburg.de/webapi/jsf/tableView/tableView.xhtml# on the number of people of Turkish and USSR descent, and on the overall number of residents in each district.

this is, however, very recently criss-crossed where a global elite not only acquires real estate but in some parts of the city also has started to reside. In these parts, English is on the fore, and the existence of a very vibrant English-speaking community can be identified both on the streets (e.g. through a blossoming infrastructure of predominantly Anglophone shops, restaurants, cultural outlets and other places of consumption) and on the web (through locally anchored diasporic communities of English speakers and their forums, expat blogs and social networks) and also traditional media like city magazines published in English.

This Anglo-dominated "expat" culture not only involves economic elites but is additionally related to the global imagination of Berlin as a supposedly "alternative" sub-cultural place. The current but also more historical discourses on the urban popular culture of Berlin attract an international crowd whose involvement in new economies – start-ups and the like – and local Anglophone-dominated "hipster" ideologies cast diversity as an element of transnational "cool". In these settings, cosmopolitanist ideals – in the sense of the voluntary adoption of meta-cultural positions – are sometimes overtly adhered to or at least tacitly taken for granted as part of the city's narrative and imagery. We can relate and contrast elite cosmopolitanism that represents a tacit cultural norm in some social spheres to urban power struggles such as anti-gentrification activism, anti-tourism discourse, a monolingual habitus in most public school and in a lack of job market accessibility for non-native speakers of German. Finally, a general increase of right-wing nationalist discourse in Germany (see Dostal 2015) affects the local situation of Berlin, too. This similarly has to be understood in the context of an increased cosmopolitanization – in the sociological understanding of the term, "[c]osmopolitanism and nationalism are not mutually exclusive" (Beck and Sznaider 2006: 8) – as monolingual Germans are, for example, indeed excluded from some prestigious sections of the local job market (as e.g. in the start-up business or in the growing tourism industry).

Finally, in the shadow of self-assumed and perceived "elite mobilities" (Birtchnell and Caletrío 2014), Berlin is home to a multitude of ethnic groups and their linguistic identities. In many cases, these forms of linguistic diversity in the city are caused by global migration under more austere socioeconomic conditions, from historically grounded communities such as Turkish and Italian *Gastarbeiter* descendants, to Polish and Russian communities resulting from Berlin's geographical proximity to Eastern Europe (the distance from Berlin to the Polish border is 80km), to recently emerging diasporic communities with an African, Arab, Asian or South American background. In this light, the influx of refugees and asylum seekers in the summer of 2015 is part of a long continuity rather than a new development for Berlin and its status as a global city. The effects of this superdiverse condition on the sociolinguistic economy of Berlin are manifold – from rather well-charted urban vernaculars such as Kiezdeutsch, to bilingual practices both on the grassroots level and in the formalised context of bilingual schools such as the Staatliche Europa-Schulen Berlin (SESB), to emerging locales such as the New African Quarter in Berlin-Wedding and uses of English in translocal spaces of consumption like third-wave coffee culture or the craft beer scene (see Heyd and Schneider in press). Considering the diversity of histories, continuities, connections and symbolic shifts of languages in Berlin, the charting of the sociolinguistic economy of Berlin is not only of interest in its own right but has implications that reach further on geographical, conceptual and discursive levels. The city of Berlin is thus a kind of boiler room for overcoming concepts on language as anchored steadily in time and national space on our way to a methodologically cosmopolitan linguistics.

5 The contributions to this volume

By looking into very different types of social contexts, this book covers language phenomena on different socio-spatial scales, from national, regional, ethnic, translocal or cosmopolitan, to local concrete spaces such as streets or houses. We start with a view on the historical linguistic development of the local variety in the national context of Germany by Peter Auer. This is followed by a more contemporary synopsis of the presence and on the distribution of the traditional local variety Berlinisch by Peter Schlobinski, which highlights changing levels of metalinguistic awareness amongst local residents. Taking up the national context and the political and language political concepts that impact on the Berlin setting, Tanager gives insight into German language policies, how they are applied in language classes for people who aim for naturalization and which effects they have on the people concerned. The following four articles deal with newer forms of identity in the city, namely Kiezdeutsch and English. Oliver Bunk and Maria Pohle discuss the indexical meanings associated with Kiezdeutsch, while Stefanie Jannedy, Norma Mendoza-Denton and Melanie Weirich discuss data from experimental phonetic studies on the local perception of Kiezdeutsch in relation Bourdieu's notion of social and symbolic capital. Both these contributions do not focus centrally on a documentation of an urban variety, but on the construction of both "Germanness" and "otherness" on the basis of predominantly German linguistic repertoires and the stereotypes associated with them.

The linguistic resources that are tied to the notion of English are another example of newly emerging local and at the same time transnationally interwoven identities. In Emily Farrell's article on the role of English in Berlin's artist community, we see how the national standard language – German – is of little value in some local settings. Leonie Schulte also discusses a context in which English plays an important role. She elaborates on the linguistic experiences of former pupils of a traditional bilingual English-German school, founded during the times of US American occupation. The pupils' use of fused "Denglish" forms constituted a symbol of local distinction during school days but, more recently, is perceived of as non-local and tied to processes of gentrification once the pupils leave school and start to move (and talk) in inner-city districts.

When we turn to processes of the commodification of language, we see that this often happens in conjunction with the commodification of other semiotized cultural products. Thus, Italian is a language that is closely tied to the Berlin restaurant business, as Edith Pichler shows. She also shows how the local image of the *Italiener* ('the Italian', a German term to refer to Italian restaurants) changes historically and in relation to the Italian and German socio-political and economic context, which displays in the naming practices of restaurant owners. Miriam Stock gives us insight into the production, performance and perception of Arabic language, food and culture in the context of Falafel stores. Surprisingly, and in contrast to the otherwise dominant attitudes on Arabic as a set of repertoires associated with working-class migrants, it is here associated with consumption patterns of upwardly mobile Berlin residents, typically living in more wealthy neighbourhoods where we find organic food shops and stylish cafés. A commodified perspective on language is very clear in Philipp Krämer's chapter on the role of Spanish in education and in the Berlin hotel business. He gives an overview of the provisions of Spanish language classes in public and private education, as well as an insight into attitudes towards practicing and learning Spanish of hotel employees, from which we learn that the product "Spanish" is more a lifestyle product, rather than necessarily associated with a particular country.

Moving into more concrete spaces, the contributions by Janet Fuller and Fatih Özcan discuss specific local linguistic landscapes, with the former focusing on the role of Anglophone resources throughout the city, the latter zooming in on two Kiezes (neighborhoods) in urban Kreuzberg and Neukölln. Both studies exemplify qualitative vs. quantitative approaches to multilingual visibility in Berlin, respectively, and thus demonstrate how written discourse operates on different levels in the city.

Studying the very local scale, we come to understand that, in a diverse urban setting, even single buildings can be relevant sites for engaging with linguistic diversity and its multiple transnational ties. Gertrud Hüwelmeier's anthropological view on a Vietnamese food and retail market in the district of Lichtenberg shows the interethnic complexity of the place and how the ties to social spaces from elsewhere continue to impact on the sociolinguistic hierarchies within the market. In the final contribution, Patrick Stevenson, closes with an essayistic meditation on the inhabitants of an apartment building, giving a glimpse into the everyday multilingual lives of Berliners and delving deeper into the language biography of one of the tenants. This final contribution, intended as a coda to the diverse studies in this book, leaves us with a highly situated account of how linguistic economies in Berlin operate at the most personal, situated and embodied level.

References

Appiah, Kwame Anthony. 2006. *Cosmopolitanism. Ethics in a world of strangers.* London: Penguin.

Baker, Philip & John Eversley. 2000. *Multilingual capital: the languages of* London's *schoolchildren and their relevance to economic, social and educational policies.* London: Battlebridge.

Beauchesne, Olivier & SCImago. 2014. Map of scientific collaboration. Data by Scopus. http://olihb.com/2014/08/11/map-of-scientific-collaboration-redux/.

Beck, Ulrich & Natan Sznaider. 2006. Unpacking cosmopolitanism for the social sciences: a research agenda. *The British Journal of Sociology* 5.1–23.

Birtchnell, Thomas & Javier Caletrío. 2014. Elite mobilities. London: Routledge.

Blommaert, Jan. 2015. Chronotopes, scales and complexity in the study of language in society. *Tilburg Papers in Culture Studies* 121. https://pure.uvt.nl/ws/portalfiles/portal/4933623/paper121_Blommaert_Chronotopes_scales_complexity.pdf.

Blommaert, Jan. 2018. *Durkheim and the Internet. Sociolinguistics and the sociological imagination.* London: Bloomsbury.

Blommaert, Jan, James Collins & Stef Slembrouck. 2005. Spaces of multilingualism. *Language and Communication* 25.197–216.

Blommaert, Jan & Ben Rampton. 2011. Language and superdiversity. *Diversities* 13.1–21.

Bourdieu, Pierre. 1992. Ökonomisches Kapital, kulturelles Kapital, soziales Kapital. In Pierre Bourdieu (ed.), *Schriften zu Politik und Kultur: Die verborgenen Mechanismen der Macht.* Hamburg: VSA. 49–80.

Brandehof, Jelke. 2014. *Superdiversity in a Cameroonian diaspora community in Ghent: The social structure of superdiverse networks.* Tilburg University: MA diss.

Brenner, Neil & Christian Schmid. 2014. The 'Urban Age' in question. *International Journal of Urban and Regional Research* 38.731–755.

Castells, Manuel. 2010. *The rise of the network society* (2nd ed.). Oxford: Wiley.

Clark, Greg. 2016. *Global cities: a short history.* Washington: Brookings Institution Press.

Clifford, James. 1994. Diasporas. *Cultural Anthropology* 9.302–338.

Creese, Angela & Adrian Blackledge. 2010. Towards a sociolinguistics of superdiversity. *Zeitschrift für Erziehungswissenschaft* 13.549–572.
Deleuze, Gilles & Félix Guattari. 1977. *Rhizom*. Berlin: Merve.
Deleuze, Gilles & Félix Guattari. 1992. *Tausend Plateaus. Kapitalismus und Schizophrenie*. Berlin: Merve Verlag.
Dostal, Jörg M. 2015. The Pegida movement and German political culture: Is right-wing populism here to stay? The Political Quarterly 86.523–531.
Elegant, Naomi. 2018. Penn removes portrait of former GSE dean with alleged history of sexual harassment. In The Daily Pennsylvanian. https://www.thedp.com/article/2018/04/gse-getup-sexual-harassment-dell-hymes-portrait-removal-upenn-penn-philadelphia
Fürstenau, Sara, Ingrid Gogolin & Kutlay Yagmur. 2003. *Mehrsprachigkeit in Hamburg*. Münster: Waxmann.
Hannerz, Ulf. 1996. Cosmopolitans and locals in world culture. In Ulf Hannerz (ed.), *Transnational connections. Culture, people, places*, 102–111. London: Routledge.
Heller, Monica. 2003. Globalization, the new economy and the commodification of language and identity. *Journal of Sociolinguistics* 7.473–492.
Heller, Monica & Alexandre Duchêne (eds). 2012a. *Language and late capitalism. Pride and profit*. New York: Routledge.
Heller, Monica & Alexandre Duchêne. 2012b. Pride and profit: changing discourses of language, capital and nation-state. In Monica Heller & Alexandre Duchêne (eds.), *Language and late capitalism. Pride and profit*. 1–20. New York: Routledge.
Heyd, Theresa & Britta Schneider. in press. Anglophone communities in Germany: the case of Berlin. In Raymond Hickey (ed.) English in the German-speaking world. Cambridge: Cambridge University Press.
Hymes, Dell. 1968. Linguistic problems in defining the concept of "tribe". In June Helm (ed.) Essays on the problem of the tribe. Proceedings of the 1967 Annual spring meeting of the American Ethnological Society, 23-48. Washington: University of Washington Press.
Koopmans, Ruud. 2001. Deutschland und seine Einwanderer: ein gespaltenes Verhältnis. *Blätter für deutsche und internationale Politik* 2.1–28.
Labov, William. 1972. The social stratification of (r) in New York City department stores. In William Labov (ed.), *Sociolinguistic Patterns*, 43–69. Philadelphia: University of Pennsylvania Press.
Maher, John C. 2005. Metroethnicity, language, and the principle of cool. *International Journal of the Sociology of Language* 175–176.83–102.
Makoni, Sinfree & Alastair Pennycook. 2005. Disinventing and (Re)constituting languages. *Critical Inquiry in Language Studies* 2.137–156.
Milroy, Lesley. 1987. *Language and Social networks*. Oxford: Blackwell.
New Oxford American Dictionary. 2009.
O'Donnell, Patrick. 1988. Administration tried to downplay allegations of sexism. In The Daily Pennsylvanian. http://www.library.upenn.edu/docs/kislak/dp/1988/1988_12_01.pdf
Park, Robert E., Ernest Burgess & Roderick McKenzie. 1925. *The city*. Chicago: University of Chicago Press.
Pennycook, Alastair & Emi Otsuji. 2015. *Metrolingualism. Language in the city*. London: Routledge.
Pries, Ludger. 2008. *Die Transnationalisierung der sozialen Welt. Sozialräume jenseits von Nationalgesellschaften*. Frankfurt am Main: Suhrkamp.

Römhild, Regina. 2007. Alte Träume, neue Praktiken: Migration und Kosmopolitismus an den Grenzen Europas. In Transit Migration Forschungsgruppe (eds.), *Turbulente Ränder. Neue Perspektiven auf Migration an den Grenzen Europas*, 211–228. Bielefeld: Transcript.

Sassen, Saskia. 1994. *Cities in a world economy*. Thousand Oaks, Calif.: Pine Forge Press.

Schneider, Britta. 2017. Lobster, tourism and other kinds of business. Economic opportunity and language choice in a multilingual village in Belize. *Journal of Language and Intercultural Communication (Special Issue 'Language, Mobility and Work', ed. by Melissa Moyer)*. 18.390–407.

Schneider, Britta. 2018. Methodological nationalism in linguistics. Language Sciences https://doi.org/10.1016/j.langsci.2018.05.006

Sennett, Richard. 2005. Capitalism and the city. In Stephen Read, Jürgen Rosemann & Job van Eldijk (eds.), *Future city*, 114–124. London: Spon Press.

Shohamy, Elana, Eliezer Ben-Rafael & Monica Barni (eds). 2010. *Linguistic landscape in the city*. Bristol: Multilingual Matters.

Simmel, Georg. 1903. Die Grosstädte und das Geistesleben. In Th. Petermann (ed.), *Die Grossstadt. Vorträge und Aufsätze zur Städteausstellung. (Jahrbuch der Gehe-Stiftung Dresden)*, 185–206. Dresden: v. Zahn & Jaensch. https://www.gsz.hu-berlin.de/de/gsz/zentrum/georg-simmel/die-grossstaedte-und-das-geistesleben.

Stevenson, Patrick & Livia Schanze. 2009. Language, migration and citizenship in Germany: discourses on integration and belonging. In Guus Extra, Piet van Avermaet & Massimiliano Spotti (eds.), *Language testing, migration and citizenship. Cross-national perspectives on integration regimes*, 87–106. London: Continuum.

Urry, John & Derek Gregory. 1985. *Social relations and spatial structures*. Basingstoke: Palgrave Macmillan.

Vertovec, Stephen. 2007. Super-diversity and its implications. *Ethnic and Racial Studies* 30. 1024–1054.

Wimmer, Andreas & Nina Glick Schiller. 2002. Methodological nationalism and beyond: Nation-state building, migration and the social sciences. *Global Networks* 2.301–334.

Section 1: **From past to present**

Peter Auer

2 *Longue durée* and social styles: Shifting indexicalities in the Berlin vernacular from the perspective of historical sociolinguistics

Dedicated to the memory of Agathe Lasch (1879–1942)[1]

1 Introduction: historical urban sociolinguistics – between *longue durée* and social styles

The beginnings of sociolinguistics are usually equated with the "invention" of the term in the 1960s. However, the interest in how linguistic variation and change are intertwined with social structure, and how social agents display their identities through language, has of course a much longer history. This

1 Agathe Lasch's groundbreaking work on the sociolinguistic history of Berlin is to this very day the single-most important contribution on this topic, on which all subsequent research (including the following remarks) is based. Born in Berlin into a Jewish merchant family, she studied in Halle/Saale and in Heidelberg, where she completed her PhD with the Neogrammarian Wilhelm Braune in 1909 on the *Geschichte der Schriftsprache in Berlin bis zur Mitte des 16. Jahrhunderts* [History of the written language in Berlin until the middle of the 16th century], published in 1910. In the first 220 pages of the thesis, Lasch gives a detailed linguistic analysis of the written documents of the time, including an exact socio-biographical reconstruction of the social field in which the local scribes in the chancelleries of the city council, the legal courts, and the Hohenzollern residence produced their documents. After a time as Associate and later (from 1913) Associate Professor of Teutonic Philology at Bryn Mawr College, Pennsylvania, during which she published her still authoritative *Mittelniederdeutsche Grammatik* (1915), she worked as the first editor of the *Hamburgische Wörterbuch*, and from 1923 as professor (extraordinaria) for Low German philology there, until she was sent into early retirement in 1934 when the Nazi government excluded all Jews from the public sector. During her ten years as a professor in Hamburg, she wrote – among many scholarly articles on Low German – *Berlinisch – Eine berlinische Sprachgeschichte* (1928). After her forced retirement, she returned to Berlin in 1937. She worked and published (abroad) until 1939, under increasingly difficult conditions. In August 1942 she was deported to Riga and either died on the way or was killed there. (All biographical details are from Kaiser (2009) and Maas ([2010] 2014), who also give an excellent evaluation of her scientific work in the context of the time.)

https://doi.org/10.1515/9781501508103-002

chapter is intended to draw attention to one tradition of "sociolinguistics" *avant la lettre* which evolved in the context of the socio-historical analysis of written documents in the urban context, and of which Agathe Lasch was a prominent and brilliant representative.[2]

Historical urban sociolinguistics is almost entirely restricted to the investigation of written language. Its empirical basis is therefore fundamentally different from that of contemporary variational sociolinguistics, which prioritizes the investigation of vernacular language on the basis of systematically composed corpora of spoken language. The documents that usually provide the basis for research in historical urban sociolinguistics were written for non-linguistic purposes, came into being outside of scientific surveys, and are unsystematic as they happened to survive the vagaries of time whereas many others did not. This has two important consequences. One is that it is usually difficult if not impossible to apply corpus-based, quantitative analytical methods, at least in one city (in most urban archives, there are not enough comparable and socially stratified data for the earlier periods). The second one is that the extant documents were written for certain purposes and survived for certain reasons. They are therefore biased. They were composed by members of the educated classes who were able to read and write and were either powerful enough to produce "endurable" ("valuable") texts themselves or to commission them. Historical urban sociolinguistics has therefore been most successful in the analysis of changes driven by the "official" (overt) prestige of the incoming innovations on a regional or even supra-regional level. Change from below often reaches the written language only after a considerable delay, which makes it difficult and often impossible to reconstruct the social mechanisms through which it originated and spread. Vernacular language itself is only indirectly visible in the documents, for instance when speakers of the lower classes are quoted (e.g., in court proceedings for reasons of documentation) or examples of their speech are given in metalinguistic treatises

2 This is of course not the place to discuss the ways in which historical urban sociolinguistics developed nor to give an overview of its chief representatives or results. Hünecke (2014) provides a bibliography of publications on historical urban linguistics from a German perspective. Unfortunately, many publications in this field are dedicated to small-scale philological details and fail to integrate their results into a theoretically motivated whole; the theoretical developments in sociolinguistics at large are often ignored. Agathe Lasch, on the other hand, was able to combine philological competence, attending with meticulous care to the details of the data, with a good view of how these results added up to an overall picture of how language developed in its embedding into the social history of the city. Her work still stands out in this respect. The field of historical sociolinguistics in general is of course large and flourishing, cf. e.g., the bibliography published by the Historical Sociolinguistics Network (http://www.hum2.leidenuniv.nl/hsl_shl/bibliography.htm) which also publishes its own journal.

or literary texts with the intent of criticizing it from the perspective of a language educator, or ridiculing it for reasons of entertainment.

Despite these shortcomings, the extant historical documents at least partially allow us to reconstruct the social reasons for which a writer may have chosen a particular variable, style or variety out of a range of alternatives. These motivations can be deduced from the writer's social status and biography, from his (or rarely her) professional aims, from the purpose of the document (e.g., a letter) and its recipients. Although these linguistic choices are to a certain degree the decision of an individual, they do not occur in a social vacuum but respond to the social constraints and linguistic ideologies under which the writer produced the text. Working within the framework of historical urban sociolinguistics therefore requires a careful interpretation not only of the texts themselves, but also of the context in which they were produced.

Agathe Lasch's 1910 doctoral thesis is a masterpiece in this respect. Based mainly on the internal municipal records of the two towns of Cölln and Berlin (which later formed the city of Berlin); the written exchanges between representatives of these towns and the residence of the Hohenzollern margrave, with whom the municipalities were in frequent conflict; letters sent to other towns; and finally reports by travelers who commented on the linguistic situation in Berlin/Cölln, she artfully puts together a sociolinguistic picture of how Berlin/Cölln shifted from Low German to High German during the late 15th and early 16th centuries. In her 1928 book she investigates the history of Berlin in the subsequent centuries, when Berlin gained economic and political importance and finally grew to become one of the largest cities in the world (cf. below). The available documents multiply during this time. Toward the end of the 18th century, the language spoken in the city of Berlin becomes enregistered as the "Berlin vernacular" (Berlinisch). Lasch takes great care in reconstructing this process by investigating numerous literary and non-literary texts and a growing number of pseudo-linguistic descriptions in which the various social personae of the "typical Berliner" are construed. By the end of the 19th century, the stereotypes linked to these social personae were known not only in the city itself, but all over the German-speaking world. Lasch's study is therefore also an early example of ethno-dialectology and of sociolinguistic enregisterment: i.e., the way in which a vernacular language is construed around certain types of speakers by its users and non-users.

In the following, I will summarize her main findings and supplement them with more recent research on the linguistic history of Berlin.[3] In the framework

3 In particular, Schönfeld (1989), Schildt (1986), Dittmar, Schlobinski, and Wachs (1986), Schildt and Schmidt (1986).

of this volume, the chapter attempts to develop a historical framework in which the following chapters, which are devoted to recent developments and the present-day sociolinguistic situation of Berlin, can be situated.

I will take a certain perspective on sociolinguistic change which loosely follows Braudel (1958) (also cf. Auer 2013) in distinguishing between historical events of *longue durée* and events of a middle-duration which he calls *conjonctures* (fashions). The latter – I think – can be equated with the formation and transformation of social styles in sociolinguistics (see, e.g., Eckert 2008). (Braudel's third category, i.e., single historical events, would correspond to the singular speech acts.) Events of longue durée persist over long periods of time, often centuries, during which changes appear to happen in slow motion only. According to Braudel, this retardation of time is due to the enduring relevance of certain structural constraints (for instance, in his case, geographical ones) which are relatively immune to single events and fashions. I propose that in the sociolinguistic history of Berlin, the period between roughly 1400 and 1950 can be characterized by two such events of long duration. The first is the shift from Low German to High German in the northern part of the German-speaking area. This process sets in in the 15th century at the latest, gains momentum in the written language and (usually later in) the spoken language of the upper classes in the 16th century. Due to the continuous influx of Low Germans speakers from the surroundings, it takes roughly until the middle of the 19th century to reach completion in Berlin. The second event of longue durée is the emergence of a common standard for spoken German and the concomitant re-evaluation of horizontal (geographical) linguistic variation in the German-speaking area on a vertical (social) scale.[4] In other words: a model of the evaluation of spoken language emerges in which the "pure" (i.e., non-dialectal), codified spoken standard holds the top position in terms of official prestige, while the most regional variants (in the extreme case, the local dialects) hold the bottom position. This process started in the late 18th century, when the most prestigious variety of German of that time (i.e. the variety spoken in Upper Saxony, particularly in the cities of Dresden, Leipzig, Meissen) was re-/devaluated on the grounds that it showed regional forms and therefore began to be unacceptable in educated speech; this process gained momentum toward the end of the 19th century and continues to the present day, although a new evaluative system appears to have been emerging over the last 30 years.

Both events of long duration must not be seen of course as teleological processes aiming at the establishment of a standard language in its written and

4 Cf. Reichmann (1988) for the term "verticalization" in this context.

spoken form, even though they retrospectively appear to have these teleological traits. In the context of their time, the outcome was unpredictable, and several competing events and processes were at play.

At first glance, the two events of long duration – the shift from Low German to (still highly regionalized) High German and the social devaluation of regionalized vernacular speech vis-à-vis the spoken standard variety – seem to amount to the same thing in Berlin: after all, Low German was the local variety spoken in Berlin before 1500. However, as we shall see, this view is inadequate. The regional variety that began to be stigmatized from the late 18th century onward was not the Low German spoken before 1500, but a very different variety, later enregistered as Berlinisch. It was not perceived nor can it be analyzed linguistically as Low German.

2 The shift from Low German to High German in Berlin/Cölln

The shift from Low German to High German in the northern German-speaking area is usually regarded as a change from above which occurred in the written language documents first.[5] Its most compelling evidence is the fact that from 1500 onward, all northern German urban chancelleries stopped writing in Low German, first in outgoing documents and later also in internal writing. Instead, they used some variant of High German. Figure 1 shows the exact time when this shift occurred. There was a clear East/West cline, with the eastern cities being ahead of the western ones. But even when compared to neighboring towns such as Magdeburg, Rostock or Schwerin, few other towns started (1510) and completed (1530) the process as early as Berlin/Cölln.

One reason is geography. Berlin/Cölln were located relatively close to the Low German/High German language border (marked by the dotted line in Figure 1). However, much more important were geo-political and geo-economic changes at the time.

Cölln and Berlin had been founded around 1230 in the margravate Brandenburg, far away from the cultural and political centers in the South, West, and North. Around 1400, Berlin had 6,110, Cölln 2,400 inhabitants; during the next 200 years, the population increased by about 30% (to 12,000 around 1618), only to drop to the old numbers as a consequence of the Thirty Years' War again

5 There is, of course, a rich tradition of research on the transition from Low German to High German in the northern cities in general; cf., among many others, Maas (1983) and Mihm (2001).

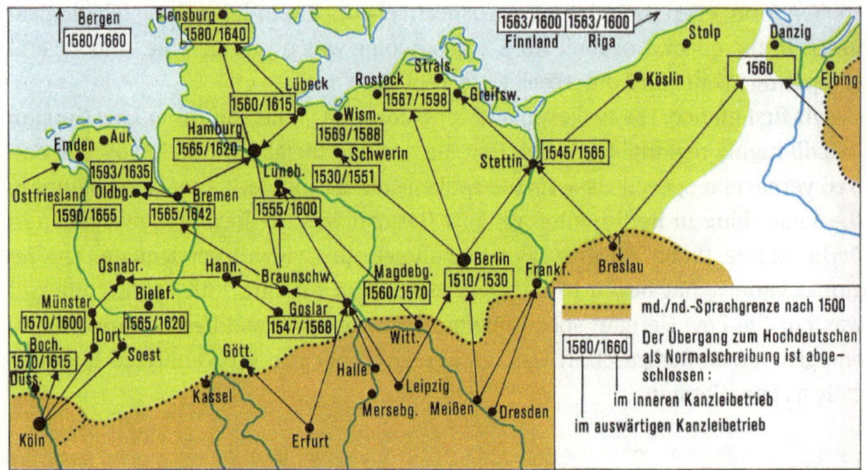

Figure 1: Transition from Low German to High German in northern German chancelleries, outgoing/internal documents (from: König [1978] 2001: 140). Copyright: dtv Verlag. INV-3780/19.

(cf. Mauter 1986). Until the Renaissance, Berlin was a minor place in terms of population size, even though the regents of Brandenburg became more and more powerful over the centuries.

The two towns (as well as others) formed alliances, and they were additionally linked by treaties and commercial ties to the Hanseatic League, which guaranteed some amount of freedom from the margraves. This northern orientation naturally combined with the use of (Middle) Low German, which was used more and more often in documents in the 14th century instead of Latin as a symbol of urban pride and self-confidence. High German documents are also not absent from the Berlin/Cölln chancelleries of this time; the language was used in documents and letters to High German-speaking addressees where language choice was motivated by the writers' wish to be understood. Lasch (1910: 29–31) argues that they may also reflect the generally higher prestige of High German already at that time. However, they are no proof that High German played a role *within* Cölln and Berlin.

The ruling margraves had been non-locals from High German-speaking areas since 1323, but they spent little time in Brandenburg and hardly had a cultural or linguistic impact. Things changed in 1415, when a member of the Hohenzollern dynasty (Friedrich VI, later Prince-Elect Friedrich I) from Nuremberg in Franconia was given the margravate as a fief. In the middle of the 15th century (1451), the Hohenzollerns built a castle in Cölln and took permanent residence there; the castle was expanded into a Renaissance palace in the 16th century as a visible sign of their power.

Not only did the Hohenzollern dynasty originate from High German-speaking Nuremberg, they also brought along with them a growing number of Franconian-speaking administrators, since they had little trust in the local town patricians. From 1411 onward, there was therefore a split in the upper echelons of the population between a small group who spoke High German, the language of the residence of the prince, and a large group who spoke the Low German of the town(s). Yet, since relations between the towns and the residence were tense, it seems that the position of Low German in the towns remained uncontested: the documents in the town chancelleries and judicial courts of the time show only very few Franconian features (Lasch 1910: 66, 99).

But there were other, more consequential changes at the time. Following the geo-political and economic power structures of the late 14th and 15th centuries, the towns of Berlin and Cölln changed their orientation from the North (Hanseatic League) to the South (Leipzig) and to the East (Frankfurt [Oder]) (Lasch 1910: 126–129). As a consequence, the scribes (and their principals, the town patricians) increasingly acted in a Low German/High German bilingual network of business contacts. Incoming High German letters or documents included in the town records were no longer translated in the 15th century, as they had been before; the leading class apparently understood High German sufficiently to deal with them in a passive form of bilingualism (while the opposite was not the case: the High German-speaking addressees would not have understood Low German). Nevertheless, all internal documents of the towns of Cölln and Berlin continued to be written in Low German.

The change came only toward the end of the 15th century, and then quite abruptly. Lasch (1910: 104–154) gives an exact description. The tensions between the Prince-Elect and his entourage and the townspeople diminished at that time; officials of the court were for the first time referred to as citizens of Berlin, and there was more and more intermarriage between the two groups. Local men, often university-educated, made a career at the Prince's court, where High German was mandatory. Germanic law, linked to Low German, ceded to Roman law, often practiced by clergymen who had enjoyed an international academic education. At the same time, commercial ties with Leipzig and Frankfurt led to numerous personal contacts. Many young men of the Berlin/Cölln leading classes, mainly merchants, went to the High German-speaking universities of Leipzig and Frankfurt/Oder for their studies (Lasch 1910: 88–89).[6] In this context, the

6 Lasch (1910: 117, 148–151) points out that the University of Wittenberg, founded in 1506, attracted only few Berliners. Wittenberg was the stronghold of Luther's Protestants, in which people in Berlin/Cölln showed little interest. The transition from Low to High German was therefore not linked to Luther and Protestantism in this area, as is often believed.

newly appointed town scribe Johannes Nether, certainly with permission and perhaps even on request of the mayor and the aldermen, shifted the official language of the town records to High German in 1504, although he himself was of Low German background. Shortly after, the judicial court appointed a new scribe who spoke High German as a first language.

From this point onward, the spread of High German was fast. Before the middle of the 16th century, the new prestige language was found everywhere: in internal documents; invoices and receipts, not only by merchants but also by ordinary craftsmen; personal notes for internal use in the chancelleries; pupils' stage productions in the newly founded Cölln grammar school (and hence presumably as the prescribed school language); even family names were adapted to High German (for instance, the family name *Schum* appears as *Schaum*, or the family name *Rycke* as *Reiche*, following the replacement of Low German /u:/ with High German /aʊ/ and Low German /i:/ with High German /aɪ/, respectively; cf. Lasch 1928: 72).

But the transition to High German was not only fast, it also had one particular feature which made the situation in Berlin/Cölln different from that in other, more northern/western German cities in the Low German area: the new language was not exclusively imported into the linguistic repertoire through the written language, but was learned directly through face-to-face contact with the High German speakers in the Upper Saxon territories, adjoining the margravate in the South. Hence, features found later – and still today – in the spoken High German of northern Germany that are due to writing pronunciation, such as the preservation of Low German initial /s/ obstruent sequences (e.g. Hamburg /staɪf/, /staɪn/ instead of Standard German /ʃtaɪf/, /ʃtaɪn/, 'stiff', 'stone'), are not observed in Berlin. A contemporary visitor from Hamburg, Albertus Kranz, reports (with regret) in his book *Saxonia*, published in 1520, that the people in the *Mark Brandenburg* (i.e., the margravate in which Cölln and Berlin were situated) had taken over the "Meißnian language".[7] (Meissen in Upper Saxony, residence of the Wettin margraves, was one of the political and administrative centers in Upper Saxony and the language was often named after it.)

The variant of High German taken over in Berlin, Lasch argues, was the one which was *heard* in Upper Saxony. Since the High German spoken there increasingly was looked upon as a particularly "good" High German, it must have been attractive to the Berliners. The most important competitor of the Upper Saxon variant of High German developed in the Southeast (the Bavarian and Franconian-speaking regions) under the influence of the Emperor's court

7 Quoted in Lasch (1928: 70).

in Vienna (the so-called *Gemeine Deutsch* 'Common German'). But even though the Hohenzollern family originated from this area, the Berlin variety of High German was clearly not under its influence. It was simply too far away.

So the re-orientation of Berlin/Cölln from the North to the South, i.e., the Upper Saxon area, was not only a straightforward consequence of the ever-increasing political and economic ties with this region, it was also attractive in terms of the attitudes and ideologies connected to it. Its prestige was enormous and increased even further in the 17th and early 18th centuries, when urban, educated Upper Saxon speech was considered the most elegant and sophisticated German, no longer challenged by the Habsburg "Common German".

The transition from Low German to High German is portrayed by Lasch as a case of language shift in which two sharply delimited varieties contrasted with each other. She insists that the language the Berlin upper classes adopted was a new, exoglossic H-variety imported *in toto* from Upper Saxony. The change came from above, as only the educated classes were able to travel and stay outside Berlin for study purposes or in the context of trading contacts. Only these people were therefore capable of learning both the written and the spoken new H-variety, and initiated a process by which in the long run the Low German vernacular spoken in Berlin/Cölln was replaced more or less entirely by the High German variety spoken in the Upper Saxon cities such as Leipzig. Lasch rejects the idea of internal variation between Low and High German; the phonology ("*Lautgrundlage*") of the new Berlin vernacular after the shift from Low to High German was in her opinion entirely Upper Saxon; only its phonetics ("*Lautproduktion*") continued to be Low German (see, e.g., Lasch 1928: 75).[8] For her, the basis of the Berlin vernacular up to the present day is therefore Upper Saxon, even though she acknowledges that the high number of immigrants from the surrounding Low German-speaking areas during the subsequent centuries reintroduced some Low German features. It was the city which took over the new prestige variety, while the surrounding hinterland for a long time remained Low German-speaking. Her model of prestige-driven language change from above is therefore a variant (though not formulated in such terms) of a "city hopping" language spread (cf. Trudgill 1986), a model which was not at all unknown in pre-war German dialectology – in fact it was favored by most

8 Her rejection of internal variation is linked to a rejection of the idea of a *Mischsprache* [mixed language] in general, which she links – like many of her contemporaries – to language decay (*Verwahrlosung*): "Das Berlinische ist nicht, wie man immer wieder lesen kann, ein regelloses Gemisch in verwahrloster Form, sondern in seiner Geschichte deutlich faßbar" (Lasch 1928: 139) [The Berlin vernacular is not, as we often read, a rule-lacking mixture in decayed form, but can be given a clear historical description].

of the "culturally" inclined social dialectologists in the interwar period (cf. Bach [1934] 1950: §109, 111, and Ch. 5 for a textbook version).

Lasch's account met with harsh criticism from traditional dialectologists who, working in the Neogrammarian framework, could only accept sound change as spreading "flatly" in geography, based exclusively on frequency of face-to-face contact among the masses of ordinary people (not on prestige).[9] But once we allow internal variation to be socially meaningful (i.e., taking part in the formation of social styles), this problem disappears. The (overt) prestige of the High German innovations cannot be explained with a Neogrammarian model of geographical spread; at the time it can only have resulted from the verbal styles of the upper classes – and they doubtlessly oriented themselves to Upper Saxony. This, however, does not imply that all Low German features disappeared – some of them simply may not have been socially salient.

Of course, language shift did not affect the whole population but proceeded in a socially stratified way. Evidence for this is the fact that the linguistic features that critically and saliently differentiated the old Low German and the new High German varieties can be observed as enregistering styles tied to certain social figurae. This means that Low German (and imperfect acquisition of High German) are now socially marked. In an anonymous Christmas play, performed for the first time by young members of the aristocracy at the court of the Prince-Elect in 1589 (from Bolte 1926: 143–144; also cf. Schmidt 1986: 139–141), most characters act in High German, as the context of its production and performance would suggest. However, some of the characters – the shepherds – represent social characters for whom the author(s) chose a different style, i.e., either Low German throughout (for the first shepherd in the following extract) or a mixture between Low German and High German which caricatures the speakers' attempts to speak High German without quite succeeding (the second and third shepherds). The members of the lower class are portrayed by their language, and both Low German and insufficiently mastered High German are presented as typical of these social strata.

For the situation in the 16th century, we can conclude

- that High German has taken over not only as the written but also as the spoken variety of the leading classes of Berlin and Cölln;
- that these leading classes are bilingual in Low and High German;

9 The critique was first – and very competently – formulated in a review of Lasch's 1928 book by the renowned Low German dialectologist Hermann Teuchert (1928/1929) who argued that Berlin/Cölln texts of the time do show Low German features, which points to a mixture of Low and High German which must also have occurred in the spoken vernacular.

- that the transition has also reached the socially ambitious lower classes who speak a "learner variety" of High German, while the remaining majority still use Low German;
- that the variety of High German spoken in Berlin is mainly oriented toward the Upper Saxon variant.

All this variation, however, remains within the overarching *longue durée* process of the shift from Low to High German and is socially meaningful in this context.

3 The re-evaluation of regional as social features

The next centuries, i.e., the period between 1600 and 1900, are still part of the same event of *longue durée* in a certain way, as the replacement of Low German by High German continues to advance among the lower classes. But this change is already complete in the leading/educated classes, who from the 16th century onward speak a Berlin-Saxon variant of High German – or, as they increasingly do in the 17th and 18th centuries, French.

The second half of the 17th century (absolutism and mercantilism) was a time of economic, military and political growth and expansion for the state of Brandenburg-Prussia. Economic growth led to a substantial influx of labor so that the population of Berlin and the adjoining area increased from around 6,000 to around 29,000 within 50 years. In 1701, Friedrich crowned himself King of Prussia, and in 1709 he united the towns and the suburbs outside the walls of Cölln and Berlin to form the city which was now called Berlin. Another 50 years later, this city already had approximately 150,000 inhabitants and was the world's fifth largest. Although immigration by religious and political fugitives from France, Switzerland, Bohemia and German states was substantial, with many of them speaking languages other than German as their L1 (Prussia accommodated around 5,000 French Hugenots alone), the majority of the new citizens, particularly the unskilled workers, came from the region and, at least until 1871, most of them would have been native speakers of Low German (Mauter 1986: 57). The dynamics between city and countryside went both ways: the incoming new inhabitants brought along their Low German dialect and used it among themselves, with often insufficient exposure to the middle class norms to learn the Berlin variant of High German well, but of course they also kept in contact with the folks back home and thereby brought the urban vernacular to the rural surroundings. Hence, the tension between Low German and High German among the lower class speakers during this time resulted from the incomplete accommodation of the High German city vernacular by Low German (and other L1) speakers.

The process of immigration of Low German-speaking labor continued during the Industrial Revolution in the 19th and early 20th centuries, when the population exploded: in 1810, Berlin had a little less than 200,000 inhabitants, in 1871 (now Berlin is the capital of Germany), it reached the size of 750,000 inhabitants, and in 1905 more than 2 million people lived in the city (Mauter 1986: 82). In 1920 the city of Greater Berlin was founded; with almost four million inhabitants it was the third largest metropolis in the world (after New York and London).

Lasch's argument that this influx of Low German speakers will have affected the High Berlin (Upper Saxon) vernacular by enhancing its Low German component is at least highly plausible. For instance, the raised variant of /a/ in the neuter pronoun *dat* 'that' mentioned above (i.e., *det/dit*), which was already on its way out of the verbal repertoire of Berlin/Cölln in the 16th century, had its comeback and is to the present day a feature of the enregistered Berlin vernacular. It is a typical dialect feature of Low German in the larger Berlin dialect area (cf. Figure 2).

In this period, however, another event of *longue durée* now becomes more important than the shift from Low to High German. This is another change from above which begins to exert its influence first on the bourgeoisie, then also on the petite bourgeoisie and the working class: the formation and ideological construction of a national standard variety of spoken German from which all regional features are eliminated. As outlined in the last section, like most other European nations, Germany had a clear prestige variety linked to one particular area, i.e., that of Upper Saxony, until around 1800. The main difference from England, France, Denmark or Sweden was that this area was not that of the capital (which, if anything, would have been Vienna), and that the political and economic power of Saxony did not last. When the economic and political power moved north to Prussia, the cultural and linguistic capital followed as well. As a consequence, the formerly prestigious variety spoken in Saxony became increasingly criticized for its regional features – and since many of these were also used in the city of Berlin, they had to be eliminated from educated speech there, too. A new generation of grammarians and language teachers propagated a spoken standard which was phonetically close to the variant spoken in the north of Germany, but whose phonology was at least compatible with, if not influenced by, the letter of the already established written standard. The process was a long and difficult one, as the new standard could not be heard anywhere in its pure form, and therefore could not be copied from model speakers as in the previous period. The national and de-regionalized new standard had to be derived from and learned on the basis of the written language, for instance in reading circles typical of the time. Here, the bourgeoisie (women in particular) practiced reading aloud according to the "correct" pronunciation norms.

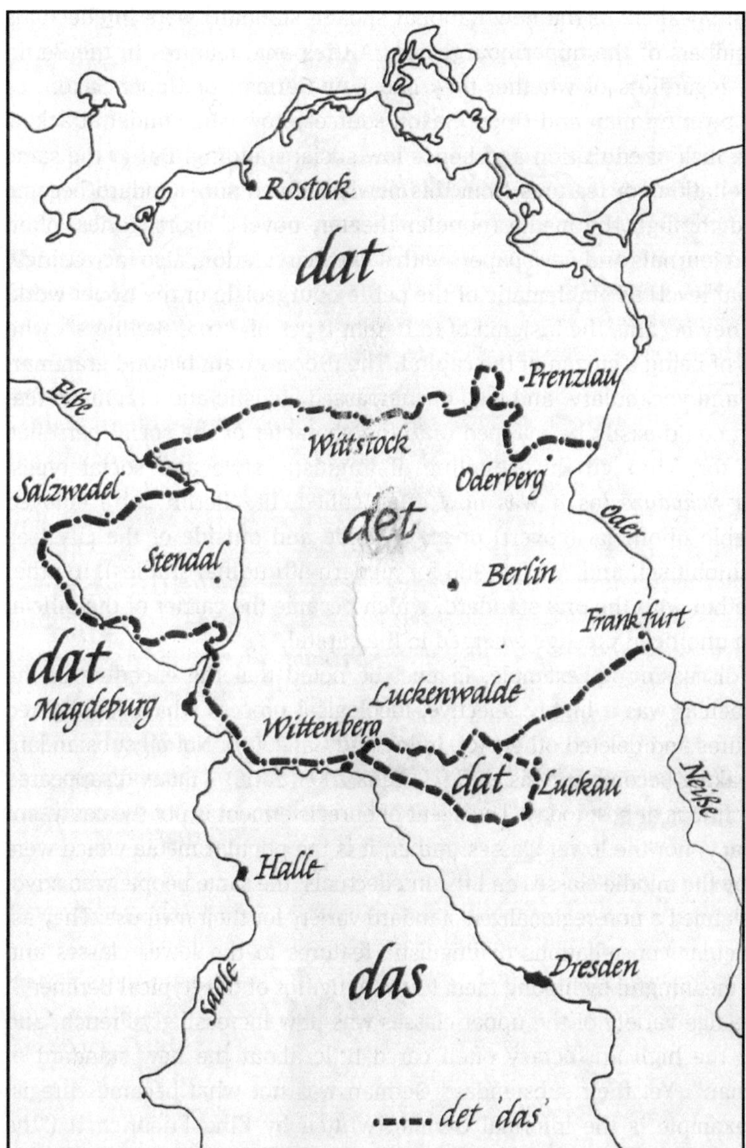

Figure 2: Geographical distribution of the variants of Standard German *das* (neuter demonstrative pronoun/neuter definite article) around 1900 according to the *Sprachatlas des Deutschen Reichs* (map from: Schönfeld 1986: 233).

The first speakers of the new national spoken standard were intellectuals and the members of the upper bourgeoisie. All regional features in the Berlin vernacular, regardless of whether they had Low German or Upper Saxon, or combined Lower German and Upper Saxon sources, now came under attack as indicating a lack of education and hence low social standing. But at the same time, constellations of features from this newly defined sub-standard became enregistered through the media (popular theater, novels, short stories, often published in journals and newspapers with a wide circulation, also increasingly on a national level) as emblematic of the petite bourgeoisie or the upper working class. They became the insignia of (different types of) "true Berliners", who were proud of being a citizen of the capital. The process went beyond grammar, phonology and vocabulary, and also encompassed stylistic and pragmatic features which could easily be mapped onto the character of the social personae they stood for. Through this coupling of linguistic style and social types, the *Berliner Schnauze* (as it was now often called, lit. 'Berlin gob') enjoyed a considerable unofficial (covert) prestige inside and outside of the city (see Dittmar, Schlobinski, and Wachs 1986 for modern attitudinal studies). In other words, together with the oral standard, which became the carrier of the official prestige, an unofficial prestige emerged in the capital.

Before discussing an example, it must be noted that the encoding of the Berlin vernacular was a highly selective, ideological process which highlighted certain features and deleted others (cf. Irvine and Gal 2000). Not all substandard ways of speaking become enregistered (cf. Agha 2003, 2006) – many disappeared and sound curious at best today. The agent of enregisterment is not the court, nor the aristocracy, nor the lower classes; rather, it is the popular media which were controlled by the middle classes and the intellectuals, the same people who advocated and claimed a non-regionalized standard variety for their own use. They ascribed particular constellations of linguistic features to the lower classes and made them meaningful by linking them to social figures of the "typical Berliner".

The prestige variety of the upper classes was now increasingly French, and particularly the high aristocracy often cared little about the new standard of "good German". Yet their substandard German was not what became enregistered. An example is the informal German written by King Friedrich II ("the Great") around 1750.[10] His official and most of his unofficial correspondence was in French, and he frankly confessed "je ne suis pas fort en allemand" [I'm not

---

10 Cf. Lasch (1928: 97–109) for other examples. For the aristocrats, these forms of speech were not yet considered substandard; they still acted in the previous first *longue durée* context in which Berlinish was the Common Language that had succeeded Low German.

strong in German] (Lasch 1928: 102; also cf. Petersilka 2005 on Friedrich's bilingualism), but with his long-standing valet and later chamberlain Fredersdorf, who became a friend to him over the years, he exchanged a huge number of informal, often personal notes. They were written in a variant of German which must have been close to his spoken variety, as it shows many traces of orality (and, by the way, disobeyed all rules of orthography, which at the time had already reached a considerable standardization). Extract (1) is a small extract from one of these letters. It demonstrates that Friedrich's German was highly divergent from contemporary as well as modern standards, but based on very different linguistic features than those which finally turned into the "Berlin vernacular":

Extract (1): Friedrich the Great writing to his chamberlain Michael Gabriel Fredersdorf in the beginning of November 1753, on the occasion of the latter's imminent marriage (from Richter 1926: 240).

01	*lasse Dihr lieber heüte wie Morgen Trauen, wann Das zu Deiner flege helfen kan;*	let yourself be married better today than tomorrow, if this can help for your [health] care;
02	*und wilstu einen Kleinen lakeien und einen Jäger bei Dihr nehmen,*	and if you want to take a little valet and a hunter with you,
03	*so könstu es nuhr thun.*	you can surely do it.
04	*wahr es Möglich, so gehe alles aus den wege, was Dihr Ergern Kan,*	if it is possible avoid everything that can annoy you,
05	*denn es Kan Dihr Den Thoht Thun.*	for it can bring you death.
06	*es Thuth mihr Sehr leidt,*	I am very sorry,
07	*daß der gestrige Zufal gekomen ist, der uns wieder zurüke-setzet.*	that yesterday's attack came, which has taken us aback again.
08	*wenn es Dihr Möglich, So continuire doch mit der Tissane.*	If it is possible for you, continue with the herbal tea.
09	*wenn du sie einen Mohnaht recht hinter-einander Drinken Könst,*	If you could drink it one month right without interruption,
10	*so würde es gewisse einen guthen effect thun, das bluht versüßen,*	it would surely do you good, sweeten the blood,
11	*die Materie ihren acreté benehmen, Dihr die Schmertzen lindren*	take away the acuteness from the matter, sooth your pains,
12	*und Dihr die heillung des geschwihrs befördern.*	and forward the healing of your ulcer.
13	*nim Dihr doch in acht, ich bitte Dihr recht Sehr darum.*	Take care of yourself, I beg you very much.
14	*gottbewahre! Fried*	God save [you]! Friedrich

Contractions as in *wilstu* < *willst du* 'want you' (02) point to the orality of these notes. Disregarding the bizarre orthography and the expectable insertions of French loans (*continuiren, Tissane* (08); *acreté* (11)), Friedrich's German shows a strange mixture of relatively standard phonological and sub-standard grammatical features. The phonology (as far as it can be reconstructed) shows only a moderate vernacular and very little Low German influence; among the few examples are the typical northern German affricate reduction in *flege* instead of *pflege* 'health care' (01), the Berlin/Upper Saxon schwa epithesis in *zurüke* instead of *zurück* (07) 'back', and the Berlin/Upper Saxon unrounding in *geschwihr* for Standard *geschwühr* 'ulcer' (12), but none of the phonological features later enregistered as "typical Berlin" and still existent in the vernacular (such as spirantization of syllable-initial /g/ or retention of Low German /k/ in the first-person pronoun *ich*).[11] The most striking substandard feature of Friedrich's language is not phonological, but morpho-syntactical: these are the numerous uses of the dative pronoun *dihr* instead of Standard accusative *dich*, as in

01 *lasse Dihr lieber heüte wie Morgen Traue* (instead of Standard *lass Dich*. . .)
04 *was Dihr Ergern Kan* (instead of Standard *was Dich ärgern kann*)
13 *nim Dihr doch in acht* (instead of Standard *nimm Dich doch in acht*)
13 *ich bitte Dihr recht Sehr darum* (instead of Standard *ich bitte Dich recht sehr darum*).

Case conflation is not restricted to the pronouns, and not to the substitution of the accusative by the dative, as

11 die Materie ihren acreté benehmen,

shows: here *die Materie* is accusative, but should be dative according to the (then and present) standard norm.[12]

Accusative/dative conflation was and is a highly sanctioned and salient feature of the Berlin vernacular, a clear substrate feature from Low German. But as a member of the high aristocracy, Friedrich could afford to disregard this norm persistently and in complete defiance of the dominant bourgeois language

11 For the first of these features, some examples can be found when a larger sample is analyzed; for the second, there is no evidence at all. Lasch (1928: 104) interprets this as evidence for her hypothesis that Low German features only entered the repertoire later from below, i.e., via immigration of Low German speakers in the 19th century. (*Ik* instead of *ich* is clearly a Low German feature; initial *g*-spirantization is associated with Low German but at the time also occurred in Upper Saxony.)

12 *Benehmen* 'take away' is a double-object verb which requires a dative for the benefactive noun phrase.

ideologies. This style was the King's individual choice, and it was neither directly copied nor did it become enregistered as linked to a typical Berlin "persona". Its most prominent feature, i.e., the confusion of the oblique cases, did enter the enregistered Berlin vernacular, but not in the same configuration with other features as in Friedrich's style.

The sources on the basis of which we can analyze the emerging *Berliner Schnauze* in the 19th century are rich (cf. Schmidt 1986: 158–168). I will pick out only one example that shows how linguistic features were mobilized for literary and political purposes by the middle of the century. This is the use of Berlin sub-standard features in political handbills, pamphlets and wall-posters during the 1848 revolution (see the detailed studies by Schildt 1986; Weigel 1979; Führer 1982). These new media for political mass communication were usually written by educated people who knew standard German perfectly well, but published anonymously in the guise of a popular figure from the (upper) lower class (such as a midwife, head mason, simple soldier, writer or rabbi). The audience were equally educated members of the middle classes who bought the handbills for little money.

Extract (2) is a small extract from a handbill published sometime after June 14, 1848. The style of this handbill is more or less the opposite of the King's style: ithas a somewhat stilted, hyperformal grammar (by and large standard-conforming, although line 03 contains an example of the aforementioned accusative/dative confusion[13]). On the other hand it includes a huge number of substandard phonological and some peculiar lexical features. Here is a list of the most important ones:

- The old, Low German stops for High German/standard German fricatives are frequent, but mostly restricted to the first-person pronoun *ik* (cf. lines 01, 03, 05, 07, 09), categorically realized as *ik*. The third-person neuter pronoun *das* is once written *'t* (in the clitic form *durch't*, Standard *durch's* < *durch das*, line 08), reflecting the Low German form, but the pronoun in its non-clitic form as well as the homophonous neuter article and subordinator are written *des*, not *det* (02, 03, 06, 07; similarly, *wie's* < *wie es* and not *wie't* in line 04). *Des* is a compromise form between Brandenburg Low German *det* and Standard *das*. Another trace of the Low German stops is diminutive *-ken* instead of Standard *-chen* (line 08, *Bisken*). Outside these few but recurrent grammatical forms, the standard forms are used.

13 *Eene jewisse anjeborene Bescheidenheit* is accusative, although the preposition *aus* requires the dative, i.e., *aus eener gewissen anjeborenen Bescheidenheit*.

Extract (2): "Offener Brief an den Ex-Bürger-General Blesson von Piefke"[14] [Open letter to the ex-general Blesson of the Civic Guards, by Piefke], signed "Piefke, mitblamierter Bürgerwehrmann; Berlin, zu haben Neue Schönhauser Str. 12, 1 Treppe hoch; Gedruckt bei Carl Lindow" [Piefke, co-blamed soldier of the Civic Guards; Berlin, to be bought in Neue Schönhauser Street 12, 1, up the stairs; printed with Carl Lindow][15].

01	*Ik habe eene janze Zeit lang daruf jewartet,*	I have waited quite a while
02	*des der General-Abmucker Isaac Moses Hersch[16] sich ooch iber Ihre werte perschon hermachen wirde.*	that the super-killer Isaac Moses Hirsch would deal with your honorable person as well.
03	*Aus eene jewisse anjeborene Bescheidenheit habe ik bisher des Maul jehalten,*	Out of a certain inborn modesty I have kept my trap shut so far,
04	*wie's ville Dependirte in de National-Versammlung dhun;*	as many deputies do in the national assembly;
05	*Aberscht ick sehe wohl in,*	But I do understand,
06	*des Hersch mir des Amt nicht abnehmen will;*	that Hersch won't do the job for me;
07	*Un da ik jloobe, des die Wuth, die in mir kocht,*	and since I believe that the rage which is boiling in me
08	*durch't Schreiben een Bisken besänftigt wird,*	will be a bit soothened through writing,
09	*So schneide ik mir'ne Jensefeder zurechte,*	I cut a goose feather for myself,
10	*stippe se in de Dinte,*	put it into the ink,
11	*und schreibe eenen offnen Brief,*	and write an open letter,

14 The well-known Berlin figure "Piefke" underwent a semantic-ideological degradation in the 20th century. First used for a typical petit bourgeois, as in this text, it was later extended to a low-ranking soldier in the Prussian army. After the 1866 defeat of Austria in the Austro-Prussian War, the term became popular in Vienna as a negative stereotype of the Prussian military in general. From there, it was generalized to become a derogatory term for Germans *tout court* in Austria and is still widespread in this function today (cf. Godeysen 2010).

15 From Schildt (1986: 184). The handbill comments on an incident that took place on June 14, 1848, when two persons were shot by the civic guards (*Bürgerwehr*) under its commander Blesson, after they had tried to seize arms from the armory.

16 Hersch is the pseudonym of another handbill writer who published in a mixture of Berlin vernacular and Yiddish, in reality perhaps the publisher S. Löwenherz, cf. Weigel (1979).

Extract (2) (continued)

12	*um Ihnen uf diesem, nich mehr unjewöhnlichen Weje meine Meinung zu sagen,*	in order to tell you in this no longer unusual way my opinion,
13	*uf Nante'sch nämlich,*	in Nante's [17] language I mean,
14	*was man deitsch nennt.*	which is called German.

- The old (Low German) high monophthongs /iː, uː, yː/ are categorically maintained in the preposition/verbal particle *auf* ~ *uf* and the verbal particle *ein* ~ *in* (see *da-r-uf* (01); *uf* (12 and 13); *in* (05)), but never elsewhere (see *aus* (03); *bescheiden, heit* (03); *Maul* (03), etc.).
- The Standard diphthongs /aɪ, aʊ/ are represented as monophthongs in *een/e/r,s* ~ Standard *ein/e/r,s* (01, 03, 08, 11), *ooch* (02), *jloobe* (07), but not in *Meinung* (12). Again, this feature is lexicalized to a handful of words.
- Spirantization of initial and medial /g/ is consistent in the text; it is highly frequent, as it also affects the participle prefix *ge-* (cf. *janze* ~ Standard *ganze* 'whole' (01); *jewisse* ~ Standard *gewisse* 'certain', *anjeborene* ~ Standard *angeborene* 'inborn' (03), and many more).
- Variable unrounding of Standard /y, ø, ɔɪ/, originally an Upper Saxon feature (cf. Lasch 1928: 226), is observed in *iber* ~ Standard *über* 'over', *wirde* ~ Standard *würde* 'would' (02), deitsch ~ Standard *deutsch* 'German' (14) (but not in *unjewöhnlich* 'unusual', line 12).

All these features were certainly recurrent features in the speech of the lower classes at the time.[18] The 1848 political writers used them in a stylized way, i.e., in high density, with high consistency and in selective lexical environments. In the typified fictional speaker "Piefke", they co-occur with other features such as an elaborate syntax (cf., e.g., the expanded gerundial in line 12: *uf diesem, nich*

17 Another well-known handbill writer's pseudonym.

18 There are some more phonological features in the text which must be considered part of the enregistered *Berliner Schnauze*, such as the shortening of *viele* > *ville* 'many' (04) and epithetic schwa as in *zurechte* ~ Standard *zurecht* 'fit' (09). The palatalization of /s/ before /r/ as in *perschon* 'person' (02) and in *aberscht*, an augmented form of Standard *aber* 'but' (05), is more idiosyncratic.

mehr unjewöhnlichen Weje 'in this no longer unusual way') and euphemisms (cf. *Ihre werte perschon* 'your honorable person' (02)), which in turn clash with non-standard vocabulary as in *Maul* ('trap', vulgar for 'mouth'), *General-Abmucker* (*abmucken* 'kill'), hyperbolic for another political writer, or the originally Low German *stippen* for Standard *tunken* 'dip' (10), as well as the mispronunciation of a loan word (*Dependirte* instead of *Deputierte* 'deputees' (04)).

From a sociolinguistic point of view it is important to note that the phonological features that became part of the *Berliner Schnauze* were no longer differentiated according to whether they originated from (formerly) low prestige Low German or (formerly) high prestige Upper Saxon. All these features were now part of one non-standard repertoire. But in order to receive a certain social interpretation, they needed to co-occur in a certain way, i.e., as a social style. This style was not invented in the political discourse of 1848; it had existed before, presumably since the late 18th century (cf. Gebhardt 1933), and it continued to exist beyond the bourgeois "revolution" well into the 20th century. Some features were added, such as a particular kind of wit, often based on innovative and sometimes absurd metaphors (cf. Dittmar, Schlobinski, and Wachs 1986: Ch. 4), or the frequent use of newly coined 'fashion words", particularly in the evaluative domain (cf., e.g., *jottvoll, (janz) famos*[19]). The number of salient phonological or grammatical features has diminished over time (cf. Schlobinski 1987). Some new features also seem to have entered the enregistered style of Berlin, such as the realization of word-final /-er/ as [a] instead of the standard [ɐ]. But it is always a constellation of features (a "style") that carries social meaning, not the individual variable in itself, and this style is consistently interpreted as a lower class/lower middle class style.

Divergent constellations of features can lead to different social interpretations, and not all non-standard features are socially salient in the same way. As a final example to prove this point, take the realization of /g/ as /j/ in syllable onset, one of the most prevalent and frequent sub-standard features in text (3). It would be wrong to ascribe to it any kind of "inherent" social meaning; *g*-spirantization in itself does not index anything. This can be seen from the fact that it also occurs outside the *Berliner Schnauze*, together with other linguistic features. A case in point is the enregistered style of the Prussian army officer (cf. Zimmermann 1987).

---

19 *Jottvoll* < *gottvoll*, lit. 'full of God', 'godly'; *famos*: originally 'famous', in the Berlin vernacular simply a highly positive evaluation.

Until 1900, the Prussian army recruited its officers exclusively from the aristocracy, mainly from the rural aristocracy of the Prussian hinterlands in Pomerania and West and East Prussia (the famous *Preussische Junker*). Stressing their rural background, these men had a tradition of distancing themselves in terms of habitus from the urban middle classes, whose striving for advanced academic education they disdained just as much as their standard German. They shared this attitude with the royals, to whom they felt deeply attached. But equally, they of course looked down on the urban and rural lower classes. Their lifestyle, etiquette and linguistic behavior distinguished them from both groups. The attitudes toward standard German that prevailed in the Prussian military class were therefore very different from, e.g., those of the English aristocracy, who became more and more loyal to "received pronunciation" at the time (Zimmermann 1987).

The influential contemporary satirical magazine *Simplicissimus* portrays the Prussian officer as a chauvinistic, stupid, vain, idle, useless and extremely arrogant member of a caste which desperately tried to keep all "intruders" out. Stiff body hexis, often symbolized by the monocle, and the fetish of the uniform combine with a particular verbal style (see the examples in Figure 3 and 4).

For the *Simplicissimus*, the most salient single feature of the Prussian officers' style is the spirantization of syllable-initial /g/ > /j/. This feature is used consistently, for instance four times in the eleven words of the text underneath the "Cavalry" drawing in Figure 3, and four times in the 24 words underneath the "Rüben" caricature in Figure 4. It co-occurs with several reductions (cf. *'ne* < *eine* and *se* < *sie*) and consonant cluster simplification (as in *nich* < *nicht* and *is* < *ist*), both of which are also part of the *Berliner Schnauze*. The crucial difference, however, between the Prussian officers' style and the *Berliner Schnauze* of the petite bourgeoisie and upper working class is the former's reduced grammatical style, in which finite verbs and grammatical words are often lacking (cf. *aber fürs Jesinde eine janz vorzügliche Speise*, with omission of the copula and co-referential pronoun *ist es*). It is this feature which makes it clear that we are not dealing with the *Berliner Schnauze*.[20]

The point is that within the range of vertically stratified features not every single deviation from the standard language has the same potential of becoming

20 Grammatical reduction is prominently used in other stylizations of the Prussian officer as well, i.e., it is not restricted to the *Simplicissimus*. Captain of the Guard Regiment von Schlettowake in Carl Zuckmayr's widely known drama *Der Hauptmann von Köpenick* (first performance in 1931, later also a movie) is another example.

Figure 3: *From Simplicissimus 1897, 2, 27, p. 212; drawing by Eduard Thöny entitled "Cavallery"*. The text reads: *Haben Kamerad nich auch das Jefühl? Jehen is eijentlich 'ne Jemeinheit.* [Doesn't the comreade feel the same? Walking actually is an insult. Available at http://www.simplicissimus.info/. Copyright permission by Dagmar von Kessel.

salient in a particular social style. Rather than indexing social class directly and univocally, the single phonological features of the Berlin substandard combine selectively with various other linguistic features and become part of a flexible and changing feature network which turns into an enregistered style, typical of a certain social persona. Two of these personae have been mentioned here as examples: "Piefke" (as he was construed in the 1848 political debate) and the Prussian army officer (as construed from the end of the 19th century onward).

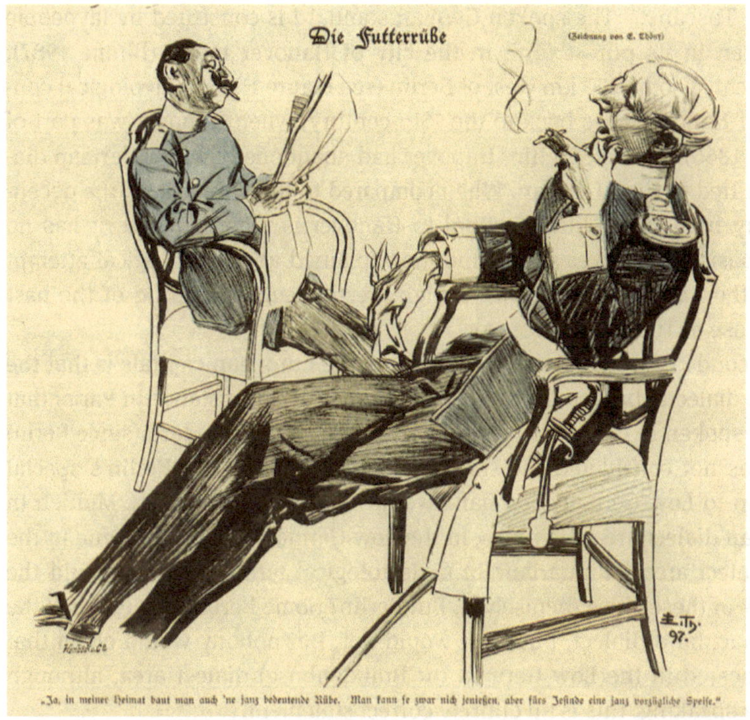

Figure 4: *From Simplicissimus 1897, 2, 24, 1897, p 189; drawing by Eduard Thöny, entitled "The mangel beet".* The text reads: *Ja, in meiner Heimat baut man auch 'ne janz bedeutende Rübe. Man kann se zwar nich jenießen, aber fürs Jesinde eine janz vorzügliche Speise.* [Yes, in my homeland they also cultivate a really important mangel beet. You can't eat it, but for the domestics, really exquisite food.] Available at http://www.simplicissimus.info/. Copyright permission by Dagmar von Kessel.

4 Conclusions

When compared to other European capitals, the city of Berlin shows at least two characteristics. The first is that the variety of German spoken in and associated with Berlin has never been considered the standard language of Germany, even during the time when the city was the capital of Germany. This is not a unique feature of the Berlin language variety; it is also true, for instance, of Rome and the Italian standard at least in pre-fascist times, which is usually ascribed to Tuscany.[21] The spoken German standard is construed by laypeople to be spoken in its purest form in the city of Hanover today (Blume 1987), which is located some 250 km west of Berlin (see Figure 1). This ideological construction of Hanover goes back to the 19th century, when Hanover was part of Prussia (in 1866). Just like Berlin, Hanover had abandoned its Low German dialect and shifted to High German. When compared to Italy (Tuscany), the decentering away from the political capital to Hanover is remarkable as it has no historical basis whatsoever and cannot be explained as an ideological attempt to anchor the national standard in a high-prestige cultural period of the past (as in the case of Tuscany/Florence).

The second characteristic of Berlin among the European capitals is that the city has no dialectal basis today. The reason is not (as for instance in Paris) that the variety spoken in the capital was simply raised to the standard (since Berlin German was not considered the standard), but it is rooted in Berlin's special relationship to Low German. Germans would not hesitate to locate Munich in the Bavarian dialect area, Hamburg in the Low German area, or Cologne in the Rhinish dialect area ("Ripuarian" in dialectological terms), and so would the inhabitants of these cities themselves. But Berlin? Some Berliners might call the Berlin vernacular a dialect, but most would not. But nobody would claim that Berlin is located in the Low German (or Brandenburg) dialect area, although historically speaking, this is an entirely correct statement.

The very brief outline of the sociolinguistic history of Berlin given in this chapter can explain these two (folk linguistic) characteristics. The absence of a dialect region into which Berlin could be included by lay speakers is easily explained by the very early shift from Low German to High German. This distinguishes Berlin both from the more southern cities (in the High German-speaking territories), for which no language shift was necessary, but also from most of the northern cities where the shift occurred much later. While in a place like Hamburg, Low German was still spoken in the middle of the last century, the Berliners had given up this variety 100 years earlier. As a consequence, the link between the city vernacular and Low German was lost. In addition, the region of Brandenburg around Berlin took over the particular variant of High German spoken in the city, so that a dialectal Hinterland is lacking. Hence the specific sociolinguistic situation of Berlin with respect to the first event of long duration discussed here (the shift from Low to High German) can account for the dialectological peculiarity of the city.

21 The fascist Italian government tried to forge a unified Tuscany-Roman standard, with some success.

With regard to the second event of long duration, the establishment of a spoken standard variety, Berlin also plays a special role: when shifting to High German, the Berliners also changed their spoken language, not only their language for writing. This was certainly due to the influence of the adjoining southern region of Upper Saxony whose prestigious German could be heard and copied by the Berliners directly, while other northern German regions had to rely on the written standard (together with their substrate dialects) when developing an oral norm. But this early Upper Saxon influence on the spoken language, which also included substrate features from Low German, also had a disadvantage: when a national norm of spoken standard German began to develop in the late 18th and 19th centuries against all regional ways of pronouncing the language, the Berlin vernacular, firmly established in the linguistic repertoire of the city and widely known all over Germany, worked against its prestige. The language of the city was stratified along a diaglossic continuum with the Berlin vernacular in its most basilectal variant (but not Low German!) as one extreme, and the new, non-regionalized standard variety as the other. But the unofficial prestige of the former was strong, and it was supported (increasingly toward the end of the 19th century) by anti-intellectual, militaristic and aristocratic circles in the capital (including the royals), who distanced themselves from the bourgeois intellectuals favoring the standard. Given this tension, Berlin offered no model for spoken standard German acceptable all over Germany; the centripetal linguistic forces were too strong.

In this chapter, I have also tried to make a more theoretical point on variation and change in the German language area. As the Berlin example shows, linguistic variables in German often have an astonishing temporal persistence. It might at first glance appear disconcerting that certain non-standard features of the Berlin vernacular as we know it today were already in use in the city five hundred years ago and earlier. Such stability despite variability could easily be misinterpreted as "variation without change" in sociolinguistics. However, it would be wrong to apply such an interpretation to the Berlin case. A closer look reveals that the features in question have repeatedly changed social meaning; in Coupland's sense, we are dealing with socio-linguistic change, even though the linguistic change never came to completion (Coupland 2014). Some of these sociolinguistic changes have been discussed in this chapter. For instance:

– Initial *g*-spirantization (a widespread process in Low German; see Lasch 1910: 300–302) is attested, but not frequent in the High German of the early period of the language shift (16th century; cf. Lasch 1910: 165–166), and even in the 17th/18th century, it occurs only sporadically (see Extract (1)). Even though we cannot be sure whether initial written <g> was perhaps pronounced [j], at least in the early period, the feature obviously was not sufficiently salient to be marked in written texts. It is only in the 19th century that *g*-spirantization becomes a highly stereotypical phonological feature of the Berlin vernacular (see Extract (2) and Figure 3/4). At the same time, its meaning changed: whereas it used to be just one among many "interferences" in the context of the shift from Low German to High German, it later became an enregistered feature of certain styles, e.g., of the *Berliner Schnauze* and the Prussian officers' style.

- Stop realization of the High German affricates/fricatives (reflecting the Low German forms) is a highly salient feature that must have been indicative of a speaker's/writer's competence in High German in the context of the Low German > High German shift. From early on, we have evidence that some grammatical words have played a special role; particularly the "irregular" behavior of the first-person pronoun High German *ich*/Low German *ik* seems to be very old. Over the centuries, only some few grammatical words have remained in which the old Low German stops are preserved (in addition to *ik*, the determiner/demonstrative *dit*/*det* ~ Standard German *das* still plays an important role in the present-day vernacular). Particularly in the case of *dit/det*, the development is not linear, but the old forms had already almost disappeared, just to re-emerge as a highly frequent feature of the Berlin vernacular in the 19th century (cf. Figure 1), now a stereotypical lower (!) class marker (hence its absence from the Prussian officers' stereotype, and its only occasional use in the 1848 texts).
- A similar lexicalization process is observed in the vocalic variables. The High German diphthongal counterparts of the Low German long high monophthongs were one of the hardest obstacles in the process of language shift, but also highly indicative of successful mastery of the new prestige language. Hence, Berlin merchant families emblematically relied on this variable to mark their belonging to the upper classes by even changing their names (cf. above, *Ryke* > *Reich(e)*, *Schum* > *Schaum*; cf. Lasch 1910: 219). Other, less skilled writers produced many hypercorrect forms, such as *aunder* for *unter* 'under' (Lasch 1910: 218; old short /u/ did not undergo the diphthongization), or combined the old monophthongs with High German consonants, as in <tziet> (a hybrid of High German *Zeit* and Low German *tiid* 'time') or <bliebt> (a hybrid of High German *bleibt* and Low German *bliivt* 'remains, stays') (Lasch 1910: 216, also 1910: 190, 193). At the end of this process, only the prefixes/grammatical words *auf* and *ein* retained the high vowel (as in *uf, ruff, rin*) – they were shortened and therefore did not diphthongize. At this point, the change stabilized (cf. Extract (2)) without carrying much social value afterwards.

- Quite differently, the most salient morpho-syntactic feature of Berlin, the conflation of accusative and dative case, a Low German substrate feature, has remained in the city vernacular from the 16th century up to today. From the 18th century onward, it was seen as a "problem" and massively sanctioned by the grammarians and schoolteachers in the city; nevertheless, as Extract (1) shows, it was widespread in the colloquial language even of the high aristocracy. (Even around 1800, highest-ranking generals in the Prussian army confessed to confusing the cases, cf. Zimmermann 1987: 39.) Only in the 20th century was this feature downgraded to a lower class stereotype.

These and many other sociolinguistic changes, so I have argued, cannot be attributed to the features themselves, but need to be seen in the context of the social styles in which they are embedded. A sociolinguistic history of Berlin needs to reconstruct these styles, only few of which have been sketched here. Their en-registerment and re-registerment is an ongoing process that continues to unfold today.

References

Agha, Asif. 2003. The social life of cultural value. *Language & Communication* 23. 231–273.

Agha, Asif. 2006. *Language and Social Relations*. Cambridge: Cambridge University Press.

Auer, Peter. 2013. Sociolinguistic change, indexical fields, and the longue durée: examples from the urban sociolinguistics of German. In: Stephen R. Anderson, Jacques Moeschler & Fabienne Reboul (eds.), *L'interface langage-cognition/The Language-Cognition Interface* (Actes du 19e Congrès International des Linguistes, Genève, 22–27 juillet 2013), 201–232. Genf/Paris: Droz.

Bach, Adolf. 1950 [1934]. *Deutsche Mundartforschung. Ihre Wege, Ergebnisse und Aufgaben*, 2nd edn. Heidelberg: Carl Winter.

Blume, Herbert. 1987. Gesprochenes Hochdeutsch in Braunschweig und Hannover. Zum Wandel ostfälischer Stadtsprachen vom 18. bis ins 20. Jh. *Braunschweigische Heimat* 73. 21–32.

Bolte, Johannes (ed.). 1926. *Drei märkische Weihnachtsspiele des 16. Jahrhunderts* (Berlinische Forschungen, Vol. 1). Berlin: Hobbing.

Braudel, Fernand. 1958. Histoire et sciences sociales: La longue durée. *Annales. Économies, Sociétés, Civilisations* 13(4). 725–753.

Coupland, Nikolas. 2014. Sociolinguistic change, vernacularization and broadcast British media. In Jannis Androutsopoulos (ed.), *Mediatization and Sociolingustic Change*, 67–98. Berlin/Boston: de Gruyter.

Dittmar, Norbert, Peter Schlobinski & Inge Wachs. 1986. *Berlinisch. Studien zum Lexikon, zur Spracheinstellung und zum Stilrepertoire*. Berlin: Berlin Verlag Arno Spitz.

Eckert, Penelope. 2008. Variation and the indexical field. *Journal of Sociolinguistics* 12(4). 453–476.

Führer, Beate. 1982. *Das Berlinische im Tagesschrifttum von 1848/49*. Frankfurt/Bern: Peter Lang.

Gebhardt, Heinz. 1933. *Glaßbrenners Berlinisch*. Berlin: Verlag des Vereins für die Geschichte Berlins.

Godeysen, Hubertus. 2010. *Piefke. Kulturgeschichte einer Beschimpfung*. Wien: Edition Vabene.

Hünecke, Rainer (ed.). 2014. *Bibliographie des Internationalen Arbeitskreises. Historische Stadtsprachenforschung*.http://tu-dresden.de/die_tu_dresden/fakultaeten/fakultaet_sprach_literatur_und_kulturwissenschaften/germanistik/gls/iak_hssf/dateien/biblio_syst (accessed 1 March 2018).

Irvine, Judith T. & Susan Gal. 2000. Language ideology and linguistic differentiation. In Paul V. Kroskrity (ed.), *Regimes of Language: Ideologies, Polities, and Identities*, 35–84. Santa Fe: School of American Research Press.

Kaiser, Christine M. 2009. Zwischen "Hoffen" und "Verzagen": Die Emigrationsbemühungen Agathe Laschs. Ein Werkstattbericht. In Mirko Nottscheid, Christine M. Kaiser & Andreas Stuhlmann (eds.), *Die Germanistin Agathe Lasch (1879–1942)*, 11–46. Nordhausen: Verlag Traugott Bautz.

König, Werner. 2001 [1978]. *dtv-Atlas zur deutschen Sprache*. München: Deutscher Taschenbuch-Verlag.

Lasch, Agathe. 1910. *Geschichte der Schriftsprache in Berlin bis zur Mitte des 16. Jahrhunderts*. Dortmund: Wilhelm Ruhfus.

Lasch, Agathe. 1928. *"Berlinisch" – Eine berlinische Sprachgeschichte* (Berlinische Forschungen, Vol. 2). Berlin: Hobbing.

Maas, Utz. 1983. Der Wechsel vom Niederdeutschen zum Hochdeutschen in den norddeutschen Städten in der frühen Neuzeit. In Thomas Cramer (ed.), *Literatur und Sprache im historischen Prozeß* (Vol. 2), 114–129. Tübingen: Niemeyer.

Maas, Utz. 2014 [2010]. *Verfolgung und Auswanderung deutschsprachiger Sprachforscher 1933–1945*. Tübingen: Stauffenburg.http://www.esf.uni-osnabrueck.de/biographien-sicherung/l/181-lasch-agathe (accessed 10 February 2015)

Mauter, Horst. 1986. Berliner Geschichte und Bevölkerungsentwicklung. In Joachim Schildt & Hartmut Schmidt (eds.), *Berlinisch. Geschichtliche Einführung in die Sprache einer Stadt*, 35–99. Berlin: Akademie-Verlag.

Mihm, Arend. 2001. Ausgleichssprachen und frühneuzeitliche Standardisierung. *Rheinische Vierteljahrsblätter* 65. 315–359.

Petersilka, Corina. 2005. *Die Zweisprachigkeit Friedrichs des Großen. Ein linguistisches Portrait*. Tübingen: Niemeyer.

Reichmann, Oskar. 1988. Zur Vertikalisierung des Varietätenspektrums in der jüngeren Sprachgeschichte des Deutschen. In Horst Haider Munske, Peter von Polenz, Oskar Reichmann & Reiner Hildebrandt (eds.), *Deutscher Wortschatz. Lexikologische Studien*, 151–180. Berlin: de Gruyter.

Richter, Johannes (ed.). 1926. *Die Briefe Friedrichs des Großen an seinen vormaligen Kammerdiener Fredersdorf*. Berlin: Hermann Klemm.

Schildt, Joachim. 1986. Berliner Umgangssprache in Flugschriften und Maueranschlägen von 1848. In Joachim Schildt & Hartmut Schmidt (eds.), *Berlinisch. Geschichtliche Einführung in die Sprache einer Stadt*, 173–213. Berlin: Akademie-Verlag.

Schildt, Joachim & Hartmut Schmidt (eds.). 1986. *Berlinisch. Geschichtliche Einführung in die Sprache einer Stadt*. Berlin: Akademie-Verlag.

Schlobinski, Peter. 1987. *Stadtsprache Berlin. Eine soziolinguistische Untersuchung*. Berlin: de Gruyter.

Schmidt, Hartmut. 1986. Die sprachliche Entwicklung Berlins vom 13. bis zum frühen 19. Jahrhundert. In Joachim Schildt & Hartmut Schmidt (eds.), *Berlinisch. Geschichtliche Einführung in die Sprache einer Stadt*, 100–172. Berlin: Akademie-Verlag.

Schönfeld, Helmut. 1986. Die berlinische Umgangssprache im 19. und 20. Jahrhundert. In Joachim Schildt & Hartmut Schmidt (eds.), *Berlinisch. Geschichtliche Einführung in die Sprache einer Stadt*, 214–298. Berlin: Akademie-Verlag.

Schönfeld, Helmut. 1989. *Sprache und Sprachvariation in der Stadt. Zu sprachlichen Entwicklungen und zur Sprachvariation in Berlin und anderen Städten im Nordteil der DDR* (Linguistische Studien A, 197). Berlin: Akademie der Wissenschaften der DDR.

Teuchert, Hermann. 1928/1929. Besprechung von A. Lasch: Berlinisch. *Teuthonista* 5(6). 295–307.

Trudgill, Peter. 1986. *Dialects in Contact*. Oxford: Blackwell.

Weigel, Sigrid. 1979. *Flugschriftenliteratur 1848 in Berlin: Geschichte und Öffentlichkeit einer volkstümlichen Gattung*. Stuttgart: J.B. Metzlersche Verlagsbuchhandlung.

Zimmermann, Gerhard. 1987. Phonetische und paralinguistische Beobachtungen zur fiktionalen preußischen und sächsischen Offizierssprache. *Zeitschrift für Dialektologie und Linguistik* 54(1). 28–60.

Peter Schlobinski

3 Berlinisch: variation and transformation processes of a city language

1 Introduction

Berlinisch, also often referred to as *Berlinerisch,* is a linguistic variety defined in linguistics as a dialect, a variety, *Halbmundart* (Schirmunski 1962), or a city language (Schlobinski 1987). In colloquial language, Berlinisch can be differentiated between strong, medium, and light (Schönfeld 2001: 37) and in everyday speech it is referred to as a dialect or jargon. The term *jargon* has primarily negative connotations, as highlighted by the author Willibald Alexis, who wrote that the Berlin dialect is a "Jargon, aus dem verdorbenen Plattdeutsch und allem Kehricht und Abwurf der höheren Gesellschaftssprache auf eine so widerwärtige Weise komponiert, daß er nur im ersten Moment Lächeln erregt, auf die Dauer aber das Ohr beleidigt" [jargon of corrupt Low German with all of the garbage and discards of higher society language, and composed in such a disgusting way that only in the first moments it incites smiles yet over time it offends the ear] (1905: 368). Carl Philipp Moritz wrote about the Brandenburg dialect in his letters, describing it as made "aus korrupten Plattdeutsch und Hochdeutsch zusammengeschmolzen, und mit Sprachfehlern durchwebt" [from corrupted Low and High German fused together, interwoven with speech defects] (1781: 17) while for Karl Nase, Berlinisch is "ein von Fehlern wimmelndes Straßendeutsch, ein Witzblattjargon" [street German teeming with mistakes, comic book jargon] (1929: 183).

Behind the terminological diversity and the depreciation of Berlinisch to a "jargon", as frequently found in everyday perceptions, lies another phenomenon, which is connected to the strong heterogeneity of this Berlin dialect. Berlinisch is dynamic and diverse, a *Varietätenraum* (space of varieties) in the sense of Klein (1974), which defies the classic view of a dialect as something relatively homogenous.[1] Following Mattheier (1980: 149), Berlinisch like other urban dialects can be said to be "nach eigenen Entwicklungsprinzipien gebildet, die bestimmt waren durch besondere Komponentenkonstellationen, die der Modernisierungsprozeß in der jeweiligen Stadt einnahm. Dazu gehören sowohl die

1 The German dialectologist Karl Haag describes cities as "Neuinseln, die wie Löcher im Lautgewebe der Landschaft sitzen" [new islands, like holes in the soundscape] (1929/1930: 34).

https://doi.org/10.1515/9781501508103-003

wirtschaftliche Bedeutung der Stadt und ihr ökonomischer Kontaktraum als auch ihre administrative Funktion, ihre soziale und politische Struktur und die konfessionelle Entwicklung, die die Stadt mitmacht" [grew according to its own principles of development, undoubtedly molded by the constellation of components of modernization unique to the city in which it is spoken. This includes the economic importance of the city, its economic sphere of contact, as well as its administrative functions, social and political structure, and religious development in which the city is involved]. Trachsel emphasizes the unique significance of the city in his *Glossarium der berlinischen Wörter und Redensarten* [Glossary of Berlin Words and Idioms], the first dictionary of Berlinisch (1873: VI):

> Bedenkt man, dass die Bevölkerung der grossen Städte nicht nur durch die Zahl der Kinder der alten Einwohner, sondern auch hauptsächlich durch Einwanderung aus den verschiedenen Provinzen und aus fremden Ländern sich vermehrt, so wird man es ganz natürlich finden, dass die neuen Bürger die sprachlichen Eigenthümlichkeiten der Gegenden mit sich bringen, aus welchen sie herkommen. Daher ist es leicht erklärlich, wenn in der Hauptstadt Ausdrücke und Redensarten vorkommen, welche auf dem Lande üblich und bekannt sind. Jedoch erleiden diese Wörter nach der Uebersiedelung in der Hauptstadt meistens eine Veränderung und erhalten einen mehr städtischen Anstrich, obgleich sie immer noch zum Volks-Dialecte gehören.
>
> [Considering that the population of large cities increases not just from the number of children inhabitants have, but also largely through the immigration from different provinces and from foreign countries, it is quite natural for the new citizens to bring with them their regional linguistic particularities. It is therefore understandable that expressions and phrases commonly used in the countryside are present in the capital. Yet, these words, after relocating to the capital, often undergo a transformation and gain a more urban character, even though they still belong to the people's dialect.]

As a city and, ultimately, a metropolis, Berlin sprawls and influences not just German slang (compare Grober-Glück 1975), but has also made a "große(n) Bresche [. . .] ins Niederdeutsche" [great breach [. . .] into Low German] (Haag 1929/1930: 35). Today, one specific type of Berlinisch prevails in Brandenburg and Low German is now spoken only by members of the grandparents' generation in Prignitz, Uckermark, and Fläming (Berner 2009: 121–122). In 1956, the "Telschet Wöderbuek", a dictionary of people's Low German from Teltow, a district on the outskirts of Berlin, was published with data from 1926 through the post-war period (Lademann 1956).

The present article will draw on processes of variation and change in order to outline the development of Berlinisch as a sociolinguistic dynamic system. Historical development will be briefly touched upon before addressing the more recent developments that took place in the second half of the twentieth century and in the twenty-first century. The analyses of the last four decades are mainly based on works by Helmut Schönfeld and myself (cf. Schlobinski 1987, 1988a/b, 1996b; Schönfeld 1981, 1996, 2001; Schlobinski and Schönfeld 1992).

2 Historical aspects

After the beginning of the Germanic settlement of the Berlin area in the middle of the first millennium A.D., Slavs migrated to the area in the sixth and seventh centuries. Numerous toponyms and hydronyms in the Spree and Havel area can only be accounted for by the incoming Slavic population of that time. Names of towns and districts ending in *-ow* (see Bretschneider 1971) such as *Teltow*,[2] *Rudow, Spandau* (> *Spandow(e)*) go back to Slavic influence, as do *Lanke* (*Scharfe Lanke*) and *Kiez* (*Sprengelkiez*).[3]

The earliest records date back to 1237 for Cölln and to 1244 for Berlin. Around this time Berlin was linguistically part of the Low German area. During the twelfth century it was significantly shaped by settlers from East Flanders, Southern Brabant, the Lower Rhine area and up to the Vorharz area. Linguistic traces of these settlers from the Rhine and Low Countries can be found some in place names (*Staaken*); the southern Eastphalian origins of some settlers are attested to in the use of the word *Heide*[4] in the sense of 'pine forest'. Bischoff (1966: 292) emphasizes that Berlin was not linguistically homogenous even in its earliest period. Language usage was divided according to social stratification, between Brandenburg and lowland farmer dialects and a stronger, Eastphalian lordly language. From the thirteenth century onwards, the historical and social conditions of the Margraviate of Brandenburg were critical influences on the linguistic history of Berlin. Berlinisch was also strongly influenced by Low German (see also Excerpt 1, Example 1). In the 15th century, Low German as a written language gradually prevails over Latin. Similarly, High German chancery conventions emerged strongly characterized by Franconian features (for details see

2 "Von besonderem Interesse ist der Name Teltow, dessen erster Bestandteil wahrscheinlich aus der vorgermanischen Zeit stammt, durch die älteren germanischen Siedler an die nachfolgenden Slawen weitergeben wurde" [The name Teltow is of particular interest, as it likely comes from the pre-Germanic era and passed down through the older Germanic settlers to subsequent Slavic settlers] (Schmidt 1992: 118).

3 *Scharfe Lanke* is a bay on the Havel in Wilhelmstadt; *Sprengelkiez* is a quarter in the Berlin district of Wedding. Lanke is a lexical relic of West Slavic origin, which remains in use for standing bodies of water such as bays; *Kiez* is likely to have originated from older Slavic forms **chyža* and **chyz* 'house, hut', but the precise etymology remains unclear.

4 Cf. *Jungfernheide*, a forest on the eastern bank of the Spandau (see Rosenberg 1986: 80).

Hier umme ist, dat wi Agnes, von der gnade godes ern woldemares marggreve tu Brandenborch und tu Lusitz wedewe, hilger dechtnisse [...] dat wi unsen getruwen radmannen beider stede, als Berlin und Colen, dorch stedicheit ore truweheit gegeven hebben und ewichliken geven[...]

(From the Berlin City Book, 1320. Book of Privileges. Renunciation of the Widow Waldemars concerning the Jews).[5]

Bonjour meschers Messieurs! Kauff sickkut Savonet! Etuits, un schön Pomat von Wacks un renlick fett. [...] Defilier nit: Ick brauch Brot. Ick nick kann borck; ick hab su Hauß Frau, un viel kind; Freß mi bal Ohr klat weck; Kauff un besahl keschwindt.

(From an etching titled *Henry Gierart, marchand des Savonettes tres renommee a Berlin. Age 82 ans*by Daniel Nikolaus Chodowiecki from 1757).[6]

Zange. (Sieht nach der Uhr.) Du bist zu früh gekommen, Tibbeke. Aber Du kannst immer rin gehn; die Richter wer'n sich gleich versammeln. –Siehfte, da kommen se schon an mit de Brillen. Geh man, un setz'Dir uf die Anklagebank.

Tibbeke. Ne, mit die Anklagebank Hab'ick nischt zu dhun; denn die Bank wird jetzt hausig selber angeklagt. Ooch würde ein Sitz uf die Bank einen schlechten Schein uf mir werfen, un sone Bankscheine lieb'ick nich; denn sie werden bei keene öffentliche Kasse vor voll angenommen, obgleich unsre volle Kassen mehr Schein als klingende Münze enthalten(Hopf 1848: 13).

Na, denn werk dir mah wat sahrn: Du bist eene janz dusslige Rotzneese, wo nich in de Zeit paßt! Ja, nu –wos mit die Dollaren aus ist, da paßt er! Na, vor dir machen se keene neue Inflation! Vor dir nich! Na, jeh doch! Na, mach doch! Du wirst den Zaun nich pinseln! Du nich! Aber det wick dir noch sahren –ick wer dir mal sahren, wat du mir kannst –du kannst mir –

(*Ein Ferngespräch*by Kurt Tucholsky [1927] 2007: 130).

Excerpt 1: Berliner Sprachproben.

Lasch 1910; Schmidt 1992; Butz 1988). The emergence of Berlinish has up to the - present day been shaped by features from the time of Low-German predominance, such as the Low German monophthongs /e:/ and /o:/; High German diphthongs /aɪ:/ and /aʊ/ (*meen* instead of *mein* and *glooben* instead of *glauben*); the g-spirantization (Berlinisch: *ne jut jebratne Jans is ne jute Jabe Jottes*); and the "Akkudativ", the merger of the accusative and dative cases, such as in *ma* for *mich/mir* originate in the time of (see Schlobinski 1988a).

Along with the decline of the Hanseatic League during the fifteenth century, the focus of Berlin's interests began to turn away from the north and towards the central and southern German regions. This brought about a growing significance of High German, particularly in the form of East Central German writing

5 http://archive.org/stream/berlinischessta00gergoog#page/n299/mode/2up.

6 http://www.zeno.org/Kunstwerke/B/Chodowiecki,+Daniel+Nikolaus%3A+Werbung.

conventions in the style of Upper Saxonia and Meissen. This went at the cost of Low German writing, although Low German continued to be the predominant vernacular through the sixteenth century. Lasch (1928: 89), in her foundational work on Berlinisch, states that the establishment of an East Central German written language was accompanied by a swift takeover of the Upper Saxon spoken language. The more dominant Low German forms still found in Berlinisch today (such as *ick* 'I' and *wat* 'what') were "erst in jüngerer Zeit neu vorgedrungen und damals nicht die allgemeine berlinische Sprechform der guten Kreise (waren)" [only recently introduced and at that time were not used in the Berlinisch of higher circles] (Lasch 1928: 104). This thesis was disputed by Teuchert (1928/1929) and Schirmunski (1962), who claimed that Low German forms were not late borrowings from the lower classes (Lasch 1928: 122) but individual relics from the Low German era. Schirmunski summarizes as follows:

> Als Umgangssprache wird das Niederdeutsche in Berlin während des 16./17. Jahrhunderts verdrängt, doch im 17. und teilweise auch zu Beginn des 18. Jahrhunderts sprachen die Volksmassen der Stadt noch niederdeutsche Mundart, die durch immer stärker werdende Einflüsse der herrschenden Form des Hochdeutschen beseitigt worden ist
>
> [Low German was replaced as a colloquial language during the 16th and 17th centuries, though in the 17th century as well as the beginning of the 18th century, the general population continued to speak a Low German vernacular which was slowly replaced by the growing influence of the dominant form of High German] (1963: 614).

The 16th and 17th centuries are characterized by bilingualism in Low and High German. Führer (1982: 73) refers to this development as diglossia. What emerged was a specifically Berlin mixed language with gradually more and more High German forms sneaking into the vernacular. The colloquial speech in Berlin was enriched through contact with French as a result of the Edict of Potsdam of 1685 and of the immigration of the Huguenots; by 1700, one in five Berlin residents was a Huguenot (see Figure 1, Example 2). This can still be seen in Berlinisch lexicon: for example, in the noun *Botten* ([rough shoes, boots] > french *la botte = der Stiefel*); in the verb *botten* (to hurry); or in the phrase *etwas aus der Lamäng erledigen* 'do something effortlessly', where *Lamäng* comes from the French *la main* 'the hand' (Harndt 1977).

In the 19th century, during the late Romanticism and the Vormärz period and with the emergence of nationalism and liberalism, there is an observable increase in focus on vernacular culture and language connected with the written use of dialects. This is reflected in political pamphlets and literary texts (see also Figure 1, Example 3). Starting around 1848 or 1849, Berlinisch began to be used as a socio-stylistically shaped "media variety" in order to "Gedanken zu scharfen Pfeilen zu gestalten und so in Kreise zu tragen, die, für ernste Untersuchungen und Belehrungen ohne Sympathie, dem Humor und Witze bereitwillige Ohren liehen" [mold thoughts into sharp arrows and thus convey them to circles who lend their willing ears to serious investigations and unsympathetic lectures humor and jokes] (Brendicke 1897: 71).[7] In the second half of the 19th century, parallel to the processes of industrialization, the population grew drastically. As Berlin becomes the capital of the new empire in 1871, the city became a political and cultural hub. The heavy immigration, above all from the nearby Mark and from eastern regions, led to new flows of migration and processes of adaptation. The immigrants adapted to new linguistic conditions and therefore appropriated the locally spoken city dialect and simultaneously contributed to its development by adding elements from their own varieties:

> Das verstärkte Wiederauftreten niederdeutscher Formen im Berlinischen des 19. Jahrhunderts, das von Agathe Lasch festgestellt und als Entlehnungen aus den unteren Schichten interpretiert wurde [see above, P.S.], ist daher eher auf den Umstand zurückzuführen, daß der größte Teil der Zugewanderten dem niederdeutschen Sprachraum um Berlin entstammten
>
> [the increasing re-emergence of Low German forms in Berlinisch in the 19th century, which Agathe Lasch identified and interpreted as a process of borrowing from lower social strata, is likely due to the fact that most of immigrants to Berlin came from Low German speaking regions near the city] (Butz 1988: 29–30).

Mass immigration and the formation of an urban proletariat reinforced the social and linguistic opposites: Berlinisch became a sign of social position, the "jargon of lower social classes" in opposition to the "upscale Berlin speech". The social differentiation of Berlinisch and its relative frequency and intensity continues through the 20th century. Now a metropolis – Greater Berlin was formed into one administrative unit in 1920 – the perceived pragmatic character of the city is now connected with the buzz word *Berliner Schnauze* [the Berlin snout]. It connotes as blunt, quick-witted, clever, aggressive, and funny (cf. Lindner 2016: 48–55). Quick and curt responses (see Excerpt 1, Example 4) can be a reflex in big city life and a "Produkt des Zusammenlebens in Enge und Menge, Eile und Wechsel" [product of living in close quarters with crowds, hurry, and change] (Lindner 2016: 54); aggressive wit can then be seen as a communicative strategy in a hectic and strongly competitive metropolis.

World War II marked a turning point for Berlin's development. By the end of the war most of the city had been turned into rubble and ash. In the postwar years, many people who had fled during the war returned to the city. While the extensive influx of refugees from eastern territories changed the

7 Führer (1982) and Schildt (1992) studied Berlinisch in everyday writing. Gebhardt (1933) and Kruse (1987) studied the Berlin dialect in the *Glaßbrenner*'s writing.

social composition of the city, the social differences between and amongst the city's districts were preserved and reflected in the linguistic composition across speakers (see Section 2). The division of Berlin into four allied occupation zones, the founding of the GDR in 1949 and the exodus from East Germany to West-Berlin (a 1961 census revealed that 21 percent of the population of West-Berlin were immigrants from the East Germany), and the closing of the border with the building of the wall in August 1961 all led to the separation of the city into two distinct communities of communication. It was only through the passing of the *Passagierscheinabkommen* in December of 1963, a treaty between West Berlin and the GDR granting visitation rights to family members, which allowed for cross-border personal communication, and the *Viermächteabkommen* [Four-Power Agreement] of 1971 that the wall began to act as a linguistic filter. Nevertheless, it remained more permeable from West to East than from East to West.

3 Divided city – divided language?

The heterogeneity of Berlinisch was the focus of a sociolinguistic project carried out in the early 1980s (Dittmar, Schlobinski, and Wachs 1986). The objective of this study was to investigate linguistic variation (selected phonetic features) and subjective speech data (language preferences and values) of the language in the city of Berlin. Next to other forms of variation within the language[8] such as gender, socioregional stratification, and social networks in the sense of Milroy (1980), the variation between the western and eastern parts of the city was a particular focus (Schlobinski 1987). To this end, in the years 1982–1984 interviews were conducted and linguistic data from street signs collected in the West Berlin middle class district Zehlendorf, the working-class district Wedding, and in the district bordering Wedding on the other side of the wall, Prenzlauer Berg.
It is particularly interesting that Wedding and Prenzlauer Berg, two districts that were traditionally blue-collar and homogenous in both social structure and with regards to urban planning, had highly significant differences in the use of Berlinisch dialects. Noticeably, Berlinisch was used in the East Berlin district of Prenzlauer Berg with a high degree of loyalty. Qualitative differences between

8 Thus it can be shown that g-spirantization in front of /l/ und /ʀ/ can no longer be found, but is particularly preferred before /ə/. This explains why in code-switching situations, a speaker in a conversation tends to say [jəle:gt], but not to show lower probability of spirantization before /e/ ([ge:gn̩]) (Schlobinski 1988b).

Table 1: Dialect use[9] by district (see Schlobinski 1987: 152–153).

	Dialect ($\bar{x}$)
Zehlendorf	28%
Wedding	52%
Prenzlauer Berg	79%

the two parts of the city in the usage of r-vocalization were later recorded (Schlobinski 1996b). This linguistic stratification and differentiation can be explained through a deeper understanding of the divergent developments of these politically divided communication communities.

Since 1945, Wedding and Prenzlauer Berg have gone down very different paths of development. Wedding took in foreign guest workers and underwent a vigorous renovation of the tenement buildings, thus taking on a heterogeneity that changed both the outward image of Wedding as well as its social structure and networks. The demographics, infrastructure, and architecture of Prenzlauer Berg, in comparison, remained stable. The eastern district had, therefore, a stable and fixed speech community and tight social networks while in Wedding, the discourse community was dynamic (breaking up traditional social networks) that mirrored the external changes happening throughout the district. The linguistic consequences of this divergent development were the different degrees of language variation and differing degrees of persistence of Berlinisch.

Berlinisch had negative connotations (vulgar, unrefined) in West Berlin that were either rare or nonexistent in East Berlin (Schlobinski 1987: 185–186; cf Schönfeld 1981, 2001). The differentiation was grounded in the fact that in West Berlin, the standard language was recognized as the norm, the legitimate language (following the definition by Bourdieu [1982] 2015: 47–97); therefore, members of middle and lower classes utilized the standard language in the pursuit of social and socioeconomic mobility. The standard language was given prestige, in juxtaposition with Berlinisch, which was considered vulgar and uneducated; Berlinisch was, in the classic sociolinguistic sense, a sociolect. In East Berlin, the situation was completely different. The Berlin way of speaking

9 The index was measured by $\bar{x}$ = number of dialect variants of six phonological variables / number of possible realizations of six phonological variables.

was needed and used in professional situations and it did not have the negative associations otherwise found in the West.

> Im Ostteil der Stadt besaß das Berlinische ein höheres Prestige als im Westteil. Es wurde von den Ostberlinern empfunden als Sprache der Identität, die auch das Gefühl einer sozialen Gleichheit vermittelte und förderte, mit der man sich wohlfühlte. Es wurde nicht nur in privaten, sondern gleichermaßen in vielen öffentlichen Situationen von Angehörigen aller sozialen Schichten verwendet
>
> [In the eastern part of the city, Berlinisch had a higher status than in the western side. Residents of East Berlin took it on as a part of their identity, which also promoted and supported a feeling of social equality and thus also wellbeing. It was not only used in private, but just as often it was used in public contexts amongst members of all social classes] (Schönfeld 2001: 48).

In East Berlin, and in Prenzlauer Berg in particular, Berlinisch was a prestigious speech variety. The difference in prestige between Berlinisch in East and in West Berlin, is correlated to the fact that the two cities had drastically different day-to-day norms, private spheres, and societal structures which led to divergent values and norms. While in West Berlin, democratic political systems and free market economics differentiated work culture from the private sphere under the imperative of social rationalization, bureaucratic socialist integration mechanisms in the East failed and led to an uncoupling of the everyday and the private sphere from the political system. The GDR citizen as an individual lived a double life as an official employee in a company and as an unofficial worker in another job. Marx and Lenin provided the interpretive lens for industrial activities while at home the western television was a primary influence. The realms of the system and of day to day life were linguistically marked by official and unofficial language use. The official language in the public domain was how newscasters and officials spoke, marked by stereotypes and linguistic clichés and often openly displaying the speakers' Saxon origins. The "gehobene Sächsisch repräsentiert bis zu einem gewissen (…) Grad innerhalb der DDR die Hochsprache; mindestens stellt es den völlig anerkannte Verkehrston auch bei offiziellen Anlässen dar" [The "upscale Saxon represents, to a certain (…) point, a language of prestige within the GDR; at the very least, it is understood as the parlance for official occasions"] (Bausinger 1972: 20). In contrast, the use of Berlinisch as an unofficial language was associated with solidarity against the governing structures, everyday culture against the ruling culture, and Berliner worker solidarity against the upper-class officials. Berlinisch took on a social use that symbolized the border against the system in power.

Between 1961 and 1989, Berlin and its linguistic region was a prime example of a single language community divided into two communities of communication due to the division of the area into two separate societal systems.

4 A reunited Berlin and its linguistic developments

After the reunification in 1989 and during the period shortly after, both the political vocabulary of East Germany and its institutional systems were deconstructed: the term *Delikatladen* disappeared; the *Team* replaced the *Kollektiv*; and *Kita* replaced *Krippe*. A slew of streets, subway stations, and train stations were renamed; for example, northbound trains from Alexanderplatz went towards *Otto-Braun-Straße*[10] instead of *Hans-Beimler-Straße*.[11] Indeed, this one-sided change in language use was also a form of reorientation towards the West and assertion of dominance from the *Besserwessis* [smart-Alec Westerners], resulting in feelings of *Ostalgie* [east-nostalgia], a phenomenon that also extends to linguistic feelings of nostalgia (Schönfeld 2001).

Many East Berliners changed their use of the dialect by speaking a less strong version and/or differentiating the contexts in which they used it. Along with objective changes in its use, Berlinisch was no longer seen as a prestigious dialect: "In Ostberlin ist die fast generelle Tendenz zur positiven Bewertung des Berlinischen und seiner Verwendung [...] nicht mehr vorhanden" [in East Berlin, there is no longer a general tendency to give Berlinisch and its usage positive associations] (Schönfeld 2001: 181). Instead, use of the dialect was stigmatized, especially in the 1990s. A 25-year old student from East Berlin described her experience:

> In de Disco in Westberlin fühl ick mich richtich unwohl. Ick trau mich kaum, 'n Mund aufzumachen, weil ich sonne Hemmungen habe davor: Guck mal, die da aus 'm Osten. [...] Die im Westen, die sprechen schon ganz anders. Man merkt das am Hochdeutschen. Wir berlinern ja ziemlich stark
>
> [In clubs in West Berlin, I don't feel comfortable. I hardly dare to speak up, because I'll out myself as from the east. [...] The guys in West Berlin, they speak differently. You can really tell with the High German. Our Berlin accent is pretty strong] (Schönfeld 1996: 89).

On the basis of his findings from research conducted in the 1990s, Schönfeld (2001: 182) posits the following:

> Der Weg Berlins von der zusammenwachsenden Stadt zu einer Stadt ohne Grenzen wird nach Ansicht unserer Probanden auch in sprachlicher Hinsicht noch ein weiter Weg sein, denn das Sprachverhalten ist in starkem Maße geprägt durch Gewohnheiten. Dazu kommt, dass die Mauer, die die Stadt in zwei Hälften trennte, noch in den Köpfen der

10 (1872–1955), a social democrat German politician in the Weimar Republic, persecuted in the Nazi era.

11 (1895–1936), German Communist member of the Reichstag, persecuted in the Nazi era.

meisten Berliner existiert. Die Ausgleichsprozesse beim Gebrauch des Berlinischen verlaufen also sehr differenziert und widersprüchlich.

[According to our respondents and with regards to language, Berlin still has a long way to go from a city growing together to becoming a city without borders; speech behavior is, to a large extent, shaped by habits. The wall, that once physically divided the city into two halves, still exists in the minds of most Berliners. The processes of adaptation between East and West in the use of Berlinisch are therefore highly differentiated and often contradictory.]

In contrast, Regener's investigation found that "im Ostteil der Stadt [. . .] der Gebrauch des Berlinischen auf relativ hohem Niveau stabil [bleibt]; im Westteil ist der tendenzielle Dialektverlust der letzten Jahrzehnte gestoppt, der Gebrauch des Berlinischen stabilisiert sich auf niedrigerem Niveau" [in the east part of the city [. . .] the use of Berlinisch [stays] stable at a relatively high level; in the western part, the downward trend in use of the dialect in the last decades stopped and the use of Berlinisch stabilized at a low level] (Regener 2002: 16). Have the communication and language barriers, caused by long-standing separation, been overcome? Or does the *Sprachmauer* [language wall], evoked in the provocative title of the study by Dittmar and Bredel in 1999, still exist?

In a study by Forsa on behalf of the GfDS (Schlobinski and Ewels 2014), a representative survey on the Berlin dialect was conducted. It focused on the assessment and evaluation of Berlinisch by residents of the capital as well as lexical content. The selection of questions and words is based on the background of existing research (see Table 2), so that comparisons and evolutions in the dialect can be examined. It is noteworthy that, since relevant research on the Berlin urban dialect in the 1980s in the East (Schönfeld 1981; Schildt and Schmidt [1986] 1992) and in West Berlin (Dittmar, Schlobinski, and Wachs 1986; Dittmar and Schlobinski 1988; Schlobinski 1987) and Schönfeld (2001[12]), no larger studies on the subject have been conducted; a sociolinguistic investigation of the use and development to date of Berlinisch is lacking.

Within the study by GfdS/Forsa, a systematically selected random sample of 1,001 men and women over the age of 14 were interviewed in the city of Berlin. The survey took place between the 10th and the 25th of September 2014 and was conducted using computer assisted telephone interviews.[13] Data was

12 These results are based on research carried out between 1991 and 1999, within the framework of a DFG project (by Reiher and Schlobinski).

13 The methodological problems with such a survey or questionnaire (see Table 1) are not discussed here (see Schlobinski 1996a).

Table 2: Comparison of studies.

	1983	1983–87	1994/96/98	1991–1999
N	550	490	876	see Schönfeld (2001: 28–29, 59)
Age	>18	>18	25–45	>12
Method	Survey	Survey	Survey	Survey, test, audio recording
East-West	West	East-West	East-West	East-West
Literature	Kruse and Schlobinski (1984), Dittmar, Schlobinski, and Wachs (1986)	Schlobinski and Schönfeld (1992)	Regener (2000, 2002), Schmidt-Regener (1998)	Schönfeld (2001)

recorded on age; gender; city district; East Berliners or West Berliners; and if they are Old Berliners or New Berliners.[14] In the following, the results of the GfdS/Forsa study are presented and embedded in the research context. The focus of analysis here is the comparison between the East and West.

4.1 Assessments of the current use of Berlinisch

The majority of respondents (62 percent) reported that they at least occasionally used Berlinisch themselves. Another 38 percent said that they did not use the Berlin dialect. There was a strong difference between ages (see Table 3). Respondents under the age of 30 were much less likely to say that they used the dialect compared to those over the age of 30. Those in the age group 35 to 59 had much stronger use, self-reporting at 71 percent.

The data reflects that there is only a minor difference between east and west in the evaluation of the use of the dialect: 66 percent of East Berliners used Berlinisch compared to 60 percent of West Berliners. Among longtime residents the difference is similarly minor: 78 percent of Old Berliners in the East compared to 73 percent of Old Berliners in the West. While studies on factual language use in the Berlin districts of Zehlendorf, Wedding, and Prenzlauer Berg showed significant differences in use (see Schlobinski 1987: 153); the

14 New Berliners are defined as residents of the city who arrived after the year 1990.

Table 3: Berlinisch use by age.

	Yes	No
14 to 29	53%	47%
30 to 44	61%	39%
35 to 59	71%	29%
>60	64%	36%

overall distribution of individual phonological features[15] demonstrated that the dialect use was at 30 percent in Zehlendorf (West Berlin), 50 percent in Wedding (West Berlin) and 80 percent in Prenzlauer Berg (East Berlin). This data seems to confirm what Regener (2000) termed *Entwicklungstendenz*, based on data from the study of linguistic attitudes, in which surveys were conducted in 1994, 1996, and 1998 in West Berlin districts of Zehlendorf and Wedding and the East Berlin districts of Prenzlauer Berg and Pankow. Given the available data, one could conclude that dialect use in the East has decreased while its use in the West has stabilized. Moreover, that there has been a convergence between East and West; either from the East or from the West or coming from both sides. It should be emphasized (again) that there are no comprehensive studies of current dialect use in the city and therefore no valid, objective speech data exists.

The majority (57 percent) of all interviewees indicated that they thought there is a difference in the Berlin dialect between East and West Berliners compared to 35 percent who indicated there is no difference, which appears to be a remarkable result. Respondents indicated that dialect differs between East and West Berliners, and in particular a significant proportion of Berliners from the western part of the city responded that there is a difference (see Table 4). The results to the question of whether respondents in the comparison studies believe the Berlin dialect sounds different in East Berlin compared to West Berlin are interesting (see Table 5).

In West Berlin investigations on the subject from the year 1983, only 20 percent of respondents agreed that Berlinisch sounded different in the East compared to the West (Dittmar, Schlobinski, and Wachs 1986: 110). The picture changed completely in the 1990s, as shown by research from Regener (2002).

15 See also: Schönfeld (2001: 86–87).

Table 4: Responses to whether the Berlin dialect is different when used by East or West Berliners (cf footnote 13).

	Yes	No	I don't know
East	43%	48%	9%
West	65%	26%	9%
Old-Berliner East	42%	50%	8%
New-Berliner West	73%	23%	5%

Table 5: Does the Berlin dialect sound different when spoken by East Berliners compared to West Berliners?

	1983 West	1994 East/West	1996 East/West	1998 East/West	1998[16] East/West
Yes	20%	49% / 75%	60% / 7 3%	48% / 63%	63% / 79%
No	60%	30% / 11%	16% / 9%	20% / 19%	
I don't know	20%	21% / 14%	24% / 18%	32% / 18%	

The survey results from Schönfeld (2001: 128–130) with data from 179 respondents show a similar picture: 79 percent of West Berliners and 63 percent of East Berliners reported that the Berlin dialect of East Berliners is different than that of West Berliners (Table 5, right column).

A possible explanation for the increase in yes-responses could be that the fall of the Wall increased contact between the East and West, allowing for more opportunities to get to know the language habits of East Berlin better. This made more exact evaluation of the linguistic reality possible, explaining the high, albeit overall lower, portion of East Berliner evaluations. Another explanation could be that the assessment is not based on actual differences in the language, but rather on the perception of use by *Wessis* versus *Ossis* and vice versa; allowing for prejudices to influence responses. However, if this were the case, the prejudice would still exist, according to data from Table 3. This shows that the mutual acceptance of West and East Berliners has increased significantly (see Table 6), even if 36 percent assume

16 Schönfeld (2001: 130). Data only exists for this component.

the acceptance has decreased, this is still significantly less than in the 1990s. Generally, Berlinisch is more accepted than it was 20 years ago. At the same time, 50 percent of respondents worry that the population of Berlin is being displaced by an influx of people from other regions (see Table 7). Differences between East and West are not relevant here. Squabbles in the media about local terms (such as the Swabian *Wecke* versus the Berliner *Schrippe* for a bread roll) are a fitting example of this concern.[17] On a more serious note, the repression of entire sections of the population, e.g. prompted by gentrification, and corresponding dialect milieus that result from immigration are relevant topics.

Table 6: Increase and decrease of acceptance of the Berlin dialect in recent years.

	increased	**decreased**	**don't know**
1994 East/West	4% / 3%	54% / 44%	42% / 53%
1996 East/West	4% / 3%	47% / 51%	49% / 46%
1998 East/West	2% / 1%	50% / 48%	48% / 51%
	increased	**decreased**	**has not changed**
2014 East/West	21% / 25%	37% / 36%	30% / 20%

Table 7: Is the dialect being displaced through newcomers from other regions?

	Yes	**No**	**Don't know**
Total	50%	47%	3%
East	53%	44%	3%
West	48%	49%	3%
Old-Berliner East	51%	46%	3%
Old-Berliner West	48%	50%	2%

17 See Spiegel online from 30.12.2012: http://www.spiegel.de/politik/deutschland/wolfgang-thierse-wettert-gegen-schwaben-in-berlin-a-875182.html.

4.2 Lexical variation

Respondents were given some Berlinisch words and phrases and asked if they a) knew the word or phrase and b) if they used it (see Table 8). The words were selected based on an analyses from Kruse and Schlobinski (1984), and Schlobinski and Schönfeld (1992).

Table 8: Use of expressions.

Item	∑	East	West	Difference
	Doofkopp	37%	37%	37%
0% Göre	53%	44%	41%	+3%
schnieke	42%	44%	41%	+3%
Piefke	27%	29%	26%	+4%
j. w. d.	57%	58%	56%	+2%
Pinte	19%	15%	22%	−7%
urst	16%	27%	9%	+16%
Stampe	10%	15%	7%	+8%
Wuppke	2%	2%	1%	+1%

As shown in Table 8, there is a significant difference in knowledge and perceived use. 82 percent of the respondents knew the word *Piefke* (little boy), while only 27 percent of Berliners indicated that they used it. *Piefke* has been used widely in Berlin since the end of the 19th century (see Mally 1974, 1984), yet "today this expression is only occasionally and often jokingly used" (Schlobinski and Schönfeld 1992: 118).

The difference between East and West regarding the words *Pinte, urst*, and *Stampe* is interesting. While *Pinte* is more commonly known and used in the West, *urst* and *Stampe* are more commonly known and used in the East. This trend is stronger among Old Berliners (see Table 9).

The word *Pinte* (bar, restaurant[18]) came to West Berlin via the northern part of West Germany from southern Switzerland and southwest Germany (Eichhoff

18 The favorite term in Berlin is *Kneipe*.

Table 9: Old Berliner knowledge of Pinte, urst, and Stampe in the East and West.

Item	East	West	Difference
Pinte	61%	77%	−16%
urst	74%	36%	+38%
Stampe	69%	48%	+21%

1977: map 32; Küpper 1990: 614). In particular, the word spread from 1945 on. Before the reunification, *Pinte* was not common knowledge nor often used in East Berlin (Schönfeld 2001: 110). In the survey from Schlobinski and Schönfeld (1992: 116), 12 percent of West Berliners compared to 0.5 percent of East Berliners responded positively to this word as a Berlin variant for bar. Today, this difference is noticeably smaller, though it still exists. It has grown since the 1990s, as shown by Schönfeld (2001: 110), who notes ratios of 12 percent in East Berlin and 36 percent in West Berlin.

The word *Stampe*, used to refer to a bar or place to drink, comes from French via the Huguenots: "Die Stampe, ursprünglich (estaminet) eine Kneipe, Budike, hat sich zum Tanzlokal 'verfeinert'" [*Stampe* originally (from the French *estaminet*), a *Kneipe* or *Budike* ['bar'], later "refined" into 'dance club'] (Lasch 1928: 166), as a result of the "Besetzung Berlins durch die französischen Truppen (1806–1813)" [occupation of Berlin by French troops] (Küpper 1990: 791). In the German dictionary Duden, *Stampe*, from Low German *stampen* ('stampfen') is accompanied with the meaning 'cheap, dive bar' (Alsleben and Grunert 2005: 42). Meyer (1925: 171), in his well-known dictionary, defines it as a lower range dance club, while in Trachsel's 1873 Berliner dictionary the word is not listed. *Stampe* is a Berliner word that existed long before the city was divided and today has negative connotations. *Stampe* is more commonly known and used in East Berlin. This can be explained by the following assumption: older lexical variants of Berlin have preserved better in East Berlin than in the West (see Section 2). In part also holds for present-day usage.

The most striking example is *urst* ('awesome, super, crazy, rad'), which in 1989 still wasn't understood in West Berlin (Schönfeld 2001: 100). In research from the 1980s, 5 percent of East Berliners gave *urst* as a variation for 'chic', along with variations on the theme such as *dufte, schnieke, fetzig, knorke*. However, not a single West Berliner knew the word. Today, 36 percent of the West Berliners indicated that they knew the word and used the word (see table 9). According to (Schönfeld 2001: 100), *urst* came to East Berlin in the 1970s. Oschlies (1981: 190) and Beneke (1982: 192) describe *urst* as youth slang, shown in use from youth (*urster Hammer*). Heinemann (1989: 88) lists the example in her East German youth slang dictionary: *urste Pose* (unique experience). Beyond the definition from the youth slang usage, *urst* appears in the East-German Berliner dictionary (Wiese 1987: 143) commonly used since the 1970s. When taking into account both the documentation listed above and the argumentation from Heinemann that youth in the GDR at large looked to Berlin's urban slang as a role model ("Berlin wird von den meisten Jugendlichen als Umschlagplatz für neue Ausdrucksmittel angesehen"), it's plausible to reason that *urst* is a youth slang term that originated in Berlin (Heinemann 1989: 30). *Urst* is, according to Heinemann (1989: 101) a synonym of *urisch*, modified by Berlinisch pronunciation, replacing [uʁʏʃ] for [uʁɪç] (<urig>). *Urst* is derived from *urig*, as a phonetically reduced form of the superlative: urigst > urst ([uʁʏʃst] > [uʁst]/[uɐst]). As an intensifying modifier, the superlative increases the degree of modification. Today, *urst* has been replaced by other intensifiers such as *krass* and *episch*.

These lexical trends show that, on the one hand, certain processes of convergence between East and West Berlin have taken place (*Pinte* vs. *urst*) while on the other hand, there continue to be differences between the knowledge and appreciation of use in the two parts of the city. The perception of difference between East and West Berlin has clearly increased after the wall fell and then stabilized at a relatively equal level, while the acceptance of Berlinisch has clearly increased since the 1990s.

5 Conclusion

Berlinisch is a variety that has evolved dynamically as a result of immigration and heterogenous social structures over centuries and will continue to do so. The result is a high degree of linguistic variation and dynamic change in the linguistic conditions in Berlin over various historical phases. The population of Berlin is currently growing rapidly; according to estimates, the city will have more than 3.8 million inhabitants in 2030 (Bevölkerungsprognose für Berlin (2016)). The correlated changes in social structures, such as the dissolution of social networks in the face of gentrification, all cause (and will continue to cause) changes in linguistic behavior in Berlin's districts and neighborhoods. The implications for Berlinisch are difficult to predict; it is challenging, if not impossible, to predict language variation and change. Moreover, the processes of reconciliation between the uses of Berlinisch are varied and inconsistent. For the conclusion of this discussion, I would like to present the following hypotheses:

1. The *Sprachmauer* [language wall] will not continue to be a deciding factor. Rather, sociolinguistic parameters such as network structures, migration flows, and the ebb and flow of subcultures are central factors that impact language variation and change. Berlinisch will continue to be reduced and disintegrate into different sociolects, eventually stabilizing at a certain level. Dialect decay in this context refers to a quantitative decrease in usage and a qualitative elimination of relic features.
2. At the same time, Berlinisch used as regiolect in the Berlin-Brandenburg region will stabilize, creating a Berliner slang (weak Berlinisch) that serves as a type of linguistic roof under which the dialect can stabilize.
3. Despite the fact that Berlin is a capital city, Berlinisch will not, in the foreseeable future, be seen as a prestigious variety like it was in East Berlin. Instead, like previously in West Berlin, it will have negative or neutral connotations. There will still be some social groups that will ascribe positive associations to Berlinisch and remain loyal speakers of the dialect. In the long term, a Berlin dialect may develop that does not have negative connotations and may even have positive connotations.
4. Migration may result in increased variation of Berlinisch, especially with influences from other non-German languages (see Wiese 2012 for more on Kiezdeutsch[19]).

But as the Berliner says: *Nüscht Jenauet weeß man nich*!

References

Alexis, Willibald. 1905. *Erinnerungen*. (ed. by Max Ewert). Berlin: Concordia deutsche Verlagsanstalt. https://books.google.de/books?id=2aAEAAAAYAAJ&hl=de&source=gbs_book_other_versions.

Alsleben, Brigitte & Brigitte Grunert. 2005. *Der kleine Duden. Deutsches Wörterbuch. Sonderausgabe Berlin*. Mannheim: Duden Verlag.

Bausinger, Hermann. 1972. *Dialekte, Sprachbarrieren, Sondersprachen*. Frankfurt am Main: Fischer Taschenbuch-Verlag.

19 Spontaneous Berlin Kiezdeutsch is a variety emerged by young speakers from multi-ethnic urban neighborhoods.

Beneke, Jürgen. 1982. *Untersuchung zu ausgewählten Aspekten der sprachlich-kommunikativen Tätigkeit Jugendlicher. Untersucht an Probanden aus der Hauptstadt der DDR, Berlin, und dem mecklenburgischen Dorf Mirow, Bezirk Neubrandenburg*. Berlin: Akademie der Wissenschaften der DDR dissertation.

Berner, Elisabeth. 2009. Niederdeutsch – Brandenburgisch – Berlinisch – Standardsprache: Entwicklungstendenzen im regionalen Varietätengefüge. In Elisabeth Berner & Karl-Heinz Siehr (eds.), *Sprachwandel und Entwicklungstendenzen als Themen im Deutschunterricht: fachliche Grundlagen – Unterrichtsanregungen – Unterrichtsmaterialien*, 121–140. Potsdam: Universitätsverlag.https://publishup.uni-potsdam.de/opus4-ubp/files/3582/sprachwandel_S121_140.pdf.

Bevölkerungsprognose für Berlin. 2016. *Bevölkerungsprognose für Berlin und die Bezirke 2015–2030. Senatsverwaltung für Stadtentwicklung und Umwelt Ref. I A – Stadtentwicklungsplanung in Zusammenarbeit mit dem Amt für Statistik Berlin-Brandenburg*. Berlin. http://www.stadtentwicklung.berlin.de/planen/bevoelkerungsprognose/download/2015-2030/Bericht_Bevprog2015-2030.pdf.

Bourdieu, Pierre. 2005 [Fr. 1982]. *Was heißt sprechen? Zur Ökonomie des sprachlichen Tausches*. Wien: new academic press.

Brendicke, Hans. 1897. Berliner Wortschatz zu den Zeiten Kaiser Wilhelms I. *Schriften des Vereins für die Geschichte Berlins* 33. 69–196.

Bretschneider, Anneliese. 1971. Havel – Hagen – Tempelhof. Ein Beitrag zur Geschichte des Ortsnamensuffixes -ow im brandenburgischen Raum. In Johannes Schultze, Gerd Heinrich & Werner Vogel (eds.), *Brandenburgische Jahrhunderte. Festgabe für Johannes Schultze zum 90. Geburtstag*, 17–33. Berlin: Duncker u. Humblot.

Bischoff, Karl. 1966. *Mittelalterliche Überlieferung und Sprach- und Siedlungsgeschichte im Ostniederdeutschen*. Wiesbaden: Steiner-Verlag.

Butz, Georg. 1988. Grundriß der Sprachgeschichte Berlins. In Norbert Dittmar & Peter Schlobinski (eds.), *Wandlungen einer Stadtsprache. Berlinisch in Vergangenheit und Gegenwart*, 1–40. Berlin: Colloquium Verlag.

Dittmar, Norbert & Ursula Bredel. 1999. *Die Sprachmauer. Die Verarbeitung der Wende und ihre Folgen in Gesprächen mit Ost- und WestberlinerInnen*. Berlin: Weidler Buchverlag.

Dittmar, Norbert & Peter Schlobinski (eds.). 1988. *Wandlungen einer Stadtsprache. Berlinisch in Vergangenheit und Gegenwart*. Berlin: Colloquium Verlag.

Dittmar, Norbert, Peter Schlobinski & Inge Wachs. 1986. *Berlinisch. Studien zum Lexikon, zur Spracheinstellung und zum Stilrepertoire*. Berlin: Arno Spitz.

Eichhoff, Jürgen. 1977. *Wortatlas der deutschen Umgangssprache. Band 1*. Bern & München: Francke Verlag.

Führer, Beate. 1982. *Das Berlinische im Tagesschrifttum von 1848/49: Studien zum Verhältnis von Idiolekt, Soziolekt und Dialekt*. Frankfurt am Main: Peter Lang.

Gebhardt, Heinz. 1933. *Glaßbrenners Berlinisch*. (Schriften des Vereins für die Geschichte Berlins, Heft 54). Berlin: Verlag des Vereins für die Geschichte Berlins.

Grober-Glück, Gerda. 1975. Berlin als Innovationszentrum von metaphorischen Wendungen der Umgangssprache. *Zeitschrift für deutsche Philologie* 94(3). 321–367.

Haag, Karl. 1929/1930. Sprachwandel im Lichte der Mundartgrenzen. *Teuthonista* 6. 1–35.

Harndt, Ewald. 1977. *Französisch im Berliner Jargon*. Berlin: Stapp Verlag.

Heinemann, Margot. 1989. *Kleines Wörterbuch der Jugendsprache*. Leipzig: VEB Bibliographisches Institut.

Hopf, Albert. 1848. *Der Bowlen-Prozeß oder Tibbeke als Angeklagter vor den Schranken des öffentlichen Gerichts*. Berlin: Leopold Schlesinger.
Klein, Wolfgang. 1974. *Variation in der Sprache. Ein Verfahren zu ihrer Beschreibung*. Kronberg: Scriptor Verlag.
Kruse, Detlef. 1987. *Glaßbrenner und der Berliner Dialekt*. Berlin: Marhold Verlag.
Kruse, Detlef & Peter Schlobinski. 1984. Frequenz- und Bedeutungsanalysen zum Lexikon des Berlinischen. *Muttersprache* 94(5). 300–312.
Küpper, Heinz. 1990. *Wörterbuch der deutschen Umgangssprache*. Stuttgart: Erich Klett Verlag.
Lademann, Willy. 1956. *Wörterbuch der Teltower Volkssprache (Telschet Wöderbuek)*. Berlin: Akademie-Verlag.
Lasch, Agathe. 1910. *Geschichte der Schriftsprache in Berlin bis zur Mitte des 16. Jahrhunderts*. Dortmund: Ruhfus.
Lasch, Agathe. 1928. *"Berlinisch". Eine berlinische Sprachgeschichte*. Berlin: Verlag von Reimar Hobbing.
Lindner, Rolf. 2016. *Berlin, absolute Stadt. Eine kleine Anthropologie der großen Stadt*. Berlin: Kulturverlag Kadmos.
Mally, Anton Karl. 1974. Piefke. Herkunft und Rolle eines österreichischen Spitznamens für den Preußen, den Nord- und den Reichsdeutschen. *Muttersprache* 84(4). 257–286.
Mally, Anton Karl. 1984. Piefke. Nachträge. *Muttersprache* 94(5). 313–327.
Mattheier, Klaus J. 1980. *Pragmatik und Soziologie der Dialekte: Eine Einführung in die kommunikative Dialektologie des Deutschen*. Heidelberg: Quelle und Meyer.
Meyer, Hans. 1925. *Der Richtige Berliner in Wörtern und Redensarten*. Berlin: H.G. Hermann Verlag.
Milroy, Lesley. 1980. *Language and Social Networks*. Oxford: Blackwell.
Moritz, Carl Philipp. 1781. *Über den märkischen Dialekt. In Briefen*. Berlin: Arnold Meyer.
Nase, Karl. 1929. Unser Berlinisch. *Berliner Lehrerzeitung* 23/24. 183–185, 192–194.
Oschlies, Wolf. 1981. Ich glaub, mich rammt ein Rotkehlchen. Jugendjargon und Soziolinguistik in der DDR. *Muttersprache* 91(3–4). 185–195.
Regener, Irena. 2000. Selbstidentifikation via Varietätengebrauch. Sprachverhalten und Spracheinstellungen in der Berliner Sprachgemeinschaft der 90er Jahre. *Linguistik online* 7(3).http://www.linguistik-online.de/3_00/regener.html
Regener, Irena. 2002. Spracheinstellungen in den 90er Jahren in Berlin: Aspekte deutsch-deutscher Identitätssicherung aus soziolinguistischer Perspektive. *conflict & communication online* 1(1). http://www.cco.regener-online.de/2002_1/pdf_2002_1/regener.pdf
Rosenberg, Klaus-Peter. 1986. *Der Berliner Dialekt – und seine Folgen für die Schüler. Geschichte und Gegenwart der Stadtsprache Berlins sowie eine empirische Untersuchung der Schulprobleme dialektsprechender Berliner Schüler*. Tübingen: Niemeyer.
Schildt, Joachim. 1992. Berliner Umgangssprache in Flugschriften und Maueranschlägen von 1848. In Joachim Schildt & Hartmut Schmidt (eds.), *Berlinisch. Geschichtliche Einführung in die Sprache einer Stadt*, 183–221. Berlin: Akademie Verlag.
Schildt, Joachim & Hartmut Schmidt (eds.). 1992 [1986]. *Berlinisch. Geschichtliche Einführung in die Sprache einer Stadt*. Berlin: Akademie Verlag.
Schirmunski, Victor M. 1962. *Deutsche Mundartkunde*. Berlin: Aufbau-Verlag.
Schlobinski, Peter. 1987. *Stadtsprache Berlin. Eine soziolinguistische Untersuchung*. Berlin & New York: de Gruyter.

Schlobinski, Peter. 1988a. Über den 'Akkudativ' im Berlinischen. *Muttersprache* 98(3). 214–225.

Schlobinski, Peter. 1988b. Code-switching im Berlinischen. In Norbert Dittmar & Peter Schlobinski (eds.), *Wandlungen einer Stadtsprache. Berlinisch in Vergangenheit und Gegenwart*, 83–102. Berlin: Colloquium Verlag.

Schlobinski, Peter. 1996a. *Empirische Sprachwissenschaft*. Opladen: Westdeutscher Verlag.

Schlobinski, Peter. 1996b. Zur r-Vokalisierung im Berlinischen. *Zeitschrift für Germanistische Linguistik* 24(2). 195–204.

Schlobinski, Peter & Andrea-Eva Ewels (eds.). 2014. *Der Berliner Dialekt in der Einschätzung der Bürger der Stadt*. Wiesbaden: Gesellschaft für deutsche Sprache. http://gfds.de/epub/berliner_dialekt.pdf

Schlobinski, Peter & Helmut Schönfeld. 1992. Zum Gebrauch einiger Berliner Wörter im Ost- und Westteil der Stadt. *Muttersprache* 102(2). 114–121.

Schmidt, Hartmut. 1992. Die sprachliche Entwicklung Berlins vom 13. bis zum frühen 19. Jahrhundert. In Joachim Schildt & Hartmut Schmidt (eds.), *Berlinisch. Geschichtliche Einführung in die Sprache einer Stadt*, 111–182. Berlin: Akademie Verlag.

Schmidt-Regener, Irena. 1998. Von der Akzeptanz des Berlinischen, von Liberalisierungstendenzen und Berührungsängsten in der Berliner Sprachgemeinschaft. In Ruth Reiher & Undine Kramer (eds.), *Sprache als Mittel von Identifikation und Distanzierung*, 153–185. Frankfurt am Main: Peter Lang.

Schönfeld, Helmut. 1981. Beschreibung einer empirischen Untersuchung zur Sprachvarianz. Analyse der phonetisch-phonologischen Ebene. In Wolfdietrich Hartung & Helmut Schönfeld (eds.), *Kommunikation und Sprachvariation*, 330–358. Berlin: Akademie Verlag.

Schönfeld, Helmut. 1996. Heimatsprache, Proletendeutsch, Ossi-Sprache oder? Bewertung und Akzeptanz des Berlinischen. In: Ruth Reiher & Rüdiger Läzer (eds.), *Von 'Buschzulage' und 'Ossinachweis'. Ost-West-Deutsch in der Diskussion*, 70–93. Berlin: Aufbau Taschenbuch Verlag.

Schönfeld, Helmut. 2001: *Berlinisch heute. Kompetenz – Verwendung – Bewertung*. Frankfurt am Main: Peter Lang.

Teuchert, Hermann. 1928/1929. Rezension zu Agathe Lasch (1928), "Berlinisch". Eine berlinische Sprachgeschichte. *Teuthonista* 5. 295–307.

Trachsel, C. F. 1873. *Glossarium der berlinischen Wörter und Redensarten*. Berlin: Plahn'sche Buchhandlung.

Tucholsky, Kurt. 2007 [1927]. Ein Ferngespräch. In Nele Lenze (ed.), *Kurt Tucholsky in Berlin. Gesammelte Feuilletons 1912–1930*, 129–30. Berlin: story Verlag.

Wiese, Heike. 2012. *Kiezdeutsch. Ein neuer Dialekt entsteht*. München: C. H. Beck.

Wiese, Joachim. 1987. *Berliner Wörter und Wendungen*. Berlin: Akademie Verlag.

Tanager

4 Learning to be German: immigration and language in Berlin

1 Introduction

After moving to Berlin in the winter of 2014, I attended two months of an *Integrationskurs* [Integration Program], a German language and civics course for foreigners planning to live in Germany long-term. Immigration law and integration policy regulate these courses; permission to reside in the country or obtain citizenship is sometimes conditional on successful completion of the program. My experience in the courses inspired my Master's thesis' focus and the ensuing study presented in this chapter. The study took place in the winter of 2016 and is composed of 80 hours of participant observation, 21 phenomenological interviews, and an analysis of the legal framework on immigration. I employed these methods in order to develop insight into how the lived experience of the participants of the courses compare to the policies that construct the program. By investigating the language ideological perspectives of participants of the Integration Program, a broader understanding of the relationship between immigration policy and the participants can be achieved.

Using an interdisciplinary approach, this chapter investigates, firstly, the specific approaches taken by the state toward promoting German language ability among immigrant populations and, secondly, the language ideologies of the participants in those approaches. While analyses of language policies often focus on the assumptions policymakers make about language use in their territory, relatively few studies bring the perceptions of participants of governmental language programs into the analysis.[1] Therefore, I also look at the lived experiences of immigrants in Germany participating in integration courses to contribute to the small but slowly growing body of empirical and theoretical studies of language policy. The *Integrationskurs* as a whole and the *Orientierungskurs* specifically serve to further distance the constructed ethnic Germanness from the "other", who is treated by the policy as if they must reshaped in order to be integrated into German society. This contrasts starkly with the German language learners' motivation for participating in the program.

1 For examples of relevant studies, see: Göktepe 2015; Martin 2005; Islam and Guven 2015; and Flores and Rosa 2015.

https://doi.org/10.1515/9781501508103-004

Part of the impetus for this research comes from a very personal interest in my role in the Berlin society and the transformation of my language ideologies as I learn German. Moreover, praise given regarding my German ability is almost always delivered in conjunction with disparaging comments about the language ability of my fellow Berlin newcomers. In these conversations, their lack of German skills is problematized. Additionally, an increase in anti-immigrant sentiment and violence in Germany make this work timely.

2 Methodology

In order to gain a well-rounded perspective into not only integration policy but also the experience of German language learners, I employ a two-fold methodological approach. This study combines a critical discourse analysis of German integration law and ethnographic research in integration classes held in two Berlin *Volkshochschulen*. Moreover, critical discourse theories also inform the analysis of the ethnographic data. This is a qualitative endeavor that incorporates multiple methods – participant observation, group discussions, phenomenological interviews, and discourse analysis of policy texts – to ensure in-depth results. Qualitative research is a multifaceted research methodology. In general, the objective of qualitative research is not to collect and test theories using numerical data, but to describe and understand a context to develop a deeper understanding about the topic at hand. Methodological triangulation, or the application of varied methods, is achieved in this study by utilizing more than one method in more than one instance of the context at hand. Ethnography, as the central qualitative method applied here, is more sensitive than a quantitative survey or another type of evaluation; treating the context in which research is conducted as a valuable space where humans interact with one another and then joining in that space allows for greater insight into the topic.

Beyond the qualitative data collected in the *Integrationskurse*, the 2000 *Staatsangehörigkeitsgesetz* (Nationality Act, henceforth StAG), the 2005/2007 *Aufenthaltsgesetz* (Residence Act, henceforth AufenthG), and the *Konzept für einen bundesweiten Integrationskurs* (Concept for a Nation-wide Integration Course, henceforth *Konzept)* were analyzed. Social categories such as *Bürger* 'citizen', *Migrant* 'migrant', *Zuwanderer* 'immigrant', *Einwanderer* 'immigrant', and *Ausländer* 'foreigner' are products of discourse created and reinforced at the individual, community, and political levels. These legal texts are extremely powerful: "the institutional authority to categorize people is frequently inseparable from the authority to do things to them" (Cameron 2001: 16). Moreover, the *Konzept* stipulates course content and serves as a guideline for the instructors teaching the *Integrationskurs*. All three policies in question have a heavy focus on the German language. In the following section, I give a brief analysis of the discourse produced by these legal texts.

3 Immigration and integration policy

Germany as a nation state and concept makes for a particularly interesting context for the study of immigration and language learning because of the tight bond in the cultural dialogue between national identity and language, as reflected in the nuanced conditioning of naturalization based on language ability.[2] German citizenship law followed the *Ius Sanguinis* principal, basing citizenship on "bloodlines" until the turn of the century, when place of birth (*Ius Soli*) replaced *Ius Sanguinis* in the naturalization law (Möllering 2010: 146).[3] In the StAG (the law regulating citizenship), language ability and understanding of and adherence to the German societal rules play prominent roles. Berlin, as the epicenter for policy creation in Germany and a dynamic, cosmopolitan capital city, is an ideal setting for investigating the impacts of immigration policy on affected individuals.

The current legal framework for immigration in Germany rests on three main events: the creation of the EU and, specifically, its freedom of movement zone; the overhaul of the StAG in 2000; and the passing of the *Gesetz über den Aufenthalt, die Erwerbstätigkeit und die Integration von Ausländern im Bundesgebiet* in the year 2004 (the law regulating residence, work, and the integration of foreigners, hereafter AufenthG) (Stevenson 2006: 150). Contemporary German society has three legally defined groups of *Ausländer* 'foreigners': EU-Citizens, third country immigrants, and asylum seekers.[4] People with German citizenship are differentiated into two categories: *Deutsche mit Migrationshintergrund*[5] 'Germans with a migration background' and those "without

---

2 For more on language and nationalism in Europe and Germany specifically, see: Barbour, Stephen and Carmichael, Cathie. 2000. *Language and Nationalism in Europe*. Oxford University Press: New York.

3 German immigration and citizenship policy have both changed substantially in the last twenty years; see Stevenson 2006 and Möllering 2010 for a discussion of the *Leitkulturdebatte*, the 2000 Naturalization Act, and the 2005 Immigration Act.

4 Note that this study does not discuss refugees or asylum seekers.

5 The Federal Statistical Office considers people who were born without German citizenship or who have at least one parent who was born without German citizenship to have 'migration background'. In public discourse, however, a German citizen born and raised in the country whose great grandfather was born in another country could be considered *Deutsche mit*

a migration background"[6] Government-run German language lessons were originally designed for *Aussiedler*, but now are available to any foreigner or German who cannot speak German with the intent of staying long-term in the country.

It needs to be noted that categories such as *Bürger* 'citizen', *Ausländer* 'foreigner', and *Einwanderer* 'immigrant' are products of discourse created at the individual, community, and political levels.[7] Both the 2001 StAG's shift to create pathways to citizenship and the 2004 AufenthG altered the national public discourse on what it means to live in Germany and how one can become a German. It is in the wake of these legal changes that current German learners participate in the *Integrationskurs*.

3.1 The integration program: *Integrationskurse*

The government sponsored integration courses take place across Germany. In Berlin, they are primarily found in the *Volkshochschulen* (VHS),[8] community learning centers for adults offering a variety of classes ranging from photography to Aramaic. German language courses have only existed in their current format since 2009, when changes recommended by an external evaluation were implemented. The standard *Integrationskurs* consists of 600 lesson hours of German language (A1–B1)[9] and 60 hours of civics knowledge (*Orientierungskurs*); both portions of the program end with a standardized test. Variations upon this basic theme range from courses designed for people entering corporate work environments, for parents, for youth aged 18–25, to courses for women only. Supplementary courses exist for those who must acquire literacy or who have previously used other alphabets. If someone fails to pass the B1 test, they may take an extra 300 hours of remedial language lessons while still receiving

---

Migrationshintergrund – thus, the categorization of someone as *mit Migrationshintergrund* also depends on factors such as country of origin, skin complexion, language competence, etc.

6 There are two other categories of German passport-holders, namely *Aussiedler* (ethnic Germans from former Eastern bloc states) and descendants of *Auswanderer* (emigrants).

7 For a witty and critical discussion of German nomenclature, see Lena Gorelik's chapter "Name Gesucht" in *Sie können gut Deutsch!* (Gorelik 2012: 31–51).

8 Some private language schools also offer Integration Courses, following the same curriculum.

9 As defined by the Council of Europe in the Common European framework of reference for languages (Council of Europe 2001).

funding. It should be noted that "hours" in this case refers to "TU"s (teaching units) and signify 45 min of teaching. Not every participant needs to take all 660 hours: "in individual cases, the number of funded TUs may be reduced. This may be the case if the participant: starts off with a higher-level course module; takes part in an intensive course; or skips a course module upon approval of the course provider" (Concept 2008: 8). The civics class (*Orientierungskurs*) is composed of a fixed 60 hours of classroom time and cannot be reduced.

Integration courses are German language lessons designed by the *Bundesamt für Migration und Flüchtlinge* [Federal Office for Migration and Refugees] (henceforth BAMF) and are oriented towards living in Germany. Early lessons include learning phases helpful for making appointments and filling out bureaucratic forms. German as a foreign language lessons, in contrast, focus on topics such as ordering food in restaurants, giving the taxi driver your address in early lessons. The integration course curriculum is set by the *Konzept fuer einen Bundesweiten Integrationskurs*[10] [Concept for a Nationwide Integration Course] (henceforth *Konzept*), addressed below. As of 2016, the tiered payment system ranged from 150 Euro per module to free (Konzept 2015). Reduced prices are available for foreigners who come from EU countries, non-German speakers with unemployment benefits from the Job Center, long-term residents with permanent visas or an obligation to attend, and for *Aussiedler* and other German citizens who do not speak German. Teachers are certified "German as a foreign language" instructors, those with whom I came into contact worked as freelancers for the city.

3.2 Integration policy as language policy

Integration, according to the *Konzept* designed by the BAMF, consists of social participation and equal opportunities. The method through which immigrants are supposed to achieve social and cultural participation and equal access to labor market participation, according to the BAMF, is language learning; immi-

10 This policy is available online in both English (2008) and German (2015), though the most recent version has not been translated to English. www.bamf.de/SharedDocs/Anlagen/EN/Downloads/Infothek/Integrationskurse/Kurstraeger/KonzepteLeitfaeden/konz-f-bundesw-integrationskurs.pdf?__blob=publicationFile www.bamf.de/SharedDocs/Anlagen/DE/Downloads/Infothek/Integrationskurse/Kurstraeger/KonzepteLeitfaeden/konz-f-bundesw-integrationskurs.pdf?__blob=publicationFile

grants must learn German. The German government policy designed to integrate immigrants into Germany is first and foremost a language policy. As outlined by official discourse, the categories between integrated and unintegrated are parallel to German speaking and non-German speaking, regardless of nationality or other signifiers. There are, of course, many other features that can cause someone to feel excluded from a community.[11]

Language policies are "practical plans to modify language practices and beliefs" (Johnson 2015: 1). Language policies can be informal, unwritten, and implied or covert, written, and official. Many are a mix between the two. Across the board, language policies are deliberate efforts to influence behavior of others regarding language use. All three legal documents addressed here (AufenthG, StAG, and the *Konzept*) have a heavy focus on the German language, making "sufficient knowledge" of German a requirement for many immigrants. Inherent in this obligation (which is sometimes legally required and other times only implied) to learn German is the idea that the government wants non-German speakers in Germany to learn and then use the German language.

One of the most straightforward examples of how language policies have the power to create social groups can be seen in the Nationality Act (StAG), which sets the groundwork for German citizenship and how one can attain it. Language ability, understanding of German social structures, and adherence to the societal norms are explicitly outlined as essential prerequisites to naturalization in the renovated naturalization law. Furthermore, non-Germans wishing to obtain a German passport must gain an understanding of the German legal system and swear allegiance to the German constitution, as well as give up their previous citizenship (a few exceptions do apply, see §12). An immigrant seeking citizenship can prove that they have sufficient understanding (§1 abs. 1.7) of the social order and way of life in Germany if they pass a naturalization test; preparation for the test is provided by the last module of integration courses, the *Orientierungskurs*. Beyond citizenship, the AufenthG makes "sufficient knowledge"[12] of German a requirement for many immigrants to retain

11 For a powerful and poetic commentary on race, racism, and whiteness in Germany, see Farah Melter's chapter "Weiß sein oder nicht sein" [To be white or not to be] in her book *Rasiss-muss? Nein Danke, ich bin satt!* (2011).

12 Sufficient knowledge is defined in the integration course policy, *Konzept für ein bundesweiten Integrationskurs* as B1, in line with the Common European Framework of Reference for Languages (Konzept 2015: 6).

residency in the country: "Ein Ausländer ist zur Teilnahme an einem Integrationskurs verpflichtet, wenn 1. er [. . .] b) zum Zeitpunkt der Erteilung eines Aufenthaltstitels nach § 23 Abs. 2., § 28 Abs. 1 Satz 1 Nr. 1 oder § 30 nicht über ausreichende Kenntnisse der deutschen Sprache verfügt (§ 44a AufenthG 2008).[13]

Naturalization comes with numerous caveats. § 9, abs. 1 stipulates that the non-German spouse of a German citizen can only be naturalized if "it is ensured that they will conform to the German way of life" (StAG English 2008), unless they have sufficient German speaking abilities (§9, 10 abs. 1 Satz 1 Nr. 6 and Abs. 4 StAG 2015). Generally, a resident of Germany who has been living in the country legally for 8 years or longer may take on German citizenship if they have sufficient German language knowledge (*Sprachkenntnisse*) and knowledge about the legal structure, societal norms, and way of life in Germany (StAG 2015).[14] The eight years required living time in Germany can be reduced to six if an immigrant demonstrates they are highly integrated, especially with proof of language knowledge (§10 abs. 3 StAG 2015). Again, value is placed on language ability, which is implied to be a particularly important part of integration. In fact, there are only a few components of integration outlined in the StAG: adherence to a German way of life; understanding of rights and German societal norms; and language ability.

The integration program is presented as a helpful sort of offering from the government to the newcomers. In the official English translation of the AufenthG from the BAMF, "[f]oreigners living lawfully in the Federal territory on a permanent basis are provided with support in integrating into the economic, cultural and social life of the Federal Republic of Germany and are expected to take commensurate integration efforts in return" (§ 44 Abs. 1 English translation AufenthG). The goal of the course is to "successfully impart the German language, legal system, culture, and history to foreigners. In this way it is intended to acquaint foreigners with the way of life in the Federal territory to such an extent as to enable them to act independently in all aspects of life, without the assistance or mediation of third parties" (§ 44 Abs. 1 English translation AufenthG).

---

13 "A foreigner shall be obliged to attend an integration course, if [. . .] he or she [. . .] b) does not possess adequate knowledge of the German language at the time of issuance of a residence title" (Federal Ministry of the Interior 2007: 44a).

14 "6. über ausreichende Kenntnisse der deutschen Sprache verfügt und 7. über Kenntnisse der Rechts- und Gesellschaftsordnung und der Lebensverhältnisse in Deutschland verfügt" (StAG 2015).

A distinction is made between foreigners who are required to attend the courses and those who are simply allowed to attend. Entitlement is extended to all foreigners from the beginning of their residence in Germany if they have a residence permit for one year, generally. Foreigners who cannot communicate in German when they receive their residence permit can be required to complete the program; however, in practice, this is only extended to certain foreigners. The state curriculum deems B1 to be adequate knowledge of the German language means in the context of this law. Furthermore, the obligation to attend is extended to those who receive social benefits in line with "Book Two of the Social Code" (§ 44a English translation AufenthG). Of the approximately 50 participants in my study sample, all of the participants who confirmed they had an obligation to attend the course received social benefits. These learners were EU nationals using social services such as unemployment benefits from the Job Center. The AufenthG has no description of what it means to have "special integration needs" or, in the reverse, someone with a "need for integration [that is] discernibly minimal". Instead, these classifications are made by the employees at the respective agencies (primarily the *Ausländerbehörde* 'Immigration Office' are endowed by this law to pass judgement on applicants for residence permits and determine, in their opinion, if someone is in particular "need" of integration.

We will see in the following section whether and how the ideologies expressed in the governmental discourses differ from those of the people who are classified as "in need of integration".

4 Language ideologies of students in *Integrationskursen*

The foci of the second part of the study are the language ideologies of German language learners and how their conceptions of belonging are transformed, if at all, by learning German in a government-run, public policy-driven context. As mentioned in section 2, the participants' language ideologies were examined in the context of an ethnographic study. Three components of ethnography have been described as most relevant: "*experiencing* through participant and nonparticipant observation, *enquiring* through formal and informal interviews, and *examining* through the analysis of documents and cultural artifacts" (McCarty 2015: 85, quoting Wolcott 2008). The following paragraphs will address these three aspects.

4.1 Three components of ethnography

4.1.1 Experiencing *Integrationskurse*

Within the broader context of Berlin, the two locations where I conducted fieldwork are at opposite ends of the same district of Mitte, and therefore have the same leadership and policies. Yet, the surrounding neighborhoods have extremely different demographics. The VHS campus in the sub-district Reinickendorf is situated in an ungentrified neighborhood with a high population density of over 10,000 residents per square kilometer (Amt für Statistik Berlin 2014: 46). On Reinickendorfer Straße specifically, 66 % of residents have a migration background, much higher than most other areas of the city (Rochmann 2011: 12). The second location was chosen because of its central location in Berlin Mitte. Despite being relatively physically close to the Reinickendorf school (approximately 5km), the Linienstraße campus is located on a well renovated street near many upscale bars and restaurants. The inclusion of two schools in contrasting locations lends the study a broader scope.

The German language learners in each of these locations came from a variety of countries; I was only able to conduct interviews, however, with a more limited sample. This data is influenced by my language abilities; it was easier for me to chat with and make arrangements with fellow German learners who spoke English, Spanish, or were comfortable with their German. A major weakness of this study, therefore, is the lack of representation of Arabic, Turkish, and Kurdish speakers in my interview data. Furthermore, it needs to be noted that my identity as an insider (a German language learner) as well as a researcher unavoidably impacts my interpretation of the data and must therefore be recognized throughout the research processes and analysis. Moreover, I may also be learning German but I truly enjoy learning languages and, though I am a migrant living in a working-class neighborhood with the highest percentage of non-passport holders in the city, I come from a position of privilege as a white, blonde, educated migrant. Moreover, I am, for example, biased towards the maintenance of heritage languages. Through active listening, purposeful observation, and encouragement I aim to report from the participants and minimize the impact of my ideologies on the research data.

Between November 2015 and February 2016, I observed approximately 80 hours of classroom time in two *Volkshochschulen* in Reinickendorf and in Linienstraße in Mitte. I attended five month-long classes, four of which were part of the integration program while the fifth was a more advanced German as a foreign language class focusing on conversation and grammar skills. There were 48 participants from 28 countries in these five classes. Additionally, I enrolled in a month long *Orientierungskurs*, the final component of the integration course, at the VHS Linienstraße campus beginning on December 14th, 2015. Before each class began, I presented myself as a researcher and asked their permission to join the course for the day. Course work, classroom discussions, as well as the relationships and interactions among the students and between the students and the teachers provided a wealth of data. In the *Orientierungskurs*, I completed homework assignments and contributed to classwork as a regular enrollee. For the participants in the integration program, attending the courses is a part of their daily routine. Ethnomethodologists, among others, believe that "social order is not created by abstract structures, but by the concrete actions of people going about their everyday business" (Cameron 2001: 88). By joining the class, I too shared the experiences of the other students; memorizing the *Bundesländer* [German states] and their capitals and learning about the German political system. I chatted at break, attended birthday parties, and visited museums with my classmates. Participating fully in the course allowed me to experience the curriculum, effectively making myself a participant in my own research project. I took notes by hand during the class, the relatively slow rate of speech allowed me to often copy entire verbal exchanges word for word. After the class, I wrote memos in which I described broader observations and reflected what I had observed. These two habits were essential methods for documenting these observations. The choice not to make audio recordings of the classroom was made so as to keep the classroom a comfortable space for the participants, in line with requests from students.

4.1.2 Enquiring through interviews and questionnaires

Between December 2015 and March 2016, I conducted 21 qualitative interviews with enrollees of Integrationskurse. Interviews were scheduled at the participants' convenience, with most interviews lasting about 90 minutes. I consider the interviews to be phenomenological interviews, which are defined as studying "human experience from a first-person perspective" (McCarty 2015: 86), wherein participants are encouraged to "reconstruct their experiences with the study topic" (McCarty 2015: 87). German language learners in the *Integrationskurse* are almost exclusively immigrants, though some were born and raised in Germany. The experience of migrating to Germany served as a mutual starting point for the interviews. The interviews began with a focused life history and move through more specific details of the experience of moving to Berlin. Language learning often comes up naturally, sometimes beginning before the move, other times only with the *Integrationskurs*. By taking naturally occurring comments as a starting point and asking for more details and reflection from the participant, this interview process serves to "draw out deeper meanings" (McCarty 2015: 89).

Of the 21 interviews completed for this study, only twelve were recorded with an audio recording device. The decision to record was made based on the comfort of the participant, as well as location. Many participants who did not speak English or Spanish fluently expressed discomfort in having the conversations recorded. Interviews that were not recorded were documented with diligent note taking and followed up by post-interview memo writing. Recorded interviews were transcribed word-for-word using f4 Transcription Software. Eleven interviews were conducted in English, though there were only three native speakers in the sample. Five interviews were conducted in Spanish and two interviews switched back and forth between English and Spanish regularly. Only one interview was conducted solely in German. Nevertheless, the German language permeated each interview.

After the first three interviews, I created a questionnaire based on the reasons why immigrants want to learn German, as articulated in the *Konzept*. The instrument provides an additional direct connection between the interview and the aim of the program as described in the official discourse.

4.1.3 Research findings

The original hypothesis at the outset of this study was that there would be a disconnect between the language ideologies in government policies and those held by the participants in the integration course. German language learners treated the language as a tool that was helpful, but not necessary, for integration; in juxtaposition, the policies-in-action emphasized German language learning as a critical aspect of integration. In the following, the reasons why participants want to learn German will be addressed using critical examinations of the observations and interviews outlined above.

4.2 Lived policy: integration as understood by immigrants and teachers

Discursively constructed by the original policy that outlines the program (see above, *Konzept* 2015, and Concept 2008), integration is the achievement of equal participation and equal opportunity for all members of a community. The "objective of the integration course is to promote integration of immigrants with regard to social participation and equal opportunities" (Concept 2008: 6).

This is supposed to be achieved through “[g]ood German language skills and knowledge of the legal and social system,” because “[g]ood language skills increase one’s chances for integrating into the labour [sic] market and are the foundation for a successful educational career” (Concept 2008: 6). Good language skills in this context is defined as matching the B1 level with reference to the “Common European Framework of Reference for Languages” (Concept 2008: 6). Moreover, the courses are supposed to teach German “in a way that relates to everyday life” and cover “basic values of society” as to facilitate “integration into the workforce” and “social and cultural integration” (Concept 2008: 6). However, results from my research show that many German language learners do not consider German to be necessary for their social or labor market participation.

The students in the Linienstaße *Orientierungskurs* had all recently taken the B1 exam. They should, according to the Concept, be able to conduct all their day-to-day activities in German. Most of the students were not capable of this. Moreover, not a single participant in my sample said that they needed German to conduct their daily activities. While two of twenty-two “could” if they had to, they were the exception. Interestingly, these two both preferred to use English when possible. Most of the participants both could not carry out daily chores in German and did not find this to be a problem. This does not mean that they did not want to learn German. Rather, they indicated that “living in the German language”[15] was not their goal and that they did not need German to go about their daily business.

On one of the final days of the module, the class discussed integration. The conversation was instigated by the instructor, who permitted the occasional use of the English language so as to let the students get deeper into the content of the topic at hand. As the learners chatted, she wrote keywords such as “participation”, “language,” and “culture” on the board as they were mentioned. In the conversation, integration as a concept was outlined as the process undertaken by an outsider joining the culture of a majority. As aspects of this process, language, and culture were mentioned by the students as critical components of integration. When integrating oneself,

15 A common phrase used by German language learners and other multilingual Berliners; “I went to the store in German yesterday” would mean “I used German while grocery shopping”. In the same vein, “I dreamt in German” is often used to mean, “the language used in my dream was German” or, “people in my dream spoke German.”

> "you should be able to keep your traditions, habits."
> "Vielleicht, auch Ihre Sprachen behalten?" [Maybe, you should also be able to keep your language?][16]

The work that goes into integration also comes from the local community, mentioned J., a trilingual hospitality professional and current stay-at-home mom. When asked which parts of integration should happen first, there were only two responses; the students agreed that learning the language was the first part of integration, followed by having a stable place to live. In the same discussion, B., the instructor, in a lecture-style delivery, steamrolled the discussion to describe integration as having failed in Neukölln, because the schools are failing and students *mit Migrationshintergrund* 'with migration backgrounds' are not doing well. She stated that the businesses oriented towards the local Turkish diaspora, noticeable by their signs and advertisements in Turkish were proof of failed integration. She advocated for mandatory preschool so as to better integrate young children and to give pent up Turkish mothers an excuse to leave the house. Her monologue was met with silence.

After the palpable silence that followed B.'s monologue, J., chimed in, declaring that "Heimat ist wo die Leute sprechen die gleiche Sprache" [home is where people speak the same language as you]. The teacher agreed, "Sprache ist auch ein bisschen Heimat" [language is also a bit like home].[17] *Heimat* 'home' quickly took over as the focus of the brainstorm. O., a Venezuelan with German citizenship, described himself as a global citizen, finding home all over the world. His decision to go to Germany was heavily influenced by his possession of a German passport; he receives financial assistance for housing and has the costs of the integration program covered. E., from Colombia, says that *Heimat* is where the family is, and her family is here, in Berlin. Integration as presented in the classroom discussion is the process of adaptation to a new home-context undergone by migrants who intend to stay long term in the country.[18] For these students, integration was as much about bringing their culture, language, and other aspects of their lifestyles to Germany as it was about incorporating German ways of life into their own.

---

16 This exchange took place in a mixture of English and German between German language learners.

17 Quotes from participants and instructors in double quotation marks were recorded word-for-word during participant observation and are verbatim.

18 This definition of integration and other conclusions drawn are based on additional data and analysis and are not addressed in this chapter due to space constrictions.

4.3 Lived policy II: Motivation to learn German

The questionnaire I developed to find out about the motivations to learn German (see Figure 1) is based on the conceptualization of the different types of motivation for learning German as outlined by the official curriculum for the integration program. The questionnaire is an adaptation of the reasons listed in the policy and was used during interviews to help ensure answers from multiple participants on the same topics. Each line is a different version of completing the statement: "I learn German to..." (see Figure 1).

Questionnaire
What are your main motivating reasons for learning German?
I learn German:

Factor	Strongly disagree	Slightly disagree	Neutral	Agree	Strongly agree
to make new friends					
because translators are too expensive					
to communicate at work					
because I enjoy learning languages					
to communicate with the government					
because I am required to					
to better understand the German culture					
so I can be independent					
so I don't have to speak my first language					
so I can read books and newspapers					
so I can communicate with my family					

Figure 1: Questionnaire on motivations to learn German.

The responses to this questionnaire (see Figure 2), as well as the interview content at large, provide evidence of a disjuncture between the official policy and the lived realities of the participants. The strongest reason for learning German was to communicate at work. Of 14 respondents, 13 agreed or strongly agreed

Motivating reasons for learning German

What are your motivating reasons for learning German?
I learn German to...

Factor	Strongly disagree	Slightly disagree	Neutral	Agree	Strongly agree
to make new friends	1		4	3	6
because translators are too expensive	6	3	5		
to communicate at work			1	2	11
because I enjoy learning languages			3	8	3
to communicate with the government	1		2	6	5
because I am required to	2	2	2	4	4
to better understand the German culture		1	1	7	5
so I can be independent	1	1		6	6
so I don't have to speak my first	10	2			
so I can read books and newspapers	1		3	6	4
so I can communicate with my family	5		2	4	3

Figure 2: Results of questionnaire on motivations to learn German.

that they learned German to communicate at work. Yet, respondents simultaneously described not needing German for their field of employment. It should be noted that the narrow sample in this study is mostly made up of a group of educated creative professionals and students. In the sample of 22 German language learners, there was one truck driver, two cleaners, two visual artists, a dancer, two filmmakers, two Jazz musicians, three architects, one corporate manager, one pastry chef, one information technology specialist, and two students. In Berlin, many of these jobs can be done without significant knowledge of the German language. I hypothesize that this is in part skewed by my influence on the data collection process; yet, this is also an accurate reflection of who has spare time to take German classes and the type of migrants presently attracted to Berlin.

The second two most common reasons for learning German were to better understand the German culture and to be independent. For both, 12 out of 14 respondents agreed or strongly agreed. Six respondents strongly agreed, explaining to me verbally that they desired to be able to read and understand their mail on their own, specifically. Another six respondents simply agreed.[19] A desire for independence is a primary factor for learning German. Yet, only two of the 22 participants had reported having ever used a professional translator. The rest of the respondents relied on friends, family, and social networks for help completing tasks for which their German was not adequate. Moreover, participants reported that they were not able to complete these tasks after completing the integration program. Independence was regularly presented as a goal that would not likely be achieved in the next five years.

Equally important, yet fundamentally different, was the emphasis on culture. In every interview, the participant talked about "the Germans". This happened without prompting but was also often done with awareness about the dangers of generalizing. Seven of the respondents agreed that they wanted to learn German to better understand the German culture. A further five respondents strongly agreed. Integration course participants perceived of the German language like a window into the German soul, and that the language itself held components of the culture within it. Understanding the German culture is, then, only possible if one can also speak German.

A need to communicate with the government was also a strong motivating factor for wanting to learn German. Six respondents strongly agreed and another five agreed. Participants had, however, very little to say on the matter. Also popular was literature, mentioned above, and an enjoyment for learning languages. Eight participants said they agreed that they wanted to learn German because they enjoyed learning languages.

There is also a noticeable contingent of temporary residents in the *Integrationskurs*, these German language learners were living in Berlin just for a year or two and enrolled in the *Integrationskurse* instead of another German language course because of the price and location of classrooms. At full price, they cost 150 Euro for one month of intensive language lessons five days a week, four hours a day. This is significantly less than language courses in other countries or at other schools in Germany, according to my participants.

---

19 More than three times, the conversation immediately veered off to a discussion of how strange it is that Germans like to use snail mail (paper mail using the postal service) and that they had expected this to be a high-tech country, only to move here and find it to be very much the opposite. Note that this is related to a tradition of discourses on data security, perhaps based on sceptic attitudes towards the government's access to data of citizens during WWII and in the GDR regime.

4.4 Lived policy III: Learning to be German in the *Orientierungskurs*

The *Orientierungskurs* instructors did not, in general, like to teach this module: "es ist ein langweiliger Kurs" [it's a boring class]. A., an instructor at Linienstraße, explained to me that she shared anecdotes about German politics in an attempt to have more fun. The resulting course content included her opinions about the Green party ("they're always telling lies, they're worthless"), Muslims, and "freeloaders" in the social security system. In contrast, B., another instructor at Linienstraße, told me that she didn't like how positively Germany was portrayed by the curriculum and therefore tries to not always show the country and the government in a positive light. In action, this was performed through comments on how bad the economy is in Berlin, how fast rent is rising, and that this was the worst place to come to look for a job. While these relatively frequent digressions were met with silence from the classroom, I believe they influenced the perception of some participants such as that of H., a man in his sixties with linguistic resources that ranged from his first language, Tamazight, through Arabic, French, and Spanish, to a new acquisition of German. He had spent the last 16 years living and working in Spain and told me "Venía aquí porque soy tonto" [I came here because I'm stupid]. He had thought there would be better opportunities for employment here. His experience seemed to be the only one that came close to matching the policy expectations for an immigrant. For the other participants, their lives, professions, and linguistic resources did not at all align with the stereotype of the uneducated monolingual manual laborer moving to Germany depicted in the German language workbooks assigned in the courses.[20]

While the objective of the *Orientierungskurs* is to facilitate the process of immigrant incorporation into society in Germany, the presentation of Germany, German the language, and Germanness as something definable and tangible

---

20 The differences in curriculum between *Integrationskurse* and other 'German as a foreign language lessons' demonstrate an underlying assumption that German as a foreign language learners, for example, spend time and money in a way that varies greatly from that of the "immigrants" envisioned to attend *Integrationskurse*. For example, coursebook content for similarly capable German learners might teach integration course participants how to apply for a job as an eldercare nurse and German as a foreign language learners how to reserve seats for the Opera. Assumptions that immigrants are poor and uneducated can be found throughout the Integrationskurs content. This does not match at all with the sample in my case study. The vast majority of the participants were well educated with experience in dynamic and engaging employment beyond the service industry and manual labor.

seems to function to further distance immigrants from this seemingly impenetrable objective. According to § 9 Abs. 1 Satz 2 of the Nationality Act, a spouse or life partner of a German can only take on German citizenship if "gewährleistet ist, daß sie sich in die deutschen Lebensverhältnisse einordnen" [it is sure that he/she will conform to the German lifestyle (StAG 2015)]. During one of the sessions of the *Orientierungskurs*, I read the English version of this section to a participant:

> T.: So, this says that the spouse of a German can only become German too if it is ensured they will conform to the German way of life.
> R.: What is the German way of life? Do I have to do yoga and jogging now?

"Strategic essentialism", as described by Buchholz and Hall, "purposefully oversimplifies complex situations in order to initiate a discussion that will later become more nuanced" (Buchholtz and Hall 2004: 367). The overwhelming assumption in the course is that the German lifestyle is a fundamental aspect of being German. The "German way of life", nevertheless, remains unspecified and is described most often in moments of frustration, as demonstrated by the quote above. And yet, frequent comments from the teachers such as "Das ist für Ausländer schwer zu verstehen" [that is hard for foreigners to understand] and "So macht man hier in Deutschland" [that's how it's done in Germany] perpetuate the dichotomy between "us" and "them", between being German and being not German.

The participants do not, in general, challenge this ideology. All three laws discussed in section 3 co-construct the boundary between "the Germans" and "the foreigners" and have a heavy focus on the German language, making "sufficient knowledge" of German a requirement for many immigrants. "Language policies can reinforce or diffuse conflict between language groups. They can be instruments of inclusion or exclusion. They can promote solidarity or stoke intolerance" (Cardinal and Sonntag 2015: 3). Despite creating a program that unequivocally provides quality language education at an affordable price, the policies I studied tacitly serve to exclude immigrants from German society, as they (re)construct a boundary between "Germans" and "foreigners". As was demonstrated above, many immigrants want to learn German language skills so as to be independent, functioning residents of Berlin. For an immigrant and language learner, this is separate from the desire to learn to be German and, furthermore, as it is unclear what this means, are not actually able to learn to be German. The multilingual, cosmopolitan fabric of contemporary society does not require immigrants to assimilate to the host culture, regardless, the immigration policies as interpreted by the German language and orientation course instructors attempt to provide the students with cultural cues and information for this style of integration.

5 Conclusion

Social categories such as "citizen", "immigrant", "foreigner", or "*Ausländer*" are products of discourse created at the individual, community, and political levels. Both the 2001 shift to create pathways to citizenship and the 2005 Integration policy altered the national, public discourse by placing German language learning at the heart of the policies. The German language is, according to the political discourse, the key to integration. Following this ideological perspective, it is the only relevant language and is absolutely necessary. However, the *Integrationskurs* participants come from immensely diverse backgrounds, their identities are created by and through connections to multiple locations, languages, and nation-states. Most importantly, they possess a wealth of linguistic resources and are adding German language ability to their toolkit. This plurality stands in stark contrast to the concept for the course created by the Government. The courses are designed to help integrate immigrants into Germany, but this case study suggests that it instead creates a concept of "being German" and presents it to the participants, separating them from the Germans and hindering the very process of integration the course is designed to promote.

The participants of my study represent an incredibly diverse group of people: young and old; introverted and charismatically outgoing; ready and willing to express thoughts in German and completely uncertain of their German language ability and unable to write or speak understandably. The political and legal framework that creates and drives integration officially predominantly addresses the German language, treating it as if only one language exists, as if only one language is relevant in the local context of Berlin, and as if the (relatively) new residents in Berlin would have to learn German to function in the city. The instructors that I met in my study presented to the participants a concept of Germanness, outlining and defining what it means to be German while teaching the language. The policies and the teachers discursively construct a Germany in which German is the only language. This clashes with the lived reality of immigrants and many Germans in Berlin. They conceive of the German language is a tangible component of German society and find that mastering it brings with it bureaucratic and social benefits. The German language learners I met treat German as a resource, a tool that helps unlock pieces of Berlin that would otherwise remain distant.

I found that the intricate relationship between the course content and the participants was the most interesting part of the data. Though the course is supposed to be a tool to help enable German language learners to integrate into the German society, the content as delivered by the teachers discursively constructed the German language and German culture as something so fixed and tangible that it felt unattainable to the participants. If a lack of German linguistic resources is like a physical barrier, a wall preventing immigrants from entering the German society or "becoming integrated", rather than functioning as a ladder for participants to climb up and over the barrier, the *Integrationskurs* strengthens the wall, paints it so it is easier to see, and adds another ten meters to the top. The official discourse in the legal framework as well as in the real-life context itself constructs "Germanness" as something very specific; it is unachievable yet very much real.

This research falls under the broad banner of language policy and planning research. There is wide variety in types of language policy and planning studies; foci in language planning and policy range from standardization and orthography development to theoretical critiques of colonial policies. Methods applied to language policy and planning research are similarly varied, drawing on multiple disciplines. In this work, the methods applied were primarily ethnographic. Future research should explore more avenues for uncovering and understanding language ideologies and linguistic resources in this context or in similar contexts. Specifically, I would recommend an in-depth investigation that includes interviews of the bureaucrats who are empowered by the AufenthG to decide if someone is to be required to learn German and if someone is in need of integration. Though this research touches upon a specific version of "how are ideologies about language formed and transformed in diverse sociolinguistic ecologies, and how [. . .] these processes relate to official and unofficial language policies" (McCarty 2015: 83), there is still much to be learned about the interaction between the discursive production of integration, language, and identity in Berlin.

References

Amt für Statistik. 2015. *Statistischer Bericht: Einwohnerinnen und Einwohner im Land Berlin am 31. Dezember 2014.*

Amt für Statistik Berlin-Brandenburg. Februar 2015. Creative Commons: Potsdam.

Amt für Statistik. 2014. *Ausländische Bevölkerung in Berlin und Brandenburg.* Amt für Statistik Berlin-Brandenburg. Creative Commons: Potsdam.

Aufenth G. 2015. *Gesetz über den Aufenthalt, die Erwerbstätigkeit und die Integration von Ausländern im Bundesgebiet (Aufenthaltsgesetz – AufenthG).* www.juris.de (accessed 2016).

Barbour, Stephen and Carmichael, Cathie. 2000. *Language and Nationalism in Europe.* Oxford University Press: New York.

Blommaert, Jan. 2010. *The Sociolinguistics of Globalization.* Cambridge University Press: Cambridge.

Buchholtz, Mary and Hall, Kira. 2004. Chapter 16: Language and Identity. In: *A Companion to Linguistic Anthropology*. Alessandro Duranti. (ed.) Blackwell Publishing: New Jersey.

Cameron, Deborah. 2001. *Working with Spoken Discourse*. Sage Publications: London.

Cardinal, Linda and Sonntag, Selma (eds.). 2015. *State Traditions and Language Regimes*. McGill-Queen's University Press: Ontario.

Concept. 2008. *Concept for a Nationwide Integration Course: A Revised New Edition*. Bundesamt für Migration und Flüchtlinge. www.integration-in-deutschland.de (accessed 2016).

Council of Europe. 2001. *Common European framework of reference for languages: learning, teaching and assessment*. Council for Cultural Co-operation, Education Committee. Modern Languages Division. Cambridge, U.K.

Flores, Nelson and Rosa, Jonathan 2015. *Undoing Appropriateness, Raciolinguistic Ideologies and Language Diversity in Education*. Harvard Educational Review 85.2 Summer 2015. President and Fellows of Harvard College. Cambridge, Massachusetts.

Gorelik, Lena. 2012. *"Sie können aber gut Deutsch!": Warum ich nicht mehr dankbar sein will, dass ich hier leben darf, und Toleranz nicht weiterhilft*. Pantheon: Munich.

Göktepe, Gökdağ. 2015. *Language Ideologies of Young Kurds towards Kurdish in Turkey*. Master Thesis. University of Luxembourg. Luxembourg.

Islam, Asadul and Guven, Cahit. 2015. *Age at Migration, Language Proficiency, and Socioeconomic Outcomes: Evidence from Australia*. Population Association of America. Maryland.

Johnson, David Cassels. 2015. Intertextuality and Language Policy. In Francis M. Hult & David Cassels Johnson (eds.), *Research Methods in Language Policy and Planning: A Practical Guide*, 166–180. Chichester, UK: Wiley-Blackwell.

Konzept. 2015. *Konzept für einen bundesweiten Integrationskurs: Überarbeitete Neuauflage – April 2015*. Bundesamt für Migration und Flüchtlinge. www.bamf.de (accessed 2016).

Martin, Peter. 2005. Talking Knowledge into Being in an Upriver Primary School in Brunei. In: Canagarajah, A. Suresh, (ed.) 2005. *Reclaiming the Local in Language Policy and Practice*. Lawrence Erlbaum Associates. Mahwah, New Jersey.

Melter, Farah. 2011. *Rassis-Mus? Nein Danke, ich bin satt!* Aurora Buchverlag: Berlin.

McCarty, Teresa L. 2015. Ethnography in LPP research. In: Hult, Francis and Johnson, David (eds.). *Research Methods in Language Policy and Planning: A Practical Guide*, 81–93. John Wiley and Sons, Inc.

Möllering, Martina. 2010. The Changing Scope of German Citizenship: From 'guest-worker' to citizen? In: Slade, Christina. and Möllering, Martina (eds.). 2010. From Migrant to Citizen: Testing Language, Testing Culture, 145–163. Palgrave Macmillan: Basingstoke

Rochmann, Ulrike. 2011. *Wer sind und wo leben die Zuwanderer in Berlin? Einwohnerinnen und Einwohner mit Migrationshintergrund*. Pressegespräch. Amt für Statistik Berlin-Brandenburg. March 30th, 2011. Berlin.

StAG. 2015. *Staatsangehörigkeitsgesetz* (StAG). www.juris.de (accessed 2016).

StAG English. 2008. Nationality Act. Unofficial Translation by the Translation Division of theFederal Ministry of the Interior. www.juris.de (accessed 2016).

Stevenson, Patrick. 2006. National Languages in Transnational Contexts: Language, Migration, and Citizenship in Europe. In: Mar-Molinero, Clare and Stevenson, Patrick (eds.). 2006. *Language Ideologies, Policies and Practices: Language and the Future of Europe*, 147–161. Palgrave Macmillan: Basingstoke.

Wolcott, Harry. 2008. *Ethnography: A Way of Seeing*. Altamira Press: Maryland.

Section 2: **New identities**

Oliver Bunk and Maria Pohle

5 "Unter Freunden redet man anders": The register awareness of Kiezdeutsch speakers

1 Introduction

In the past two decades,[1] there has been a growing interest in Kiezdeutsch as a new German variety associated with young people in multiethnic urban neighborhoods like Kreuzberg or Neukölln in Berlin[2] (e.g., Wiese 2006, 2012; cf. also Jannedy, Mendoza-Denton, and Weirich this volume). Considerable attention has been paid to Kiezdeutsch from a grammatical perspective (cf. Wiese 2006, 2009, 2012, 2013; Freywald et al. 2015; on analyses of bilingual, in particular Turkish-German adolescents cf. Auer 2003, 2013; Kern and Selting 2006) and more recently also in the fields of media representation (cf. Androutsopoulos 2007, 2010; Androutsopoulos and Lauer 2013) and language attitudes in public discourse (cf. Wiese 2015). While studies focusing on public perception have shown that Kiezdeutsch speakers are constructed as being incapable of distinguishing between Kiezdeutsch as the informal variety and Standard German as the formal variety (cf. Androutsopoulos 2007; Hellberg 2014; Wiese 2015), Wiese and Pohle (2016) have shown that Kiezdeutsch speakers distinguish between these registers on a grammatical level. Within this context, a central topic that has yet not been focused on concerns the internal perspective, that is, the way Kiezdeutsch is perceived by its speakers, e.g., in how far they see Kiezdeutsch as a social and linguistic register, i.e., a distinct language praxis that is associated with certain social meanings (cf. Agha 2007).

---

1 The data presented in this article is part of the dissertation project "Kiezdeutsch im Sprachrepertoire" (Pohle in prep.) The research was supported by funding from the German Research Foundation (DFG) for the "Emerging Grammars in Language Contact Situations: A Comparative Approach" (FOR 2537), Project P6 (PI: Heike Wiese). For helpful comments and suggestions, we thank the editors of this volume and two anonymous reviewers. For all remaining errors and shortcomings we of course take full responsibility.

2 Apart from Kiezdeutsch in Berlin, we find similar varieties in multiethnic and multilingual areas in other major German cities. In southern Germany, Keim (2008) investigates the variety spoken by adolescents in multiethnic areas in Mannheim. In addition, as the data in section 4.1. illustrate, our participants mention Hamburg, Lüneburg, and Bielefeld as cities where Kiezdeutsch is spoken by adolescents.

https://doi.org/10.1515/9781501508103-005

In this paper, we investigate the perception of Kiezdeutsch, analyzing which social meanings speakers associate with Kiezdeutsch. We present qualitative and quantitative analyses of data from adolescent Kiezdeutsch speakers and adults, based on results from two open guise studies and semi-structured interviews.

Our analysis points to two major tendencies: First, the internal perception of Kiezdeutsch partly mirrors negative ethnic and linguistic stereotypes that appear in the external perception and support an othering of Kiezdeutsch speakers (cf. Wiese 2015 on such stereotypes in the external perception). However, the concept "ethnicity" as such is not a core element in the self-perception of Kiezdeutsch speakers. As we will demonstrate, for our in-group and some of the out-group informants Kiezdeutsch is not bound to geographical descent of the speaker's parents. Rather, "ethnicity" seems to be allocated by the majority society, referring to specific social markers, family being only one among them.[3] Rather, the focus is on social aspects associated with Kiezdeutsch in the majority society, in particularly socioeconomic disadvantages, educational failure, and a gangster-image. Second, speakers locate Kiezdeutsch as part of a broader repertoire: they explicitly distinguish between Kiezdeutsch as an informal register and Standard German as a formal register, allocating the two varieties to specific communicational contexts.

This paper is structured as follows: Section 2 provides an overview of relevant studies on the media representation and the internal and external perception of multiethnolects in Northwestern Europe, with special focus on Kiezdeutsch, and the role of these representations in the identity building processes of adolescents. In Section 3, we describe our methods and the design of our study. Section 4 presents and discusses our findings, while Section 5 summarizes our results.

2 The external and internal perception of multiethnolects in Northwest Europe

Over the last decades, multiethnolects in Europe have received a lot of attention from both a grammatical and a sociolinguistic perspective (cf. Quist 2008;

3 In this paper, we approach "ethnicity" from a very general and colloquial perspective, i.e., the geographical descent and the cultural background of a person's parents. In doing this, we try to grasp the differentiation between "German" and "foreign" that our participants made very frequently. However, note that ethnicity is not a predetermined category but an attribute that is associated with socially constructed groups (cf. Wiese to appear a, note 4 and references).

Wiese 2009). A number of studies investigated the external perception of multiethnolects, exploring the media representation of multiethnolects and their speakers, language attitudes, and the sociolinguistic dynamics of labeling. These studies show that in contrasting multiethnolects with the standard language of the respective countries, the media presents multiethnolects as inferior, incorrect versions of the majority language (cf. Androutsopoulos 2007; Quist 2016; Jonsson and Milani 2010; Svendsen 2014). The speakers themselves are often referred to as non-native, foreign, masculine, aggressive, and uneducated young migrants with a gangster-image (cf. Androutsopoulos 2007; Milani, Jonsson and Mhlambi 2015; Quist 2016). Hence, the media creates and feeds an image of linguistic and ethnic otherness, restricting the use of the multiethnolect to speakers with specific social and/or ethnic backgrounds.

In the public discussion, this image is picked up and contributes to establishing predominantly negative stereotypes of speakers and their languages. In a corpus study on the public debate on the dialectal status of Kiezdeutsch, Wiese (2015) identifies "overwhelmingly negative attitudes and ideologies" regarding Kiezdeutsch and its speakers based on "particular delimitations of social in- and out-groups" (Wiese 2015: 362). Thereby, central topoi in the public discussion substantially mirror the negative medial image of Kiezdeutsch and its speakers. One of these is the presumed mono-repertoire of Kiezdeutsch speakers, i.e., the view that speakers of Kiezdeutsch do not have other ways of speaking within their repertoire: Kiezdeutsch is not acknowledged as a distinct variety among other varieties but is seen as broken language and the result of language decay. This is in line with Hellberg (2014), who investigates out-group adolescents, who do not speak Kiezdeutsch. Hellberg (2014) reports negative attitudes and language ideologies towards Kiezdeutsch, again including the opinion that Kiezdeutsch speakers have a mono-repertoire.

In sum, from an external perspective, the repertoire of Kiezdeutsch speakers only consists of one single register, i.e., they have a mono-repertoire. In the definition of the term register, we follow Agha (2007: 145) who describes registers as "cultural models of action that link diverse behavioral signs to enactable effects, including images of persona, interpersonal relationship, and type of conduct". The term is closely related to the term enregisterment (Agha 2007: 81), which Agha describes as the process of allocating performable signs to distinct registers.

While previous research has concentrated on external perceptions of Kiezdeutsch, in particular in the media, the internal perspective remains widely underresearched. However, there is evidence that adolescents themselves reproduce stereotypical images, suggesting that the media's stylizations of a multiethnolect contribute to the identity-establishing process in young adults (cf. Quist 2008; Madsen and Svendsen 2015). This points to an interplay between media representations, external attitudes in public discourse, and the internal perception of multiethnolects.

In the context of identity building Auer (2013: 37) sees Kiezdeutsch as a sign of self-identification of its speakers as "outsiders of society". Other studies point out that multiethnolects do not only isolate their speakers from the societal majority but also allow the establishment of new social in-groups (Keim 2008; Christensen 2010; Aarsæther 2010; Bijvoet and Fraurud 2010). This aspect plays a major role in analyzing the register awareness of Kiezdeutsch speakers, as our findings will show below. Before we turn to that, we provide an overview of the methods and the design of our study.

3 Methods and design of the study

In our study we follow a mixed-methods research-design, avoiding the methodological dilemma between quantitative/indirect and qualitative/direct approaches (cf. Teddlie and Tashakkori 2006, 2009; Dörnyei 2007) by analyzing the data from both perspectives. The method we used is located between the fields of folk linguistics and language attitude research.

3.1 Data

In our study, we conducted an open guise study (cf. Soukup 2013), followed by a semi-structured group interviews. In open guise studies, participants listen to different recordings in which the same speaker uses different varieties of a language. Contrary to the matched guise method (cf. Lambert et al. 1960), in open guise designs, the informants are told that it is the same speaker who uses different varieties in the recordings. The informants are then asked to describe the speaker according to his/her language usage. Hence, open guise designs allow for an explicit judgement with respect to stereotypes that are associated with specific varieties (cf. Soukop 2013: 281). The transparent character of the design can give insights into stereotypes that the informants consciously attribute to different varieties, noticing them as different "coats of identity" (Soukup 2013: 282). In turn, making use of this method might reveal which strategies the informants use to apply these "coats of identity" themselves.[4] Instead of making use of closed scaled

4 For advantages of the open guise method in comparison to matched guise study cf. Soukup (2013: 271).

questionnaires, which is common in perceptual studies, we decided to conduct semi-structured interviews with open questions, because, in accordance with Studler (2014: 182), we considered this approach more flexible and more suitable to reveal the beliefs, attitudes, and self-portrayal of the informants.

3.2 Informants

Our in-group informants consisted of 16 students (eight male, eight female, average age: 16 years; SD = 0.6), all of whom lived in Berlin-Kreuzberg, a highly multiethnic district. They attended a high school with a high rate of multilingual students.[5] 15 of the 16 informants spoke at least one language in addition to German (Turkish, Arabic, Kurdish, Bosnian, and/or Polish) at home and/or with their friends. Turkish-German was the most frequent combination (11 out of 16). The out-group perspective was represented by five adult speakers (two male, three female, average age: 39 years; SD = 11.4) all of which were German speakers who grew up monolingually and speak only German at home and with their friends. The informants worked as police officers and social workers in different urban areas in West Germany (Hamburg, Lüneburg, Bielefeld, Berlin) and thus were regularly in contact with Kiezdeutsch and Kiezdeutsch speakers.

3.3 Stimuli

Our stimuli consisted of four recordings of two adolescents (male and female) that were collected as part of a dissertation project on "Kiezdeutsch im Sprachrepertoire" (cf. Pohle 2013).[6] For these recordings, Kiezdeutsch speakers were asked to describe a fictional situation (a car accident presented via visual stimuli) in four different communicative situations, illustrated in Table 1.

Only the spoken data were used in the open guise study. The open guise study was similar to the study in Bijvoet und Fraurud (2010), who explored the perception of adolescents in multilingual areas in Stockholm.[7] Two adolescents,

---

5 Cf. Bureau of Statistics Berlin-Brandenburg.

6 For the methodology cf. Wiese (2012, to appear b); for a more detailed description of the study cf. Pohle (2013), Wiese & Pohle (2016: 193ff).

7 In contrast to the study described in Bijvoet and Fraurud (2010), in which the speakers were asked to imagine the communicative context and the dialog partner, the speakers in our study were asked to describe an accident to a real person, being either a friend or the police officer, represented by one of the instructors.

Table 1: Linguistic contexts in the “Language Situation”–study.

	spoken	written
formal	oral police report	written police report
informal	telephone conversation to a friend	SMS/Whatsapp message to a friend

one male and one female, 18 and 19 years of age, appeared as the speakers in our study. Both of them were born in Berlin and had a bilingual background (Turkish-German), with Turkish being the dominant family language. Among their friends, they used both German and Turkish. Both participants stated that they used German as their dominant language outside these private contexts. At the time of the elicitation, the speakers attended a secondary school (*Gymnasium*) in Berlin-Neukölln, an area that, like Berlin-Kreuzberg, displays a high number of people with “migration background”[8] (67.19%) and students with “nichtdeutscher Herkunftssprache” (i.e., German is not the “language of origin”) (89.9%).[9] In the audio recordings, the two speakers made use of different linguistic means in the different contexts: In the formal context both speakers used a variety of German close to the standard, and in the informal contexts, we identified features that are typical for Kiezdeutsch, e.g., some /ç/ → /ʃ/ coronalization, optional V3 structures after initial adverbials, and some prepositional phrases without determiners.[10]

3.4 Procedure

The elicitation of the in-group data took place at the students' school, in a room that was reserved for the students' spare time activities. After filling out a questionnaire concerning the students' linguistic biography, the open guise study was conducted after having played the two recordings (informal and formal) separately. The open guise study was balanced for order of the informal and the formal recordings. Furthermore, in half of the cases only the male or the

8 All figures hold for 2013, when the recordings were made. Concerning the problematic term *Migrationshintergrund* (migration background) cf. Scarvaglieri and Zech (2013).

9 Students of *nichtdeutscher Herkunftssprache*: those whose parents state that the main language spoken at home is not German.

10 For an overview of the linguistic features of Kiezdeutsch cf. Wiese (2006, 2012).

female speaker was played. Finally, a semi-structured group interview of about ten minutes each was initiated by asking four questions. This way, we conducted four interviews, each including two male and two female informants. The out-group informants were interviewed in Hannover. Because this group was only meant to function as a control group, the group size was much smaller. For that reason, only the recordings of the male speaker in the formal context were played. Table 2 illustrates the different interview configurations[11] and the speaker numbers[12] that were confronted with the respective configuration.

Table 2: Setting of the open guise study.

	Male speaker	**Male speaker**	**Female speaker**	**Female speaker**
in-group	**informal → formal**	**formal → informal**	**informal → formal**	**formal → informal**
1JmIF	speakers J1–J4			
2JmFI		speakers J5–J8		
3JwIF			speakers J9–J12	
4JwFI				speakers J13–J16
out-group				
5EmIF	speakers E1–E4			

3.5 Data analysis

The data were analyzed qualitatively using a structured qualitative content analysis (cf. Kuckartz 2012) to identify categories and stereotypes that previous studies have found to be of major importance in the media's representation and the external perception of multiethnolects (cf. Section 2): "ethnicity", "language competence", "educational status", "language repertoire" and "local affiliation".

11 The interview codes provide the following information: interview number, age group of the participants (J=adolescent, E= adult), gender of speaker in den recording (m=male, w=female), order of the registers played (I= informal, F= formal).

12 The speaker codes themselves (see section 1.4 and onwards) provide the following information: age group of the participant (J=adolescent, E= adult), gender of the participant, additional languages spoken by the participant.

We focused on the question whether Kiezdeutsch speakers refer to their variety as a register that is used only in specific communicative contexts or whether Kiezdeutsch speakers use Kiezdeutsch in formal and informal contexts indiscriminately. Furthermore, we investigated which social and sociolinguistic characteristics our in-group adolescent and out-group adult informants associated with Kiezdeutsch, especially with respect to perceived ethnicity. In addition, the spoken data were analyzed quantitatively: we annotated utterances for semantic domains that related to social meanings and stereotypes and calculated their frequency in both groups. Table 3 summarizes the findings for this:

Table 3: Distribution of different topic in the interview data.

Semantic domain	**All informants**		**In-group informants**				**Out-group informants**	
					Male speaker	Female speaker		Male speaker
	n	%	n	%	n	n	n	%
Ethnicity	**64**	**17**	**59**	**17.3**	25	34	**5**	**7.6**
Language Competence	**130**	**32**	**114**	**33.3**	55	59	**16**	**24.2**
Educational Status	**33**	**9**	**22**	**6.4**	18	4	**11**	**16.7**
Local Affiliation	**53**	**14**	**49**	**14.3**	12	34	**4**	**6.1**
Language Repertoire	**110**	**28**	**81**	**23.7**	45	36	**29**	**43.9**
Total	**408**	**100**	**342**	**100**			**66**	**100**

We interpreted the most frequently mentioned semantic domains as particularly relevant topics for the respective group and included this aspect in our analysis.

4 Results and analysis

We present our data in two parts. The first part concerns the categories "ethnicity" and "local affiliation", the second part concerns linguistic repertoire and educational background.

4.1 "Ein Deutscher, der wirklich Deutsch ist; Vater Deutsch, Mutter Deutsch": ethnicity and local affiliation

Prima facie, "ethnicity" seems to be the most salient category relating to the social meaning of Kiezdeutsch: our in-group informants describe the speakers predominantly as foreign, as illustrated in (1) and (2).[13]

(1) J8mP: *N Ausländer. Kanake. Spricht Kanakisch.*
'A Foreigner. Kanake. Speaks Kanakisch.'

(2) J14mA: *ja genau Ausländer, kanakisch halt*
'Yes exactly – foreigner, kanakisch.'

Using of the pejorative *Kanake* / *Kanakisch* does not only refer to a specific ethnic group but more strongly reflects the social stratification of Kiezdeutsch as the language of societal outsiders (Auer 2013; Hellberg 2014; Wiese 2015): *Kanake* is typically associated with socially discriminated, uneducated foreign people, who speak broken German (*Kanakisch*), which corresponds to the characteristics of the stereotypical Kiezdeutsch speaker in both media and public discourse (cf. Section 2). However, the fact that Kiezdeutsch speakers make use of the term *Kanake* might point to its re-interpretation in order to signal the affiliation to a specific group outside of society (cf. Androutsopoulos 2007). In the process of identifying with a group, reproducing medial stereotypes like a specific perceived ethnicity might play a significant role. This implies that, at first glance, the in-group informants associated Kiezdeutsch with foreignness. Hereby, the informants based their perception of what is German not on cultural features, which are acquired when being born and raised in Germany. Rather, the adolescents determine Germanness following some kind of *ius sanguinis* principle (cf. Wiese 2015):

(3) J14mA: *Die ist vielleicht hier geboren oder lebt hier, seit eh, seit 10 Jahren oder so aber sie ist keine Deutsche.*
'Maybe she was born here or lives here, since well, since 10 years or so. But she is not a German.'

13 This is in line with the findings in Maegaard (2010), Christensen (2010), Bijvoet & Fraurud (2010).

(4) J1mT: *Ein Deutscher, der wirklich Deutsch ist; Vater Deutsch Mutter Deutsch, der würde niemals solche Wörter benutzen.*
'A German, who is really German, father German, mother German, he would never use such words.'

This attitude reflects a social separation in the larger society into Germans without and Germans with migration background[14] (cf. Scarvaglieri and Zech 2013). Even though this does not reflect the legal situation in Germany, (3) and (4) imply that the in-group participants conceptualize German based on this principle. In (3), the informant admits that the speaker might be born in Germany and has lived in the country for a long period of time, however he strongly rejects that the speaker is German. This becomes also clear in (4), where the speaker makes the Germanness of both parents the key factor for being really German.

The importance of *ius sanguinis* as a tool for the construction of societal in- and out-groups is also visible in the external perception of Kiezdeutsch as a new German dialect, indicating that this is a widespread principle used for demarcating social in- and out-groups in public discourse (cf. Wiese 2015). Our data suggest that multilingual Kiezdeutsch speakers reproduce this perception, referring to themselves as *Ausländer* and with the pejorative *Kanake*, perceiving themselves not as members of the German society.

Further evidence for this comes from (5) and (6). In addition, the data reveal that for the adolescent informants Kiezdeutsch marks the speakers as members of a social group that is characterized by specific socioeconomic features. To make this more obvious, consider the examples (5)–(7):

(5) J1mT: *Migrant. Türke.*
'Migrant. Turk.'

(6) J2mT: *So Araber ein bisschen so.*
'A little Arabic.'

(7) J14mA: *Türkin. Hundert Prozent / Also südländisch.*
'Turk. One hundred percent / Well Mediterranean.'

14 According to the report by the Federal Bureau of Statistics Demographic (2016), people with migration background are defined as people who were born in a foreign country, who have not had German citizenship from birth on or who have at least one parent for whom this holds.

At first glance, it seems, the informants associate Kiezdeutsch with speakers of Turkish or Arabic heritage. According to the Commissioner of the Federal Government for Migration, Refugees and Integration for the situation of immigrants in Germany (2014: 28ff), people with Arabic and Turkish cultural backgrounds are socially most discriminated in Germany. Naming these groups might imply that the informants implicitly associate Kiezdeutsch not with perceived ethnicity itself, but also with a specific socioeconomic status of its speakers. (8) and (9) illustrate this even more[15]:

(8) J10mT: *so ein Pennermädchen so*
'such a hobo-girl'

(9) J4mT: *Son Assi. Asozial.*
'such an antisocial person'

The terms *Pennermädchen* and *Assi* do not evoke any associations with specific cultural backgrounds but denote a social class, typically characterized by a low income and low educational success. Hence, perceived ethnicity itself does not describe a Kiezdeutsch speaker. Rather, our in-group informants do explicitly include *komplett Deutsche* in the group of Kiezdeutsch speakers. The criterion for these people to be part of the Kiezdeutsch speech community is the fact that they live in the same socioeconomically underprivileged area. (10) depicts how the adolescent informants allocate Kiezdeutsch to this group of people:

(10) J14mA: *Das reden halt alle, die in diesem Ghettogebiet leben*
'Everybody who lives in this ghetto area speaks like that.'
J13wD: *Auch komplett Deutsche.*
'The completely German too.'
J14mA: *Ja es gibt auch viele Deutsche die so sprechen.*
'Yes there are a lot of Germans who speak like that.'
J13wD: *Assi-Deutsche*
'Asocial Germans'
J13wD: *Assi-Deutsche, wisst ihr nicht diese Chantals und Pascals.*
'Asocial Germany, you know, those Chantals and Pascals.'

However, as the example illustrates, the adolescent informants distinguish between themselves and *komplett Deutsche* as separate groups that are related by

15 Cf. Wiese (2012) for the relation between social and economic properties of Kiezdeutsch speakers.

language use. Language seems to function as an indicator for specific socioeconomic features of its speakers, who live in *Ghettos* regardless of their ethnic background. Informant J13wD refers to the speakers as *Chantals* and *Pascals*. These names represent public stereotypes of German monolingual adolescents with low educational success, living in financially underprivileged households (cf. John 2014). This, in turn, allows for a very distinct and complex perception of the Kiezdeutsch speech community. On the one hand, the adolescent informants perceived Kiezdeutsch as a way to express their local identity, assuming that the speaker is a member of the local community, as (11) illustrates:

(11) J13mA: *Auf jeden Fall Kreuzberg oder Neukölln, sowas alles. Allein wie sie spricht.*
'Definitely Kreuzberg or Neukölln something like that / just the way she speaks'

Here, perceived ethnicity might play a role in demarcating the local in-group. On the other hand, assigning Kiezdeutsch to monolingual German speakers implies that, apart from the multilingual and multiethnic composition, the socioeconomic composition of these areas play a very important role.

Previous studies from Scandinavian countries indicate that in-group informants associate multiethnolects not predominantly with a certain minority cultural background (cf. Aarsæther 2010; Bijvoet und Fraurud 2010; Christensen 2010; Madsen and Svendsen 2015) but rather with "something more local, associated with a city, or one or more districts in the city" (Kerswill 2014: 18). Our data are in line with these findings.

While the adolescent informants described a heterogeneous Kiezdeutsch speech community in Berlin, the adult informants perceived Kiezdeutsch speakers as a homogenous speech community in different major cities in Germany:

(12) E2mD: *Hamburg, Berlin, Lüneburg, ich glaube das eh findet man in jeder Stadt auf jedem Schulhof, dass sich die Jugendlichen so unterhalten.*
'Hamburg, Berlin, Lüneburg, I think you can find it on every school yard, that pupils talk like that.'

The significance of "local affiliation" for the adolescent informants is also visible quantitatively: The adolescents addressed "local affiliation" twice as much as the out-group informants (n=49, 14.3% vs. n=4, 6.1%). For the former group it might be much more important to express the affiliation to a local group, perhaps also as part of the identity building process. Additionally, the adolescent informants displayed a fine graded understanding of the Kiezdeutsch speech community in Berlin, identifying the speakers not based on heritage but also on the socioeconomic and multiethnic status of the area they live in. The out-group informants on the other hand referred to Kiezdeutsch as a global phenomenon amongst adolescents even in different cities. They did stress the possibility of monolinguals to be part of the same speech community. One informant admitted that also monolinguals might speak Kiezdeutsch in some cases:

(13) E2mD: *Zuerst dachte ich auch erst an Migrationshintergrund (. . .) ich hab aber die Erfahrung gemacht, dass viele der deutschen Schüler das schon übernommen haben. Die unterhalten sich tatsächlich so auch wenn sie keinen Migrationshintergrund haben.*
'At first I also thought about migration background (. . .) but I made the experience that a lot of the German students have adapted this [kind of language, M.P. & O.B.]. They indeed talk like this, even though they don't have a migration background.'

Although this informant also did not exclude Germans without migration background from the group of Kiezdeutsch speakers, he pointed out that the German students group adopted a type of language that is typically used by adolescents with migrant background. Our data in Section 4.2 indicate that such a distinction between the Kiezdeutsch speakers is also reflected in differences in educational success and cognitive abilities. While multilingual speakers are still judged to be unsuccessful and incapable of switching between registers, monolinguals appear to be the opposite. Due to the fact that (13) is the only example of this kind in our data, we prefer not to over-intellectualize. However, together with Section 4.2, the analysis described above seems not entirely far-fetched.

Apart from this example, we observe the overall impression that the speaker has a migration background of a specific kind:

(14) E1mD: *Ehm. Migrationshintergrund, Nordafrika, wegen dieses yallah.*
'Well migration background. North Africa because of this yallah.'

The informants mention that the speaker has a migration background, descending from North-Africa. Also Turkish was mentioned very frequently. The out-group informants highlighted the migration background of the speakers, excluding any other adolescents. However, when the informants were asked to evaluate the speaker in the formal recordings, this picture changes:

(15) E5fD: *Eine Form von Migrationshintergrund könnte man jetzt auch daraus nicht mehr basteln.*
'You cannot make up a migration background anymore.'

The in-group participants where much more critical in this respect:

(16) J4mT: *Also er hat schon den Akzent, den türkischen Akzent, was jeder Ausländer hat, aber ja er hat sich halt, ja gut ausgedrückt. Aber das war halt perfekt, es war ein perfektes Deutsch.*
'Well he has got the accent, the Turkish accent, as every foreigner has, but he expressed himself well. / But it was like perfect, it was like perfect German.'

The data show that for the in-group participants, language competence is not related with perceived ethnicity. Even though they used phonological cues for identifying the speaker's ethnicity, this did not influence their perception of the "good" or even "perfect" proficiency of the speakers' Standard German. However, for the adolescents it did play a role to address the speaker's potential ethnic background, reflecting once more the significance of 'ethnicity' as a topic within the interviews. This is also evident quantitatively. The adolescents addressed "ethnicity" in 17.3% (n=59) of all cases, whereas the adult out-group addressed this only in 7.5% (n=5). A possible reason for this might be that in their everyday life and especially in the phase of growing up and in the identity building process, ethnicity might be a major topic for adolescents. Remember that our in-group participants referred to the Kiezdeutsch speakers as foreigners, even though they are born and raised in Germany. The data suggest that the in-group participants are much more critical in distinguishing between German, foreign, and German with migration background based on the speakers' language use. The slightest deviation from the standard German pronunciation marked the speaker as a "foreigner".

Summarizing this section, the data strongly suggest that apart from perceived ethnicity certain socioeconomic factors are crucial for the internal perception of Kiezdeutsch: Kiezdeutsch functions as a wide linguistic "one-of-us" marker (Christensen 2010) in peer-groups of adolescents of multiethnic underprivileged urban "ghetto"-areas. Even though our in-group participants refer to themselves as foreigners who speak Kiezdeutsch, Kiezdeutsch does not per se function as a marker for foreignness or migration background. Rather, Kiezdeutsch is defined as a language praxis used by a social fringe group of adolescents living in urban "ghetto"-districts. This group also includes monolingual speakers living in these areas. Put differently, Kiezdeutsch appears to be enregistered in the sense of Agha (2007) as a language form with low "social value" (Auer 2013: 32). Another major finding in our analysis concerns the register awareness in in-group speakers. We turn to this in the next section. We also illustrate the correlation between educational background and register awareness.

4.2 "Unter Freunden redet man anders": Language repertoire and educational background

The data demonstrate, that the adolescent informants were completely capable of assigning the correct communicative contexts to the recordings as illustrated in (17)–(19).

(17) J15mT: *Spricht mit der Freundin.*
'She's talking to a friend.'

(18) J11mT: *Polizei könnte es sein [mit der sie spricht]*
'Could be [talking to; M.P. & O.B.] the police'

(19) J9wT: *ja nicht die Freundin*
'Yes, not a friend.'

While this observation was very clear, it is far from trivial as it differs massively from the adults' perspective. (17) indicates that Kiezdeutsch is associated with peer-group conversations, whereas (18) illustrates reactions to the formal recordings. Here, the participant explicitly rejects that the speaker talks to a friend but rather to a police officer. The examples show that the adolescent participants have a strict opinion about when Kiezdeutsch is the appropriate register and when it is not. The most important factor in choosing the register was the peer-status of a dialog partner. Our informants explicitly identified Kiezdeutsch as a typical way of talking to peers, in contrast to the formal language, which is reserved for group-external communication with adults. The following illustrates this:

(20) J2wT: *Also, es hängt doch damit ab, ob man mit nem Freund redet oder wie hier mit einer anderen Person, mit Erwachsenen halt.*
'Well it depends on whether she is talking to a friend or like in this case with another adult.'

Also in conversations with teachers Kiezdeutsch was strictly forbidden. Our data suggest two reasons, why adults and teachers were named in particular.

On the one hand, using Standard German is a way to express politeness towards adults:

(21) J4mT: *Eigentlich kann man unter Freunden reden, so wie man will, aber wenn man jetzt mit einem Erwachsenen redet oder so, dann muss man doch richtig reden und respektvoll und höflich sein.*
'Actually you can talk among friends as you like, but when you talk to adults or something like that, then you have to speak well and be respectful and polite.'

Among friends, the informant reports, it is allowed to talk however one would like but towards adults the speaker needs to be respectful and also express this in their language. Kiezdeutsch functions as an internal code which signals a relaxed atmosphere among like-minded peers, outside societal pressures and monolingual norms. Hence, the usage of Kiezdeutsch is strongly restricted to in-group-communication.

On the other hand, Kiezdeutsch is also predominantly used by adolescents as an in-group marker, setting Kiezdeutsch apart from Standard German which is a tool for communicating with the world outside of the peer-group. As Thimm (2008) reports, youth languages refer to the group identity and in this respect they mark common in-group values and ideologies. In addition, they indicate a distance to out-group alternatives. Referring to Schlobinski (1989), Thimm (2008) also highlights that youth languages signal the distance of the dominant norms and values within a specific culture, reproducing these values at the same time. Thus, Kiezdeutsch speakers identify themselves through specific features, already indicated in the previous section: Kiezdeutsch speakers come from urban areas that are socioeconomically disadvantaged and they struggle with the prejudice of educational failure. These features are also salient in the medial representation of multiethnolects. By reproducing these features and assigning Kiezdeutsch to a specific group of speakers, the speakers set themselves apart from values and norms that are shared by adults.

Turning to the use of Standard German, our informants were also confident about when Standard German is the appropriate variety to use. The participants strictly exclude Kiezdeutsch in out-group-settings (cf. 22), in which they preferred to speak "proper German". We interpret the term "proper German" as a reference to Standard German. At the same time, this paraphrase again shows how the informant distinguishes between good German and bad German, good German (Standard German) being reserved for official matters and appointments:

(22) J10mT: *Unter Freunden redet man anders so, wie die jetzt mit Türkisch und so, aber würde ich einen Termin irgendwo haben, dann würde ich also dann würden die auch so richtig Deutsch sprechen.*
'Among friends you talk differently, like she was doing with Turkish and so on, but if I had an appointment somewhere, I would well, then they would speak like proper German.'

When the adolescent participants talked about the reason for speaking Kiezdeutsch, they stressed that this variety allows them to speak freely in a relaxed atmosphere with like-minded friends. Another important aspect is visible in (23):

(23) J3wT: *Für mich ist ja so, wenn ich mit dem Staat rede [...] ich versuch dann auch gut zu reden. Aber halt wenn es mein Freund ist, dann brauch ich doch nicht ein auf Dings zu tun. Ich kann dann so reden wie ich es will, ohne es mir schwer zu machen.*
'For me it is like, when I talk to the state, then I try to speak well. But among friends I can talk like however I want to talk, without making it too hard for me.'

Using the multiethnolects in these informal contexts has the advantage of avoiding the pressure of speaking "good" German. The informant reports that she has to make an effort to speak Standard German in formal contexts and thus she does not feel as comfortable as when speaking Kiezdeutsch. At first glance, one could argue that the informant struggles with Standard German in general. However, it seems more likely that using Standard German in formal contexts demands more effort in general also for monolingual speakers. From this perspective, Kiezdeutsch is not different from other informal varieties of German (cf. also Wiese to appear a for similar results in urban languages in Africa).

The analysis so far depicts that the informants explicitly highlighted the importance of Standard German for interacting with the out-group majority society. Kiezdeutsch speakers seem to be aware of the fact that a high language competence and mastering the standard variety is the key to social and cultural integration and success in the monolingual aligned German society. However, not all of our participants share this attitude of a register awareness of Kiezdeutsch speakers. (24) shows that some of the adult informants assume a mono-repertoire in Kiezdeutsch speakers:

(24) E1mD: *Ich hab schon Jugendliche kennengelernt, die nur so eh Ghettosprache drauf hatten. Die hatten nichts anderes drauf, ich*

hab mich gewundert, ich hab versucht, da was Normales heraus zu kitzeln, aber das ging nicht.
'I got to know adolescents, who were only capable of speaking well ghetto language. They couldn't speak differently and I was surprised. I tried to tease out something normal, but that was not possible.'

The informant labels Kiezdeutsch as *Ghettosprache* expressing a negative attitude towards the variety. On the other hand, this label, which also occurred very frequently in our in-group data, again reflects the association with a socioeconomic disadvantages group of people living in urban areas. The informant states that, in his experience, adolescents were not always capable of speaking standard German, also when the informant tried to trigger the standard variety. He refers to this variety as "normal" in contrast to the *Ghettosprache.* While Kiezdeutsch is limited to low socioeconomic status, Standard German is the language of the societal norm. In addition, the informant seems to assume that this proficiency in Standard German is typically accessible for speakers, which is the reason for the informant's attempt to trigger Standard German. However, as the speaker reports, Kiezdeutsch speakers do not always have access to this standard variety.

Not all of the adult participants shared the idea of a mono-repertoire of Kiezdeutsch speakers:

(25) E2mD: *Es ist tatsächlich ganz unterschiedlich, je nachdem in welcher Situation man ist. Man hat tatsächlich Jugendliche, die dann so ankommen und sagen wir wirklich eh vernünftiges Deutsch mit einem sprechen und die wollen verstanden werden. Es gibt aber auch Situationen, [. . .] wo die nur so mit einem reden wollen und dann ist es wiederum die Aufgabe des Empfängers, das auch zu verstehen und verstehen zu wollen.*
'Actually it is quite diverse, depending on the situation. You really can find adolescents who can speak, let's call it like that, proper German and they want to be understood. But there are also situations, [. . .] where they only want to talk like that. And then it's the task of the listener to understand them and to want to understand them.'

In this example the informant draws a more nuanced picture. He admits that some adolescents can speak "proper" German in order to facilitate a communicational situation in which both parties can communicate. According to the informant, the motivation behind this is that the speaker desires to be understood. This requires the speaker to know when Kiezdeutsch is not the adequate variety. While Kiezdeutsch signals in-group coherence and separation from the external community, Standard German serves as linguistic bridge between the in- and the out-group. This becomes even clearer in the second part of (25) where the informant mentions that not all Kiezdeutsch speakers switch into Standard German in conversations with adults. The reason for that, however, does not necessarily imply that the speaker is not capable of speaking Standard German. Rather it shows that the speaker actively chooses Kiezdeutsch as a tool for signaling the difference between the in- and the out-group. According to another informant this is a strategy that some adolescents consciously use for provoking adults in disputes:

(26) E4fD: *Ich glaube auch, dass es bei einigen Jugendlichen manchmal dieser Wechsel der Sprachen auch so zum bisschen Rollenverständnis, vielleicht auch Machtdemonstration ist. Auch grad in Vernehmungen, ich erinnere mich an eine wo ein Jugendlicher im Bereich Graffiti sämtliches Fachjargon, aus dieser Szene benutzt hat, und ich glaube das sollte auch einfach so seine Hierarchie so ein bisschen erhöhen in der Vernehmung, indem er gezielt diese Wörter benutzt hat, vielleicht in der Hoffnung das wir damit überhaupt nix anfangen können. Und insofern ist das auch teilweise gezielt eingesetzt wird, wenn man natürlich denn beide Seiten beherrsch.*

'I think that teenagers make use of switching between the languages to establish their own role and demonstrating power. Especially in examinations, I remember a situation where a teenager used terminology in the field of graffiti and I think he was doing that in order to raise his own position in this examination. Using this word he might have hoped that I cannot follow at all. So when you are capable of mastering both sides [registers, authors] they might do that on purpose.'

According to the informant, some speakers use Kiezdeutsch to question hierarchical configurations. This also challenges social roles and demonstrates power. At the same time, the speaker marks the adult communicative partner as an out-group member, demonstrating a different social affiliation. However, this is not typically just for Kiezdeutsch, but for youth languages in general (cf. Thimm 2008).

In sum, our out-group informants partly agreed on the speaker's ability to switch between registers in different contexts. At first glance, this seems to match our in-group data. The major difference between these two groups, however, is the argument behind this assumption. According to the adolescent participants, Kiezdeutsch speakers naturally switch to Standard German when speaking to adults or in out-group settings. On the other hand, as can be seen below, the adult informants report two major reasons for the capability of adapting the language to certain situations: educational background and specific cognitive abilities of speakers. Example (27) illustrates the latter reason:

(27) E2mD: *Ich glaube, es ist tatsächlich von der Situation abhängig, und je besser die* [Jugendlichen, M.P. & O.B.] *die Situationen einschätzen können, umso mehr trau ich denen auch im Kopf zu. Also es gibt genug Jugendliche die sprechen in der, wie in der ersten Phase* [informal recording, M.P. & O.B.], *auch mit dem Polizisten und wollen dann irgendwas, und wundern sich warum sie es nicht kriegen und anders rum genauso. Und wiederum die die ein bisschen mehr im Kopf haben, ähm wenden das dann tatsächlich auch situationsangemessen an.*
'I believe, it really depends on the situation and the better the teenager can estimate situations, the more I think they can do intellectually. There are a lot of teenagers who talk he the one in the first recording [=informal, M.P. & O.B.], also with police officers and then they want something and are surprised why they can't get it. But it's also the other way round. And again, those who are a little more intelligent, well they adapt their language to different situations.'

The informant assumes that being able to evaluate a communicative situation correctly is a performance that requires certain cognitive abilities. Adolescents who are not capable of evaluating a situation correctly lack these abilities and thus fail in applying the adequate variety. This line of argumentation becomes even more salient when our participants raise the topic of the educational status of the speakers. The adolescent informants expressed a close relationship between good German and a high educational status of the speakers[16]:

(28) J8mP: *Er ist gut in der Schule. Weil er so gut Deutsch spricht. Vielleicht Gymnasium.*
'He's good at school. Because he speaks German so well. Maybe Gymnasium.'

16 The results are in line with results from similar study on Rinkebysvenska (cf. Milani & Johnson 2012).

In (28) the informant clearly identifies the speaker as a good student, attending a Gymnasium (grammar school) due to the fact that he uses Standard German. In contrast, the usage of Kiezdeutsch in the informal context was regarded as a sign for failing at school.

The argument is in line with the study in Madsen, Møller, and Jørgensen (2010) and Madsen (2013) on the register awareness of Danish students. These students explicitly distinguished between Standard Danish and the informal multiethnolect. While the former register was conceptualized as an advantage for success at school, the latter was a factor for failing at school. Note, however, that our in-group participants only addressed the differences between the educational backgrounds of Standard German speakers and Kiezdeutsch speakers. The ability for a speaker to switch between the registers is, as argued above, not a question of educational status. This is in strong contrast with the out-group perspective.

According to the adult informants, the ability of switching between Kiezdeutsch and standard German heavily depends on the speaker's educational background. Students with a high educational background, i.e., attending a Gymnasium, are assumed to be capable of switching registers, whereas students with a low educational background are not. The informants disqualified the latter group of students from being capable to switch registers, due to the fact that their heritage language prevents them from developing a certain proficiency in Standard German:

(29) E2mD: *Ich glaube es kommt darauf an, wenn ich Leute vor mir habe, die, denen ich zu einem gewissen Bildungsstand einfach mal unterstelle [. . .] also die können sich schon normal unterhalten, haben aber für ihren Kreis eine eigene Sprache entwickelt, wo ich sage Hut ab, der ist zweisprachig, es gibt aber auch genug, die wirklich den ganzen Tag und sich nur so unterhalten, da ist es für mich schon ein Zeichen davon, dass sie anders nicht können, weil einem auch ganz oft eh ihre Sprache, also ihre Heimatsprache dazwischen kommt, weil sie bestimmte Wörter gar nicht ins Deutsche übersetzen können und anders rum, das sind Leute mit denen möchte ich mich nicht unterhalten.*
'I think it depends. There are people that I ascribe a specific educational background to, then I assess this as a foreign language more or less. So they can communicate normally, but for their peer group they developed an own language. In that case I say hats off! That guy is bilingual. But there are also enough people, who really talk like that all day long. That indicates to me that

they cannot speak differently because their native often language intervenes, because they cannot transfer certain words into German or vice versa. I don't want to talk to these people.'

Even though the informant acknowledges the existence of Kiezdeutsch as a variety on its own and even refers to its speakers as bilinguals, he highlights that there are many speakers, who cannot switch to Standard German due to the influence of their native language. According to the informant, the speakers are not capable of translating certain words from their native language into German and vice versa, because they only know them in one of these languages. This strongly resembles the myth of the *Doppelte Halbsprachigkeit*, i.e., the lack of full language proficiency in either of the two languages bilinguals grow up with. As Wiese (2011) demonstrates, this attitude is missing an empirical basis. Furthermore, language users evaluate each other socially and in this process speech styles and dialects play a significant role (Wiese 2011: 82). Accordingly, this holds for Kiezdeutsch, too. The social stigmatization becomes even clearer in the last sentence of the utterance, in which the informant adds, that he would rather not communicate with these people, who cannot speak "proper" German.

After listening to the informal recording, two of the five adult participants assumed low educational achievements, hence mentioning that the speaker might attend a Hauptschule (cf. Keim 2008 for similar observations), where he is utterly failing:

(30) E5fD: *Ich hatte irgendwie so ein Wort vor Augen, Hauptschule mit B geschrieben, also Haubtschule also jemand der eh sich möglicherweise noch um den Hauptschulabschluss bemühen muss, weil er aus dem normalen System schon raus ist.*
'I had a special term in mind, Hauptschule, written with a B, so Haubtschule, someone who is really struggling with graduating from Hauptschule, because he is already out of the normal system.'

The informant sees the speaker as an adolescent that is located outside of the "normal system", struggling with educational success and attending a Hauptschule. This again reflects the social stratification of Kiezdeutsch speakers as members of a social group, that is to be situated outside the society. Some of the informants confirm this impression but mention that this might be a stereotype (cf. 31). They question their attitude based on their personal experience with adolescents, attributing the usage of Kiezdeutsch to students with very diverse educational backgrounds, including Gymnasium:

(31) E3fD: *Die erste Reaktion ist wahrscheinlich immer das man denkt eher niederer Schulbesuch aber ich glaube das sind Vorurteile [...] aber Schulformen könnten alle sein.*
'The first reaction is always I think low education, but I think those are prejudices. (...) But the school type could be any.'

(32) E2mD: *Ich hab die Erfahrung gemacht das auch am Gymnasium die Jungs so reden.*
'I've had the experience that even at academic high schools the boys talk like that.'

Taking into consideration the claim mentioned above, that out-group speakers assume higher cognitive capacities for speakers that can switch between registers, we interpret the underlying attitude in (31) and (32) in the following way: Kiezdeutsch speakers in Gymnasien are able to switch into Standard German due to higher intellectual capacities. This does not hold for Kiezdeutsch speakers in Hauptschulen. Here the stereotypical Kiezdeutsch speaker struggles with educational success and lacks intellectual capacities of switching between Kiezdeutsch and Standard German. Hence, from the out-group perspective, Kiezdeutsch speakers have a different social status depending on whether they attend a Gymnasium or a Hauptschule. Our adolescent informants, however, clearly perceived Kiezdeutsch as the language of low education background and Standard German with educational success. This in turn, highlights the close relationship between Kiezdeutsch and certain socioeconomic features for the adolescent informants (cf. Section 4.1).

The differences in the perception of the relation between Kiezdeutsch and educational success are also reflected on a quantitative level. Educational status appears to be a more relevant topic for the out-group informants (n=11, 16.7%) compared to the in-group informants (n=22, 6.4%). The differences between adolescents and adults might be due to age effects: Adults might to a much higher extent regard educational success as an important factor generally. In addition, the data reveal that adults feel that Kiezdeutsch also appears at a Gymnasium, where, as we conclude, their speakers are able to switch between registers. This might also explain why language repertoire was the most addressed topic (n=29, 43.9%), for the out-group informants and language competence (n=16, 24.7%) was the second most addressed category. This distribution was reversed for the in-group informants (language competence n=114, 33.3%, language repertoire, n=81, 23.7%). The distribution might reflect the awareness of Kiezdeutsch speakers that using the standard language increases educational success.

5 Conclusion

In this paper, we investigated internal and external perceptions of Kiezdeutsch, focusing on the question how Kiezdeutsch-speakers reflect their own language usage as a social and linguistic register. In order to reveal the role of standard language ideologies for the enregisterment of Kiezdeutsch, we carried out an open guise study presenting both Kiezdeutsch and Standard German. We furthermore conducted semi-structured interviews with adolescents from Kreuzberg. We also included the out-group perspective, interviewing a test group of adults in the same way. Analyzing the data qualitatively and quantitatively revealed the following:

First, one of the major aspects in the internal and external perception of Kiezdeutsch is ethnicity. At first glance, our adolescent informants seemed to make a connection between Kiezdeutsch and ethnicity. However, on closer examination this connection seems to be a reproduction of media stereotypes rather than sociolinguistic reality, due to the fact that the adolescents included monolingual Germans in the group of Kiezdeutsch speakers. Perceived ethnicity might play a role in identifying as a group, due to the media's representation of Kiezdeutsch, but it seems the informants did not only refer to ethnicity as such, but more to "projections of stereotypes associated with ethnicity" (Madsen and Svendsen 2015: 227). None of our adolescent informants excluded adolescents without migration background from the group of Kiezdeutsch speakers, as long as they displayed the same low socioeconomic and educational status and lived in the same equally underprivileged urban areas. In this sense, Kiezdeutsch speakers perceive Kiezdeutsch as a linguistic symbol of being a social outsider, which is in line with the indexical meanings of Kiezdeutsch in public discourse.

Second, our data reveal some major differences between the internal and external perception of Kiezdeutsch, in particular with respect to linguistic repertoire. Our adolescent informants displayed high sensitivity concerning the situational restrictions for the usage of Kiezdeutsch: The adolescents allowed Kiezdeutsch only in informal peer-group-communication associated with a relaxed atmosphere among like-minded friends. In other settings, especially in out-group-situations, all adolescent informants agreed on the usage of the German standard variety. This was motivated by the desire to avoid prejudices and social exclusion and to express politeness and respect. Switching between these registers was seen as a natural ability in our adolescent informants. On the other hand, our adult participants tied the ability of register switching to intellectual capacities and education, distinguishing between Kiezdeutsch speakers with high educational background and lower educational background.

In sum, our findings contribute to recent language attitude research in multiethnolects and provide new insights from an internal perspective. Most importantly, the study points out metalinguistic reflections of in-group speakers, concerning their register awareness in contrast to an external point of view. In addition, the study reveals the internal motivation for making use of a multiethnolect as a linguistic marker of belonging to a specific peer group within the speech community. In our analysis, we were also able to strengthen and confirm different aspects that were pointed out in earlier studies on language attitudes towards multiethnolects in Northwest Europe but that have yet not been explicitly examined for Kiezdeutsch.

However, due to the limited amount of data, we were not able to conduct a statistical analysis. Especially the size of the sample of our adult informants needs to be increased to provide a more detailed, statistically analyzable data set. Furthermore, our data point to an interesting aspect that we were not able to go into depth here: In contrast to other multiethnolects in Northwest Europe, Kiezdeutsch does not seem to be predominantly associated with male speakers, but also with female speakers. This is just one of the aspects that we leave for future research, as a closer look into this topic might be especially fruitful in comparing Kiezdeutsch to other multiethnolects in Northwest Europe.

References

Aarsæther, Finn. 2010. The use of multiethnic youth language in Oslo. In Pia Quist & Bente Ailin Svendsen (eds.), *Multilingual Urban Scandinavia: New Linguistic Practices*, 111–126. Clevedon: Multilingual Matters.

Agha, Asif. 2007. *Language and social relations*. Cambridge: Cambridge University Press.

Androutsopoulos, Jannis K. 2007. Ethnolekte in der Mediengesellschaft. Stilisierung und Sprachideologie in Performance, Fiktion und Metasprachdiskurs. In Christian Fandrych & Reinier Salverda (eds.), *Standard, Variation und Sprachwandel in germanischen Sprachen*, 113–155. Tübingen: Narr.

Androutsopoulos, Jannis K. 2010. The study of language and space in media discourse. In Peter Auer & Jürgen Erich Schmidt (eds.), *Language and Space: An International Handbook of Linguistic Variation. Volume I: Theory and Methods*, 740–758. Berlin & New York: Mouton de Gruyter.

Androutsopoulos, Jannis & Katharina Lauer. 2013. 'Kiezdeutsch' in der Presse: Geschichte und Gebrauch eines neuen Labels im Metasprachdiskurs. In Şeyda Ozil, Michael Hofmann, Yasemin Dayıoğlu-Yücel (eds.), *Jugendbilder: Repräsentationen von Jugend in Medien und Politik*, 67–94. Göttingen: V&R Unipress.

Auer, Peter. 2003. 'Türkenslang' – ein jugendsprachlicher Ethnolekt des Deutschen und seine Transformationen. In Annelies Häcki Buhofer (ed.), Spracherwerb und Lebensalter, 255–264. Tübingen & Basel: Francke.

Auer, Peter. 2013. Ethnische Marker im Deutschen zwischen Varietät und Stil. In Arnulf Deppermann (ed.), *Das Deutsch der Migranten*, 9–40. Berlin & Boston: Mouton de Gruyter.

Bijvoet, Ellen & Kari Fraurud. 2010. Rinkeby Swedish in the mind of the beholder. Studying listener perceptions of language variation in multilingual Stockholm. In Pia Quist & Bente Ailin Svendsen (eds.), *Multilingual Urban Scandinavia. New Linguistic Practices*, 170–188. Clevedon: Multilingual Matters.

Christensen, Mette Vedsgaard. 2010. One of my kind? Language and Ethnicity among Danish adolescents. In Pia Quist & Bente Ailin Svendsen (eds.), *Multilingual Urban Scandinavia: New Linguistic Practices*, 207–224. Bristol: Multilingual Matters.

Commissioner of the Federal Government for Migration, Refugees and Integration for the situation of immigrants in Germany. 2014. *10. Bericht der Beauftragten der Bundesregierung für Migration, Flüchtlinge und Integration über die Lage der Ausländerinnen und Ausländer in Deutschland*.https://www.bundesregierung.de/Content/Infomaterial/BPA/IB/10_Auslaenderbericht_2015.html?view=trackDownload (accessed18 June 2018).

Dörnyei, Zoltán. 2007. *Research methods in applied linguistics*. New York: Oxford University Press.

Freywald, Ulrike, Leonie Cornips, Natalia Ganuza, Ingvild Nistov & Toril Opsahl. 2015. Beyond verb second – a matter of novel information structural effects? Evidence from Norwegian, Swedish, German and Dutch. In Jacomine Nortier & Bente Ailin Svendsen (eds.), *Language, Youth and Identity in the 21st Century. Linguistic Practices across Urban Spaces*, 73–92. Cambridge: Cambridge University Press.

Hellberg, Aïsha. 2014. "Ich jage Dich mit dem Duden durchs Ghetto". Sprachideologie und Sprachreflexion in schülerVZ-Gruppen. In Helga Kotthoff & Christine Mertzlufft (eds.), *Jugendsprachen: Stilisierungen, Identitäten, mediale Ressourcen*, 189–214. Frankfurt am Main: Peter Lang.

John, Linda. 2014. *Sprachliche und soziale Normen. Quantitative Studie zum Einfluss von Abweichungen des sprachlichen Standards und ethnisch markierten Vornamen bei der Leistungsbewertung von Schulaufsätzen*. Unpublished Master's thesis.

Jonsson, Rickard & Tommaso M. Milani. 2010. Youth styles in Sweden: Representations and practices. *Copenhagen studies in bilingualism* 55(1). 10–51.

Keim, Inken. 2008. *Die "türkischen Powergirls". Lebenswelt und kommunikativer Stil einer Migrantinnengruppe in Mannheim*. Tübingen: Narr.

Kern, Friederike & Margret Selting. 2006. Einheitenkonstruktion im Türkendeutschen: Grammatische und prosodische. *Zeitschrift für Sprachwissenschaft* 25(2). 239–272.

Kerswill, Paul. 2014. The objectification of 'Jafaican': the discoursal embedding of Multicultural London English in the British media. In Jannis K. Androutsopoulos (ed.), *The Media and Sociolinguistic Change*, 428–455. Berlin & New York: Mouton De Gruyter.

Kuckartz, Udo. 2012. *Qualitative Inhaltsanalyse. Methoden, Praxis, Computerunterstützung*. Weinheim & Basel: Beltz Juventa.

Lambert, Wallace E., Richard C. Hodgson, Robert Gardner & Samuel Fillenbaum. 1960. Evaluational reactions to spoken language. *Journal of Abnormal and Social Psychology* 60(1). 44–51.

Madsen, Lian Malai. 2013. "High" and "Low" in urban Danish speech styles. *Language in Society* 42(2). 115–138.

Madsen, Lian M., Janus S. Møller & Normann J. Jørgensen. 2010. "Street language" and "Integrated": Language use and enregisterment among late modern urban girls. In Lian M. Madsen, Janus S. Møller & Normann J. Jørgensen (eds.), *Ideological Constructions and Enregisterment of Linguistic Youth Styles*, 81–113. Copenhagen: Københavns Universitet.

Madsen, Lian Malai & Bente Ailin Svendsen. 2015. Stylized voices of ethnicity and social division. In Jacomine Nortier & Bente Ailin Svendsen (eds.), *Language, Youth and Identity in the 21st Century. Linguistic Practices across Urban Spaces*, 207–230. Cambridge: Cambridge University Press.

Maegaard, Marie. 2010. Linguistic practice and stereotypes among Copenhagen adolescents. In Pia Quist & Bente A. Svendsen (eds.), *Multilingual urban Scandinavia: New linguistic practices*, 189–206. Bristol: Multilingual Matters.

Milani, Tommaso M. 2010. What's in a name? Language ideology and social differentiation in a Swedish print-mediated debate. *Journal of Sociolinguistic* 14(1). 116–142.

Milani, Tommaso M.& Rickard Jonsson. 2012. "Who's afraid of Rinkeby Swedish? Stylization, complicity, resistance." *Journal of Linguistic Anthropology* 22(1). 44–63.

Milani, Tommaso M., Rickard Jonsson & Innocentia J. Mhlambi. 2015. Shooting the subversive: When non-normative linguistic practices go mainstream in the media. In Jacomine Nortier & Bente A. Svendsen (eds.), *Language, Youth and Identity in the 21st Century*, 119–138. Cambridge: Cambridge University press.

Pohle, Maria. 2013. *Registerdifferenzierung bei Kreuzberger Jugendlichen*. Universität Potsdam MA thesis.

Pohle, Maria. In prep. *Kiezdeutsch im Sprachrepertoire*. Universität Potsam. Doctoral Dissertation.

Quist, Pia. 2000. Ny københavnsk 'multietnolekt'. Om sprogbrug blandt unge i sprogligt og kulturelt heterogene miljøer. *Danske Talesprog* 1. 143–211.

Quist, Pia. 2008. Sociolinguistic approaches to multiethnolect: Language variety and stylistic practice. *International Journal of Bilingualism* 12(1–2). 43–61.

Quist, Pia. 2016. Representations of multiethnic youth styles in Danish broadcast media. In Nikolas Coupland, Jacob Thøgersen, Janus Mortensen (eds.), 217–234, Oslo: Novus Press.

Scarvaglieri, Claudio & Claudia Zech. 2013. "Ganz normale Jugendliche, allerdings meist mit Migrationshintergrund". Eine funktionalsemantische Analyse von "Migrationshintergrund". *Zeitschrift für angewandte Linguistik* 58(1). 201–227.

Schlobinski, Peter. 1989. "Frau Meier hat Aids, Herr Tropfmann hat Herpes, was wollen Sie einsetzen?" Exemplarische Analyse eines Sprechstils. *Osnabrücker Beiträge zur Sprachtheorie* 41. 1–34.

Soukup, Barbara. 2013. On matching speaker (dis)guises – revisiting a methodological tradition. In Tore Kristiansen & Stefan Grondelaers (eds.), *Language (De)standardisation in Late Modern Europe: Experimental Studies*, 267–285. Oslo: Novus Press.

Studler, Rebekka. 2014. "Einige Antworten habe ich *contre coeur* so angekreuzt". Zur Relevanz offener Fragen in Fragebogenstudien zu Spracheinstellungen. In Christina Cuonz & Rebekka Studler (eds.): *Sprechen über Sprache. Perspektiven und neue Methoden der Spracheinstellungsforschung*, 169–204. Tübingen: Stauffenburg Verlag.

Svendsen, Bente Ailin. 2014. Kebabnorskdebatten. En språkideologisk forhandling om sosial identitet. Tidsskrift *for* ungdomsforskning 14(1). 33–62.

Teddlie, Charles & Abbas Tashakkori. 2006. A general typology of research designs featuring mixed methods. *Research in the Schools* 13(1). 12–28.

Teddlie, Charles & Abbas Tashakkori. 2009. *Foundations of Mixed Methods Research: Integrating Quantitative and Qualitative Approaches in the Social and Behavioral Sciences*. Los Angeles: Sage.

Thimm, Caja. 2008. Generationsspezifische Wortschätze. In D. Alan Cruse, Franz Hundsnurscher, Michael Job & Peter Rolf Lutzeier (eds.), *Lexikologie. Handbücher zur Sprach- und Kommunikationswissenschaft* 21(1),880–888. Berlin & New York: Mouton de Gruyter.

Wiese, Heike, Ulrike Freywald & Katharina Mayr. 2009. *Kiezdeutsch as a Test Case for the Interaction between Grammar and Information Structure* (Interdisciplinary Studies on Information Structure 12). Potsdam: Universitätsverlag Potsdam.

Wiese, Heike. 2006. "Ich mach dich Messer" – Grammatische Produktivität in Kiez-Sprache ("Kanak Sprak"). *Linguistische Berichte* 207. 245–273.

Wiese, Heike. 2009. Grammatical innovation in multiethnic urban Europe: New linguistic practices among adolescents. *Lingua* 119(5). 782–806.

Wiese, Heike. 2011. Führt Mehrsprachigkeit zum Sprachverfall? Populäre Mythen vom "gebrochenen Deutsch" bis hin zur "doppelten Halbsprachigkeit" türkischstämmiger Jugendlicher in Deutschland. In Şeyda Ozil, Michael Hofmann, Yasemin Dayıoğlu-Yücel (eds.), *Türkisch-deutscher Kulturkontakt und Kulturtransfer. Kontroversen und Lernprozesse*, 73–84. Göttingen: V&R unipress.

Wiese, Heike. 2012. *Kiezdeutsch. Ein neuer Dialekt entsteht.* München: C.H. Beck.

Wiese, Heike. 2013. What can new urban dialects tell us about internal language dynamics? The power of language diversity. [Special Issue]. *Linguistische Berichte* 19. 207–245.

Wiese, Heike. 2015. "This migrants' babble is not a German dialect!" – The interaction of standard language ideology and "us"/"them" dichotomies in the public discourse on a multiethnolect. *Language in Society* 44(3). 341–368.

Wiese, Heike. to appear a. Urban contact dialects. In Salikoko Mufwene & Anna María Escobar (eds.), *The Cambridge Handbook of Language Contact*. Cambridge: Cambridge University Press.

Wiese, Heike. to appear b. Language Situations: A method for capturing variation within speakers' repertoires. In Yoshiyuki Asahi (ed.), *Methods in Dialectology XVI*. Frankfurt am Main: Peter Lang.

Wiese, Heike & Maria Pohle. 2016. "Ich gehe Kino" oder "...ins Kino"? Gebrauchsrestriktionen nichtkanonischer Lokalangaben. *Zeitschrift für Sprachwissenschaft* 35(2). 171–216.

Stefanie Jannedy, Norma Mendoza-Denton
and Melanie Weirich

6 Social capital and the production and perception of fine phonetic detail in Berlin

1 Introduction

In a city like Berlin, which exhibits both tremendous postwar historical changes for Berlin natives, as well as a high rate of in-migration and immigration, how might perceptual linguistic habits – linking linguistic categories and social categories – in the majority, ethnic-German population result in the prevention of accumulation of social capital in the minority, multi-ethnic population?

The core of this paper will lay out our experimental phonetic evidence and link the outcome of our studies to Bourdieu's ideas of social power and social identity through linguistic capital. We begin by laying the groundwork necessary to 1) understand migration as a phenomenon in Berlin, 2) trace an example from our data collection and tie it to Social Identity Theory and linguistic variation, and 3) follow this introduction by discussing Bourdieu and the theory of social capital.

1.1 The multiethnic side of Berlin

According to the census office at Berlin-Brandenburg, at the end of 2017, Berlin, the capital of Germany consists of 3.7 million inhabitants[1] of whom almost 19% (711,282) are foreigners and more than a third of whom, 1,207,052 (32.5%), have an immigrant background. The two largest immigrant communities are Turks and Arabs. Berlin, as a diasporic place, is home to about 178,223 Turks (roughly 5% of the total population), some of them the direct migrants who came to Germany during the 1960s, and some their descendants who have been born and raised in Germany. It is also home to about 138,607 Arabs (3.7%) descended from about 20 different countries. Crucially, both Turks and Arabs now live in working class West Berlin neighborhoods along the former Berlin Wall which used to

1 https://www.statistik-berlin-brandenburg.de/publikationen/Stat_Berichte/2018/SB_A01-05-00_2017h02_BE.pdf (accessed 23 August 2018).

https://doi.org/10.1515/9781501508103-006

belong to the American sector post-WWII. Due to cheap housing, the districts of Kreuzberg, Wedding and Neukölln became settlements for the new immigrants. Nowadays, these districts are in the process of gentrifying and characterized by a multi-ethnic, multinational and multilingual (Turkish, Palestinian, Lebanese Arab) immigrant-descent population, coexisting with monoethnic and multiethnic Germans (Amt für Statistik Berlin-Brandenburg 2015, 2016).

While there are currently no reliable statistics on language use in the aforementioned neighborhoods, data from the 2017 Berlin census report released by the Berlin/Brandenburg office of statistics states that approximately 33% of the Berlin population has a migrant background – defined as someone who has at least one parent who immigrated to Germany after 1949 or who does not have German citizenship. Wiese (2015) interpolates from the 2009 and 2010 census data released by the German Federal statistical office that approximately 31% of people under the age of 18 years in Germany and approximately 46% of minors living in a city with a population exceeding 500,000 people have a migrant background.

Second- and third-generation descendants of immigrants are more integrated culturally, linguistically and socially than their first generation forebears in terms of their engagement with the apparatus of the state: they attend German day-care, schools and after school programs, later participating in the labor force, all while speaking German. With the influx of hundreds of thousands of refugees and new immigrants to Germany since 2015, the political question of their integration has become a hot-button issue. Social democratic parliamentarian Aydan Özoguz, herself a second-generation Turkish-German, has stated on the German daily news (*Tagesschau* December 12, 2015) that the "mistakes of the past" pertaining to the lack of social and cultural integration and formal language training shall not be repeated, asserting that new immigrants to Germany must be formally instructed in mandatory language and integration classes.

Many of the first generation of primarily male migrant workers, largely excluded from state institutions, spoke their first languages while also innovating a type of pidgin German termed – *Gastarbeiterdeutsch* [foreign workers' German] (Keim 1978). The Berlin-raised second- and third-generation descendants of the foreign *Gastarbeiter* now often speak a version of their heritage language as well as a unique version of German, *Kiezdeutsch* (Jannedy 2011; Jannedy and Weirich 2012), which displays some features of *Gastarbeiterdeutsch*. By displaying the internal regularities inherent in any dialect variety, Kiezdeutsch today would be considered neither a pidgin nor a collection of features, but rather a full-fledged variety or dialect of German (see also Wiese 2012).

Transcending its immigrant roots, today Kiezdeutsch is spoken among both the multilingual, multiethnic youth and their ethnic-German peers living in the same quarters and attending the same schools. Although in the majority ethnic-German public perception Kiezdeutsch is still associated with multiethnic and multilingual speakers, in practice this relatively new variety with its grammatical and phonological innovations also serves as one vector for the creation and display of local identification with the originating urban neighborhood, and this applies to all youth in the neighborhood. Kiezdeutsch is a resource in the practice of being from particular areas of Berlin. Nonetheless, the use of grammatical forms or pronunciation variants that do not match the local, ambient majority-dialect is stigmatized, and perceived by listeners from outside the relevant neighborhoods as "wrong" and "bad" German (Wiese 2015). Newspaper reports on research work done on Kiezdeutsch become targets of negative reader commentaries aimed not only at the content of the article but also at the investigating scientists.

Because of its stigmatization and the continuing negative language ideologies toward it, Kiezdeutsch has been saddled with many unfortunate and some outright insulting names such as *Kanaksprak* (Zaimoğlu 1995) or *Türkenslang* (Auer 2003), *Türksprech* (*Berliner Zeitung*) or *Türkensprache*. We consider *Kiezdeutsch* a neutral term making reference to a geographically-localized variety found most robustly in certain smaller parts of neighborhoods which in Berlin are called *Kieze*. In that, urban Berlin German is no different from varieties in other European cities where adolescent speakers from multicultural backgrounds are also the driving forces behind grammatical innovation and phonetic variation. To name a few: *Multicultural London English* (Torgersen, Kerswill, and Fox 2006; Kerswill, Torgersen, and Fox 2008), Dutch *Straattaal* (Nortier 2001; Appel, 1999), Swedish *Rinkebysvenska* (Kotsinas 1992, 1998), or the Danish *Kobenhavnsk multietnolekt* (Quist 2005).

Kiezdeutsch is characterized by various morpho-syntactic features such as the omission of articles (*hast Du __ Auto?* [do you have __ car?]), prepositions (*ich geh __ Schule* [I go __ school]), copula verbs (*Ich __ Leila* [I __ Leila] or *mein Bruder __ stark* [my brother __ strong]) (Wiese 2012; Auer and Dirim 2003; Auer 2003). There are also some phonetic-phonological features like the fronting of the diphthong /ɔɪ/ as in *Leute* or *Euro* (Jannedy and Weirich 2014b), and the perceptually salient coronalization of /ç/ to [ɕ] or [ʃ] (Jannedy and Weirich 2014a, 2017).

1.2 A discourse example

In 2010/2011 and in 2017/2018, we conducted sociolinguistic interviews with students from a high school in Kreuzberg and Wedding. While first and foremost, as linguists, we were interested in the word- and phonological forms chosen, it became apparent that many youth struggle with their dual identity:

> *Ja, weil, ich meine, wir, ich bin also ich persönlich bin nicht äh deutsche Staatsbürgerin und ich fühle mich selber ein bisschen ähm als Deutsche und nicht also – okay auch als Türke. Aber in der Türkei sagt jeder "Deutsche" zu mir, und hier sagt jeder "Ausländer" zu mir und ich finds irgendwie nicht so okay.*
> 'Yes, because, I mean, we, I, me personally, I am not a German citizen [German citizenship is not automatically bestowed on those born in Germany] and I do feel a bit German and not – ok, also as Turkish. But in Turkey everybody calls me "German", and here people call me "outsider/foreigner", and I don't think that's ok.'

In our follow-up interviews conducted in 2015 and 2018, especially young German-born women of Turkish and Arab descent reported that many ethnic Germans wouldn't acknowledge them as authentic Germans, presumably because of their names, because they might wear a headscarf, or because they are of a different ethnicity. However, the vast majority of our adolescent interviewees with Turkish or Arab roots also say that they could not conceive of a partner that was not raised in their respective culture and belief system, perhaps anticipating problems which they do not want to create for their families. Our interviews are notable in that they reflect the difficulty that ethnic minority members exhibit in laying a claim to German-ness despite having been born and raised in Germany and carrying a German passport. We understand this as a difficulty in laying claim to the social capital of German-ness. But what is the relationship between speaking German and German-ness?

Foroutan et al. (2015) report that – based on data from a large scale, Germany-wide telephone interview with 8,270 participants older than 16 years – 95.5% of the adults and adolescents maintain that speaking German is an indispensable criterion for being German. Almost 34% of the adolescents and 42% of those older than 25 say that speaking German without an accent is a criterion for German-ness. Popular language ideologies in Germany hold that children growing up in bilingual contexts acquire neither language they are exposed to to the fullest extent. The supposed inability to natively speak either of these languages is termed in German *Doppelte Halbsprachigkeit* which translates to 'double semilingualism' (Stroud 2004; Wiese 2015). A statement (press release[2] on *Doppelte Halbsprachigkeit*) signed by many German linguists asserts that *Doppelte Halbsprachigkeit* is a modern language myth, serving to demote bilingual language usage and especially low income speaker groups or speakers to the bottom of the social hierarchy.

2 https://www.sfb632.uni-potsdam.de/en/press/press2010-12.html (accessed 22 June 2018).

The daily paper *Berliner Kurier*[3] ascribes the demise of the German palatal fricative sound orthographically represented as *-ch* to the speech of Turks (*Türksprech*). Thus, if media coverage and repeatedly communicated popular beliefs (as displayed in newsgroups and reactions to interviews, see Wiese 2015) suggest a connection between the demise of the German language, multilingualism and multiethnic adolescent speaker groups, probabilistic inferences may be drawn by parts of the population implicitly subscribing and believing in such causal relationship.

Van Berkum et al. (2008) measured the amplitude of electrical activity in different brain areas and showed that biases based on probabilistic inferences are manifested neuro-physiologically and thus yield an immediate brain response. They tested neurophysiological responses to two types of stimuli: First, an incompatibility between objects leading to the interpretation of semantic anomalies (*You wash your hands with soap/horse and water.*) eliciting a classic N400 effect (higher amplitude of the curve) in the infelicitous condition; and second, an incompatibility between speaker and message of the sort of *Every evening I drink some wine before I go to sleep*, spoken in a young children's and in an adult voice. Speaker inconsistencies and semantic anomalies both elicited the classic N400 effect known to reflect an early sense-making process in language comprehension. What this data suggests is that biases (possibly based on probabilistic inferences) drive our expectations of what may be felicitous and true about the social world surrounding us.

Work in social psychology has also explored the role of unconscious or implicit biases (Banaji and Greenwald 2013) which is rooted in the human capacity for social categorization. According to Social Identity Theory (Tajfel and Turner 1979), three cognitive processes are involved: 1. social categorization, 2. social identification, and 3. social comparison. Social categorization makes humans decide which social group they or others belong to based on age, gender, social class, ethnicity, etc. This in essence creates an "in-group" versus an "out-group". The second process is the social identification in which people associate and identify with a specific group more overtly and openly. And the third process is the comparison between the own group that somebody identifies with ("in-group") and others ("out-group"). These processes are believed to be innate to humans and are said to have evolutionary underpinnings (Sidanius and Pratto 1999). Thus, identifying with specific groups and not identifying with others is the basis for implicit social attitudes and biases. Banaji and Greenwald (2013), well known for their ground breaking methodological work on implicit attitudes towards race,

3 Berliner Kurier (2010) Das "-ch" stirbt aus, October 21, 2010.

are quoted to say (Johnson 2009): "our data, obtained from millions and millions of people, show a real disparity between who we think we are, who we say we are [...] and what actually goes on in our heads." For this reason, we have conducted a series of experiments that tap implicit knowledge and beliefs in the processing of acoustic stimuli – following an exemplar theoretic approach (Goldinger 1996) in which instantiations of usage (exemplars) are stored along with other type of information which then allows for generalizations over these exemplars.

1.3 Linking social perception and identity

Labov's work (1966, 1972) has shown that alternate pronunciations can have social meaning serving to express group membership. Kiezdeutsch is a social practice used by many urban adolescent speakers in multiethnic and multilingual neighborhoods that cannot be divorced from social context (Duranti and Goodwin 1992). Eckert (Eckert 2008; Eckert and Labov 2017) showed the complexity of social meaning, as alternations themselves do not have social meaning but are indexical of social meaning. In the context of two current vowel shifts like the American Northern Cities Chain shift or the California Vowel shift, speakers differentiate themselves from each other by much variation in the implementation and context specific usage of specific vowel forms. There is, however, much less evidence for such systematic patterns of variation for consonants. Campbell-Kibler (2008) however was able to show that varying implementations of the suffix *-ing* in American English triggered changes of the social perception of the speaker. For German the topic of social perception and social meaning or indexical relationships between social meaning and acoustic forms is largely unexplored, as most variationist work is done in the vein of dialectology rather than social variation. Just a few studies provide some evidence that phonetic variants in German may have social meaning (Jannedy and Weirich 2014a). Variants are generally associated with specific speaker types, speech styles or speaker groups, and in this particular study we were able to show that the link between certain consonantal variants and a specific speaker group was especially strong in older listeners. We will come back to this study later on.

Our experimental evidence suggests that certain phonetic variants observed in the speech of young Kreuzberg middle-school students are indexically used to both indicate social identity and infer social meaning (Experiment 1, section 3.1). Consistent with the broader sociophonetic literature, we show that speech perception is highly contextualized and therefore mediated and bootstrapped by inferred and assumed knowledge about the speaker and situation (Niedzielski 1999; Hay and Drager 2010; Jannedy and Weirich 2014a). This implies that the perception and interpretation of fine phonetic detail is dependent on top down information and can shift depending on who a listener believes the speaker is or who the listener is made to believe the speaker is (Experiment 2, section 3.2). Also, we are able to show that the cultural prestige of a language and the ethnicity of a speaker inferred by their name contribute to the outcome of the experiment (Experiment 3, section 3.3).

Furthermore, empirical data implies that listeners not only notice semantic incongruencies but also try to plausibly integrate the social characteristics of a speaker with the message while drawing probabilistic inferences between speaker and message (Van Berkum et al. 2008). In addition, this also leads to the erroneous attribution of grammatical irregularities, with one potential outcome being the prevention of social upward mobility among minorities, especially given the ethnic majority's ideology equating Standard German usage and grammar with Germanness.

Social meaning is not directly linked to linguistic forms, rather, it is fleeting as speakers can shift in and out of personas they construct of themselves, they can take different stances or align themselves in different ways with interlocutors or propositions in the discourse. This is subsumed under the term indexicality (Silverstein 2003), linguistic forms have no social meaning in themselves. Rather, in the construction of identity, speakers use stylistic variants as part of their own language ideology in which these coinciding linguistic forms are linked to specific personas or social groups to which they long to belong or can express specific stances. In that sense, *Indexicality Theory* is rather compatible with *Social Identity Theory* in that it provides the theoretical and somewhat abstract frame by which group identification is expressed verbally. In this paper, we will lay out the work that shows how phonetic variation indexes social qualities and meaning by which speakers make social moves or take stances and how this seems to be internalized (probabilistically inferred) knowledge by specific listener groups. Moreover, the social meaning of fine phonetic detail directly influences listeners' perceptions, and is a key piece in the ability of speakers to lay claim to linguistic capital.

2 Theoretical background on Bourdieu and social capital

The works of Pierre Bourdieu (1977a, 1977b, [1980] 1990, 1986, 1985, 1991) occupy a central place in modern sociology and, by extension, in sociolinguistics. Concepts such as habitus, linguistic capital, and the linguistic market (Coupland

2014; Sankoff and Laberge 1978; Eckert and McConnell-Ginet 1992) have long been used to elucidate patterns in the quantitative study of language. For the purposes of this paper, we follow Bourdieu in understanding language as constituting a type of capital that is in many ways transmitted across the generations, but which transcends economic capital, though under certain circumstances it can be converted to economic benefits. In Bourdieu's conception, social structuring arises as a kind of habitus, a set of durable dispositions which biases agents to act and react in certain ways. These dispositions of manners, dress, taste, language and other symbolic practices, even bodily hexis, are inculcated from an early age, and thus not only give clues to our social standing in the world but also serve as scaffolding for the structuring of further input from the world.

For Bourdieu, broader cultural forms such as musical taste and education as well as the minute details of language such as phonology and word order are acquired as part of our social capital, which connects us to the actual and potential resources of people in our social group. However, because of the embodied quality of habitus, social capital is thought to be as natural to the person as their deportment. We understand social capital then as the range of cultural skills, verbal and nonverbal behavior, attitudes and interactional styles belonging to (and as we will see below, attributed to) certain groups of speakers.

More than Butler's (1997) approach to identity, which in some ways privileges performance, play, and agency of individuals to identify with a group, Bourdieu's notion of the passing down of social capital deals much more with the environment and conditions of our upbringing. For a Berliner, this effectively means the type of neighborhood in which they have grown up, the type of language that they have heard spoken around them, the type of food they have grown to love and the social moves they have internalized and which they exercise in their lives. For example, Zehlendorf and Wedding, or Kreuzberg and Neukölln have distinctive neighborhood flavors and in those cases we might say that the respective neighborhood accents stand as metonymic of larger social attributes and of broader constellations of behaviors that are attributed to neighborhood residents.

3 Evidence from experimental work

We will discuss the social meaning of some of the phonetic-phonological characteristics of Kiezdeutsch (Jannedy and Weirich 2012) by describing the results of a production study (section 3.1.; Jannedy, Weirich, and Helmeke 2015) and two perception experiments (section 3.2.; Jannedy and Weirich 2014a; section 3.3.; Weirich and Jannedy 2014). While there is evidence for morpho-syntactic and phonetic-phonological features to be characteristics of Kiezdeutsch, here, we concentrate on the /ç/ – /ʃ/ alternation as phonetic cue known to be a particular salient feature of this urban multiethnolect. In the speech of some adolescents, the palatal fricative /ç/ and the post alveolar fricative /ʃ/ phonemes have completely merged towards [ʃ] or [ɕ]. In the production study, speakers came from Kreuzberg, while, for the perception studies, the concept of Kiezdeutsch was triggered by naming particularly this neighborhood.

3.1 Production and social identity

In this production study (Jannedy, Weirich, and Helmeke 2015), we examined the realizations of the fricatives /ç/ and /ʃ/ by 32 adolescents (19 female, 13 male, mean age 13.9, SD 0.9). All of them attended the same class (8th grade) at an integrated secondary school in Berlin Kreuzberg. We collected information about the speakers including speaker sex, language background (mono- vs. multilingual), self-rated national and local identity, language of father and mother, language spoken at home, and language spoken with friends. These factors were tested for their potential impact on the realization of the fricative contrast by adding them as test variables in our statistical model.

The fricatives were part of three minimal pairs and were read embedded in a carrier sentence as well as part of a word list. Acoustic analyses were conducted to parameterize the shape of the fricative spectra, and, in particular, the realization of the contrast between /ç/ and /ʃ/ for each participant. Analyses included the spectral moments (Forrest et al. 1988) and Discrete Cosine Transformation (DCT, cf. Watson and Harrington 1999). The spectral moments consist of the centroid frequency or Center of Gravity (COG), the standard deviation (SD), the skewness (expressing whether the frequencies are skewed towards the higher or the lower frequencies), and the kurtosis (revealing the spectral peakedness of the distribution). DCT decomposes the fricative spectrum into a set of half-cycle cosine waves, and the resulting amplitudes of these cosine waves are the DCT coefficients reflecting the mean amplitude of the spectrum (DCT0), its slope (DCT1) and curvature (DCT2), and the amplitude of the higher frequencies (DCT3). While the spectral moments have a long tradition in the phonetic analysis of fricative spectra (Hughes and Halle 1956; Forrest et al. 1988; Jongman, Wayland, and Wong 2000; Newman 2003), DCT has been shown to be very effective in separating the very similar spectral shapes of /ç/ and /ʃ/ in German (Jannedy and Weirich 2017).

Overall, results indicated that there was a strong tendency for /ç/ and /ʃ/ to merge in the speech of young Kreuzberg adolescents (regardless of speech material). However, there was also a great amount of inter-speaker variability regarding the size of the acoustic distance between these two fricative sounds. While for some speakers the contrast seemed to be nearly lost (and thus the fricatives merged towards /ʃ/), others still produced the fricative contrast in a measurable way.

One reason for this inter-speaker variability was the language background (monolingual vs. multilingual), with multilingual speakers producing /ç/ more often as [ɕ] or [ʃ]. However, several monolingual mono-ethnic Germans also showed a strong tendency for merging and dismissing this contrast. An additional analysis of a subset of the speakers included information on their national and local identity. Results revealed that the speakers' self-ascribed local identity (Berliner vs. Kreuzberger [the specific local neighborhood]) significantly affected the contrast realization, with speakers identifying specifically as someone from Kreuzberg showing stronger tendencies to merge the fricatives – and, most interestingly, this was the case independent of language background.

Our finding that the merged variant is also used by speakers with a mono-ethnic background identifying with the neighborhood/speech group, we take as evidence that the variant is becoming a more widely accepted feature of a youth style sociolect which begins to spread through a wider community in Berlin.

3.2 Perceptual divergence and social meaning

In Jannedy and Weirich (2014a), we conducted a perception experiment similar to other studies examining perceptual divergence effects, where listeners are asked to categorize identical stimuli across different priming conditions (e.g., Strand and Johnson 1996; Strand 1999; Niedzielski 1999; Hay, Nolan, and Drager 2006; Brunelle and Jannedy 2013; Hay and Drager 2010). These studies show that acoustically identical stimuli can be categorized differently phonologically depending on language external factors, such as what the listener believes to know about the speaker (regarding, e.g., age, sex or language background). That is, we are here exploiting the idea of specific acoustic forms being associated with indexical meaning. In other words, this implies that in speech perception, there always is a component of interpretation. In particular, in Jannedy and Weirich (2014a), we tested three listener groups in a categorical perception experiment, asking them to categorize words that were played to them either as *Fichte* [spruce] or *fischte* [1st and 3rd p. sg. past tense of 'to fish']. Stimuli were taken from an artificially created acoustic continuum starting at

FICHTE on the one side (/fɪçtə/) and ending at FISCHTE (/fɪʃtə/) on the other. For two out of three listener groups, we co-presented names of Berlin neighborhoods by writing them on the response pad: these were KREUZBERG (KB) vs. ZEHLENDORF (ZD) vs. a control condition (CO, no added info). Kreuzberg is a younger neighborhood than Zehlendorf: the mean age of inhabitants in 2016 was 37.8 years in KB vs. 46.3 years in ZD (Amt für Statistik Berlin-Brandenburg 2016). Also, the districts differ in the percentage of inhabitants with migration background: KB = 40.5% vs. ZD = 24.9% (Amt für Statistik Berlin-Brandenburg 2016) and in the distribution of income (percentage of inhabitants with a net salary of more than 1500 Euro = 29.7% in KB vs 39.6% in ZD, cf. Amt für Statistik Berlin-Brandenburg 2016).The idea was to test if naive listeners would perceive higher rates of *fischte* (with the merged variant) when primed with the concept Kreuzberg (young and multi-ethnic) as opposed to no prime or to Zehlendorf (older, less multi-ethnic and more affluent in contrast to KB). If so, this in fact would indicate that listeners draw on preconceived notions of how people speak in different urban spaces when processing speech.

In addition to the different priming conditions, we tested three age groups of listeners: the mean age for the younger listeners was 22.7, 30.2 for the middle aged group, and 51.5 for the older ones. The oldest group of listeners (right plot of Figure 1) perceived significantly more often *fischte* when seeing the word *Kreuzberg* on their response pad. They perceived much less *fischte* in the control condition with no added information or when primed with the concept *Zehlendorf*. The middle aged group of listeners (middle panel of Figure 1) also perceived most *fischte* when being co-presented with *Kreuzberg* or when not being prompted with anything; least *fischte* perceptions occurred in the context of *Zehlendorf*. Interestingly though, youngest listeners perceived least *fischte* in the *Kreuzberg* condition followed by *Zehlendorf*, and most *fischte* in the control condition (Jannedy and Weirich 2014a: 108).

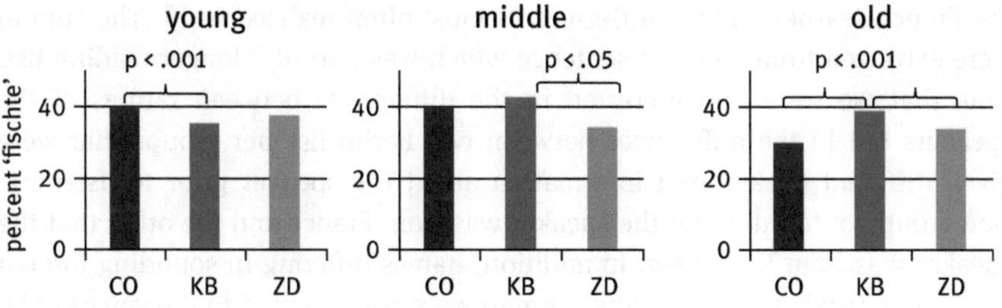

Figure 1: Percentage of fischte ratings separated by neighborhood (KB: Kreuzberg, ZD: Zehlendorf, CO: control, no added information) for the three different age groups (taken from Jannedy and Weirich 2014a).

The data shows that middle aged and older listeners especially associate the merged form (*fischte*) with *Kreuzberg*. For younger listeners the merged forms seem to have become the norm so that these forms are not saliently connected to specific locations or speaker groups. Similar to the production study described above, these results point to a sound change in progress with the /ç/ – /ʃ/ merger spreading and becoming more accepted among younger people in Berlin.

3.3 Phonetic variation, listener attitudes and social meaning

The second perception experiment (Weirich and Jannedy 2014) was conducted within the framework of the *Social Connotation Hypothesis* (van Bezooijen 2002), which states that language external social factors (speaker heritage, ethnicity, social status, economic or cultural background, etc.) determine the perceived status and pleasantness of a language, and are responsible for the ideological weighting of language varieties. Here, we focused on the potentially differential prestige of French and Turkish. In contrast to Turkish, French in Germany is viewed in a positive light: According to a study from the Institut für Deutsche Sprache (IDS) in 2009, French was the foreign accent rated to be most likeable ("sympathisch") to the participants (36%) and thereby seen as Germans' most favored foreign accent[4] (Eichinger et al. 2009). In our study we examined whether speakers associated with a high prestige language will receive better ratings than those associated with a low prestige language, and whether that interacted with the listeners' age.

Fifty-four listeners from Berlin (aged between 18 – 66 years, mean age 35.7) were asked to rate several speakers on personality traits and the speakers' knowledge of German. Recordings from 8 male and 8 female students from a secondary school in Berlin-Kreuzberg were used. Each stimulus consisted of a single word containing the palatal fricative /ç/, which in Kiezdeutsch and in the French learner variety of German is most often realized as [ʃ]. The stimuli were extracted from a carrier sentence which was part of a longer reading list. Note that we were not interested in the differences between ratings of the speakers but in the differences between two Berlin listener groups that were given different background information about the speaker prior to listening. One group got to infer that the speaker was from France and the other that the speaker was from Kreuzberg. In addition, names differing in sounding foreign (French or Turkish) vs. sounding German were co-presented to the voices to be

4 http://www1.ids-mannheim.de/aktuell/presse/pr090617.html (accessed 22 June 2018).

judged. Statistical analyses using linear mixed models were conducted with the fixed factors priming condition (France vs. Kreuzberg) and origin of name (German vs. foreign) and the random factors listener and stimulus. A significant interaction between priming condition and origin of name (German vs. foreign) was found ($\chi2(2) = 7.97$, $p < .05$). The name of the speaker influenced the listeners' judgments depending on the priming condition (see Figure 2): for the speakers assumed to come from Kreuzberg, stimuli with a German name were rated better regarding their knowledge of German than stimuli with a foreign sounding name. This influence of name disappeared for speakers assumed to come from France. Thus, for a speaker from Kreuzberg the name seems to be extremely important, it affects his/her rated knowledge of German, while for an (assumed) French speaker this information does not play a role.

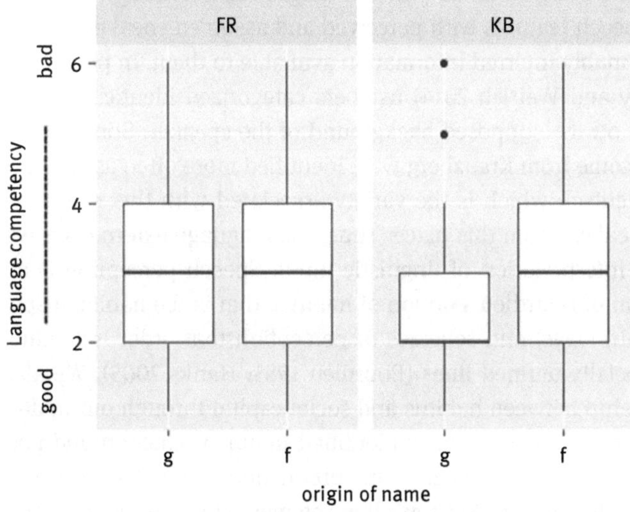

Figure 2: Language competency ratings separated by priming condition (FR = France, KB = Berlin-Kreuzberg) and origin of name (g = German, f = foreign).

In addition, we found a tendency for older listeners to rate the stimuli that supposedly were produced by French speakers more positively; while younger listeners rated the stimuli that supposedly came from Kreuzberg speakers more positively. Since the stimuli/speakers did not differ between the two conditions and the only difference was the added information on the origin of the speaker (France vs. Kreuzberg), we interpret any differences in the ratings to be affected by the added information. The added information affected listeners differently depending on their age. We therefore assume that for older listeners France (still) has a positive connotation, while younger listeners seem to prefer Kreuzberg. This can be interpreted in the way of an ongoing change of prestige of the different concepts and thereby facilitate the spread of the youth variety Kiezdeutsch among adolescents.

4 Concluding discussion

This paper has sought to integrate our experimental work on sociophonetic variation and auditory perception with the concept of social capital. We have reviewed the results of our research program showing that the imagined information that listeners have about speakers affect the perception of their ethno-national origin, and that this is tied to perception of migrants' language capabilities.

Our perception data shows that as part of interpreting a message, listeners associate speakers' speech features with perceived and assumed speaker characteristics and any reasonably inferred information available to them. In particular, in our study (Jannedy and Weirich 2014) listeners categorized identical stimuli differently depending on the supposed background of the speaker. Stimuli from speakers assumed to come from Kreuzberg were identified more often as /ʃ/ – the variant used in Kiezdeutsch which is the variety associated with this neighborhood and with the speakers from this place. Thus, the language-external knowledge determined the interpretation of linguistic input. Speech perception is an embodied instantiation of Bourdieu's notion of habitus, that is the habits, dispositions to act in certain ways, and schemes of perception that order individual perspectives along socially defined lines (Bourdieu 1985; Hanks 2005). We also theorized the relationship between habitus and social capital through our understanding of the linguistic change we have identified in our production and perception studies on the merged variant. The production study (section 3.1.; Jannedy, Weirich, and Helmeke 2015) shows that the merged variant is used also by monolingual, mono-ethnic adolescents identifying with the speech group and a particular neighborhood in Berlin. The perception study (section 3.2.; Weirich and Jannedy 2014) shows that the association of this variant and the particular neighborhood is made by listeners older than 30 but not by younger listeners. For younger listeners, there is no longer a link between the merged variant and particular speakers of a particular neighborhood. We interpret these results in light of a sound change in progress with the merged variant spreading among younger people in Berlin.

While we were able to show in controlled experiments that top-down processing has an effect on the outcome of perception and interpretation of stimuli, and that prior expectations in form of stereotypes, attitudes and prejudice drive our categorizations and interpretations, this pattern of behavior can also be observed in the real world and in the broader European context, as we will discuss in some of our future work.

We follow Hansen-Thomas (2007) who asserts that the one-nation-one-language ideology and the closely related idea of language as an indicator of German-ness have been crucial to the creation of the modern German state. This has profound implications for immigrants (and their children).

This brings us to the case of the purported *Doppelte Halbsprachigkeit* [double semilingualism]. The term has been criticized by a number of scholars not only because it is disparaging, but because it implies that bilingualism is a subtractive state, one that would take away from otherwise "full" language. As Colin Baker ([1993] 2011:9) writes:

> The danger of the term *semilingualism* is that it locates the origins of under-development in the internal, individual possession of bilingualism, rather than in external, societal factors that co-exist with bilingualism. Thus the term may be a political rather than a linguistic concept.

Nonetheless, we venture to suggest that educating and training listeners' awareness of what kind of effect non-linguistic factors have on speech processing and perception, combined with deliberate metalinguistic training for speakers in learning on how to switch at will from variety 1 (Kiezdeutsch) to variety 2 (Standard German) and to acquire competence in maneuvering addressee- or situationally-appropriate register changes, may go far in convincing adults (like teachers or employers) not to label innovative youth as lacking in cultural and linguistic capital.

We are hopeful for change in the next generation. As we have mentioned above, Foroutan et al.'s (2015) data and our own perception and attitude studies show that acceptance of Germanness despite accented speech is growing in the population of 16–25 year olds compared to those 25 and older.

Acknowledgements: We sincerely thank the editors of this volume and two anonymous reviewers for their valuable comments and suggestions. Any remaining faults are our own.

References

Amt für Statistik Berlin-Brandenburg. 2015. *Statistisches Jahrbuch 2015*. Brandenburgische Universitätsdruckerei. Potsdam.

Amt für Statistik Berlin-Brandenburg. 2016. *Statistischer Bericht: Einwohnerinnen und Einwohner im Land Berlin am 30. Juni 2016*. Brandenburgische Universitätsdruckerei. Potsdam.

Appel, René. 1999. Straattaal. De mengtaal van jongeren in Amsterdam [Street language; the mixed language of young people in Amsterdam]. *Toegepaste Taalwetenschap in Artikelen* 62. 39–55.

Auer, Peter. 2003. Türkenslang: Ein jugendsprachlicher Ethnolekt des Deutschen und seine Transformationen. In Annelies Häcki Buhofer (ed.), *Spracherwerb und Lebensalter*, 255–264. Tübingen: Francke.

Auer, Peter & İnci Dirim. 2003. Socio-cultural orientation, urban youth styles and the spontaneous acquisition of Turkish by non-Turkish adolescents in Germany. In Jannis K. Androutsopoulos & Alexandra Georgakopoulou (eds.), *Discourse constructions of youth identities*, 223–246. Amsterdam: John Benjamins.

Baker, Colin. 2011 [1993]. *Foundations of bilingual education and bilingualism*, 5th edn. Bristol, Buffalo & Toronto: Multilingual Matters.

Banaji, Mahzarin & Anthony Greenwald. 2013. *Blindspot: Hidden biases of good people*. New York: Bantam Books.

Bourdieu, Pierre. 1977a. The economics of linguistic exchanges. *Social Science Information* 16(6). 645–668.

Bourdieu, Pierre. 1977b. *Outline of a Theory of Practice*. Cambridge: Cambridge University Press.

Bourdieu, Pierre. 1985. The genesis of the concepts of habitus and of field. *Sociocriticism* 2. 11–24.

Bourdieu, Pierre. 1986. The Forms of Capital. In John George Richardson (ed.), *Handbook of Theory and Research for the Sociology of Education*, 241–258. New York: Greenwood Press.

Bourdieu, Pierre. [1980] 1990. *The Logic of Practice*. Stanford, CA: Stanford University Press.

Bourdieu, Pierre. 1991. *Language and symbolic power*. Cambridge: Polity Press.

Brunelle, Marc & Stefanie Jannedy. 2013. The cross-dialectal perception of Vietnamese tones: Indexicality and adaptability. In Daniel Hole & Elisabeth Löbel (eds.), *Linguistics of Vietnamese – An international survey*, 9–34. Berlin & New York: Mouton de Gruyter.

Butler, Judith. 1997. *Excitable speech: A politics of the performative*. New York & London: Routledge..

Campbell-Kibler, Kathryn. 2007. Accent, (ING), and the Social Logic of Listener Perceptions. *American Speech* 82(1). 32–64.

Campbell-Kibler, Kathryn. 2008. I'll be the judge of that: Diversity in social perceptions of (ING). *Language in Society* 37(5). 637–659.

Coupland, Nikolas. 2014. Language Change, Social Change, Sociolinguistic Change: A meta-commentary. *Journal of Sociolinguistics* 18(2). 277–286.

Duranti, Alessandro & Charles Goodwin (eds.). 1992. *Rethinking Context: Language as an interactive phenomenon*. Cambridge: Cambridge University Press.

Eckert, Penelope. 2008. Variation and the indexical field. *Journal of Sociolinguistics* 12(4). 453–476.

Eckert, Penelope & William Labov. 2017. Phonetics, Phonology and Social Meaning. *Journal of Sociolinguistics* 21(4). 467–496.

Eckert Penelope and Sally McConnell-Ginet. 1992. Think practically and look locally: Language and gender as community-based practice. *Annual Review of Anthropology* 21. 461–490.

Eichinger, Ludwig M., Anne-Kathrin Gärtig, Albrecht Plewnia, Janin Roessel, Astrid Rothe, Selma Rudert, Christiane Schoel, Dagmar Stahlberg & Gerhard Stickel. 2009. *Aktuelle Spracheinstellungen in Deutschland. Erste Ergebnisse einer bundesweiten Repräsentativumfrage*. Mannheim: Institut für Deutsche Sprache / Universität Mannheim.

Ersanilli, Evelyn & Sawitri Saharso. 2011. The Settlement Country and Ethnic Identification of Children of Turkish Immigrants in Germany, France, and the Netherlands: What Role Do National Integration Policies Play? *International Migration Review* 45(4). 907–937.

Foroutan, Naika, Coşkun Canan, Benjamin Schwarze, Steffen Beigang & Dorina Kalkum. 2015. *Deutschland Post-migrantisch II: Einstellungen von Jugendlichen und jungen Erwachsenenen zu Gesellschaft, Religion und Identität*. Berlin: Berliner Institut für empirische Integrations- und Migrationsforschung, Humboldt-Universität zu Berlin.

Forrest, Karen, Gary Weismer, Paul Milenkovic & Ronald N. Dougall. 1988. Statistical analysis of word-initial voiceless obstruents: Preliminary data. *Journal of the Acoustical Society of America* 84(1),115–123.

Goldinger, Stephen D. 1996. Words and voices: Episodic traces in spoken word identification and recognition memory. *Journal of Experimental Psychology: Learning, Memory, and Cognition* 22(5). 1166–1183.

Hanks, William F. 2005. Pierre Bourdieu and the Practices of Language. *Annual Review of Anthropology* 34. 67–83.

Hansen-Thomas, Holly. 2007. Language ideology, citizenship, and identity: The case of modern Germany. *Journal of Language and Politics* 6(2). 249–264.

Hay, Jennifer. & Katie Drager. 2010. Stuffed toys and speech perception. *Linguistics* 48(4). 865–892.

Hay, Jennifer, Aaron Nolan & Katie Drager. 2006. From fush to feesh: Exemplar priming in speech perception. *The Linguistic Review* 23(3). 351–379.

Hughes, George W. & Morris Halle. 1956. Spectral properties of fricative consonants. *Journal of the Acoustic Society of America* 28. 303–310.

Jannedy, Stefanie. 2011. Urbanes Deutsch und seine Rezeption. *Jahrbuch der Geisteswissenschaftlichen Zentren Berlins. Bericht über das Forschungsjahr* 16. 74–95.

Jannedy, Stefanie & Melanie Weirich. 2012. Phonology & the interpretation of fine phonetic detail in Berlin German. Paper presented at Interspeech 2012, the 13th Annual Conference of the International Speech Communication Association, Portland, OR, USA, 9–13 September.

Jannedy, Stefanie & Melanie Weirich. 2013. /oy/ as an identity marker of Hood German in Berlin. Paper presented at the ICA 2013 Montreal, Proceedings of Meetings on Acoustics, Acoustical Society of America, 2–7 June.

Jannedy, Stefanie & Melanie Weirich. 2014a. Sound change in an urban setting: Category instability of the palatal fricative in Berlin. *Laboratory Phonology* 5(1). 91–122.

Jannedy, Stefanie & Melanie Weirich. 2014b. Linguistic Influences on Diphthong Realization of /oy/ in Hood German. Paper presented at the 10th International Seminar on Speech Production (ISSP), Cologne, Germany, 5–8 May.

Jannedy, Stefanie & Melanie Weirich. 2017. Spectral moments vs discrete cosine transformation coefficients: Evaluation of acoustic measures distinguishing two merging German fricatives. *Journal of the Acoustical Society of America* 142 (1).395–405.

Jannedy, Stefanie, Melanie Weirich & Luisa Helmeke. 2015. Acoustic analyses of differences in [ç] and [ʃ] productions in Hood German. Paper presented at the 18th International Congress of Phonetic Sciences (ICPhS), Glasgow, 10–14 August.

Johnson, Carolyn Y. 2009. Research shows key role for unconscious bias. *The Boston Globe*. Thursday, 30 July.
Jongman, Allard, Ratree Wayland & Serena Wong. 2000. Acoustic characteristics of English fricatives. *Journal of the Acoustical Society of America*. 108. 1252–1263.
Keim, Inken. 1978. Gastarbeiterdeutsch: Untersuchungen zum sprachlichen Verhalten türkischer Gastarbeiter. Tübingen: TBL Verlag Gunter Narr.
Kerswill, Paul, Eivind Nessa Torgersen & Susan Fox. 2008. Reversing "drift":Innovation and diffusion in the London diphthong system. *Language Variation and Change* 20(3). 451–491.
Kotsinas, Ulla-Britt. 1992. Immigrant adolescents' Swedish in multicultural areas. In Cecilia Palmgren, Karin Lövgren & Goran Bolin (eds.), *Ethnicity in Youth culture*, 43–62. Stockholm: Stockholms Universitet.
Kotsinas, Ulla-Britt. 1998. Language contact in Rinkeby, an immigrant suburb. In Jannis K. Androutsopoulos & Arno Scholz (eds.), *Jugendsprache – langue des jeunes – youth language. Linguistische und soziolinguistische Perspektiven*, 125–148. Frankfurt a. M.: Peter Lang.
Labov, William. 1966. The Social Stratification of English in New York City. Washington: Center for Applied Linguistics.
Labov, William. 1972. Sociolinguistic Patterns. Philadelphia: University of Pennsylvania Press.
Newman, Rochelle S. 2003. Using links between speech perception and speech production to evaluate different acoustic metrics: A preliminary report. *Journal of the Acoustical Society of America* 113(5). 2850–2860.
Niedzielski, Nancy. 1999. The effect of social information on the perception of sociolinguistic variables. *Journal of Language and Social Psychology* 18(1). 62–85.
Nortier, Jacomine. 2001. „Fawaka, what's up?" Language use among adolescents in Dutch mono-ethnic and ethnically mixed groups. In Anne Hvenekilde & Jacomine Nortier (eds.), *Meetings at the Crossroads. Studies of Multilingualism and Multiculturalism in Oslo and Utrecht*, 61–73. Oslo: Norvus Forlag.
Quist, Pia. 2005. New speech varieties among immigrant youth in Copenhagen – a case study. In Volker Hinnenkamp & Katharina Meng (eds.), *Sprachgrenzen überspringen. Sprachliche Hybridität und polykulturelles Selbstverständnis*, 145–161. Tübingen: Gunter Narr.
Sankoff, David & Suzanne Laberge. 1978. The linguistic market and the statistical explanation of variability. In David Sankoff (ed.), *Linguistic Variation: Models and Methods*, 239–250. New York: Academic Press.
Sidanius, Jim & Felicia Pratto. 1999. *Social Dominance: An intergroup theory of social hierarchy and oppression*. Cambridge: Cambridge University Press.
Silverstein, Michael. 2003. Indexical order and the dialectics of sociolinguistic life. *Language & Communication* 23(3–4). 193–229.
Strand, Elizabeth A. 1999. Uncovering the role of gender stereotypes in speech perception. *Journal of Language and Social Psychology* 18(1). 86–100.
Strand, Elizabeth A. & Keith Johnson. 1996. Gradient and visual speaker normalization in the perception of fricatives. In Dafydd Gibbon (ed.), Natural Language Processing and Speech Technology, 14–26. Berlin: Mouton de Gruyter.
Stroud, Christopher. 2004. Rinekby Swedish and semilingualism in language ideological debates: A Bourdieuean perspective. *Journal of Sociolinguistics* 8(2). 196–214.

Tajfel, Henri & John Turner. 1979. An integrative theory of intergroup Conflict. In William G. Austin & Stephen Worchel (eds.), *The social psychology of intergroup relations*, 33–47. Monterey, CA: Brooks/Cole.

Torgersen, Eivind, Paul Kerswill & Susan Fox. 2006. Ethnicity as a source of changes in the London vowel system. In Frans Hinskens (ed.), *Language variation – European perspectives. Selected papers from the third International Conference on Language Variation in Europe (ICLaVE3)*, 249–263. Amsterdam: Benjamins.

Turner, Victor W. 1969. *The Ritual Process: Structure and Anti-Structure*. Chicago: Aldine Transaction.

Van Berkum, Jos J. A., Danielle van den Brink, Cathelijne M. J. Y. Tesink, Miriam Kos & Peter Hagoort. 2008. The Neural Integration of Speaker and Message. *Journal of Cognitive Neuroscience* 20(4). 580–591.

van Bezooijen, Renée. 2002. Aesthetic Evaluation of Dutch. Comparisons across Dialects, Accents, and Languages. In Daniel Long & Dennis R. Preston (eds.), *Handbook of Perceptual Dialectology. Volume 2*, 13–31. Amsterdam & Philadelphia: John Benjamins Publishing Company.

Watson, Catherine I. & Jonathan Harrington. 1999. Acoustic evidence for dynamic formant trajectories in Australian English vowels. *Journal of the Acoustical Society of America*. 106(1). 458–468.

Weirich, Melanie & Stefanie Jannedy. 2014. Evaluating attitudes towards Hood German and speakers with French foreign accents. Paper presented at the 10. Tagung Phonetik und Phonologie im deutschsprachigen Raum, Universität Konstanz, 9–10 October.

Wiese, Heike. 2012. *Kiezdeutsch. Ein neuer Dialekt entsteht*. München: C. H. Beck.

Wiese, Heike. 2015. "This migrants' babble is not a German dialect!": The interaction of standard language ideology and "us"/"them" dichotomies in the public discourse on a multiethnolect. *Language in Society* 44(3). 341–368.

Zaimoğlu, Feridun. 1995. *Kanak Sprak: 24 Mißtöne vom Rande der Gesellschaft*. Hamburg: Rotbuch.

Emily Farrell

7 Language, economy, and the international artist community in Berlin

1 Introduction

Artists are the consummate contingent, late-capitalist workforce. Often highly educated and skilled, concentrated in metropolitan areas, they rely overwhelmingly on part-time and freelance work, both inside of and outside of the art world (Menger, 2006: 2014). Concurrently, artists are often the first wave, the pioneers, of gentrification. Artists move where art markets and communities cluster, where living and studio space is affordable, where galleries, artists' studios, music venues, and other creative spaces and businesses provide the possibility of income and connections. While studies have focused on artists, the art world, mobility, and gentrification (see Deutsche & Ryan, 1984; Ikeda, 2017), few have examined the role language plays at this intersection. This paper, which draws from an ethnographic study with twenty international artists living in Berlin, attempts to examine language "as one of the key ways in which mobility, like any other social process, actually happens, and how it plays a role in the making of social categories which either facilitate or impede (or alternatively, force or protect against) engaging in mobility or rootedness." (Heller, et al, 2015: 35). International artists, particularly English-speaking artists, who migrate to Berlin are prime examples of the tensions between mobility and situatedness, between local, national, and global, where the "'local' no longer opposes but constitutes the global" (Burawoy, 2001: 158). Language practices are an integral site where these tensions are made visible/audible.

Why Berlin? The international art market has become an important mainstay for the city. Built up through its circulating mythos as a haven for artists, the state has used the expansion and strengthening of this market as a central strategy for reviving an economically depressed city after German reunification. Artists have become a commodity to the city. Non-EU citizen artist migrants to Berlin are in a position to take advantage of state sponsored structures that privilege their migration through the existence of a specific artist visa (*Aufenthaltstitel für Künstler/innen*) particular to the city-state (Büro für Künstlerberatung, 2017). While the two-year renewable visa includes economic requirements, for example that you are making a base salary annually from your art work, it does not include a German language requirement. English-speaking artists with no German language, therefore, have a relatively easy path to obtain a work permit. And yet,

https://doi.org/10.1515/9781501508103-007

while the city encourages the growth of international artistic presence in Berlin in order to contribute to its reputation as a creative city and its economic growth, it is also not necessarily focused on long-term migration and stability for this community. Artists often find themselves in a cycle of two-year visas without clear potential for more permanent residency. For a non-permanent residency permit as a freelance artist, *Niederlassungserlaubnis für Selbständige*, an applicant must have held a visa for five years and have a B1 level of German language according to the Common European Framework of Reference for Languages (Landesamt für Bürger- und Ordnungsangelegenheiten, 2018). It is not until the process of application for residency that German language becomes a formal requirement. Berlin represents, then, a site that attracts mobile, English-speaking artists through its desirability, as well as the structures the city itself has put in place. It is a perfect meeting place of local and global, or the global in the local, where ideologies and practices that "represent the perception of language and discourse that is constructed in the interest of a specific social or cultural group" (Kroskrity, 2010: 195) challenge and reinforce boundaries of the nation.

The prevalence of English in Berlin is one part of this puzzle (see also Schulte, this volume, Fuller, this volume). In the equation of European Union multilingualism, where "the ideal is for each speaker to control a lingua franca, a mother tongue, plus a freely chosen language of affinity" (Gal, 2012: 33), English is the most commonly shared language. English-speaking artists in my study then, migrate into a context where English is already assumed as shared in the EU context and where they are not required to speak the national language, German. While this is not surprising within the context of English as an international lingua franca, and in particular English use in Europe (Wilton & De Houwer, 2011: 5–6), examining the circulation of English in this specific time and space reveals something of the workings of neoliberalism in late capitalism (Piller & Cho, 2013: 32). English language education, and the dominance of English as the first foreign language, has a long history in Germany (Linn, 2016: 15). English is a required school subject and is frequently now assumed to the point that job ads in Germany do not necessarily explicitly ask for English knowledge as some competency is expected (Gerhards, et al, 2015: 18). English-speaking artists in Berlin frequently rely on the language work of German speakers and the underlying German education system that ensures English is seen as "a prerequisite for successful communication in Europe" (Gnutzmann, et al, 2015: 188). In contrast, particularly for artists who have migrated from Australia and the US, where second language learning rates are lower (Lo Bianco & Slaughter, 2009: 49), as are the perceptions of the utility of a second language, in this case even where German is the dominant national language, this assumption provides a privileged fallback for English-speaking artists in Berlin. Taken for granted, English use in Berlin reveals itself as a form of "'banal globalization', the everyday textual realization and interactional enactment of global capitalism" (Jaworski and Thurlow, 2010). The privileging of English can also make invisible the language investment that these artists may make in learning German. As my informants often reported, where German speakers hear accented German they frequently switch to English, whether out of politeness for the speaker who they assess to be less proficient, or for other reasons, such as a desire to use the language. In these cases, English speakers frequently follow the path of least resistance and continue in English, otherwise they must actively choose to switch back and continue in German, a more threatening act. In these interactions, the local and global run headlong into each other, where the national is both challenged and reinforced.

In this study, the mythos of Berlin as a haven for artists, coupled with the encouragement of the state for international artists to migrate, intersect at the site of the city and English language use. English, as the lingua franca of the international art market, becomes the dominant language of communication for this scene in Berlin. At the same time, German is the dominant language of the society and of the nation. It is the language in which all interactions with bureaucratic mechanisms operate. While nominally operating in a transnational or global space, the privilege these artists have to operate in English while living in Germany, points to the power of English within the local city and global sphere. There is a contestation whereby these artists generally resist the logic of the nation-state by (often) staying outside of the German-speaking world. At the same time, there is the power of globalization seated in the use of English as a lingua franca, which vests L1 English speakers with a power to refuse to be drawn into either the national language or EU policy on multilingualism. In addition, however, artists must navigate local policies, practices, and institutions. In the next section of the paper, I will introduce the thirteen artists who I reference in this chapter, followed by a discussion of the context of the city of Berlin itself. Section four provides examples to explicate the ways in which tensions between the local, the nation and the city, and the global and migratory, are made salient through language practices and ideologies.

2 Studying international artists in Berlin

The data for this paper derives from an ethnographic study, conducted from 2009 to 2010, with follow up data in 2017, with twenty artists living in Berlin exploring the intersection of language, artistic practice, and the city. I conducted one round of semi-structured formal interviews, using a set of pre-determined questions that also allowed room for informants to extrapolate and expand the direction of talk. The interviews were, on average, an hour long, with the shortest interview lasting just over half an hour and the longest eighty minutes. Three informants were not interviewed: two participants I observed moved back to Australia before an in-person interview could take place. The final participant declined to do an interview. Over the course of the year, I observed these artists in Berlin, at gallery openings and art events in the city, attending to language attitudes and practices. This paper draws from thirteen informants: Robert & Anna, Mia, Olivia, Sam, Dan & Varsha, Zoe & Sasha, Lucy, Zach, Luc, and Stefan (for a full list of informants see Appendix 1). These informants came primarily from English language majority countries: England (Varsha), the US (Robert, Anna, Mia, Zach, and Sam), Canada (Olivia), Australia (Zoe, Sasha, and Lucy), and New Zealand (Dan). Luc, who is French, and Stefan, who is Dutch, were included as artists who worked in the core art studio where I recruited informants, where English was the primary language of communication. All interviews were conducted in English, with some German words used primarily for institutions or phrases in discussing specific interactions. The majority of participants were painters broadly defined (Robert, Anna, Zach, Dan, Sam, Lucy, Luc, Stefan, and Olivia), one a musician (Zoe), one a performer (Mia). Two were the partners of artists: Varsha moved along with Dan and worked at a creative internet start-up; Sasha, Zoe's partner, worked as a DJ and journalist. All the artists moved with a developed art practice of some form, whether, for example, they had studied and worked as sculptors or painters, that they planned to establish in Berlin. Where artists had migrated with a partner, or had a partner that was an artist (here Dan & Varsha, Zoe & Sasha, and Robert & Anna), I interviewed the couple together. Taking a sociolinguistic ethnographic approach (Heller, 2011), I thus examined language practices and ideologies in this art community in Berlin.

I recruited artists into the study initially through one artist's studio, what I call the "core" art studio in this chapter, and beyond this through their networks. This core studio artist had moved to Berlin from the US for a project in 2008 and had brought a number of her US based assistants with her. The artist was well established and was able to hire other artists for this particular project to help in creating new artworks, a common practice for contemporary artists who often do not fabricate their works on their own. The studio then advertised Berlin positions for a period of work around 18 months, looking for Berlin-based artists. The process of recruiting artists to the studio provides important insights for the intersection of art labor, globalism, language, and the city. The jobs were advertised on the New York Foundation for the Arts (NYFA, https://www.nyfa.org/) website in English. They received hundreds of applications from people who were willing to move from US cities to Berlin for the job. The studio was, however, interested in hiring people who were already based in Berlin, despite advertising on a New York City focused, English language jobs site. The assumption that, due to the international nature of the art community, advertising in this manner would be a viable way to get job candidates in Berlin, did indeed work as a strategy. The studio did recruit US artists, based in Berlin, who found the job ad through their networks. By the time I was interviewing, the core studio had completed its project and shut down. The artists I spoke with had remained in Berlin and moved on to other job opportunities.

Similar to the studio advertising on a New York City art website, many artists found work and apartments through websites and resources they were already familiar with in New York or the US generally. Many used the Berlin Craigslist website (http://berlin.craigslist.de) for job searches and housing, the majority of the postings being in English. They also made use of other Berlin or Germany-specific online resources like Toy Town Germany (https://www.toytowngermany.com) and the website for the so-called "expat" community magazine Ex-Berliner (www.exberliner.com). Very few relied on German resources, such as the Berlin city magazine, *Zitty*, though one couple mention using it for job listings.

My informants, as international artists, find themselves inhabiting an in-between space: not quite tourists, not quite home. The way they talk about life in Berlin and the relationship to where they migrated from often resonates with tourists consuming a foreign culture, where experiences in Berlin's art scene and "snippets of language" are brought back to New York or LA (Jaworski and Thurlow, 2010). Simultaneously, their presence in Berlin affects the fabric of the city. In this sense they fit into the privileged and problematized category of the "expatriate" who, as Yeung states, is "constructed as a global knowledge-worker, an agent who evades territorial emplacement and nationalizing linguistic regimes", a global agent extraordinaire who is a participant in the spreading of English as part of the "processes of neoliberal market expansion" (Yeung, 2016: 743). In part, they can be viewed through the lens of elite transmigration (De Fina, 2016: 164). They see themselves as migrational. Some are unsure whether they will stay in Berlin, some have plans to stay in Berlin for the foreseeable future, or even to continue to live part-time in Berlin, part-time elsewhere where it may be easier to earn more money more quickly. All have transnational connections to their countries of origin, to artist communities in multiple other cities. This is also the case economically. Artists often rely on grant money from their country of origin, for example through the Canada Council for the Arts or the Australia Council for the Arts, which provide support for artists external to the Berlin economy while bringing income into the city.

At the same time, as my data shows, resisting the German language is not ultimately possible, both in that many interactions must be done in or through German and also that informants did find a need or desire to invest in German learning.

On the global level, they are also operating within the logic of the contemporary art market, where, in 2010, at the time the interviews for this study took place, despite the recent global financial crisis, art works were continuing to break records at auctions. As Pénet and Lee (2014) point out, on the same day that "Lehman Brothers filed for bankruptcy protection, (…) Damien Hirst sold an unprecedented $270 million worth of art at Christie's." (2014: 2). In examining the relationship of artists to cities, Zhang notes that "'pioneer but eventually sacrificed' is regarded as the conventional role that artists play in the urban chain of capital accumulation." (2015: 438). While these artists were mostly working in unstable, art world related jobs, they were also highly aware of the economics of art market success. My informants, then, are economically and culturally valuable to Berlin where they are given access to the city through the artist visa, contributing to the economy of the city, facilitating "global expansion and circulation" (Duchêne and Heller, 2012: 10). At the same time, Berlin presents an international creative space to these artists that allows them to live and identify as artists.

3 The mythos of Berlin

Berlin has long been a mythical place for artists and musicians. From the art and culture of the Weimar period with its cabarets, the theatre of Berthold Brecht, the architecture of Walter Gropius (Weitz, 2013), to the late 70s infamy of David Bowie's most iconic albums and songs, *Low* and *Heroes*, recorded in the city. After the wall fell, rents in former East Berlin were infamously cheap. Squatter culture proliferated. Empty space, the stuff of artists' dreams, was rife. Berlin, since reunification, has been constructed, both in the *arm, aber sexy* (poor, but sexy) (Focus, 2006; Klee and Wehnert, 2013) speeches and policies of Berlin mayor Klaus Wowereit, as well as in international English language media (see for example Lee, 2006), as an idealized creative haven offering space and time to survive as a practicing artist. The city now capitalizes on this mythos with more commercial enterprises: the annual Berlinale film festival and Berlin Art Week, which in 2015 attracted around 100,000 international visitors (Investitionsbank Berlin, 2016). In their work on lifestyle migration to Berlin, Griffiths and Maile (2014) see "the city as an imagined space, as a repository and enabler of fantasy and representation" (140).

Berlin had to reinvent itself after reunification in an environment where there was increasing

> recognition of the *economic and social value of culture* ... inner cities have become a preferred site for cultural and creative production. And in the same way that cities support cultural heritage or high-art institutions in order to promote the culture-based redevelopment of urban spaces and economies, policy makers also have to acknowledge citizens and the specific meanings they attach to a place [...]. (Merkel, 2012: 160–161, emphasis in original)

The relationship between the international art community and Berlin's economic redevelopment are inseparable. Berlin still relies heavily on EU funding to continue to place culture as its primary industry and asset (Merkel, 2012: 162). Since 2009, the cultural sector in Berlin has grown by 4% to 8.5% of the gross value added, in comparison to the European average of 3%, with one in five employers being in the cultural sector (Senatsverwaltung für Wirtschaft, 2014). The strategy for the city to focus on the cultural sector has strengthened its economic power and despite increased rents, creative industries, such as galleries, continue to move or stay in Berlin (Investitionsbank Berlin, 2016: 2–4). Another consequence of increased migration to the city is the decrease in available housing. Vacant rentals in Berlin decreased from 5.2% in 2006, to 1.8% in 2013 and with high turnover of housing stock, "rents tend to rise from year to year" (Ikeda, 2017: 76). The creative city not only attracts tourists, but also highly mobile professionals who value the city's cultural infrastructure. More than anything, for artists moving from other creative urban centers, Berlin presents a situation in which time to make creative work is financially viable. These artists hope to be able to find the promised time and space for art in Berlin and are ultimately able to benefit from the prestige provided to English speaking artists. Despite its importance to the city, a clear and detailed picture of the art community in Berlin is not easy to gather. Moser (2013) draws together various data to examine the nature of art and artists in Berlin, including identifying 400 professional galleries in the city (90), and circa 8,702 visual artists alone (earning a minimum of €3,900 annually) insured through the *Künstlersozialkasse*, which has provided insurance for self-employed artists in Germany since 1983 (97–98). The existence of an insurance specifically for artist shows the significance of this community to the nation.

Inhabiting a precarious yet privileged space, international artists move to Berlin, rather than Germany. The city, not the nation, for these artists, becomes the space where being an artist is possible. No longer viable in New York, Berlin takes the place of "New York in the 80s" (Artsy, 2016). As Dogramaci (2016: 52) notes, the "principle of the wandering, mobile and transnational artist and nomadic models of thought bar themselves from this [national] classification and canonization as national", where resistance to the national can be seen through language practices, in the resistance to learning German. This mobility presents a "potential challenge to the borders of the nation, a possible rethinking of the nation-state as the primary means of political, economic, social, and cultural organization" (Heller, et al, 2015: 3). In this case there is a push towards focusing on Berlin and its art scene as a way to revitalize the city where there is awareness that "the arrival and presence of artists [...] is linked not only with residential gentrification but also with new retail capital and new types of services, leading to profound social changes." (Murzyn-Kupisz & Działek, 2017: viii). There is a tension between the artist conception of a city outside of the national that allows a freer creative life, and the economic and state structures in place to support this migration. For these artists who have chosen Berlin, the city could also have been Brussels, "the new Berlin" (Lynch, 2015) or Mexico City, the "Berlin of Latin America" (Cabrera, 2018), where, embedded in a diverse, international, multilingual population, English is the lingua franca. Artists talk of hurrying to move to Berlin before it's "over" or considering a move to Barcelona when Berlin is no longer viable. At the same time, as a creative city, artists lay claim to belonging in the city, even after living in Berlin for short periods of time. Berlin, in a sense, becomes an abstracted, global creative city that belongs to the international art community. Artists desire Berlin, and Berlin desires the cultural capital of the international art world. Artists frame Berlin metaphorically into familiar spaces, seeing Melbourne or New York in these new spaces they inhabit.

Galleries and artists' studios, prime spaces for employment for this community in Berlin, frequently operate in English. While these jobs are often unstable, low-paid, and short-term, they are balanced by the access that Berlin provides to the most prestigious art world spaces, to works, exhibits, and performances that an artist in Australia, for example, would wait a lifetime to see. Concurrently, Berlin presents opportunities that other cities don't, particularly within the English-speaking art bubble. English-speaking artists stand out for jobs in American and international artist studios where in a larger city, like New York, they would be vying for work in a much greater pool of qualified candidates. On the other side, the artist visa restricts income to art related activities. Where artists tend to have multifaceted skill-sets out of necessity, with histories of contingent, freelance, and part-time work in balancing making art and making a living, they are therefore often unable to legally mobilize these skills to make a living. Where usually an artist might supplement income through bar or café work, or using other skills, in Berlin on an artist visa, this must be done illegally, for example as a cash job off the books.

The mythos of the creative city draws this artistic community from other art centers that are too expensive, no longer viable, and/or do not hold the allure of Berlin. They are drawn by the appeal of the city that they see as allowing them to wholly embrace an art practice and the identity of an artist. But this desire is outside the national and, therefore, outside the German language. These artists move with English as their primary linguistic resource and the dominance of English in the international art world that has taken root in Berlin provides an open space for them to inhabit.

4 The privilege and privileging of English in Berlin

English is privileged in the international art scene in Berlin. It is possible to exist in an English-speaking bubble, limiting the number of interactions outside of this safe space, while simultaneously benefitting from access to this English-speaking art world. In addition, English exists as the lingua franca for interactions between German and other L1 language speakers. Here, I provide examples from my informants as to how English circulates in this world. Artists do grapple with varying ideologies about the German language, both acknowledging that they feel they should know or invest in learning the language, while also often struggling to see the utility.

4.1 Swimming and floating in the bubble of English

Robert grew up in New York City and spent summers in Germany as a child. His mother migrated to the US from Ecuador, his father from Germany. They met in Germany when his mother worked on the American Army base in Munich. Robert, however, did not grow up speaking German, though he was immersed in the language around his father's family. He holds German citizenship. On arriving in Berlin, he and his American partner had been concerned about not speaking German:

> *I remember one of the first like kind of, encouraging things in our early days in Berlin when everything was kind of like frightening [. . .] ah whether it was like realistic to be herê was our friend T told us about HIS friènd D. who was Italian. And he was telling us how SHE was an artist and she had lived here for n- like over a year and a half nòw or two years and didn't speak like a word of German. And she was doing fine. [. . .] and so I heard that and I was like alright then things might not be às [. . .] terrifying as /they were/ you @knów@.* (Robert)

His major concern in the move was at the intersection of language and economic survival: would they, without German, be able to find work. He was relieved to discover others getting by without a word of German. Despite having a relationship to German through family, his response was positive in discovering he would not need the language. Robert expresses and embraces the privileged position of being an English speaker in Germany and Berlin. He does not want to have to increase his German proficiency. English as a lingua franca allows Robert to stay in his comfort zone.

More than anything, the draw of the city and its international art scene is the priority, rather than learning German or thinking within the national frame. The world that these artists find themselves in tends to be an English-speaking one as a consequence of the dominance of English in the international art market. For Robert the move to Berlin was:

> *all aboùt kind of the hypè. [...] Berlin is this hot art scene kind of a thìng. [...] and it's kind of lived up to thàt but in a more subdued wày. [...] likè ... it's definitèly an ideal place tò have a studiò pay cheap rént meet other young artists kind óf àhm ... but it's àh ... kind òf the art scene that I'm interested in is kind of a bubblè you knów it's like separated from German cultùre and separated fròm German Berliners.* (Robert)

Robert finds himself primarily in a separated world, seeing the boundary between the German world and even Germans in the creative city. There are German Berliners and other Berliners. While negotiating the creative city space, he also discursively enacts national spaces. He acknowledges that his interest is primarily in American art or non-German art. He realized "that there's a whole world in Berlìn b- fòr ... the non-German speàk [...] or for specifically for just English speakers" (Robert). These global migratory flows and economic forces compel artists to migrate from places like New York City, where one would expect this art world to be based, to Berlin, only to find themselves immersed in an art community that is overwhelmingly populated by American art and artists speaking English, while surrounded by the cheap rent and studio space of Berlin.

Mia, an artist who also migrated from New York, finds inspiration in existing in the liminal space of not understanding the German around her. She relates this back to artistic practice, that by not understanding the language, she is able to exist in a more intuitive space, rather than an intellectual one. That she is able to ignore what may be any criticism from people expressed in German, because she doesn't understand. This contrasts, she notes, to more frequent encounters with strangers that she has on the street in the US, for example. She says:

> *There's an acceptance somehow that comes with like ignorance. [...] I don't necessarily always want it to be that wấy [...] bùt for this past year it's been a nice kind of state of swimming. Swimming through things instead of likè [...] beìng be- trying to be four steps ahead of where you are inste- and just being able to be like okay. Shh. [...] floating and- ànd letting things roll.* (Mia)

She can float along as a consequence of her refusal to learn German, allowing her to inhabit the identity of artist, an identity she can inhabit in Berlin. While she reflects that this ignorance should not always be the case, for now she feels that there is a certain "submission to the unknown" that sometimes requires "not understanding", providing a rationale for her current lack of investment in German language learning. She links this back to art practice by saying that living in this bubble has allowed her to just let her work "do its thing", that "art is all about doing something, things that you don't u- really understand". She recognizes that she is used to "the privilege of my bubble", of being shocked at times when people engage her in German on the street. While she sees her current state as not necessarily sustainable, she is quite content to stay detached from Germany surrounding her on the street.

The privilege of the English bubble is salient in art employment contexts. Olivia migrated to Berlin from Vancouver. She had seriously considered moving to New York, but ultimately came to Berlin with her German partner. In New York, she feels, she would have been invisible in the crowd of more qualified artists with Masters' degrees. In contrast, she has found that in Berlin she had access to privileged art world spaces and jobs specifically as a consequence of being an English speaker:

> *JUST because I speak English too. [...] like I speak Englísh so I'm friends with like English speaking peóple [...] like I'm in that communitý with no like question whether or not I'm likè you know likè, .h whatever likè, we- likè, there's no confusiòn [...] as to what like I need or want or whatever.* (Olivia).

She feels this has given her "an odd leg úp for some reason. Like I'm living in Germany and getting like more uhm what's it called likè more of- like of the bene- like I'm likè benefitting I don't know! It's SO weird." (Olivia) Rather than weird, it reveals the neoliberal forces at work in the dominance of English in the international art market, privileging the privileged. German language is then not only not the priority, if the job in the important artist's studio, for example, operates in English, German fluency is both irrelevant and counterproductive. English in Berlin then serves as a way into the art world, into the community, but also into privileged art job opportunities.

4.2 English as a lingua franca

English-speaking artists in Berlin, often rightly, assume that English is a lingua franca in the art world. They either encounter other L1 English speakers or others who have high levels of English proficiency. It is the notion of English as "crucial to access global markets" (Heller, 2010) taken to its extreme point, whereby English allows English-speaking artists access to the international art world, dominated by American artists, in the local context of the city.

English has become the default second language choice for many service encounters. As Mia frames it:

> *I've seen this happén between uhm lìke non ahh like say for example an Italian person and a German per- or a German-speaking person on the other side of the countér thàt [...] the Italian person tries to speak some Germàn [...] doesn't work out. The person- @@ @you know or so it doesn't work out@ so wèll so that- like the person behind the counter tries Englìsh. [...] and the Italian perso- person speaks Englìsh. And so then they converse in English.* (Mia)

Here, English presents the most likely option for successful communication in an international city. Mia remarks that rather than a switch to English being a reflection on the Italian person's ability to speak German, it is rather a practical issue, one of being able to complete a transaction. English is a resource in Berlin, a language that allows the flow of communication and commerce.

In comparison to English, German does not have the same utility to these artists beyond very basic interactions and service encounters. Mia compares the utility of German in Berlin to her experiences of living short-term in Italy and using basic Italian. Compared to Italian in Italy, she finds the "function" of German in Berlin not as necessary:

> *I get past the like initial function of like ordering òr like basic neéds [...] and there'll be a flip to English. [...] If I were more diehard about practicíng I would ... I would probably like ... I don't know! I guess I would try- I guess I woúld would just try really hard to be lìke please don't speak to me in En- let's try let's try as hard as I can but like I'm not!* (Mia)

There is no need to practice German, because English is enough. She remarks that the intensive German class she took was "a little overload for me". She does use some German, for example, with a friend who is more comfortable speaking German. In this case, Mia speaks back in English, but is continuing the flow of conversation through her comprehension of German. Unlike her experiences of Italian in Italy, in Berlin she can assume she shares English as a common language. There is no incentive for German learning.

Even for German artists and musicians in Berlin, the prestige and "cool factor" of English in creative circles prevails. Sam, having moved from LA, passed the university entrance exam and was about to start an MFA program in German. She questions the use of English by German musician friends in Berlin who play in a band:

> *And they're all German. [. . .] but when you go to their shòws they talk to the audience in English! [. . .] lìke and I just am always lìke @oh my god@ like why why! [. . .] I just think it's so funny! Lìke like you guys are German and you're in Germany. [. . .] half the audi- or most of the audiencé Is Germans! Like why it's just such a weird thing to me that they think it must be cool! To speak in English.* (Sam)

Lingua franca English even extends to people who share German as a first language. Like the art world, the music business often operates in English. Zoe, who came to Berlin with her partner, Sasha, from Sydney to pursue her music career finds that "ninety nine percent of the time it's in English" (Zoe) when she is booking shows and negotiating with promoters. When Zoe has spoken in German with a venue, it tends to be situations where she has actively said to them "I am going to write to you in German from now on because I have to practice my @German@ @@." Likewise, she has actively made the choice to speak with the bass player in her band in German. Having invested in a number of intensive German classes and living in a German speaking country, she still must actively insist that people engage with her in German. If not, when speakers hear her accent or see she is struggling to find a word, they switch to the lingua franca, English.

There is the additional benefit for English speakers who use German in Berlin that they can rely on code-switching. Anna, Robert's partner who worked in an international artist's studio that was very multilingual and where she used German in her day-to-day work, describes a "trade-off between German and English all the tìme so that you càn like if someone says something to you in German you don't understand then they'll say it to you in English." (Anna). She remarks that it would be difficult not being an English speaker in Berlin and not having this language fallback. With the assumption of English, there can be a collaborative process in negotiating a conversation in German. Robert follows similar patterns. He speaks some German with his great aunt, but acknowledges that if he does not know a word, he is able to use the English word and, because she speaks English, she is able to understand and they can continue the conversation with his language use supported through her language skills.

The scaffolding of German through English as a lingua franca even appears in the language classroom in Berlin, where students tend to have a large variety of language backgrounds. Dan and Varsha, who migrated as a couple from the UK, took a German class together. They ultimately left the class, because they had a change of teacher. This new teacher, who they did not like, "refused to speak any English with us" (Varsha) unlike their previous teacher. There is an expectation, a normalization of this sort of English language support. At the same time, Varsha recognizes how this assumption of shared English is particularly inward looking: "Yeah. It's just, you- kind of makes you feèl, ... almost boorish you knów [. . .] come to this country that's not your own country and demand that everyòne speaks to you in your own languâge you know it's kind ôf when you think about it @just@ seems really hm self-absorbed @@." (Varsha) While Dan is monolingual, Varsha grew up speaking Mirpuri Punjabi and then learned Urdu, which is now the language she speaks primarily with her family in England. She has the perspective of a bilingual, but this does not initially translate into a practice of investing in German language learning. In following up in 2017, Varsha, who had recently left Berlin to move back to England, reported that she had spent an intensive six months investing in learning German. She successfully complete level C1 and was very happy with the level of German she reached, that she was able to develop more German friend networks and thereby feel more established in Berlin. She plans on joining a German conversation group once she is settled in a new city in the UK.

English speaking artists in Berlin, then, resist the logic of the nation by choosing not to learn German. In contrast, for two of the artists in the study who worked at the core artist studio who were not L1 English speakers, proficiency in both German and English was integral. Luc and Stefan, my French and Dutch informants, had both increased their fluency in English and in German as a consequence of work and social contexts in Berlin. Both had found it necessary to have some German proficiency upon arrival in order to survive financially. Both dove headlong into jobs where they used German, despite feeling their language skills were not ready. As a consequence, their German improved allowing them both to continue to find a steady flow of freelance work in German. They both arrived in Berlin with English language skills gained through formal education, as well as consuming English language media growing up. Working in the core studio surrounded by American artists only reinforced their English language skills. The prevalence of English as a lingua franca allowed Luc and Stefan to both connect to the global, international art community, while also operating in the national language.

4.3 Ideologies of German

Despite the privilege of English, there also exists a discourse surrounding the advantages and use of German, which may or may not result in language learning. Zach, a painter who moved to Berlin from New York and worked in the core artist's studio, recognizes the value of German, despite making minimal investment into learning:

> *I'm not contènt though I can go every single dày w- barely speaking any Germàn mostly speaking Engl̃ish and everybody that I interact with is Engl̃ish I would like tò speak better German. Uhm ... but I think it does help [...] I think you would get more respêct from people if you could speak Germán [...] uhm I think it would help get jóbs.* (Zach)

He sees the economic advantage, as well as the cultural capital attached to German. His girlfriend at the time of this interview, who was Swedish-Hungarian, was highly multilingual speaking German, English, Swedish, Hungarian, and a number of other languages at a high level of proficiency. She was undertaking a degree in German in Berlin. Zach notes that in interactions where she was speaking to someone in German, he felt infantilized not knowing the language. At the same time, Zach makes no effort to understand more formal communications, for example phone bills and other "bureaucratic things", "I kind of ignore them" allowing bills to pile up, past their due date. While there is an acknowledgement of the utility of German for official communication, this has not been enough to encourage learning and use of the language. Zach is able to not take these overdue notices seriously, as he believes he will eventually return to New York and any debts will no longer have consequences.

Another strategy for navigating outside the English bubble in Berlin is to buy German language help. Varsha and Dan used Craigslist to find German speakers when they needed them for more formal interactions with the German system: for example, they hired someone to accompany them to their visa interview. The person they found ultimately refused to take any payment, happy to provide free language labor. They also hired a German speaker to read their rental contract before they signed it. German resources are available for the right price when needed.

English-speakers do find, and are often surprised to discover, that navigating the day-to-day, in particular in institutional contexts, cannot be done without German. Sam, in the early days of the core studio, found herself as the go-to person for German language labor. The majority of people in the studio spoke little German. She was called in to speak to the artist's doctor on her behalf, which Sam found "somewhat uncomfortable". She explains the situation in the studio:

> *Because a lot of the art world here is in- is operate- operates in English, and so she probably assumed that she could get bý [...] or maybe that we could as the studio get by without using German at all and thèn [...] realized along the wày oh shit! @this is a problem@.* (Sam)

The artist did come to see the oddity of the situation. Sam notes that she remarked: "We need more Germans, like it's so weird that we're in Germany and we're all American, so she made- she would- she made that kind of clear that, [. . .] w- this is weird that we're all American @@@ so that was nice." (Sam) Moving the core studio to Berlin, advertising jobs on an English language, NYC-based website, resulted in low levels of German language skills in the studio. The artist realized, belatedly, that German language was a vital resource for navigating local structures in Berlin, despite its English bubble.

Even in a city where so much English circulates and dominates, the lack of German proficiency presents difficulties. Escaping the logic of the nation entirely is not feasible. Lucy, an Australian artist who supports herself working as a nanny for an English-speaking family, wonders, "maybe I should be in an English-speaking city. S- because this I've got a handicap". Mia wonders "at what point Berlin is going to become resentful. Or IF it is ever." She links her future possible German learning to making the choice to stay in Berlin, but for her this is a proposition that is left for a future time. For some informants, this commitment to remain in the city, or feel more settled, has resulted in German learning. Mia, in 2017, continues to live in Berlin, has invested in German learning, which she uses at work in a bar and in her art business.

Overall, German remains useful primarily in institutional and bureaucratic contexts for the artists in this community. Artists acknowledge that not speaking German is a problematic position, but frequently use a discourse of utility to rationalize a lack of investment. Rarely do these artists find themselves excluded from society as a consequence of not learning German. Varsha, however, provides a further example where an active investment in German learning has given her a sense of integration, despite now having left the city. In the art world in particular, as Mia says, everyone "speaks so many languages, but English is the granddaddy of them all."

5 Conclusion

There is a paradox at work here that covers an economic logic, benefitting both the city-state and international, English-speaking artists. As English is privileged as a lingua franca of the international art world, it becomes both the path of least resistance for English-speaking artists, as well as, often, their access to privileged art world jobs. Both disincentivize the difficult process of learning German. Artists migrate for an idealized creative world and are unavoidably part of a process of gentrification that assists the city-state in economic revitalization, whilst also ensuring change that alters the ideal fabric of the artist space. Rents rise, cost of living increases, available space decreases.

English-speaking artists in Berlin desire German language ability, as Varsha reflects, because without it there is a feeling one is not integrated. The logic of the nation-state remains. As Burawoy notes "the nation-state, even if decentered, is alive and well" (2001: 149). But language learning is ultimately deprioritized after economic survival and commitment to an art practice. While my informants do acknowledge that there is something "boorish" about not speaking German, or that it is not a contented position, they are able to remain outside of the German speaking world, drawing on a discourse of "utility" to explain the lack of investment. The expression of desire for German fluency tends to be framed as something that comes from a position of shame or embarrassment, particularly when an artist had lived in Berlin a number of years. The resistance to learn or invest is also linked to economics: the cost of classes and the justification of financial investment when commitment to staying long-term in Berlin is uncertain. There is a utilitarian stance taken towards language. Where artists do not see a clear use for German, they often do not see the justification for the time and financial investment. In addition, English-speaking artists are in a position to choose not to learn, in many cases, because they do not feel forced to learn. The contrasting cases here are Stefan and Luc, who found that for economic survival, as speakers of Dutch and French, respectively, they had no choice but to learn. As a consequence, both have high level proficiency in conversational English and German. This English-speaking art community lives in a space where they are not happy about their lack of German knowledge and yet simultaneously, most continue to operate primarily in English, with friends, in the art scene, in their jobs. Finally, there remains a preference, where possible, even for those who do speak proficient German, for work and life to function in English in Berlin.

Because English is privileged in this sphere, when these artists invest in German learning, the investment often remains invisible. German speakers, on hearing an accent, will very often switch to English, assuming they have a higher proficiency. On the other side, German is often invisible or silenced to those who are lured to Berlin through the chatter in art cities like New York, LA, and through English language media like the New York Times. This explains the fact that an artist can plan and set up a studio in Berlin without considering the need for German language skills in daily operations. But there is also a space for collaboration in these bilingual or multilingual spaces. Artists in this study talk of contexts where they speak English and their interlocutor normally responds in German. Both speakers operate in the language they are most comfortable in. German speakers, like Robert's aunt, provide translation assistance when a German word is not available to him, the English speaker.

Despite existing in a particularly English-speaking, mobile, migratory sphere, international artists lay claim to Berlin as a creative city they belong to, that belongs to them, even when residence in the city has been short-term. Artists lay claim to ownership of the city, because of its mythos as an artistic, creative center. There are complex forces at work to make this so: global flows of artists from cities that have been gentrified where developing an art practice is becoming financially untenable; the role of English as a lingua franca, in particular for the art world, encourages these flows, supported at the policy level by the city-state. The creative city becomes the product, discursively constructed, of post-reunification Berlin. International artists, and the cultivation of a vision as an artistic center, holds economic value for a city in need of economic revival, making Berlin and its artists a part of a globalized economy. This community of artists represents elite, global, migratory flows. The ways in which language practices move with artists, the way local investments in English as a lingua franca both aid and hinder this mobility and the ways these artists navigate belonging in Berlin illustrate the tensions between mobility and situatedness, local and global. Berlin, as a city, is changed as a consequence.

Transcription conventions

stréss	rising tone
strèss	falling tone
!	rising falling tone
-	truncation
CAPITALS	emphatic stress
. . .	long pause
@laugh@	spoken laughingly
[. . .]	ellipsis/intentional omission

References

Artsy. 2016. *Chinese dissident artist Ai Weiwei on responding to the Syrian refugee crisis and his new life in Berlin.* https://www.artsy.net/article/artsy-editorial-ai-weiwei-speaks-about-his-divisive-responses-to-the-syrian-refugee-crisis-lego-and-his-new-life-in-berlin. Accessed March 28, 2018.

Burawoy, Michael. 2001. Manufacturing the global. *Ethnography*. 2.147–159.

Büro für Künstlerberatung. 2018. Aufenthaltstitel/Visum für Künstler/innen. *Kulturwerk des bbk berlin GmbH*. http://www.bbk-kulturwerk.de/con/kulturwerk/front_content.php?idart=3193. Accessed March 28, 2018.

Cabrera, Gabriel. 2018. *The Mexico City guide for art, food, and design lovers*. https://www.artfuldesperado.com/the-mexico-city-guide-for-art-food-and-design-lovers/. Accessed April 2, 2018.

De Fina, Anna. 2016. Linguistic practices and transnational identities. In Siân Preece (Ed), *The Routledge handbook of language and identity*. Abingdon: Routledge. Chapter 10: 163–178.

Deutsche, Rosalyn, and Cara Gendel Ryan. 1984. The fine art of gentrification. In October. 31.91–111.

Dogramaci, Burcu. 2016. Migrant, nomad, traveler – Towards a transnational art history. In Hans Kippenberg and Birgit Mersmann (Eds), *The Humanities between global integration and cultural diversity*. Berlin, Boston: De Gruyter. 50–69.

Duchêne, Alexander, and Monica Heller. 2012. *Language in late capitalism: Pride and profit*. New York: Routledge.

Focus. 2006. *Wowereits Berlin-Slogan: "Arm, aber sexy"*. https://www.focus.de/politik/deutschland/wowereits-berlin-slogan_aid_117712.html Accessed March 31, 2018.

Gal, Susan. 2012. Sociolinguistic regimes and the management of "diversity". In Alexandre Duchêne and Monica Heller (Eds). *Language in late capitalism: Pride and profit*. New York: Routledge. 22–42.

Gerhards, Jürgen; Silke Hans; Sören Carlson; and Daniel Drewski. 2015. Die Globalisierung des Arbeitsmarktes: Die Veränderung der Nachfrage nach transnationalem Humankapital im Zeitverlauf (1960-2014) und im Ländervergleich auf der Grundlage einer Analyse von Stellenanzeigen. *BSSE Working Paper No. 35*. Berlin: Freie Universität Berlin.

Gnutzmann, Claus; Jenny Jakisch; and Frank Rabe. 2015. Communicating across Europe. What German students think about multilingualism, language norms and English as a lingua franca. In Andrew Linn, Neil Bermel, and Gibson Ferguson (Eds). *Attitudes to English in Europe*. Berlin, Boston: De Gruyter. 165–191.

Griffiths, David, and Stella Maile. 2014. Britons in Berlin: Imagined cityscapes, affective encounters and the cultivation of self. In Michaela Benson and Nick Osbaldiston (Eds.). *Understanding lifestyle migration: Theoretical approaches to migration and the quest for a better way of life*. London: Palgrave Macmillan. 139–159.

Heller, Monica. 2010. Language as resource in the globalized new economy. In Nikolas Coupland (Ed.), *Blackwell handbooks in linguistics: the handbook of language and globalization*. Oxford, UK: Blackwell Publishers. Retrieved from http://i.ezproxy.nypl.org/login?url=https://search.credoreference.com/content/entry/bllg/language_as_resource_in_the_globalized_new_economy/0?institutionId=1961

Heller, Monica. 2011. *Paths to post-nationalism: A critical ethnography of language and identity*. New York: Oxford University Press.

Heller, Monica; Lindsey A. Bell; Michelle Daveluy; Mireille McLaughlin; and Hubert Noël. 2015. *Sustaining the nation: The making and moving of languages and nation*. Oxford: Oxford University Press.

Investitionsbank Berlin. 2016. *Die Bedeutung von Kunsteinrichtungen als Image- und Wirtschaftsfaktor*. https://projektzukunft.berlin.de/fileadmin/_migrated/news_uploads/Kunsteinrichtungen_als_Wirtschaftsfaktor_2016.pdf Accessed March 28, 2018.

Ikeda, Mariko. 2017. Artists as initiators of urban transformation: Are gentrification and touristification inevitable? A case study of the Reuter Quarter in Neukölln, Berlin. In Monika Murzyn-Kupisz and Jarosław Działek **(Eds)**, *The impact of artists on contemporary urban development*. New York: Springer. 67–90.

Jaworski, Adam, and Crispin Thurlow. 2010. Language and the globalizing habitus of tourism: Toward a sociolinguistics of fleeting relationships. In Nikolas Coupland (Ed.), *Blackwell handbooks in linguistics: The handbook of language and globalization*. Oxford, UK: Blackwell Publishers. 255–286.

Klee, Andreas, and Hendrikje Wehnert. 2013. So kreativ wie Berlin… *Raumforschung und Raumordnung*. 71.85–86.

Kroskrity, Paul V. 2010. Language ideologies – evolving perspectives. In Jürgen Jaspers, Jef Verschueren, Jan-Ola Östman (Eds), *Society and Language Use*. Amsterdam: John Benjamins Publishing Company. 192–211.

Landesamt für Bürger- und Ordnungsangelegenheiten. https://www.berlin.de/labo/willkommen-in-berlin/dienstleistungen/service.245683.php/dienstleistung/326564/ Accessed February 23rd, 2018.

Lee, Denny. 2006. *36 Hours in Berlin*. New York Times. Online: http://www.nytimes.com/2006/12/10/travel/10hours.html Accessed March 29, 2018.

Linn, Andrew. 2016. *Investigating English in Europe*. Berlin: De Gruyter.

Lo Bianco, Joseph, and Yvette Slaughter. 2009. *Second languages and Australian schooling*. Camberwell, Victoria: ACER Press.

Lynch, Eimear. 2015. *Why Brussels is the new Berlin*. New York Times. Online: https://www.nytimes.com/2015/12/11/t-magazine/travel/brussels-travel-guide-hotels-restaurants.html Accessed March 29th, 2018.

Menger, Pierre-Michel. 2006. Artistic labor markets: Contingent work, excess supply and occupational risk management. In *Handbook of the economics of art and culture*. Victor A. Ginsburg and David Throsby (Eds). Amsterdam: Elsevier. 765–811

Menger, Pierre-Michel. 2014. *The economics of creativity: Art and achievement under uncertainty*. Boston: Harvard University Press.

Merkel, Janet. 2012. "Creative governance" in Berlin? In Helmut Anheier and Yudhishthir Raj Isar (Eds). *Cities, cultural policy, and governance*. London, Thousand Oaks, California: SAGE. 160–166.

Moser, Valerie. 2013. Bildende Kunst als Soziales Feld: Eine Studie über die Berliner Szene. Bielefeld: transcript Verlag.

Murzyn-Kupisz, Monika and Jarosław Działek. 2017. Preface. In Monika Murzyn-Kupisz and Jarosław Działek **(Eds)**, *The Impact of Artists on Contemporary Urban Development*. New York: Springer. V–x.

Pénet, Pierre, and Kangsan Lee. 2014. Prize & price: The Turner Prize as a valuation device in the contemporary art market. *Poetics*. 43.149–171.

Piller, Ingrid, and Jinhyun Cho. 2013. Neoliberalism as language policy. In *Language in society*. 42.23–44.

Senatsverwaltung für Wirtschaft, Technologie und Forschung. 2014. *Dritter Kreativwirtschaftsbericht: Entwicklung und Potenziale*. https://projektzukunft.berlin.de/fileadmin/_migrated/news_uploads/01_KWB13_Inhalt_small.pdf Access March 31, 2018.

Weitz, Eric. 2013. *Weimar Germany: Promise and tragedy*. Princeton: Princeton University Press.

Wilton, Antje, and Annick De Houwer. 2011. The dynamics of English in a multilingual Europe. In Antje Wilton and Annick De Houwer (Eds), *English in Europe today: Sociocultural and educational perspectives*. Amsterdam: Benjamins. 1–3.
Yeung, Shirley. 2015. From cultural distance to skills deficits: "Expatriates", "migrants", and Swiss integration policy. *Multilingua*. 35.723–746.
Zhang, Chao. 2015. When the artistic field meets the art worlds: Based on the case study of occupational painters in Shanghai, In Laurie Hanquinet and Mike Savage (Eds). *Routledge International Handbook of the Sociology of Art and Culture*. London & New York: Routledge. 437–454.

Appendix

Participant overview:

1. Robert, US. Worked as an artist assistant in the core studio. Partner of Anna. Robert's father is German and his mother is from Ecuador. He spent summers in Germany with his father's family. He speaks some German and understands it, but has taken very little formal German language education.
2. Anna, US. Worked in a Danish artist's studio where German is the dominant language used. Partner of Robert.
3. Mia, US. Partner of Luc. Minimal formal German classes. Moved to Berlin from New York after completing a Master of Fine Arts (MFA) degree. Worked as an art teacher using English.
4. Zach, US. Worked as an artist assistant in the core studio. Came to Berlin as part of his university exchange program. Took formal German classes through university.
5. Luc, France. Worked as an artist assistant in the core studio. Partner of Mia. Luc is a L1 speaker of French and speaks both German and English.
6. Sam, US. Worked as an artist assistant in the core studio. Sam spent two periods of time living in Germany with her family as a child. Learned German in school. Was at the start of a graduate art Master's program in German.
7. Lena, Australia. An artist who had residencies in Berlin. Written response to interview questions. No formal interview. No formal German classes. Oona's partner.
8. Oona, Australia. As with Lena, primarily lived doing artist residencies in Berlin. No formal interview. Did not take any formal German classes. Lena's partner.
9. Sasha, Australia. Journalist. Partner of Zoe. Took the German integration course for migrants, as well as a number of intensive German courses.

10. Zoe, Australia. Musician. Trained as an interior designer. Partner of Sasha. Has taken a number of intensive German courses. Makes an effort to speak German with her band members.
11. Olivia, US/Canada. Worked as an artist assistant in the core studio. Moved to Berlin with her German partner who had been living in Canada and spoke fluent English. She took German classes at the Goethe Institut in Canada before she migrated. She tries to speak German with her partner's family, who do also all speak English.
12. Lucy, Australia. Trained as an artist. Worked as a nanny. Taking formal German lessons in Berlin at the A2 level. Has a German partner whose family does not speak much English. She uses some German with him and his family.
13. Viola, The Netherlands. Artist working as a chef. No formal interview. L1 Dutch speaker. Speaks fluent German, as well as English. Attended graduate school in Berlin, where she studied in German. Partner of Stefan.
14. Stefan, The Netherlands. Worked as an artist assistant in the core studio. L1 Dutch speaker. Speaks fluent English. Learned German in high school in Holland and then on the job in Berlin. Partner of Viola.
15. Jane, US. Worked as an artist assistant in the core studio. No formal German classes. Uses Rosetta Stone to learn German basics. Partner of Paul.
16. Paul, US. Worked as an artist assistant in the core studio. No formal German classes. Partner of Jane.
17. Juliet, US. Artist, working on a residency in Berlin. Speaks French, spent time as an exchange student in France.
18. Varsha, UK. Working for an internet start-up. Partner of Dan. L1 speaker of Mirpuri Punjabi. Also speaks Urdu. As of 2017, she has taken formal German classes through C1.
19. Dan, New Zealand by way the UK. Artist, working for an internet start-up. Partner of Varsha. No formal German classes.
20. Andy, US. Photographer. Speaks German at a high proficiency, actively invested in German language learning. Works as an English language teacher for businesses.

Leonie Schulte

8 Stancetaking and local identity construction among German-American bilinguals in Berlin

1 Introduction

This paper examines the role of discursive stancetaking in local identity construction among a group of German-American (Ger-AmE) Berliners. In so doing, I analyze speakers' personal narratives about the changing relationship between repertoire use, place and identity. The speakers at the center of this study are alumni of a German-American bilingual school in Berlin, Germany. The school – which will not be explicitly named in this paper – was founded in 1960 during the American allied occupation of (parts of) West Berlin. It has since been known for its combined German and American English language education from kindergarten through secondary school (henceforth high school). The school is also known for its predominantly German-American student body. *German* and *American* are broad categories in this context; while the school officially uses these to indicate the students' nationalities, participants in this study define these categories based upon a) their parents' or legal guardians' nationalities and b) the languages they predominantly use (in this case, German, American English, or as many describe, "a mix of both"). In this paper, I will orient my discussion around the definitions my informants use.

Situated in the relatively suburban, affluent and predominantly German-speaking district of Zehlendorf in south-west Berlin, many of the school's students are easily identifiable due to their particular style of German-AmE code-mixing. The speakers involved in this study refer to this linguistic practice as *speaking Denglisch, denglisching* or *mixing*. Denglisch speakers make use of their linguistic repertoires in fluid and creative ways, often involving both inter- and intrasentential code-switches "Wir waren gestern im Kino, but the film was so bad. Wir sind sofort gegangen." [We went to the movies yesterday, but the film was so bad. We left right away], "Cooles Foto! Looks like a lot of fun, ihr Süßen!" [Cool photo! Looks like a lot of fun, you cuties!], but also some

https://doi.org/10.1515/9781501508103-008

morphological innovations such as the affixation of English verbs with a German past-tense form: *ge-stepped, ge-downloaded, ge-watched, ge-talked.*[1] This practice is comparable to such concepts as *translanguaging* and *metrolingualism*, whereby speakers "select and deploy particular features from a unitary linguistic repertoire to make meaning and to negotiate particular communicative contexts" (Garcia and Vogel 2017: 1). Speakers, furthermore, negotiate fixed and fluid linguistic and cultural, as well as local and national identities within urban contexts of interaction (Otsuji and Pennycook 2010). Though comparable to the abovementioned terms (and other related concepts), I will refer to these hybrid linguistic practices as speaking Denglisch, denglisching and mixing throughout this paper, as these are the locally relevant, emic terminologies used by my informants.

Berlin, as the site of this investigation, is particularly significant as a context for the study of German-AmE bilingualism; on the one hand, due to the city's history with American allied occupation, and, on the other, due to its contemporary position as an urban hub for elite tourism, life-style travel and expat culture (Novy 2018). The gentrification of many Berlin districts is increasingly being linked to the spread of English in the city as well as with the changes in Berlin's linguistic landscape in some neighborhoods. Today, gentrified areas such as Kreuzberg, Mitte and parts of Neukölln are flooded with English signage (see also Fuller this volume), from high-end design shops, galleries, artisan cafés, to up-scale restaurants, which are pushing out local businesses. This means there is a growing indexical link between gentrification and English: the language of global business and tourism.

As an alumna of the bilingual school in Zehlendorf, I was confronted with the changing position of English-speakers in Berlin and my role in it as a local, particularly after graduating high school. I found that while speaking AmE and Denglisch was a sign of local in-group membership in Zehlendorf, speaking English in Neukölln (where I later moved to), was associated with a kind of foreign elitism that I did not want to be identified with. This experience led to a re-evaluation of my own linguistic repertoire and its function in my performance of localness.

I conducted a study in 2015 in order to examine whether fellow alumni had undergone similar experiences. Based on the findings of my 2015 study, this paper focuses on the ways in which relationships to repertoire use change and shift over biographical time. These shifts are linked to broader lifestyle changes, such as

1 These examples are taken from recorded interviews conducted during a 2015 study, upon which this paper is based, as well as from the researcher's private emails and text messages.

higher education, employment and relocation (both within the city of Berlin and abroad). As Woolard (2011) discusses in her longitudinal study of Castilian-Catalan speakers, linguistic identities change over biographical time, and relationships to certain linguistic practices, codes, and styles change through life experiences. This means that speakers accumulate, redefine and negotiate new and changing indexical links between ways of speaking and their social identities (see also Jaffe 2009; Bucholtz 2009). This paper is not based on longitudinal data, but instead analyzes the biographical narratives of seven German-American Berlin locals, as they discuss their changing relationship to English, German and speaking Denglisch. What emerges in their speech is a pattern of self-positioning in which speakers align themselves with or distance themselves from other individuals and groups, leading them to continuously form and reform their own local identities. This discursive enactment of self-positioning is referred to as stancetaking (Jaffe 2009; Du Bois 2007; Johnstone 2007).

I employ concepts from the stancetaking framework in order to investigate the dialogical links that German-American bilingual Berliners construct between local identity and repertoire use, and further, how this link is informed by their evaluation of and positioning towards different local groups (such as AmE speaking tourists and monolingual Germans). In the following, I track the sequence of my informants' personal narratives from high school bilingual group identity to encounters with other English-speaking groups in Berlin post-adolescence and to the ways in which they perform their local identity in different Berlin neighborhoods as adults. Here, I specifically focus on the ways in which stance is expressed through code-switching, reference to local terms and place names, and generalized categories. These denote alignment and disalignment with given topics and speakers. By disaligning themselves from American expats and tourists, speakers create ideological representations of themselves whereby they can lay claim to local Berlin identity.

This paper contributes to ongoing scholarship on urban, fluid linguistic practices, by analyzing the ways in which speakers create indexical relationships between repertoire use and local group membership. Stance is used as an analytical tool through which to investigate the ways in which group membership is defined and negotiated discursively.

2 Stancetaking

The concept of stancetaking, the interactional process of taking perspectives in discourse (Johnstone 2007) is widely used in sociolinguistics and linguistic anthropology. The primary focus of this analytic tool is to capture and explore discourse *positionality*, or rather the means by which speakers position themselves in relation to the entities or propositions they are talking about in a given period of discourse (Jaffe 2009). Due to the wide reach and use of the term, stance carries several working definitions. For the purposes of this paper, I orient myself along Du Bois' definition, in which stance is more broadly defined as "a public act by a social actor, achieved dialogically through overt communicative means (language, gesture and other symbolic forms), through which social actors simultaneously evaluate objects, position subjects (themselves and others), and align with other subjects, with respect to any salient dimension of the sociocultural field" (Du Bois 2007: 163). As Du Bois' definition indicates, evaluation simultaneously involves acts of alignment and disalignment with other subjects (Jaffe 2009: 5). I use the terms *alignment* and *disalignment* to indicate the ways in which individuals demonstrate their relative positions towards (or away from) given concepts, as well as other individuals or groups.

The concept of stancetaking thus allows for an investigation of the ways in which speakers form social categories and relationships, evaluate objects and other subjects, and position themselves discursively within their sociocultural fields. Importantly, acts of stancetaking allow us to understand the indexical relationships that speakers construct between social groups, ways of speaking, and other socio-cultural practices, and how these are entailed in their discursive self-positioning (Silverstein 2003: Jaffe 2009; Johnstone 2007). Within this framework, a general distinction is drawn between epistemic and affective/evaluative stance, whereby affect denotes the emotional and evaluative position of the speaker towards the object of discourse, while epistemic stance is related to the speaker's certainty and commitment concerning that object. Following Jaffe, both affective and epistemic stance are socially and culturally grounded and consequential (Jaffe 2009: 7), meaning that both offer insight to the ways in which social relationships are constructed, negotiated and entailed by individual stance. Affective stance indexes individual or community value systems in that it does the work of evaluation, self-presentation, and positioning. Importantly, affective stances index shared, culturally specific structures of feeling and can thus be used to draw social boundaries, construct differences and social categories, as well as allow speakers to lay claims to particular identities and statuses (Jaffe 2009). Epistemic stance, on the other hand, concerns a speaker's demonstration of authorial or authentic knowledge or claim to social capital in relation to a given topic. Johnstone's (2007) Pittsburghese study, for example, demonstrates how locals perform the Pittsburgh dialect by drawing on stereotypically local phonological and lexical variants. In so doing, speakers demonstrate their authoritative stance as local actors, equipped with the knowledge and linguistic competence to perform the local dialect.

Stance is enacted through a range of linguistic and extra-linguistic resources such as lexical items and grammatical constructions, including stance-related generalizations. Generalizations are also understood as expressions of position and attitude, and these kinds of utterances index and evaluate certain categories (or classes). These generalizations are not categories that I take to be fixed or universally given, but instead are created by speakers based on their personal and social expectations and beliefs. As Scheibman points out, generalizations such as in subject noun phrases, e.g., *these people, the French, those Brits,* are used in conversations to evaluate, demonstrate solidarity with one another and authorize opinions (Scheibman 2007: 112). The use of generalized subject noun phrases allows for speakers to forge generalized indexical relationships between the subjects and their characteristics, thus allowing for the construction of contrast between subject groups (Scheibman 2007: 113–114). What is more, as Jaffe, Heller and many others point out, stance can also be enacted through code-choice, as for example in multilingual contexts where code-choice can mobilize the distinction between tourist and local (Heller, Jaworski, and Thurlow 2014). Code choice can also do the work of linking styles of speech to local ethnic and social categories and identities, such as in Kiesling's (2005) work on *wogspeak* or Eckert's (1989, 2000) *Jocks* and *Burnouts*.

The sociolinguistic notion of stance is "fundamentally performative" (Jaffe 2009: 11) in that a stance-based approach reveals how social identities are discursively constructed rather than being predetermined and static. In that sense, social identity can be seen as the "cumulation of stances taken over time" (Jaffe 2009: 11) meaning that social identity can be negotiated and redefined over time through the process of constant re-evaluation and self-positioning within the speaker's socio-cultural field. In what follows, I discuss the contemporary and historical position of English in Berlin, before analyzing the ways in which my informants negotiate the changing indexical relationships between repertoire use, identity and localness.

3 Gentrification, touristification and English in Berlin

Today, Berlin is one of the fastest growing tourist economies in Europe (Novy 2018). Unlike other, comparably popular tourist destinations in Europe, such as London and Paris, Berlin was divided for decades during the Cold War (1949–1990), and its large-scale and fast-moving urban development, since the reunification in 1990, has brought on considerable economic and social changes. Tourism and gentrification-induced changes mean that, on the one hand, the city has been quickly rebuilt and refurbished, with ongoing construction work becoming a common feature (for better or for worse). The booming tourist industry and growing start-up, industrial, commercial as well as art scene (see also Farrell this volume) mean that the city is growing economically and culturally. On the other hand, the pace of these developments has led to a vast increase in rental and property prices across the city, which is pushing out many local businesses and working-class groups. Increasingly, as Füller and Michel (2014) and others, point out, the city is catering to the needs and tastes of the young, mobile, affluent and cosmopolitan consumers who continue to flock to the city. Like London's East End and Paris' Canal Saint Martin area, several boroughs in Berlin are becoming targets of what Novy refers to as "touristification" or the urban transformation processes caused or associated with tourism (Novy 2018: 423). Neighborhoods (depicted in Image 1 below) like Neukölln (8) and Kreuzberg (6) in the former West and Mitte (5) and Friedrichshain (6), in the former East are not only hubs of international tourism, but also for young urban professionals, experienced travellers and temporary city users, who are in search of the "sophisticated experiences away from established tourism zones" and who share many of the "amenity demands and preferences of city dwellers and commuters" (Fainstein, Hoffman, and Judd 2003: 243). There are, therefore, not only increasing numbers of established "tourist zones" that offer the stereotypical amenities of tourist sites (e.g., guided tours, historical monuments, "authentic German" food stalls, and souvenir shops), but long-term and short-term visitors are beginning to blend into and co-construct the local scene. This second point is significant because this so-called blending of tourist, visitor and local is particularly being spurred by the affluent middle-class life-style traveller, young-urban professional and artist markets. This is increasingly leading to a commodification of Berlin not only as a destination for travel, but as a place that is consumable and can be shaped by the elite consumer, in many sections of the city.

Significantly, this has led to the spread of new shops and businesses that are largely English-speaking or cater to an English-speaking market, contributing to a rapidly changing urban linguistic landscape with English-speaking high-end designer shops, artisan bakeries and coffee shops, art galleries and up-scale restaurants. This is indicative of a shift in the linguistic market place, whereby, following Cameron, "the traditional motives for acquiring or maintaining particular languages are increasingly yielding to a more calculating economic rationalism, which favours those forms of linguistic capital that are most readily convertible into the literal economic kind" (Cameron 2012: 354). In this sense, there is an increasing dialogical link between the social and economic changes in Berlin and the spread of English as a "global semiotic commodity" (Cameron 2012: 354).

This has quickly become a contentious issue in German media and politics. As Novy (2018) and others have pointed out, in the context of increased tourism, there is a concern of the commodification, homogenization and disruption of local life. Conservative politicians such as Jens Spahn of the Christian Democratic Union (CDU), lament the spread of English by elite hipster communities and the growing presence of English-speaking service staff in cafés and restaurants, which apparently dilutes Berlin's rich culture of "Dichter und Denker" [poets and thinkers] (Spahn 2017). Füller and Michel discuss the rise in anti-tourist protest and critique among – particularly left-leaning – locals in areas like Kreuzberg (Füller and Michel 2014: 1305). While the debate around the cultural and economic integration of migrants in Germany has led to the introduction of German language proficiency requirements for many newcomers (Bundesamt für Migration und Flüchtlinge 2016; see also Tanager this volume), English continues to spread as a language of elite communities.[2] This leads to a shift in power dynamics not only between local communities and newcomers, but also between different migrant and diaspora groups.[3]

Though the increased presence of English speakers has caused contentious debate in recent years, their presence is not new. Berlin has a long history with BrE and AmE speakers, most notably in its recent history through the allied-occupation of Berlin. During the occupation, from 1949 – 1990, the city was divided into four sectors; American, British, French in the former West and the Soviet-controlled GDR (German Democratic Republic) in the former East. For the purpose of this paper, I turn my attention primarily to the American sector, which comprised the three districts Steglitz-Zehlendorf, Neukölln and Tempelhof-Schöneberg in the south-west (represented by numbers 4, 7 and 8 on the map).

Zehlendorf, the most suburban of the three American sectors, became a residential hub for American soldiers, with clusters of housing blocks, baseball fields and shops with American food and goods, as well as governmental institutions like the American consulate, which is still seated in Zehlendorf today. In the 1960s, a German-American bilingual school was built for the children of American soldiers. From the beginning, it was designed to combine German and American education styles, offering both the German Abitur and the American High School

2 Gentrification is not solely being led by English speakers. It is also caused by the migration of many other affluent Europeans, but also other Germans (particularly from the south) in areas like Prenzlauer Berg. However, for the purpose of this paper, I am focussing on the role of English-speaking groups.

3 Due to the space constraints in this paper, I only briefly mention the multilingual and multicultural context of Berlin, as well as the effects these social, economic and linguistic developments have on other migrant diasporas.

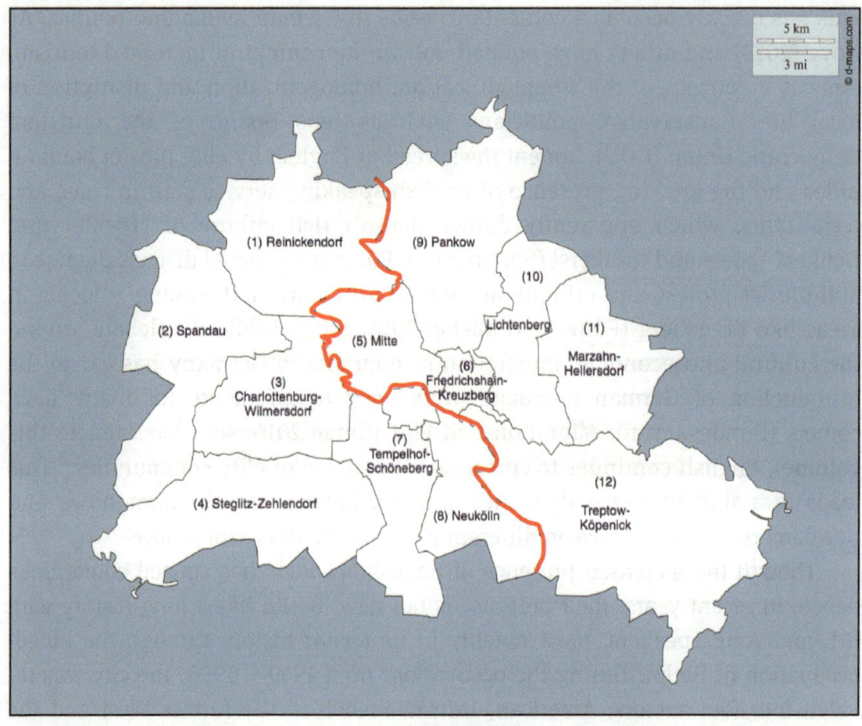

Figure 1: Map of Berlin with demarcation of Berlin Wall (Source: d-map.com/carte.php?num_car=27352&lang=en – with additions by the author.).

Diploma. There has thus been a significant English-speaking presence in Berlin since the Cold War, and it is in this context that the informants in my study have grown up.

Today, aside from the presence of the bilingual school, Zehlendorf remains largely German monolingual, in a district that has a comparatively low rate of diversity with only 22.2% of residents with migration backgrounds – meaning the individuals themselves – or at least one of their parents – have migrated to Berlin from another country. This is comparatively low in relation to other districts in Berlin, such as Friedrichshain-Kreuzberg at 35.9%, Neukölln at 39.6% and Mitte at 45%[4] (Statistik Berlin Brandenburg 2016). Though the American

4 It should be noted that Zehlendorf does not have the lowest percentage of residents with migration backgrounds. Areas such as Treptow-Köpenick at 7.1%, Marzahn-Hellersdorf at 10.4% and Pankow at 11.1 %, in the former East, are comparatively much lower (Statistik Berlin Brandenburg 2016).

presence in most of the formerly occupied zones is dissipating, the school continues to thrive with ca 1700 students overall.

4 Participants

In what follows, I analyze four conversations with seven Denglisch-speaking Berliners. The interviews were semi-structured and focused on my informants' reflections on their linguistic practices both during school and after graduation.

As an alumna of this school myself, I noticed a shift in my repertoire use in my early 20s, where I became particularly aware of my AmE usage in certain parts of Berlin, combined with a re-evaluation of my own localness (which I had never previously questioned). I wondered if other alumni from the bilingual school had experienced the same shifts in their repertoire use. In my original (2015) study, I tapped into my own friendship network and used the friends-of-friends method to survey a total of 30 alumni through an online questionnaire, as well as more in-depth discussion through interviews. Questions were generally kept quite broad, while revealing little of my own experience or perspective (so as to reduce researcher effects). Some informants were interviewed individually and others in pairs.

The seven informants in the study I present here include: (1) Anne and Katherine, both have a German and an American parent. I skyped with them from Oxford while they were both completing their studies in New York. Anne graduated from the bilingual school in 2012 and Katherine graduated in 2009. At the time of our interview, Anne was in her early 20s and Katherine was in her mid-20s. (2) Alex and Sarah, graduated from the bilingual school in 2005. The couple, then in their late 20s, lives in Neukölln, but studied in the UK. Both have German parents.[5] (3) Marie, graduated in 2009. Both parents are German. Marie studied in the UK and has since moved to several different countries in her work with NGOs. (4) Eric and Roland both graduated in 2012. Both have a German and an American parent. The two were in their early 20s at the time of the interview, and have been living, working and studying in Berlin since graduation. The group is composed of mobile, white, middle-class, educated

5 Alex uses gender inclusive personal pronouns, and has asked me to use they/them throughout this paper. I will, henceforth, be using they/them in the third person singular when referring to Alex.

20-something-year-olds, who, through their post-adolescent educational, vocational and social developments have various social ties to international English-speaking communities.

The following section specifically explores the role that *Denglisch* played in group-identity formation while growing up in Zehlendorf. All participants in the original study attended the school for at least seven years, meaning their entire highschool experience took place there. The speakers I focus on in this paper have all attended the school for 13–14 years, meaning kindergarten through Abitur/American HighSchool Diploma (graduation from secondary school). To track the patterns and strategies of alignment and disalignment in the informants' narratives, I begin by addressing the kinds of dialogical links these speakers form when reflecting on their school experience. In so doing, I identify key aspects of identity formation across the group, which become salient in their narratives of identity construction throughout our conversations.

5 Speaking Denglisch: group membership and localness from Zehlendorf to Neukölln

5.1 Group membership: us kids, the real bilinguals

When I asked my participants to characterize the linguistic practices typical of their school, all reported that academic and social life was oriented around German and AmE interaction, and in most cases a "mix" of both (i.e., Denglisch). I then asked them if they personally spoke Denglisch at school and with their friends, which often led to in-depth discussions about the social significance of Denglisch for social organization.

In the following excerpt of my conversation with Katherine and Anne – both of whom have a German and an American parent – I asked them if speaking Denglisch was something that all of their classmates engaged in. In other words, was it common to hear kids speak Denglisch at school? This prompts Katherine to quickly clarify that not all students spoke Denglisch; it was only one specific group, the "bilinguals". Below, they begin mapping out a social microcosm in which social groups are ordered into three generalized classes; "Americans", "Germans" and "bilinguals", whereby evaluations of linguistic practices are used by speakers to construct national categories.

(1) K: I found that at [name of school] there were certain subgroups (.) like,
there's a spectrum again (.) there was the American diplomat kids (. . .)
but they did not learn German (. . .) and then there was all the (. . .) us kids
(. . .) like the bilingual kids with two different nationality parents,
or who grew up going to the school the entire time (.) well its almost (.) no,
then there's the kids who had like,
two different nationality parents and then (. . .)
I think there was the kids who had like all German parents [–]
A: [–] Or the Germans who
just never really learned English.
K: There were a few of those too [–]
[–] *Nach zehn Jahren* [after ten years]! Like,
are you kidding me? [laughter][6]

In this conversation, Katherine and Anne create distinct groups by indexing them through generalized categories: "the American diplomat kids", "the bilingual kids", "the Germans". These categories, referred to by subject noun phrases, are then evaluated in their accompanying predicates: "they do not learn German", "never really learn English". These evaluative predicates signal Katharine and Anne's attitudes towards these groups, implying a perceived inability or unwillingness to make use of certain linguistic resources. By contrast, the class of "the bilingual kids" at once, specifically designates those students whose parents have two different nationalities, while also presupposing the ability to use resources from both AmE and German. The use of the personal pronoun *us* as in "us kids" furthermore demonstrates that Katharine includes Anne in the bilingual group, while strengthening the dichotomy between their group and other groups.

Katherine's exclamative interjection in German, and the subsequent code switch, is a demonstration of her authoritative position as a bilingual: "*Nach zehn Jahren*! Like are you kidding me?" Katherine's inter-sentential code-switch here is a performance of her identity as one of the bilingual kids and can be understood as a form of epistemic stancetaking in which she demonstrates her knowledge of the codes of in-group membership (i.e., being able to code-switch). This not only establishes authoritative knowledge but it also legitimates further acts of evaluation (Jaffe 2009: 7), as seen in the proceeding utterance "you must be kidding

6 Transcription conventions: (.) short pause; (. . .) long pause; [–] interruption/overlap; *italics* German word/phrase/code-switch; ~ pseudograph (name change to preserve anonymity); [words] researcher's comments and contextual information; '' reported speech; . full stop: end of phrase/sentence;, continuative; wor- truncated word; ? interrogative; ! exclamative.

me", which expresses her disapproval and disbelief over other speakers' inability to learn English despite having attended a bilingual school for ten years.

In this brief excerpt from my interview with Katharine and Anne, the two create direct links between national categories and language practices. These categories are, on the one hand defined by the nationalities of the students' parents wherein bilingualism is specifically related to dual nationality (or having parents of two different nationalities), but also through the ability to speak Denglisch.

In my conversation with Marie, a similar pattern of evaluation and categorization becomes evident. In this excerpt, I had just asked Marie if all students spoke Denglisch at school. Like Katherine and Anne, Marie creates similar distinctions between groups that did and groups that did not speak Denglisch. Both of Marie's parents are German. However, in contrast to Katherine and Anne, Marie's account of bilingualism does not necessarily preclude Germans from this category.

(2) M: There were really German people at our school.
I'm not sure how much they mixed.
Maybe because they didn't want to or have to,
but also maybe cause they were seen as Germans.
You know?
And then there were (.) *ja* (.) the real bilinguals.

Marie draws a distinction between the "really German people" and the "real bilinguals". Here, "mixing" refers to speaking Denglisch, which the "really German people" did not, to her memory, engage in. Again, we find the use of generalized subject noun phrases which function to create distinctive classes of speakers. The use of the generic *they* form on the other hand, demonstrates Marie's disassociation from the "really Germans". Unlike Katharine and Anne, Marie is not solely defining these groups according to parents' nationalities, but rather constructs an image of Germanness and bilingualism through difference in repertoire use. In so doing, she demonstrates her disalignment from the German group, despite her German background. This example at once disrupts the notion of languages as straightforwardly linked to community or territory (e.g., Germans speak German), while demonstrating the situated and emergent act of identity and meaning making in multilingual contexts (see also e.g., Heller, Jaworski, and Thurlow 2014).

Going further, like Katherine and Anne, Marie draws a link between social group and ability or willingness to learn German and English and to code-switch, as expressed in the utterance "they didn't want to or have to". Here, Marie is attributing intent to the group, by assuming they either do not want or do not have to mix, implying that she sees a social motivation behind speaking and not speaking Denglisch. Significantly, Marie alludes to a further link in her utterance “cause they were seen as Germans”, which further suggests a relationship between social expectation and code choice.

In the examples above, the definition of bilingualism specifically describes students who speak Denglisch. Though most students at the bilingual school learned both English and German, this factor alone is not enough to include everyone in the “bilingual” category that my informants are constructing. It is the practice of speaking Denglisch specifically that is understood as a resource of in-group membership. This linkage is further exemplified in the below conversation between Eric and Roland – both have German-American backgrounds – who attempt to characterize typical Denglisch speakers. As I had in my conversation with Katherine, Anne and Marie, I asked the two to describe students who used Denglisch. In this excerpt, Roland and Eric refer to Denglisch as “mixing”. Unlike the previous excerpts, Roland and Eric are not creating national categories, but instead refer to students who code-switched as “the popular kids”.

(3) R: Yeah,
I think (.) yeah (. . .) No,
there were definitely people who just generally tried to avoid mixing[–]
E: [–] Yeah,
like the more popular kids [–]
R: [–] Yeah.
E: [–] Would be more prone to do it [mixing].
The ones who,
I guess,
were more social.

To Eric and Roland, code-mixing or denglisching are indexical traits of popular and social kids. Roland begins by explaining that some students tried to avoid mixing. Before he can elaborate, Eric interrupts him and explains that it was the “popular kids” in particular who were most likely to mix. Like Marie, Roland attributes intent to some speakers but he is also underscoring the social value of this linguistic practice. Significantly, Eric and Roland’s conversation substantiate Marie’s implication in (2), strengthening the notion of the indexical relationships between social group, status and repertoire use, while highlighting the role of social expectation in the subjective and intersubjective associations among the student population. Similar to Goodwin’s (2006) study of school girls’ talk, speakers in these excerpts “make visible their current alignment or disalignment with regard to others who are present or talked about” (191), which is a key way in which social actors take up stances and form groups of shared values and characteristics. Just as the girls in Goodwin's study organize themselves into cliques based on their leisure activities, consumption preferences and family wealth (Goodwin 2006: 182), Denglisch speakers form groups around repertoire use (though perhaps not as overtly or intentionally).

The establishment of these social categories further underscores the fact that personal stance is achieved through comparison and contrast with other relevant persons and categories. Comparison and contrast with other groups saturates both their in-group identification among their classmates, as well as their evaluation and social categorization of other Zehlendorf locals. In so doing, the group draws distinguishing lines between themselves as students of the bilingual German-American school and the surrounding environment which they described to me as predominantly German-monolingual.

5.2 Group differentiation in Zehlendorf

From the narratives offered by Anne, Katherine, Marie, Eric and Roland emerges a system of identification and categorization in which social groups are organized along their language practices. These further become indexical generalized classes of nationality and social position. The bilinguals argue that they identified themselves with their ability to speak Denglisch, which is associated with popularity and an ambiguous or fluid relationship to national categories (such as in Marie's distinction between herself and other Germans). This identification remains central to the ways in which the bilingual group says to have interacted with their local environment outside of school: in Zehlendorf. Here speaking AmE and Denglisch is a particularly prominent marker of differentiation, which speakers report to have deployed in order to consciously perform difference. Marie's commentary below offers a particularly helpful overview of the relationship between Denglisch and performances of identity:

(4) M: Yeah,
I think we did it more and more on purpose in public spaces,
like on busses (.) especially in Zehlendorf or in the *S-Bahn*.[7]
I'm hundred percent sure there was so-some mixing on purpose (.) just to let other people know that we're different maybe?
And,
I mean (.) I still hear it now when I'm in Zehlendorf.

7 S-Bahn is the over-ground train. This term is used throughout Germany.

There's always a group of students in the S1[8] speaking English,
but they mix it (. . .) it's not like they do- (.) they speak English because they don't understand German,
but they mix it maybe on purpose,
maybe to be cool.
I think it was a sign of coolness (. . .) yeah,
you're just (.) you're different than other people.

Marie establishes another system of contrast. Here she explicitly describes how Denglisch was employed to mark difference by not only overtly attributing intent to her own repertoire use but by extending it to other generations of German-American school students. Marie clarifies that mixing is not a result of inability to speak one or another language but is a purposeful strategy of differentiation and a marker of "coolness". As alluded to in the previous section, Marie now makes explicit how she and members of her group manipulated and made use of their linguistic repertoires to take up stance, and to align and disalign themselves from others. As Heller, Jaworski, and Thurlow point out, code-switching as a means of stancetaking allows for speakers to draw social boundaries and mark difference, such as between local groups and tourists (Heller, Jaworski, and Thurlow 2014). Denglisch is used here as a resource by bilingual speakers in order to manage identities in interaction (Cashman 2008; Wei 2005), which are contextually emergent and locally grounded.

From these narratives, we can gather that local adolescent identity was characterized by an ability to code-mix, which allowed speakers to distinguish themselves from groups that didn't (e.g., what was conceptualized as *Americans, Germans* and *Zehlendorf* locals). Denglisch was thus a means of marking difference and claiming membership in a socially distinct, hybrid group.

5.3 Re-imagining localism: sounding local

During the interviews with my participants, I asked them to reflect, not only on their language use during school but also on post-adolescent life in Berlin. Here, I inquired whether and how their language practices changed after they

8 The S1 is a public train line which runs between the stations Wannsee and Oranienburg, and is the only line which stops directly in Zehlendorf.

left school, and how their relationship to their repertoires may have evolved in the years since.

As Woolard notes, in the case of her Catalan-Castilian bilingual informants, there are "qualitative differences between the ways that adolescents and adults orient to sociolinguistic distinctiveness and particularly in the way they relate to distinctions to sense of self and social identity" (Woolard 2011: 641). This also means that relationships to repertoire use change over time, and these changes are triggered by broader social and biographical changes. After leaving highschool, as their networks with school friends weakened and they began pursuing higher education, travelling, working, and relocation to other Berlin districts, many of my informants describe how the linguistic practices that they had once associated with group membership, local identity, hybridity and popularity, no longer had the same currency. In fact, moving to more linguistically diverse neighborhoods in Berlin such as Kreuzberg, Neukölln, Friedrichshain and Mitte – areas that are becoming increasingly gentrified and popular for tourism – challenged the relationship they had constructed between identity and linguistic practice. They quickly were encountered with a diverse and multilingual environment in which speaking English was indexical of foreignness, tourism, gentrification, and expat culture, but never with the local speech of local actors. What was once a straightforward link between linguistic practice and local group identity was now being questioned; many participants offered stories about strangers remarking on their code-switching, their accents and their seemingly ambiguous nationalities. Sarah – whose parents are both German – describes these encounters to me during our interview:

(5) S: My memories of post-graduation,
of people commenting on the fact that,
either why does one speak with an American accent if one is not in fact American? (.) Or when one is mixing,
people just kind of picking up on it,
and it's like,
"oh, that's interesting, why do you do that?"

Post-adolescent encounters with Berlin are described as a confrontation with the ways in which other local (and non-local) groups evaluated and interpreted their linguistic performance of identity, which triggered a reassessment of the ways in which my informants make use of the linguistic codes and styles at their disposal. It also implies a re-evaluation of the kinds of local and non-local groups they wanted to align themselves with. At this point, there is a clear shift in the biographical narratives, whereby emphasis is placed on the notion of localness which was always presupposed in highschool. In excerpt 5, emphasis is placed on what it means to "sound" local and how it is possible to navigate personal identity through linguistic repertoires.

In the – rather long – extract below, Alex, Sarah's partner, describes the shift they[9] experienced from being identifiable as a local, bilingual student in Zehlendorf, to encountering new forms of association. The couple now lives in Neukölln, and because of the ways in which they feel their linguistic practices are being associated by others, they begin to develop new contextual strategies for the way they use their linguistic repertoire and organize categories of identification. Alex speaks Denglisch throughout our entire two-hour interview, which I associate with the fact that they knows I am a fellow Denglisch-speaker as well as an alumna of the bilingual school. The main transcript is given on the left and translations of the German portions are given on the right:

(6) A: *Irgendwie habe ich schon das Gefühl dass, ich mein (.) das haben wir schon ein paar Mal gehabt (.) wenn*	somehow, I do have the feeling that I mean (.) we've had this a few times
man irgendwie inner Eckkneipe sitzt in Neukölln, hier in der Gegend, dann achte ich schon teilweise sehr bewusst drauf, dass ich nicht unbedingt auf Englisch spreche, weil es schon in dem Moment dann nicht assoziiert wird (.) zumindest gehe ich davon aus (.) dass es nicht assoziiert wird damit, dass ich an einer bestimmten Schule war wo man bilingually up-growed,[10]	when we are sitting in a corner bar in Neukölln, here in the area, then I do, partly very consciously, pay attention not to necessarily speak in English because in that moment it is not being associated with (.) at least I assume it is not being associated with the fact that I went to a specific school where you *grow up bilingually*
sondern dass es in dem Moment in die Richtung geht, von wegen, "oh are you perhaps an expat or a tourist living here", and that the association is very different and, also, being	but instead, in that moment that it might go in the direction of something like

9 I use they/them pronouns in the 3rd person singular to refer to Alex.

10 This seems to be an idiosyncratic construction in Alex's speech: a direct transfer of the German adj + split infinitive verb: *bilingual aufgewachsen*.

conscious of the fact, *dass es in dem Moment vielleicht nicht unbedingt als* like something like elite, select *gewertet wird, sondern eher als* someone who is not necessarily welcome in the community that one is now living.	that in that moment it won't necessarily ben evaluated as something like elite and select, but rather as

Through the phrase *inner Eckkneipe sitzen* 'sitting in a corner bar' Alex takes up an epistemic stance as a local. Following Johnstone (2007), this is an index of their knowledge of locally significant linguistic forms and local customs. *Inner* representing either *in der* 'in the' or *in einer* 'in a' is a non-standard contraction of the preposition *in* and the dative determiner *der* 'in the' / 'in a'. Though preposition-article contraction is common in standard German dative cases such as *in* + *dem* = *im*, the form *inner* for *in* + *der* is only found in regional colloquial speech and is commonly associated with the Berlin dialect (see also Schlobinski this volume). *Eckkneipe* or corner bar (local pub) is a further claim to local identity, as Berlin corner bars – of which each neighborhood has dozens – are usually frequented by locals, particularly by the middle-aged working class. Despite this alignment with local practices and the demonstration of local knowledge, in the next sentence, Alex explicitly mentions their attention to code-choice because English is associated with tourists and expats in Neukölln, and not with locals. Their discussion of code-choice here is significant because it demonstrates how they metapragmatically creates new links between local forms and social contexts – all of which are explicitly linked to place or neighborhood. Alex is not only re-evaluating the way in which their speech is appraised by others in different local environments, but they is also forming new indexical links between the ways in which speaking English in areas with a lot of tourists and expat communities becomes associated with something foreign, and even unwanted in an environment that is being gentrified so quickly, and where the unequal power-dynamics between local communities (such as the large Turkish and Arabic-speaking diasporas) and incoming affluent Englishspeakers is so pronounced. There is a clear shift of the conventional indexicalities in Alex's narrative: their reference to American English being "elite" and "select" is a reference to the indexical relationship between American English and "coolness" and "difference" as an adolescent in Zehlendorf. This relationship shifts to an understanding of American English as disruptive and unwelcome in Neukölln. Alex's metapragmatic assessment and reorganisation of the indexical links between AmE and social evaluation are anchored in considerations of the local environment and specifically, the particular Berlin neighborhood they is in.

Following Blommaert, it becomes clear that the "values and functions of resources" attributed in local environments, which become meaningful "on the basis of codes, conventions, hierarchies and scales available" (Blommaert 2003: 44) are not necessarily transferrable to other local environments. That being said, Alex, Sarah, Katherine and Anne all report about the ways in which they were able to adapt to these changing circumstances by switching to German. As Ag and Jørgensen point out, this is an example of the ways in which "speakers navigate, and in which they position themselves and others according to situation" (Ag and Jørgensen 2013: 530), and in which they deploy their fluid linguistic resources for identification and authentication (Heller, Jaworski, and Thurlow 2014).

A notable theme that emerges from my informants' narratives is that they describe that they have become increasingly concerned with the notion and performance of localness. This concern appears to be linked to their implicit awareness of the fact that they can lay claim to an international, AmE-speaking, mobile group, and that this group is partly associated with greater urban changes brought on by touristification and gentrification. Their conscious avoidance of AmE, and their shift to German and other locally salient forms is an instance of self-positioning in which speakers attempt to extricate themselves from that group membership. Marie expresses this sentiment in the excerpt below:

(7) M: In Berlin,
you want to be seen as a Berliner.
You want that,
and so comes with speaking German and maybe even having (. . .) you know like (.) being the direct German,
Berliner Schnauze kind.
But in Zehlendorf; Zehlendorf is a little bit different (.) there everyone is (.) I mean everyone is German.
There's no tourists,
there's no expats (.) this (. . .) I don't know (. . .) this problem of tourists, of expats,
or of not being identified as a German (. . .) if you're in Zehlendorf you are definitely from there,
so there it's nice to set yourself apart because there (.) that's how we grew up.

Marie juxtaposes two forms of localness in this excerpt that are each based on two different forms of alignment and disalignment. In the first part, she explicitly expresses her desire to be able to lay claim to Berlin identity. She associates Berlin identity with a specific regional style often referred to colloquially as

"Berlinerisch" in which speakers are described as having a *Berliner Schnauze* or 'Berlin snout'. This has several implications. First, Marie is setting out to define what it means to "sound local" and second, she is attributing a regional style to a certain kind of behavior: "directness" (or even rudeness, which is typically associated with the *Berliner Schnauze*). Finally, she links this to her own performance of Berliner-ness. Arguably, this can be taken as the establishment of a further generalized category in which she evaluates the qualities of a specific way of speaking that she links to being a Berliner. "Berliner-ness" is then set in contrast to "Zehlendorf-ness", whereby she determines that local Berliner-ness is already implied in Zehlendorf-ness because a) "everyone is German" and b) "there's no tourists, there's no expats". Though technically, all the Americans at the bilingual school could be considered expats, Marie reserves this category for the Americans she encounters outside of Zehlendorf. In the local Zehlendorf environment, there is the necessity to perform cosmopolitanness, whereas in the presence of tourists and expats in other parts of the city, there is a necessity to perform localness.

5.4 Performing the local: us Berliners and these Americans

Denglisch-speakers construct local identity through adapting their linguistic resources to the expectations they perceive in other local environments. Another way of constructing local identity is by contrasting themselves with non-locals discursively. In the following excerpt, Katherine, who studied and is currently living in the US creates a contrast between herself and Americans currently moving to Berlin:

(8) K: Kreuzberg is where all the *Amis* move now.
Where it's really hip to live so (.) I think there is an influx of young Americans (. . .) that's also a problem I had when I was graduating,
cause a lot of people I knew from Bard[11] (. . .) kept saying like "I am moving to Berlin"
and I'm like,
"yeah but Daddy's going to pay for you and you don't have anything you're doing there.
You're not learning German,
but it's not your primary thing you just want to go there and see art" (.)
which is fine but (.) I think I'm very attached to like the wellbeing of Berlin.

11 Bard is a wealthy, private liberal arts college on the East Coast of the United States.

Though Katherine is half American and attended university in the US, she draws a distinction between herself and her course mates. In so doing, she first identifies the qualities of the group. Her use of the term "Ami" – a slighting abbreviation for *Amerikaner* 'Americans' used widely throughout Germany – demonstrates an affective stance, whereby she uses a German culturally specific term to mark difference (and perhaps even disdain). She then precedes to attribute and evaluate their intent: Moving to Kreuzberg because it's "really hip". What is striking about this example is that Katherine is drawing similar links between the generalized category, "the Amis" and their perceived unwillingness/inability to learn German, as she did when talking about "the American kids" at school. As she alleges that her classmates from Bard are "not learning German", she is creating a similar picture of in-group membership, whereby belonging is linked to repertoire. She is also adding new characteristics to this group, which echo stereotypes about the kinds of English-speaking newcomers in Berlin: privilege/elitism (studying at Bard, wealth through family funds) and place consumption (art scene, hipster culture), but she also mentions her own sense of concern about "the wellbeing of Berlin", which seems to reference the demographic and urban changes taking place in the city. Katharine can arguably lay claim to this group, having studied at the same private liberal arts college, but in order to perform localness she positions herself in contrast to the group, both by defining and evaluating it as separate, and by elaborating her concern over the effects of their presence in Berlin.

In the following excerpt, Anne, like Katherine, describes the differences she identifies between herself and American speakers she hears in the underground train (*U-Bahn*). As she recounts conversations she has had with friends where she has tried to explicitly distinguish herself, she also is negotiating the degree to which she can or would like to lay claim to Americanness, and by contrast, localness.

(9) A: I feel like we (.) when there's Americans (.) with my friends who are still there [in Berlin] who are not American,
they'll be like "~Anne, look, like, there's Americans, like, you should go talk to them."
And I'm like "no like they're not like me" like,
just cause I live there [in the US, where she is living at the time of the interview] and I speak American English I don't (.) I see these Americans in Berlin and I feel,
like,
a little bit of (-) like,

> it kind of hurts me a little bit to hear this like strong American accent in the *U-Bahn* and like those (.) the people from our schools [Universities] who go there after college and,
> like,
> listening to them,
> like,
> "yeah I'm so cool, like, I'm living in like an apartment in Neukölln that costs like a thousand dollars, like, so cheap" you know,
> like people who are just,
> like,
> living there and,
> like (.) these Americans who I don't (. . .) I don't relate to them as Americans living in Berlin because I feel like I'm a different kind (.) or I don't want to be put in that box.

In this situation, Anne negotiates between the associations her interlocutors are making about her identity and the ways in which she feels she is distinguished from this assumed identity. Like Katherine, Anne can make a claim to American identity; she is half American and is studying in the US. Though she uses "typically American" forms, such as the filler-word *like*, she takes steps to disalign herself through explicit differentiation, such as in: "they're not like me", "I don't relate to them", "I don't want to be put in that box". Like Katherine, she also makes it a point to distance herself from her course mates at university, whom she is associating with the gentrification process by renting expensive apartments in previously working-class neighborhoods. She also separates herself from them on a lexical level, again – through the use of the subject noun phrase "these Americans" she creates a generalized category, which allows her to indicate her separateness. She then distances herself more by placing her classmates from her university in the US in the same category as the Americans in the train. The "strong American accent" she hears on the train is a signal of difference: Americans with strong accents are those who move to Berlin and live in expensive apartments in Neukölln. Jaworski and Thurlow (2009) find a similar phenomenon in their work on "elite tourism" whereby up-scale tourists take up affective stances that firstly generalize and distinguish low-scale tourists from their ways of travel, place consumption and leisure activities. Through what Rampton refers to as "processes of symbolic differentiation" (Rampton 2003: 68) "elite" tourists are able to draw an ideological distinction between the kinds of consumption activities, class backgrounds, and social qualities that separate them from other, presumably less sophisticated forms of tourism (Jaworski and Thurlow 2009: 199). The significant class-distinction in Jaworski and Thurlow's study is not applicable in this case, in fact, Katherine, Anne and the Americans they describe are arguably all middle-class; however, there is a similar process of ideological distinction. As Heller, Jaworski and Thurlow point out, stancetaking is also characterized by "the struggle over who gets to decide what the nature of the commodity is (what will count as "place", "language" and "identity") and who can legitimately participate in its production, distribution and circulation" (Heller, Jaworski, and Thurlow 2014: 450). In this sense, though Katherine and Anne can both lay claim to American identity, they are defining what it means to legitimately participate in Berlin life, forming new contrasting links between Americans living in Berlin and themselves: half Americans, who speak AmE, who are, nevertheless, local Berliners.

Through their, often stereotypical descriptions of American, or expat American social interests (the art scene), place consumption (moving to expensive apartments in Kreuzberg and Neukölln), language competence/speech attributes (not learning German, strong accents) they create implicit evaluations that index distinction. It is mainly through discursively identifying and representing other social groups (Americans, Germans, Amis) that they are able to create ideological representations of themselves, and thereby distance themselves from groups whom they associate with cultural chauvinism.

6 Conclusion: localness as commodity

In their disalignment with tourist and expat groups, the participants in this study engage in both new and evolving processes of indexicalization and linguistic identity performance, but their specific positions as middle class, AmE-speaking locals place them on an intersection between claims to localness and claims to international identity, which they negotiate linguistically through the deployment of their fluid Ger-AmE repertoires. Denglisch is thus a resource for them to adapt to the various indexical fields through which they move as they cross through different neighborhoods in Berlin and as they move through different life stages.

While it is described as a sign of distinction, coolness and hybrid identity to speak English in the context of Zehlendorf, while still being considered local, speaking English in gentrified parts of Berlin reduces their claim to local identity. Notably, the informants are mainly critical of other English speakers who are often, arguably, part of the same socio-economic class. In this sense, being able to claim local identity in a city like Berlin is a form of social currency, a claim to authentic localism–as–commodity, and a claim to authority over the nature of what it means to belong to the local community. In order to do so, speakers draw on linguistic and cultural forms that they understand to be locally relevant, such as speaking German and distancing themselves from the gentrification process, which is so often linked to English-speaking newcomers. They thus demonstrate their desire to be able to take part in defining what the nature of the local commodity is, and to take part in the *sociolinguistic economy* (Blommaert, Collins, and Slembrouck 2005), or rather, the field in which social capital is intersubjectively and continually co-produced, and in which locally recognized practices have the most currency. The ability to deploy linguistic resources to adapt to new and changing local contexts is an example of, following Heller, Jaworski, and Thurlow, "social actors strategically orient[ing] to appropriate, recycle, challenge or ignore a wealth of semiotic resources, imbuing them with symbolic connotations and indexicalities, linking linguistic variables with specific groups and contexts" (Heller, Jaworski, and Thurlow 2014: 429). In so doing, the participants in this study engage in the intersubjective and co-produced economy of social and linguistic meaning, laying claim to a sense of Berlin identity which is in constant flux.

Transcription Conventions

(.)	short pause
(...)	long pause
[–]	interruption/overlap
italics	German word/phrase/code-switch
~	pseudograph (name change to preserve anonymity)
[words]	researcher's comments & contextual information
""	reported speech
.	full stop: end of phrase/sentence
,	continuative
wor-	truncated word
?	interrogative
!	exclamative

References

Ag, Astrid & Jens Normann Jørgensen. 2013. Ideologies, Norms, and Practices in Youth Poly-Languaging. *International Journal of Bilingualism* 17(4). 525–539.

Bundesamt für Migration und Flüchtlinge. 2016. *Deutsch Lernen*. http://www.bamf.de/DE/Willkommen/DeutschLernen/deutschlernen-node.html (accessed 14 August 2017).

Blommaert, Jan. 2003. Orthopraxy, writing and identity: Shaping lives through borrowed genres in Congo. *Pragmatics* 13(1). 33–48.

Blommaert, Jan, James Collins & Stef Slembrouck. 2005. Polycentricity and Interactional Regimes in 'Global Neighborhoods'. *Ethnography* 6(2). 205–235.

Bucholtz, Mary. 2009. From Stance to Style: Gender, Interaction, and Indexicality inMexican Immigrant Youth Slang. In Alexandra Jaffe (ed.), *Stance: Sociolinguistic Perspectives*, 146–170. Oxford: Oxford University Press.

Cameron, Deborah. 2012. The commodification of language: English as a global commodity. In Terttu Nevalainen & Elizabeth Closs Traugott (eds.), *The Oxford Handbook of the History of English*, 352–365. Oxford: Oxford University Press.

Cashman, Holly R. 2008. Accomplishing Marginalization in Bilingual Interaction: Relational Work as a Resource for the Intersubjective Construction of Identity. *Multilingua* 27(1–2). 129–150.

Du Bois, John W. 2007. The Stance Triangle. In Robert Englebretson (ed.), *Stancetaking in Discourse: Subjectivity, Evaluation, Interaction*, 139–182. Amsterdam & Philadelphia: John Benjamins Publishing Company.

Eckert, Penelope. 1989. *Jocks and Burnouts: Social Categories and Identity in the High School*. New York: Teachers College Press.

Eckert, Penelope. 2000. *Linguistic Variation as Social Practice: The Linguistic Construction of Identity in Belten High*. Oxford: Blackwell.

Englebretson, Robert. 2007. *Stancetaking in Discourse: Subjectivity, Evaluation, Interaction*. Amsterdam & Philadelphia: John Benjamins Publishing Company.

Fainstein, Susan S., Lily M. Hoffman & Dennis R. Judd. 2003. Introduction. In Lily M. Hoffman, Susan S. Fainstein & Dennis R. Judd (eds.), *Cities and visitors: Regulating people, markets, and city space*. 1–21. New York, NY: Blackwell.

Füller, Henning & Boris Michel. 2014. 'Stop Being a Tourist!' New Dynamics of Urban Tourism in Berlin-Kreuzberg. *International Journal of Urban and Regional Research* 38(4). 1304–1318.

Garcia, Ofelia & Sara Vogel. 2017. Translanguaging. In George W. Noblit & Luis C. Moll (eds.), *Oxford Research Encyclopedia of Education*, 1–21. Oxford: Oxford University Press.

Goodwin, Marjorie Harness. 2006. *The Hidden Life of Girls: Games of Stance, Status, and Exclusion*. Malden, MA: Blackwell.

Heller, Monica, Adam Jaworski & Crispin Thurlow. 2014. Introduction: Sociolinguistics and Tourism: Mobilities, Markets, Multilingualism. [Special issue]. *Journal of Sociolinguistics* 18(4). 425–458.

Jaffe, Alexandra. 2009. Introduction: The Sociolinguistics of Stance. In Alexandra Jaffe (ed.), *Stance: Sociolinguistic Perspectives*, 3–28. Oxford: Oxford University Press.

Jaworski, Adam & Crispin Thurlow. 2009. Taking an Elitist Stance: Ideology and the Discursive Production of Social Distinction. In Alexandra Jaffe (ed.), *Stance: Sociolinguistic Perspectives*. 195–226. Oxford: Oxford University Press.

Johnstone, Barbara. 2007. Linking Identity and Dialect through Stancetaking. In Robert Englebretson (ed.), *Stancetaking in Discourse: Subjectivity, Evaluation, Interaction*, 49–67. Amsterdam & Philadelphia: John Benjamins Publishing Company.

Kiesling, Scott F. 2005. Variation, stance and style: Word-final *-er*, high rising tone, and ethnicity in Australian English. *English World-Wide* 26(1). 1–42.

Novy, Johannes. 2018. 'Destination' Berlin Revisited. From (New) Tourism Towards a Pentagon of Mobility and Place Consumption. *Tourism Geographies* 20(3),418–442.

Otsuji, Emi & Alastair Pennycook. 2010. Metrolingualism: Fixity, Fluidity and Language in Flux. *International Journal of Multilingualism* 7(3). 240–254.

Rampton, Ben. 2003. Hegemony, social class and stylisation. *Pragmatics* 13(1). 49–83.
Scheibman, Joanne. 2007. Subjective and intersubjective uses of generalizations in English conversations. In Robert Englebretson (ed.), *Stancetaking in Discourse: Subjectivity, Evaluation, Interaction*, 111–138. Amsterdam & Philadelphia: John Benjamins Publishing Company.
Silverstein, Michael. 2003. Indexical Order and the Dialectics of Sociolinguistic Life. *Language and Communication* 23(3–4). 193–229.
Spahn, Jens. Sprechen Sie doch Deutsch! *Die Zeit*, August 24, 2017. Accessed September 14, 2017. https://www.zeit.de/2017/35/berlin-cafes-hipster-englisch-sprache-jens-spahn
Statistik Berlin Brandenburg. 2016. *Statistischer Bericht: Einwohnerinnen und Einwohner im Land Berlin am 30. Juni 2016.* https://www.statistik-berlin-brandenburg.de/publikationen/stat_berichte/2017/SB_A01-05-00_2017h01_BE.pdf
Wei, Li. 2005. "How can you tell?": Towards a common sense explanation of conversational code-switching. *Journal of Pragmatics* 37(3). 375–389.
Woolard, Kathryn. 2011. Is there linguistic life after high school? Longitudinal changes in the bilingual repertoire in metropolitan Barcelona. *Language in Society* 40(5). 617–648.

Section 3: **Commodification**

Edith Pichler

9 Lifestyles, milieu languages and the economy: the presence of Italian in the urban spaces of Berlin

1 Introduction

The Italo-Berliner Community is characterized by the presence of various milieus and their members who were and are in possession of different kinds and degrees of financial, social and cultural capital (Bourdieu 1983), which in combination with their different lifestyles contributes to manifold economic, cultural and social activities. Berlin's Italians are prevalent in the gastronomy and food trade, and these activities give some of the *Kiezes* (a Berlin term for 'neighborhood') a touch of a Mediterranean character. The Italian restaurants thus leave their mark on the public space in the quarters of Berlin. In this article, I want to focus on the observation that there is interdependence between milieu provenience, cultural capital of the Italian entrepreneurs, time of immigration and the type and the naming of the restaurants.[1] This is a result of milieu-specific sociolinguistic practices, where naming is connected with the habitus of the owner and is a symbolic sign of distinction to attract clients with the same "habitus" (see Bourdieu [1979] 1987).

I first introduce the concepts of milieu and habitus from a sociological perspective and then present a milieu-typology of Italian immigrants. I give an overview of community-formation and the diverse typologies and milieus of Italians living in Berlin. This is followed by a chapter on gastronomy and the role of the various milieus, lifestyles and consumer trends in its historical development. The transformation of consumer behavior reflects the variety of milieus in the local Italian population to which the strategies of shaping/

1 The article contains data based on many years of empirical research and participant observations in the Italian communities of Berlin (for example, on the diverse migrant types), which have already been discussed in earlier articles (see reference list). Furthermore, living in Berlin, being a representative and consultant of Italians abroad at the Italian Ministry of Italian Affairs in Rome (Consiglio Generale degli Italiani nel Mondo / General Council of Italians Abroad) and taking part in the Italian emigration work group at the Italian Embassy in Berlin, I am in continuous contact with Italians in Berlin.

https://doi.org/10.1515/9781501508103-009

structuring the restaurants and their naming is connected. I give insight into the sociolinguistic contributions of Italians in the transformation of urban spaces in Berlin by studying the different milieus and the style and naming of the restaurants.

2 Milieus, habitus and lifestyles

While the concept of milieu did not play a significant role in the analysis of social structure, it has once again resurfaced in the course of the 1980s – not least with a comprehensive reception of Bourdieu – to explain social differences which are not only class-specific and imagined as vertical. Social milieus influence socialization, and in the respective classes there are several milieus existing next to each other (Hradil 2006). Social milieus are defined as groups of people who each have similar "values, principles of life-shaping, and mentalities" (Hradil 2006: 4, translation EP). In particular, Vester et al. (2001) are pioneers in this research field, investigating the social milieus in Germany in relation to social structural change, and have thus made Bourdieu's concepts (Bourdieu 1983, 1987) well-known in Germany.

In his studies of class structures, Bourdieu introduces theories of distinction and styles of life that correspond to a particular habitus – the attitude of the individual in the social world, their habits, disposition and values (Bourdieu 1983, 1987). A habitus contains the schemata that serve to perceive social reality, the aesthetic criteria to evaluate cultural products and practices, as well as schemes that initiate the production of actions. Accordingly, the habitus is the expression and result of the situation of the groups in the context of social inequality; in short, it is a class habit (Bourdieu 1983).

Habitus and lifestyle are in part the result of different distributions of economic, social and cultural capital. Economic capital is directly convertible into money, and represents all forms of material wealth. Social capital, on the other hand, is the means of access to social resources that are mediated through social relations (networks and associations). Bourdieu distinguishes between three forms of cultural capital: an objective form (books, works of art, etc.), an institutionalized form (educational titles, academic titles), and an incorporated form (knowledge, education, cultural skills). In the latter form of capital, social origin plays an important role, that is, growing up in a particular milieu implies a particular lifestyle (distinction) and a particular habit. At the same time, classification and hierarchization of lifestyles take place, which are accompanied by symbolic power and position struggles (Bourdieu 1983).

For a long time, and including by experts, the opinion dominated that migrant communities are homogenous formations with internally similar milieu and habitus. At least in the German context, it was assumed that the majority of their members appertain to the working class with low education and low professional levels. Yet, particularly through transformations within the communities and through immigration of diverse types of migrants, it becomes more apparent that migrant communities have always been diverse. Today, we can observe that the milieus are subject to ongoing change, for example, within the Italian community, where a multicultural, intellectual-cosmopolitan milieu has become more visible, besides the milieu associated with the traditional *Gastarbeiter*.

A detailed study of the life-worlds and life styles of individuals with a migration background was published by Sinus-Sociovision in 2007, which adopted and adapted the milieu typology in their study of the German migrant population. In their survey "Migrants in Germany – socio-economic environments and housing-related interests" (2007), one important result was that "migrants from varying original cultures can be seen to adopt common life-world models. Factors such as ethnic affiliation, religion and migration history inevitably influence day-to-day culture and the cultural background, however they seldom shape the milieu nor give identity" (Perry and Beck 2009: 45). Consequently, ethnic origin is not the only factor in the determination of socio-economic environment and milieu affiliation.

The study describes a total of eight migrant milieus with their own distinctive values, lifestyles, everyday aesthetics, levels of integration and housing preferences. What connects the members of each milieu is a certain class-specific habitus that provokes different lifestyles. The milieus unfolding within different communities need not necessarily be identical to the categories developed in the Sinus Sociovision (2007) study. For example, different migration experiences, immigration modalities, as well as the political, social and cultural conditions of the countries of origin contribute to the fact that they can vary.

3 Italian migration to Germany: a short overview

Already at the beginning of the 1950s, on the initiative of Italy, negotiations began between the Italian and German governments for the recruitment of migrant workers, which ended in 1955 with a bilateral agreement between the two countries[2] (Dohse 1981). The number of Italian workers increased constantly, apart from a short recession period 1966–1967 with more repatriation; in the end, it reached the peak of 450,115 Italian employees in 1973. After that, because of the "oil crisis" and the recruitment stop, the number of Italian employees began to decrease (Motte, Ohliger, and von Oswald 1999). In the beginning, Italian migration had been characterized by workers commuting between Italy and Germany, depending on economic cycles and the demand of the labor market. The fact that they were citizens of the EEC1 favored this movement between the two countries. This aspect common to this generation of migrants with the so-called *nuovi mobili*, who were moving into Europe from one labor market to another, was also favoured by low cost flights.

Destinations of this migration were the industrial regions of western Germany, particularly the Munich area (BMW), Stuttgart area (Mercedes, Bosch, etc.), Frankfurt area (Airport, Opel), Cologne (Ford), and the Saarland region (mining industry, steel industry). Characteristic is the case of the city of Wolfsburg (Volkswagen) – due to a recruitment policy that favored the employment of Italian factory workers, and unlike other industrial areas, in Wolfsburg, Italians are the largest foreign group. Because of this, the city is also a destination for newer waves of Italian migration (Prontera 2009).

After a period of stagnation in the 1970s and 1980s, during which the Italian communities stabilized through family reunion, in the 1990s, we can observe a revival of Italian emigration to Germany. The increase in arrivals is constant: from 23,894 people in 2010 to 57,191 in 2015; in 2016, the number of newcomers fell slightly to 52,564 people (Statistisches Bundesamt 2018: 19) (Table 1).

Initially, this "new European mobility" was promoted by various EU cooperation projects such as the Erasmus Project. With the financial and economic crisis in Europe in 2007/2008, a new migration period has started, dictated by need and economic reasons (Tirabassi and del Prà 2014). Among the most recent newcomers, there are not only young, singles and graduates – 26% of Italian newcomers to Germany in 2016 had a university degree (Istat 2017) – but there are also many families and many people holding a secondary school degree. The destinations for this new wave of Italian migration to Germany are partly the western, economically strong regions, in which the Italian population increases. In addition, Berlin has experienced a significant upswing of the Italian population in recent years, too (see below).

---

2 After this agreement, similar agreements with other countries followed, like, for example, Turkey, Greece, Spain, Portugal, Morocco, Tunisia, and Yugoslavia. Because of the oil crisis and the crisis of the mass-industries in 1973, the German government stopped this policy of recruitment. Consequently, migrants began to bring their family to Germany (Nikolinakos 1973).

Table 1: Arrival from Italy (italian citizens). Source: Statistisches Bundesamt 2017.

Year	Total	Men	Women	%
2016	52,564	31,509	21,145	40.2
2015	57,191	34,342	22,849	40.0
2014	56,700	34,562	22,138	39.0
2013	47,485	29,284	18,201	38.3
2012	36,896	22,821	14,075	38.0
2011	28,070	17,456	10,614	37.8
2010	23,894	15,099	8,795	36.8

With more than 500,000 people on December 31, 2016, the Italian community represents 8.5% of foreigners and is, after the Polish community (740,962 people), the largest immigrant group from within the EU. If we add people of Italian origin but with German or both German and Italian citizenship, the number of Italians in Berlin amounts to 861,000 (of which 41.9% are women, see Statistisches Bundesamt 2017: 63, 87). Unlike in the 1950s and 1960s, migrants are no longer employed mainly in the industry (27.2% in June 2017) but mostly in the service sector (71.2% in June 2017). Only 29.4% (75,038) work in the manufacturing sector (see Bundesagentur für Arbeit 2018). Within the service sector, the two most important employment sectors for Italians are gastronomy and trade (mainly import and sale of Italian products, see Bundesagentur für Arbeit 2018). The general German public stereotypically conceives of Italians as working in precisely these sectors, so that in colloquial speech, the expression *der Italiener* 'the Italian' refers to a restaurant (Table 2).[3]

4 Community formation in Berlin

Because of its peculiar cultural and social history, Berlin has always been attractive to quite diverse groups of people. Berlin's industry prevalently recruited workers coming from Turkey and from Greece (Gillmeister, Fijalkowski, and Kurthen 1989). Hence, Italian immigrants who arrived in Berlin have been quite

3 This stereotype is frequently reproduced in the media. In an interview with the social-democratic politician Steinmeier, he was asked about a meeting with another politician and he replied: "Manchmal treffen wir uns sogar zufällig beim Italiener" [Sometimes we even meet each other accidentally at the Italian] (*Tagesspiegel* 19.08.2013), to emphasize that he had a good relationship with the person in question. In this example, the reader will know that *der Italiener* is not a person but an Italian restaurant.

Table 2: Number of employees and activity rate of Italian population in Germany in the economic sector (Manufacturing / Service Sector) at June 2017 in selected Regions. Source: Bundesagentur für Arbeit 2018.

Region	Total	Manuf. %	Service %	Gastrono. %	Comm. %
Hamburg	4,066	10.0	90.0	21.1	15.3
Niedersachsen	10,928	32.0	68.0	23.9	8.5
Nordrhein-Westfalen	48,607	31.1	68.9	13.8	14.2
Hessen	29,807	22.1	77.8	15.9	15.6
Rheinland-Pfalz	11,021	28.8	70.9	18.6	12.9
Baden-Würtemberg	81,717	38.6	61.4	9.5	14.3
Bayern	45,508	23.1	76.8	22.8	14.1
Saarland	6,237	43.2	56.8	9.2	14.4
Berlin	10,459	5.0	95.0	31.3	12.3
Germany	255,498	29.4	70.5	16.3	13.8

different from those groups that came to Western Germany, who were mainly labor migrants. Thus, the formation of an Italian community in Berlin took a different course than in other German cities such as Munich, Stuttgart or Cologne (see also Tamponi 1991). This process went through different stages and was characterized by varying types of immigrants. The decisions by Italians to move to Berlin and to settle there were determined by several factors. The particular political, economic and social characteristics of the city have favored the immigration of different types of Italians who, with their different habits and lifestyles, contributed to the development of a heterogeneous migrant community. Among Italian women who arrived in Berlin at the turn of the 1960s and 70s, for example, there were some who migrated not only for economic reasons but were impelled by curiosity. These women often state that they wanted to get to know a new life. For some of them, emigration from southern Italy meant building up a more independent life and to emancipate from family dependence (see Pichler 2002, 2017).

As can be inferred from the Table 3 below, 1,364 Italians used to live in Berlin in 1960. After the Berlin Wall was built, the figure rose to 2,626 in 1961, to 5,798 in 1970, and to 6,368 in 1973. In 1982, it increased to 7,199, and grew to 8,549 in 1990 and, again, to 12,858 in 2000 (10,558 in the neighborhoods of West Berlin and 2,146 in the neighborhoods of East Berlin). While West German cities experienced a decline in Italian residents in times of recession, there has been a steady increase in Berlin, especially after the fall of the Berlin Wall. Moreover, the reunification process was accompanied by major changes in Berlin which a growing social, cultural and economic status of many areas of city life. This, in turn, brought about an increase of immigration of freelancers,

Table 3: Italian residents in Berlin. Source: Amt für Statistik Berlin-Brandenburg, diverse year issues of 2018.

Year	Italians
1950	1,078
1960	1,364
1970	5,798
1990	8,549
2000	15 842
2011	17,441
2013	22,693
2014	25,250
2015	26 715
2016	28,167
2017	29,405

journalists, managers, architects, and the like. Additionally, new exchange programs among European universities, such as Erasmus and Socrates, have raised the number of exchange students, of which some stayed on, not seldom working for two or three days per week in restaurants and pizzerias. They often come from an economically well-off background, but with a degree of social and cultural dissatisfaction and in search of alternative environments and aspiring self-realization (Yildiz 2013).

If we include people German passport holders with Italian background into the category of Italians in Berlin, their number reaches 36,533 in 2017 (Amt für Statistik Berlin-Brandenburg 2017). In contrast to the more prototypical *Gastarbeiter* regions like the Saarland, where only 44% of Italians are first generation immigrants, 78% of the Italo-Berliners have migrated themselves (Statistisches Bundesamt 2017: 132, 134).

Italians in Berlin are scattered across the different districts of the city but most of them settle in the inner city area. Table 4 shows that the districts of Mitte, Friedrichshain-Kreuzberg and Pankow have been the preferred residential areas for more recent Italian immigrants.

After the German reunification, two cases of a district merger between one Eastern and one Western city disctrict were carried out in the context of a general reform of administrational districts: Mitte was formed by combining the former districts of Tiergarten, Wedding (both West) and Mitte (East), and Friedrichshain-Kreuzberg results from a merger of Friedrichshain (East) and Kreuzberg (West). The new district of Mitte thus includes traditional immigrant neighborhoods Tiergarten and Wedding, while Kreuzerg used to be a kind of utopia for both young people from West-Germany and other immigrants for years. In addition

Table 4: Italian residents in the Berlin districts. Source: Amt für Statistik Berlin-Brandenburg 2018.

Districts						**Years**
	2010	**%**	**2015**	**%**	**2017**	**%**
Mitte	2,389	15.0	4,524	16.9	5,182	17.6
Friedrichshain-Kreuzberg	2,559	16.1	4,376	16.4	4,602	15.6
Pankow	1,363	10.3	3,010	11.3	3,391	11.5
Charlottenburg-Wilmersdorf	2,670	16.8	3,674	13.7	3,935	13.4
Spandau	546	3.4	888	3.3	1,098	3.7
Steglitz-Zehlendorf	1,187	7.5	1,422	5.3	1,547	5.3
Tempelhof-Schöneberg	2,065	13.0	2,759	10.3	2,981	10.1
Neukölln	1,700	10.7	3,396	12.7	3,455	11.7
Treptow-Köpenick	226	1.4	512	1.9	698	2.4
Marzahn-Hellersdorf	85	0.5	211	0.8	244	0.8
Lichtenberg	213	1.3	642	2.4	840	2.8
Reinickendorf	839	5.3	1,301	4.9	1,432	4.9
Berlin	15,842	100	26,715	100	29,405	100

Prenzlauer Berg became a popular destination for many foreign young people. Nowadays, Mitte, Friedrichshain-Kreuzberg, and, more recently, Neukölln are very much en vogue and are a destination for students, "hipsters" and creatives from everywhere, and thus also from Italy (Holm and Schulz 2016).

Because of the recruitment practice of the Berlin industries, Italians were and still are prevalently active in the gastronomy and food trade (restaurants, specialty shops, wine bars), and it is these activities that give certain *Kiezes* a Mediterranean character (see Table 5 and Figure 1 below).

Table 5: Number of employees and activity rate of Italian population in Berlin in the economic sector (Manufacturing/Service Sector) – annual development4. Source: Bundesagentur für Arbeit 2017, 2018: Tab 4).

Year	Total	Manufactory %		Service %		Gastronomy %		Trade %	
2017	10,459	522	4.5	9,937	95.5	3.274	31.3	1,282	12.3
2016	9,341	459	4.9	8,882	95.1	3.141	33.6	1,175	12.6
2015	8,023	399	5.0	7,624	95.0	2.843	35.4	1,002	12.5

Figure 1: Mediterranean Lifestyle in Berlin. Source: Gino Puddu.

5 A typology of Italo-Berliners and their milieus

As mentioned above, different migration experiences, immigration modalities, as well as the political, social and cultural conditions of the countries of origin affect the development of social milieus (in the sense of the categories presented in Table 6 below). This also applies to Italo-Berliners. In the 1960s, Italy developed from an agrarian country to a modern industrialized nation. These changes, often referred to as the *miracolo economico*, also had a significant impact on southern Italy. Internal migration and information technology (radio, television, etc.) contributed significantly to the modernization of the country. Socially, a new legislation on divorce, abortion, and family affairs enhanced social

Table 6: A typology of Italians in Berlin.

Migrants	Organisations
Arbeitsmigranten	Italian parties (PCI/PSI, MSI) Organisations of migrants associated to political parties
Rebels	Non-parliamentary leftists, *Casa di Cultura popolare* Initiatives of women
Post-moderns	Independent organisations often with (inter)cultural character Parents initiative for bilingual schools Civil movement like *Mafia nein Danke*
New Mobiles	Indignati: girotondini, Movimento Stop-Berlusconi, Potere al popolo Virtual Networking (blogs), information for newcomers. professional, about parties/amusement

modernization (Gambino et al. 1980; Pombeni 2018). At the same time, compulsory education was extended and qualitative improvements in the school system were made. In the late 1960s, an inclusive school system was introduced, by which special schools were abolished (Gambino et al. 1980; Pombeni 2018). One of the claims of the 1968 student movement was an extension of the right of third-level education also for people from economically disadvantaged families. In this context Italy saw students and workers fighting side-by-side in a struggle for more social equality (Capanna [1988] 2006; Tridente 2011). As a consequence of these processes the Italian society became socially and culturally more diverse and differentiated. Already at the beginning of the 1980s, Fabris and Mortara (1986) identify eight different types of milieus in Italy: the *arcaici* (pre-industrial and traditional, church and family); the *puritani* (egalitarianism, austerity, anti-consumerism, social engagement); the *cipputi*[4] (working class, unionized, left-oriented, laborious, work ethic); the *conservatori* (respectability, decorum, social ascent, dutiful); the *integrati* (mixture of tradition and innovation, values of an industrial society, consumerism); *the affluenti* (individualistic, consummate and hedonist lifestyles, self-realization, success, money); the *emergenti* (moderate, innovative, laity, rejection of social and political extremism, expanded experiential and geographical horizons); the *progressisti* (heirs of the 1968 generation, alternative culture, aspiring an egalitarian, anti-authoritarian society, rejecting

4 *Cipputi*, a communist industrial worker, is a famous character of Francesco Tullio Altan, an Italian comic artist and satirist.

conventional rules). The different types of Italian immigrants in Berlin and their milieus, which I try to define below, partly reflect the different milieus as they had developed in Italy. We can observe similarities and overlaps across these groups, as for instance between the Italian *Arbeitsmigranten* (labor migrants) and the *rebels* in Germany, who reflect the 1968 movement in Italy.

In the following, I present a taxonomy of different milieus that can be made out in the wider Italo-Berlin community. The taxonomy is based on earlier research (see Pichler 2002); for illustration, I add ethnographic extracts, based on observation and interviews which describe central agents in the respective milieus.

5.1 The *Arbeitsmigranten* (labor migrants)

A substantial part of Italians who arrived in Berlin during the 1960s came from West Germany, to which there had been immigration from Italy since the 1950s. For many, the incentive to move to Berlin was caused by the economic benefits the Berlin's administration granted to workers who moved to the city. According to the date I have collected for an earlier study it is safe to say that even for the few Italians who arrived in Berlin in the 1960s and 1970s, the choice to move to a large city, anonymously, had an adventurous aspect, in the sense of a search for independence, emancipation, autonomy and freedom (see also Pichler 2002). They did not come to Berlin primarily for economic reasons only but mainly because they were attracted by the city, by the opportunities it offered for young people from the Italian province. So, this group includes people who took advantage of the recruitment policy, took on factory jobs in Berlin, and then focused on pursuing projects in other areas of their lives. These Italians found work above all as construction workers – a business strongly dependent on the ups and downs of the overall economic situation – and in the clothing industry – a field with a strong tendency to move the production to countries with lower wages. With the beginning of the labor migration, political parties in Italy, particularly the communist party (PCI) and the socialist (PSI) party, began to cooperate also with the emigration associations in Germany (Pichler 2002, 2014). The ethnographic description below depicts one active member of this group.

> Giorgio M., born in 1950, comes from the region of Molise in southern Italy. After completing compulsory school at the age of 14, he initially worked as an unskilled worker. In 1968, he attended a training course in Pisa as machine-locksmith. The course was financed by the EEC [the predecessor of EU] and most of the graduates went to Germany as recruited workers. Giorgio M. came to Bielefeld in January 1969. There, he immediately became a member of the IG Metall [the dominant metalworkers' union in Germany]. In 1970, after his employment contract expired, Giorgio M. decided to go to Berlin with other

Italians. It was popular to go to Berlin, and the financial help of the Senate and the Berlin allowance were, among other reasons, incentives to change the place of residence. Giorgio M. was hired by Siemens for one year and lived in a company-owned dorm. He then signed on with Waggon-Union and rented his own apartment. A Spanish colleague told him that the Berlin section of the PCI (Partito Comunista Italiano) organized a "Festa de l'Unità"[5] in the old cafeteria of a university in West Berlin. This way he came into contact with other Italians who were active in the PCI (and in the affiliated migrant organization) and in other leftist movements like "Lotta Continua". In 1976, he founded with them the 'Circolo Carlo Levi', and in the 1980s he was for some years secretary of the PCI. Together with other Italians and Germans, he was the initiator of "Coro Carlo Levi", which still exists today under the name "Il Coro Italiano", and performs on different occasions in the city's neighborhoods.

5.2 The rebels

Around 1970, some young Italians who immigrated to Berlin represented a left-wing political culture. They were attracted by the myth of Berlin as a city of the students' revolt (Pichler 2002). While some of them already held a university degree, others continued their studies in Berlin. In order to make a living, they took on work in different local spots, such as waiting in local bars or teaching Italian.

For this group, which I refer to as *rebels*, the city was a place of refuge in which they sought emancipation from the constraints of traditions and fulfilment. Socio-politically and culturally they aligned with the migrant workers. The rebels were often organized in groups connected to left wing movements (e.g., *Lotta Continua*). They established a cultural center (*Casa di Cultura Popolare* [House of Culture of the People]) and many were committed to political-cultural projects among migrants. Other rebels functioned as intellectual avant-garde in traditional left-wing organizations. An important personality among the student movements, and also for the rebels, was a professor of Italian origin, Johannes Agnoli (1925–2003, see, e.g., Agnoli and Brückner 1967; Agnoli 1996), originally from Pieve di Cadore, who in 1962 first became assistant and then professor of political theory at Otto-Suhr-Institut of Freie Universität. In 1967, Agnoli was one of the founders of the "Union of Progressive Italian Migrants", which published the newspaper *L'emigrante in lotta* [Migrants in struggle]. For these "migrants in

5 The celebration of unity (Festa dell'Unità) is a cultural and political festival organized regularly in numerous communes of Italy by the Italian Communist Party now Democratic Party. In addition to political debates and a sociocultural offer, the festival offers food specialties prepared by the members of numerous stands.

struggle", Agnoli held courses in Political Studies and Marxism at Technische Universität Berlin (Görres Agnoli 2004).

The rebels were the founders of the first women's initiatives, which were also concerned with the difficulties of migrant workers or their wives. Inspired by the example of the then-spreading parent-run kindergartens (so called *Kinderläden*, initially associated with highly liberal education ideals), some co-founded an Italian kindergarten in which an antiauthoritarian education policy. In addition to this integrative function – it was difficult for Italian children to get a place in kindergarten at the time – Italian culture and the Italian language was fostered and taught as many children only spoke local dialects at home. By contrast, the 1980s rebels were more involved in alternative projects, often orientated toward art projects. During this time, the squatter movement in Kreuzberg attracted young Italians of the rebel type. These connections occasionally brought about jobs in the various local alternative projects (Pichler 2002, 2014). Giovanna can be seen as representative of this milieu.

> Giovanna M. was born in Florence and grew up in Viareggio. After graduation, she studied biology at the University of Pisa and graduated at the age of 23. Already during school, she attended seminars and thematic workshops of the PCI. In the study period – Pisa was one of the strongholds of the 1968 protests – Giovanna M. was involved in various leftist groups; together with workers, they organized strikes, demonstrations, etc. She wanted to finish her studies quickly, "per poi volare, andare via di casa" [to fly and leave home]. During a working camp for international youth in Czechoslovakia, Giovanna M. met a young student from Berlin who became her partner. She came to Berlin in November 1970. She had left Italy and wanted to see what happened elsewhere. The idea of a life in Italy, where everything was predictable and one-dimensional, frightened her. In contrast, Berlin with its "comuni" offered thousands of opportunities and an unruly life outside of the family. In Berlin, everything was possible, for example, to go to the theater or to the opera, dressed as one wanted. It was a life without classes. In 1971, Giovanna M. received a three-year doctoral scholarship. In Berlin, she had contacts with Italians from the left scene. Initially, they met privately in the various residential communities, later they founded the Casa di Cultura Popolare. During this time, co-operation with other Italian women created a kind of "colettivo femminista" [feminist collective]; the group was co-founder of an Italian kindergarten.

5.3 The postmoderns

The increase in Italians in Berlin during the 1990s constituted a new type of migrants, distinctly different from those of the preceding periods. For these young people, often with a diploma or a university degree, emigration was chosen freely, inspired by the desire to make new experiences and to live in a different country with different people, rather than necessitated by economic needs. The

Postmoderns, who were often committed to food issues and shaped the catering industry, were among the instigators of the Slow Food movement in Berlin.

These young people initiated new business activities quite different from those of the previous migrants, even when they were employed in the traditional gastronomy sector. A new understanding of life quality, changing consumer behavior, individualist lifestyles in combination with changes in the city created new, postmodernist niches. They profited from the post-1990 changes and proved flexible with respect to economic innovation. An example of this innovative spirit are *enoteche* (Italian style wine bars) or espresso bars. The design of these restaurants reflects part of their "post-material" way of life among the young restaurant staff, who are often recruited from this postmodern milieu. We can notice the tendency of these postmoderns to create self-run intercultural associations. At the same time, the postmoderns showed hedonistic attitudes in a big city and its multicultural environment, butv they productively engaged in these (inter)cultural connections, for instance, by setting up their own associations.

> Elisa B. comes from the Marche. In 1983, she went to Berlin, where she stayed, as she was fascinated by the cultural vivacity of the city. Besides, this allowed for her to leave small-town Italy, where she felt shackled. In Berlin, she initially did a traineeship in child psychology, before she had the opportunity to acquire a restaurant along with a partner. For Elisa B., this meant making a dream come true, which had already been that of her mother. For Elisa B., the restaurant was her "second passion", to which she dedicated herself, introducing innovative ideas, such as cultural-culinary trips across some regions of Italy or through the recipes of Cinecitta – the Italian version of Hollywood. In recent years, Elisa followed the growing production of organic products in the area of Brandenburg, obtaining some of the products that she cooks directly from farmers and growers. From the beginning, her establishment was supposed to be not only a restaurant but also a meeting place for Italians and for Germans interested in Italian culture. Today, there are photography exhibitions by Italian and German artists, as well as from other nationalities, and the restaurant is endowed with a small library of books, newspapers and magazines in the two languages. Italian films and videos are shown in non-dubbed versions, and Italian language classes are organized. The Deutsch-Italienischer Freundschaftskreis e.V. (DIF [Circle of German and Italian Friends]) and Tubo Kurvo associations have offices in the establishment. Elisa B., along with her partner and other guests of the establishment, was the co-initiator of the Slow Food culinary movement in Germany. Among the personnel, Elisa's recruits are young people who are working to pay off their studies and who consider themselves members of the same "alternative-postmodern" milieu. In a nutshell, the establishment operates as a meeting place for a new generation of Italians who are looking for an opportunity to live and work in Germany and Berlin.

5.4 New mobiles

More recently, Berlin has been confronted with a new type of mobility. Mobility is part of present-day Europe as managers and freelancers but also young people, irrespective of their educational level, work in temporary jobs like catering, call centers, logistics, in the cleaning sector or in start-ups. This type of economy creates forms of exclusion and precariousness (e.g., food deliverers). Precarious working conditions are generally typical for this milieu sometimes referred to as the *precarious creatives* (Castel and Dörre 2009). This new type of migrants has a critical attitude toward traditional religious or political groups and patters and they thus founded their own groups.

> Tina S. was born in 1986 in southern Italy. She studied Industrial Design at the University of Naples. She had no previous work experience in her field of study and no further experience abroad when she came to Berlin without friends or any significant information. Job search and the hope to specialize further were the motives for her decision. Tina S. is currently working as a waitress in a well-known Italian restaurant in Berlin, whose owner is also very active in the social and cultural sector. Berlin, she adds, is beautiful, but the integration is difficult. Berlin is not a simple, easy city, even if it initially seems so. So, her expectations have not been completely fulfilled. Tina S. hopes that after the bureaucratic hurdles and difficulties of an immigrant, the fact that she has left her family and home will be rewarded. She wants to improve her language skills and finally work in her profession rather than in restaurants or similar jobs. She emphasizes though that these jobs are suitable options without high language skill requirements. Due to her work in gastronomy, Tina has only Italians friends.

Besides the typical associations with emigration, the migrants of the 1990s and 2000s founded some formal or informal associations which mirror their cultural needs and their political orientation. These associations serve as social networks for the new immigrants or for Italian entrepreneurs who recruit their staff from a specific milieu. The new types of migrants, however, take on a critical stance on these associations, create their own initiatives and found other organizations which corresponded more to their social and cultural needs and interests. Some of these initiatives, again, founded bilingual German-Italian kindergartens, which shape the image of the *Kiezes*. Additionally, bilingual German-Italian European schools (grammar schools, secondary schools and *Gymnasien*) convey Italian culture on families of whichever nationalities.

With the arrival of the new mobiles, a new form of protest, the "indignados", was established. The so-called "girotondini" (self-run) brought a certain playfulness to the scene of political protest in Berlin. Both Germans and Italians of different age groups and migration experiences organized, for instance, an "anti-Berlusconi party" in front of the Italian Embassy. Some of these new mobiles are active in various support groups for refugees and asylum seekers, who, in some cases, first arrived in Italy and then moved on to Berlin (see the activity of the Association Koinè).

Let us summarize these brief insights into the different milieus of Italians in Berlin. While the *Arbeitsmigranten* (labor migrants) were characteristic of a period of the past, we nowadays find types such as the *postmodernists*, the *rebels* and the *new mobiles* among more recently arriving immigrants. The boundaries between the different types can be fluid and the different groups may share some of their typical characteristics. The *Arbeitsmigranten* and the *rebels* for instance have their political leftist attitudes in common – the former in more traditional parties like the PCI, the latter in groups outside traditional political parties. The biographies above also show that there are connections between the politically active *Arbeitsmigranten* and the *rebels*, for instance in the activities concerned with the Festa dell'Unità, the Casa di Cultura Popolare, etc. The *rebels* and the *postmoderns* are united in part in an academic habitus with respective university degrees or the aspiration to a higher cultural capital. This also applies to some of the *new mobiles*. *Arbeitsmigranten* and *new mobiles* have in common that the choice to emigrate was also triggered by economic pressure. Finally, politically active members can be found among the new migrants, which resembles characteristics of the *rebels* albeit without the latter's ties to established parties or other groups. Table 7, shows a synopsis of these the shared characteristics of the different types of migrants.

Table 7: Differences and similarities between the types of milieus.

Type	Political Engagement	Institutional Cultural Capital/ University Degree	Economic Factor/ Push factor
Arbeitsmigranten	+	–	+
Rebels	+	+	–
Postmodernists	–	+	–
New Mobiles	+/–	+/–	+

In sum, we are facing new types of immigration from Italy to Berlin in the recent years. They are more and more diverse in terms of political activity and of their levels of education (Tirabassi and del Prà 2014). As will be elaborated in the following, the diversification into different cultural milieus can be associated with the presence of different types of Italian restaurants in Berlin, which sell different ideas of Italy.

6 Milieus, lifestyles and consumers: the establishment and transformation of Italian gastronomy in Berlin

Germany, as well as Italy and the rest of Western Europe, experienced Americanization of consumption and became a consumer society after World War II.[6] Following the experience of fascism, war and poverty, consumption allowed to create some distance from the unpleasant past; the consumption of products assumed a role of purification – moral catharsis, repentance and an attenuation of painful memories, loss, hunger, etc. As a result, the discredited ideologies, values and visions of the past were no longer regarded as targets of identification and orientation. The integrative ideology of the nation was disputed. The cultural and social needs were increasingly met through the consumption of products (Siegrist 1997). While the Federal Republic of Germany was critically depicted as a consumption democracy, it became a politically and socially stable construct exactly through the experience of the well-being which its citizens had achieved (Wildt 1997).

With the achievement of a relative economic well-being in the post-war period, eating out in a restaurant was no longer an exceptional event reserved for important festivities like weddings and baptisms for the middle and lower classes in Germany (Schwendter 1995). Italian catering successfully established in Germany and found its place in a new democracy of consumption. There was soon no German town or country, in both the West and in what used to be the GDR, where you could not find an Italian restaurant or pizzeria (Möhring 2012).

In the 1960s, the legendary *Rosario*, the king of pizza, introduced pizza in Berlin. American soldiers stationed in the city are said to have been the first enthusiastic costumers and they allegedly already were familiar with pizza from Italy. It is equally plausible that they already knew it from their home country, where Italian immigration had started long before (Tamponi 1991). Pizza pioneers were facing a market that did not always supply the appropriate goods and ingredients. Restaurant owners were forced to improvise, this way creating a new form of "Italian gastronomy". For the pizza toppings, ingredients were used that were available on the Berlin market: *Plockwurst* and cheese had to replace mozzarella and the *salamino piccante*. What initially appeared as a makeshift solution soon turned out a successful recipe. With these adjustments, the pizza

6 The following section is based on ethnographic observation in Berlin, and gives an overview on restaurants, which were and are important for the development of Italian gastronomy.

satisfied the German taste so that Germans gradually took to it. It was the beginning of the *pizza alla tedesca*, the German-style pizza (Pichler, 1997: 160).

The boom of Italian cuisine in Berlin started in the late 1960s and continued throughout the 1970s with the help of the *Arbeitsmigranten*. At that time, a large number of Italian restaurants opened, which, different from Italian traditions, were often restaurants and pizzerias at the same time, where a large variety of foods was offered, though often not very "Italian". Encouraged by the success of these venues, many Italians extended their presence in different districts of the city. Often the owners did not possess specific knowledge in the field of cooking.

> For Ugo R., born in Tripoli, Libya, his migration to Germany was the second "migration" in his life. After the Second World War, his family had left Tripoli, where the father owned several shops, and returned to their hometown C. There, Ugo R. learned the traditional handicraft of a ceramist and at the same time attended evening courses at a technical school until graduation, as his family, who had financial difficulties through the forced return migration, could not finance his studies. In 1964, Ugo R. got a job at a German company in Bavaria. One year later, he came to Berlin, where he first worked as tiler. Inspired by the example of other Italian restaurant owners, Ugo R. opened a ristorante pizzeria in the mid-1970s.

The success of these places may be partly attributed to the development of mass tourism, which in the 1960s brought more and more Germans to Italy. Rimini for example earned the nickname *Teutonengrill* ('Teuton grill'). On their return to Germany after vacation, many Germans were eager to enjoy their vacation experience at home and made going to Italian restaurants a habit. Italian restaurants were generally cheaper than German restaurants, also because it was still possible to recruit Italian low cost labor (Corni and Dipper 2012). This type of vacation substitute may also explain the interior design of many Italian restaurants in Berlin. They are, for example, often decorated with fishing nets, oyster shells, or, in other cases, in an antique manner imitating ancient Roman columns and temple vestiges.

The 1980s marked a crisis, especially for traditional restaurants and pizzerias. Many were taken over by immigrants from other countries, who continued to operate them as typical Italian restaurants but using cheaper staff. Some Italian restaurant owners tried to overcome the crisis by improving the quality of the food and the decor (by taking off rough plaster walls, fishing nets, etc.). There went along with a rediscovery of what was considered traditional food and many establishments began to emulate the *osterie* of Italy. Indeed, the new Italian restaurants in Berlin's suburbs began to resemble the Italian *trattorie* and *osterie*. Restaurant owners of this type successfully made use of the niche between luxury or home-style restaurants and the old *ristorante* pizzerias. These places respond to the needs of a new generation of the post-industrial era with less conventional styles and interests who do not understood themselves as bourgeois and who, quite distinct from 1950s German tourists in Italy, are in tendency hedonistic.

> Mario F. is from the province of Agrigento in Sicily. At the beginning of 1980, his two brothers met him in Germany, and one found work in construction and the other as a pizza-maker as well. In the summer of 1980, Mario F. decided to go and see his relatives in Germany, after having finished his secondary school studies. Even without having a clear migration plan, he knew that he had a reference point, while in those years it was not rare for young Italians without contacts to spend the night in dormitories or on the benches of the Bahnhof Zoo (the train statoin at the zoo). As he still did not know the language very well, he began to work as a barman (following the typical career in Italian catering in Germany, moving on from barman to waiter, from dish-washer to cook). Later, Mario F. was able to open his own restaurant in a centrally-located and elegant neighborhood of West Berlin, where he began to propose a different type of gastronomy. Using his cultural and social capital, he created a "Promi Lokal" (a place for celebrities to meet), frequented by politicians, people of the world of culture, etc. Taking advantage of the rediscovery of Tuscany by the Berlin population, with its plain, simple and "authentic" cuisine, Mario F. (although from Sicily) opened a Trattoria Toscana, where the cooking was finally free from compromises made in the past.

For that period, we can observe a paradigm shift with regard not only to the debate on consumption and consumerism but also to its practices. Ecological consequences of consumerism are now perceived as a global issue (Andersen 1997). With the globalization of consumption, social distinctness is no longer performed through discrimination against the common-place and ordinary alone, but in much more complex ways, by drawing on a multitude of opportunities and through developing new styles of distinction (Bourdieu 1987). Social differences are not only encoded by the job, the professional position or the academic degree, but predominantly by different lifestyles (Wildt 1997).

For a new generation – consumers and caterers alike, all grown up in a post-industrial society, critical towards consumerism and familiar with certain values and alternative lifestyles – abundance and immoderation are not any longer crucial for their social identity. A lot more relevant now are the authenticity of the consumed products and frugality in one's consumer behaviour.

The spread of postmodern-alternative values further encouraged the ongoing existing trend within the Italian gastronomy to focus a more elaborate lifestyle, with an altered, often critical attitude towards mass consumption and with a stronger focus on particular food habits. These new developments coincide with the re-emerging interest of Italian regional cuisines. In this process, young Italian immigrants play an important role, as they are often, more open toward taking new paths and occupying new niches in the food market. The success of Italian restaurants has opened up new market of niches for other Italians: as producers of pasta and dairy products or as importers of wines and products from their regions of origin.

A generational change among Italian restaurant owners helped transforming the supply lines. The new Italian restaurants no longer provide a mass cuisine but a cuisine that signifies differentiation. This implies the offer of a differentiated regional cuisine. A pioneer of this offer was Pino B., originally from Basilicata, who opened a restaurant called *A Muntagnola* in 1991, offering not that much an Italian cuisine in disguise but, according to his self-decription, a "poor cuisine rich in ideas, traditions and culture". The restaurant uses regional products, products that were "rediscovered", often from cooperatives, small family producers from Lucania, and thus contributing to sustainable production in the region of origin.

Even for the younger generation of migrants, trade and supply of products from the region of origin instead of mass-produced goods, represent an alternative and a resource in which family members are also involved. Now we can observe that "new" Italian restaurants also offer a vegan cuisine, especially in neighborhoods where this type of customer is believed to be predominant (e.g., in Kreuzberg, Mitte or Friedrichshain).

Moreover, it is possible to observe a revival of what was once idealized as small and beautiful. Surely, this is partly because capital is available for investment. Several places have recently opened as small taverns. The dishes characteristic of the Venetian, Bolognese or Neapolitan tradition are simple, rustic and minimalist. The ingredients and the wines come from family farms and wineries of the restaurant owner's areas of origin.

7 Milieus, restaurants and names

In his book *Die Gesellschaft der Singularitäten*, Andreas Reckwitz describes how a post-industrial economy has created a society of singularity, which stands in contrast to the social logic of the "universal" of standardized industrial societies (Reckwitz, 2017: 27). Whenever a particular scenery is important for self-realization, food is an important symbol of this singularity of culture and lifestyle: "Das Essen ist in extensiver Weise zu einem Gegenstand der Sorge, des Genusses und Erlebens, des Wissens und der Kompetenzen, der Performanz und des sozialen Prestiges geworden, ausgestattet mit einer identitätsbildenden Kraft: Man ist, was man isst" [In extensive ways, food has become an object of care, pleasure and experience, of knowledge and competence, of performance and social prestige, equipped with the power to constitute identity: You are what you eat] (Reckwitz 2017: 309). Authenticity and acentric construction in a society of singularity find their clearest expression in food culture, according to Reckwitz (2017: 309). One could argue that while the democratization of eating habits in the 1960s (eating out) and the popular Italian food of the 1960s/1970s represent the general (*das Allgemeine*), the changes in gastronomy and tastes of customers elaborated above, including the different types of the habitus of customers (*rebels, new mobiles*, etc.) are symbols of a tendency to produce singularity. The furnishing of rooms, the dishes offered (the menu) and, in particular, the names of restaurants are codes of these transformations: from the *Allgemeine* ('the Italian') of the popular (touristic) time to the various different singularities.

It is possible to find a connection between the above-mentioned types of migrants and different styles of restaurants. Changing consumer behavior, urban changes and a larger number of items available lead to new opportunities. The ability to exploit their cultural and social capital allows today's restaurant owners to offer not only "ethnic food" but also a milieu-orientated culture. They thus play with the imagination of the Italian way of life, targeting a diverse array of customer milieus from the dolce vita lifestyle evoked in the Italian films, books or songs to the left-radical chic (Pichler 2013). In this context, we can observe an interdependence between milieu provenience, cultural capital of the entrepreneurs and time of immigration on the one hand and the naming of the restaurants on the other. It was indicated above that tourism had an important impact on the development of the Italian gastronomy in Germany. Therefore, the names of many restaurants that opened at the time recall the tourist sites either from the experience of German visitors or through famous films, songs, etc.

Naming connects with the habitus of the owners but also with the possible clients. It is a result of milieu-specific sociolinguistic practices and an example of symbolic distinction. In the political climate in the 1970s, for instance, young Italians would take advantage of their cultural and social capital by opening places with a "left-wing" image, like a mix between brewery and tavern. Italian left-wing culture fascinated many Germans, who wanted to show their solidarity with this movement and with the culture of migration, between a glass of red wine and a plate of *lasagna*. Some new establishments after German reunification, in an air of nostalgia, rediscovered the 1970s left-wing environment. This type of memory, which in part had some folkloristic connotations, became an environment of identification for contemporary anti-globalization activists. Accordingly, restaurants, pizzerias or pubs from this context have the names of popular heroes and rebels or add *Cucina Popolare* to their names, in the tradition of the Festa dell'Unità in Italy.

With processes of individualization, personal or family names are used increasingly. A personal name guarantees authentic Italian-ness and symbolically means that *mein Italiener*, 'my Italian (restaurant)' is truly Italian. Other young restaurant owners adhere to practices of "glocalism" by importing and offering organic wines and other products from their homeland – benefiting from a new trend towards organic products. The names of their restaurants also aim at expressing both authenticity and archaism and sometimes make use of local dialects. Thus, Gaia N., an Italo-Berliner belonging to the generation of *new mobiles*, opened a branch of Gusto Nudo-Independent Winegrowers, who, with respect to biodiversity, refuse to cooperate with the chemical industry.

The following Table 8 gives an overview of the different migrant groups, the types of economy they work in and the kinds of names the respective establishments tend to carry.

Table 8: Migrant typologies and restaurant names.

Migrants	Economy	Names
Migrant Workers	**Industry/ construction, ristorante-Pizzeria**	**Often connected with touristic-places:** *Bardolino, Portofino, San Marco, Venezia, Rapallo, Roma, Capri, Il porto, La Baja, Rimini*
Rebels	**Student-Pub-osterias, bars,university, alternative projects**	**Often connected with an imagination of leftist lifestyles:** *Osteria 1, Il Casolare Cucina Popolare* **Folk-heroes or social rebels (Hobsbawm):** *Masaniello, I Golosi Briganti*
Postmodern	**New lifestyle (trattorias/enoteca, bars), creative industries**	**Individualistic-modernist, e.g. names of the owners:** *Da Mario, Francucci`s, Anna & Bruno, Osteria Sippi* **Tuscany-fraction:** *Trattoria Toscana, La Maremma, Gallo Nero* **New touristic destinations with distinction: Salento/ Cilento:** *Masseria, Tropea* **Literature/Film/Arts:** *Gattopardo, Il Cenacolo, Arcimboldo, Fellini*
New Mobiles	**Higher services sector/ freelancer/ university students catering trade creative industries**	**Glocalism: Dialect and regional heritage** *Malafemmena, Osteria In Bacan, Jamme Ja, De Noatri, Masteca e tasi* **Ironic-Dadaistic** *Muret la Barba* *To Beef or not To Beef* **International** *The Winery, Switch 21* *Thal wine bar*

Interestingly, it is occasionally also possible to observe a link between socio-demographic characteristics of different Berlin neighborhoods and the names of Italian restaurants. The following Table 9 provides examples, or rather, possible impressions, of these associations. Charlottenburg and Zehlendorf/Dahlem are mostly quarters with high and middle class inhabitants (professionals, teachers, professors, etc.). Accordingly, the names of the restaurants are connected either with constructions of "luxury" or "culture". Marienfelde is more inhabited by lower class citizens (workers, craftsmen, lower civil servants), thus, the names of restaurants are more linked to constructions of popularity and not so much a symbol of distinction (Amt für Statistik Berlin-Brandenburg 2017). The new lifestyle-intellectuals and young hipsters are meanwhile establishing in traditional working class quarters like Kreuzberg und Neukölln, attracted by the urban character of the different *Kiezes*. With the renewal of some neighborhoods, the inhabitants' socio-demographic and ethnic structure also changed (Holm and Schulz 2016).

Table 9: Links between naming and Berlin quarters.

(Charlottenburg) Luxury	(Zehlendorf/ Dahlem) Culture	(Marienfelde) Popular	(Kreuzberg/ Neukölln) Glocal/International
Via Condotti	Villa Medici	Il Falco	Jamme Ja/ Osteria el bacan
Brunello	Galileo	Ristorante Colombina	The Winery

The menus have also undergone change: while in the past and in the old-fashioned restaurants, many different varieties of newly invented spaghetti dishes were to be found, now the menus are rather minimalistic and more "authentic", depending on whether a restaurant tends toward either posh or frugal. With the opportunity to present their localities online, further possibilities have arisen to give an individual touch to Italian businesses. Besides presentation in Italian or German, there is an increasing tendency to have English-language menus, especially in quarters like Friedrichshain, Kreuzberg or Neukölln, Kreuzkölln where the public is often anglophone or touristic.

The Table 10 below presents examples of an "old style" menu and a menu more typical for the creation of newer, "authentic" styles

Table 10: Dishes, milieus and distinction/singularity.

Old Style	New "authentic" Style
Pasta	*Pasta e Risotto*
Spaghetti Pomodoro E Basilico mit Tomatensauce und Basilikum	Tagliatelle ai porcini e bietola croccante (Tagliatelle mit Steinpilzen und frittiertem Mangold)
Spaghetti Bolognese mit Fleischsauce	Ravioli di zucca e ricotta di bufala con salsa di scamorza (Ravioli gefüllt mit Kürbis und Büffel-Ricotta an Scamorzasauce)
Spaghetti Carbonara mit Schinken, Ei, Sahne und Parmesankäse	Gnocchi di patate con calamaretti e bottarga (Kartoffel-Gnocchi mit jungen Tintenfischen und getrocknetem Rogen von der Meeräsche)
Spaghetti Diavolo mit Olivenöl und Knoblauch, scharf	Straccetti al finocchietto con ragù di salsiccia Fenchel-Straccetti (Pasta mit Kalbs-Salsiccia Ragout)
Spaghetti Amatriciana mit Speck, Zwiebeln und Knoblauch	Spaghettini alle vongole veraci (Spaghettini mit frischen Venusmuscheln)
Spaghetti Orient mit frischen Paprika, frischen Tomaten, Zwiebeln und Knoblauch	Risotto al limone con crudo di gamberi e pesto di basilico (Zitronen-Risotto mit Garnelentatar und Basilikum-Pesto) (http://www.boccadibacco.de/speisekarte)
Spaghetti Al Pesto mit Basilikumsauce	
Spaghetti Caprese mit Sardellen, Thunfisch, Oliven und Mozzarella in Tomatensauce	*Gli Antipasti*
Spaghetti Mare E Monti mit Meeresfrüchten, frischen Champignons, Knoblauch in leichter Tomatensauce	(Appetizer) Burrata, olio al basilico e pomodori secchi (Burrata, basil olives oil and dry tomatoes)
Spaghetti Con Broccoli mit Broccoli und Fetakäse überbacken in feiner Tomatensauce	Baccalà, vellutata di ceci e rosmarino (Stockfish, chickpeas cream and rosmary oil)
Spaghetti Barolo mit Schweinefiletspitzen und Pfifferlingen in Rahmsauce	Carciofi alla romana (Artischockes roman way)
Penne All`Arrabiata Makkaroni mit Knoblauch in scharfer Tomatensauce	Carpaccio, rucola, Parmigaino e Balsamico al lampone (Beef Carpaccio, Rucola, Parmigiano Reggiano 18 months and raspberry balsamico)

Table 10 (continued)

Old Style	**New "authentic" Style**
Penne Alla Sicilliana Auberginen, Mozzarella, Schweinefiletspitzen, Knoblauch und Zwiebeln in Tomatensauce \Penne All`Ortolana Makkaroni mit Fetakäse, Broccoli und Knoblauch in feiner Tomatensahnesauce Penne Al Quattro Formaggi Makkaroni mit vier verschiedenen Käsesorten überbacken And more and more and more.........pasta & Co. (http://www.barolo-lieferservice.de/#cat7)	Misto della casa, formaggi, salumi e nostre verdure sott'olio (Mix Antipasti, cheese, salami und vegatables) (https://www.mastecaetasi.de/en/our-menu/dinner/)

8 Conclusion

The Italo-Berliner community is characterized by the presence of various milieus, which, in combination with their different lifestyles, contribute to manifold economic activities also in the gastronomy and food trade. Italian restaurants and their names are a result of milieu-specific sociolinguistic practices. Naming is connected to the habitus of the owner but also to the sociocultural and economic characteristics of the quarters in which the restaurants are located. It is the result of interrelations of different factors and it can be regarded as a symbol of change from a universal, standardized mass society to a post-industrial and postmodern society of competitive singularities. The presence of Italian establishments is attractive for Berlin's inhabitants. In fact, parts of the quarters of the city have won urban quality through the activity of ethnic entrepreneurs. The presence of these places attracts a different clientele, and they are an attraction for young people. Thus, the names of the restaurants indicate cultural transformation and transnational interaction in an increasingly globalized world.

References

Agnoli, Johannes. 1996. *Subversive Theorie. "Die Sache selbst" und ihre Geschichte. Eine Berliner Vorlesung*. Freiburg: Ça ira-Verlag.

Agnoli, Johannes & Peter Brückner. 1967. *Die Transformation der Demokratie*. Berlin: Voltaire Verlag.

Amt für Statistik Berlin-Brandenburg. 2017. *Regionaler Sozialbericht Berlin und Brandenburg 2017*. Potsdam.

Amt für Statistik Berlin-Brandenburg. 2018. *Statistischer Bericht. Einwohnerinnen und Einwohner im Land Berlin am 31. Dezember 2017*. Grunddaten. Potsdam.

Andersen, Arne. 1997. Mentalitätswechsel und ökologische Konsequenzen des Konsumismus. Die Durchsetzung der Konsumgesellschaft in den fünfziger Jahren. In Hannes Siegrist, Hartmut Kaelble & Jürgen Kocka (eds.), *Europäische Konsumgeschichte: Zur Gesellschafts- und Kulturgeschichte des Konsums (18. bis 20. Jahrhundert)*, 763–791. Frankfurt & New York: Campus.

Bourdieu, Pierre. 1983. Ökonomisches Kapital, kulturelles Kapital, soziales Kapital. In Reinhard Kreckel (ed.), *Soziale Ungleichheiten* (Soziale Welt Sonderband 2), 183–199. Göttingen: Schwartz.

Bourdieu, Pierre. 1987 [1979]. *Die feinen Unterschiede. Kritik der gesellschaftlichen Urteilskraft*, German edn. Frankfurt am Main: Suhrkamp.

Bundesagentur für Arbeit. 2017. *Beschäftigte nach Staatsangehörigkeiten – Deutschland, Länder und Kreise (Quartalszahlen) – Juni 2016*. Nürnberg: Bundesagentur für Arbeit.

Bundesagentur für Arbeit. 2018. *Beschäftigte nach Staatsangehörigkeiten – Deutschland, Länder und Kreise (Quartalszahlen) – Juni 2017*. Nürnberg: Bundesagentur für Arbeit.

Capanna, Mario. 2006 [1988]. *Formidabili quegli anni*. Milan: Garzanti Libri.

Castel, Robert & Klaus Dörre (eds). 2009. *Prekarität, Abstieg, Ausgrenzung. Die soziale Frage am Beginn des 21. Jahrhunderts*. Frankfurt & New York: Campus.

Corni, Gustavo & Christof Dipper (eds.). 2012. *Italiener in Deutschland im 19. und 20. Jahrhundert. Kontakte, Wahrnehmungen, Einflüsse*. Berlin: Duncker & Humblot.

Dohse, Knuth. 1981. *Ausländische Arbeiter und bürgerlicher Staat. Genese und Funktion von staatlicher Ausländerpolitik und Ausländerrecht. Vom Kaiserreich bis zur Bundesrepublik Deutschland*. Königstein: Hain.

Fabris, Giampaolo & Vittorio Mortara. 1986. *Le otto Italie. Dinamica e frammentazione della società italiana*. Milan: Mondadori.

Gambino, Antonio, Giorgio Galli, Lucio Colletti, Tullio de Mauro, Giorgio Ruffolo, Nora Federici, Carla Ravaioli & Gianni Borgna. 1980. *Dal '68 a oggi. Come siamo e come eravamo*. Bari: Laterza.

Gillmeister, Helmut, Jürgen Fijalkowski & Hermann Kurthen. 1989. *Ausländerbeschäftigung in der Krise? Die Beschäftigungschancen und -risiken ausländischer Arbeitnehmer am Beispiel der West-Berliner Industrie* (Beiträge zur Sozialökonomik der Arbeit Band 21). Berlin: Edition Sigma.

Görres Agnoli, Barbara. 2004. *Johannes Agnoli. Eine biografische Skizze*. Hamburg: konkret Literatur Verlag.

Holm, Andrej & Guido Schulz. 2016. GentriMap: Ein Messmodell für Gentrification und Verdrängung. In Ilse Helbrecht (ed.), *Gentrifizierung in Berlin: Verdrängungsprozesse und Bleibestrategien*, 287–318. Bielefeld: transcript.

Hradil, Stefan. 2006. Soziale Milieus – eine praxisorientierte Forschungsperspektive. *Aus Politik und Zeitgeschichte* 44–45. 3–10.

Istat. 2017. *Migrazioni internazionali e interne della popolazione residente*. Rom.

Möhring, Maren. 2012. *Fremdes Essen: Die Geschichte der ausländischen Gastronomie in der Bundesrepublik Deutschland*. München: Oldenbourg Verlag.

Motte, Jan, Rainer Ohliger & Anne von Oswald (eds.). 1999. *50 Jahre Bundesrepublik, 50 Jahre Einwanderung: Nachkriegsgeschichte als Migrationsgeschichte*. Frankfurt & New York: Campus.

Nikolinakos, Marios. 1973. *Politische Ökonomie der Gastarbeiterfrage. Migration und Kapitalismus*. Reinbek: Rowohlt.

Perry, Thomas & Sebastian Beck. 2009. Migrants in Germany – Socio-Economic Environments and Housing-Related Interests. In Brüning Henning & Elke Mittmann (eds.), *Die anderen Städte, Bd 8: Stadt und Migration: The other cities*, 43–51. Dessau: Stiftung Bauhaus Dessau.

Pichler, Edith. 2002. Pioniere, Arbeitsmigranten, Rebellen, Postmoderne und Mobile: Italiener in Berlin. *Archiv für Sozialgeschichte 42*. 257–274.

Pichler, Edith. 2013. *Von Arbeitssuchenden, Empörten und kreativem Prekariat. Die neue italienische Einwanderung nach Berlin*. Berlin: Heinrich Böll-Stiftung.

Pichler, Edith. 2014. Dai vecchi pionieri alla nuova mobilità. Italiani a Berlino tra inclusione ed esclusione. In Elettra de Salvo, Gherardo Ugolini, Laura Priori (eds.), *Italo-Berliner. Gli italiani che cambiano la capitale tedesca*. 25–40. Milano-Udine: Mimesis.

Pichler, Edith. 2017. Double Emigration: Geographical and Cultural? The Participation of Italian Women in the German Labour Market. *International Review of Sociology* 27(1). 25–36.

Pombeni, Paolo. 2018. *Che cosa resta del '68*. Bologna: Il Mulino.

Prontera, Grazia. 2009. *Partire, tornare, restare? L'esperienza migratoria dei lavoratori italiani nella Repubblica Federale Tedesca nel secondo dopoguerra*. Milan: Guerini e Associati.

Reckwitz, Andreas. 2017. *Die Gesellschaft der Singularitäten*. Berlin: Suhrkamp.

Schwendter, Rolf. 1995. *Arme Essen – Reiche Speisen. Neuere Sozialgeschichte der zentraleuropäischen Gastronomie*. Wien: Promedia.

Siegrist, Hannes, Hartmut Kaelble & Jürgen Kocka (eds.). 1997. *Europäische Konsumgeschichte: Zur Gesellschafts- und Kulturgeschichte des Konsums (18. bis 20. Jahrhundert)*. Frankfurt & New York: Campus.

Sinus Sociovision. 2007. *Die Milieus der Menschen mit Migrationshintergrund in Deutschland*. Heidelberg: Sinus Sociovision GmbH.

Sinus Sociovision. 2008. *Zentrale Ergebnisse der Sinus-Studie über Migranten-Milieus in Deutschland*. Heidelberg: Sinus Sociovision GmbH.

Statistisches Bundesamt. 2017. *Bevölkerung und Erwerbstätigkeit. Bevölkerung mit Migrationshintergrund. Ergebnisse des Mikrozensus 2016*. Wiesbaden: Statistisches Bundesamt (Destatis).

Tamponi, Mario. 1991. *Italiener in Berlin. Alle Wege führen nach Rom – manche von Rom nach Berlin*. Berlin: Ausländerbeauftragte des Senats von Berlin.

Tirabassi, Maddalena & Alvise del Prà. 2014. *La meglio Italia. Le mobilità italiane nel XXI secolo*. Torino: Accademia University Press.

Tridente, Alberto. 2011. *Dalla parte dei diritti. Settanta anni di lotta*. Torino: Rosenberg & Sellier.

Vester, Michael, Peter von Oertzen, Heiko Geiling, Thomas Hermann & Dagmar Müller. 2001. *Soziale Milieus im gesellschaftlichen Strukturwandel. Zwischen Integration und Ausgrenzung*. Frankfurt am Main: Suhrkamp.

Wildt, Michael. 1997. Die Kunst der Wahl. Zur Entwicklung des Konsum in Westdeutschland in den 1950er Jahren. In Hannes Siegrist, Hartmut Kaelble & Jürgen Kocka (eds.), *Europäische Konsumgeschichte: Zur Gesellschafts- und Kulturgeschichte des Konsums (18. bis 20. Jahrhundert)*, 307–348. Frankfurt & New York: Campus.
Yildiz, Erol. 2013. *Die weltoffene Stadt. Wie Migration Globalisierung zum urbanen Alltag macht*. Bielefeld: transcript.

Miriam Stock

10 From authentication to distinction – consuming Arabic in Berlin's gentrifying falafel economies

1 Introduction

Florian, a Berlin resident in his early thirties, is a huge fan of falafel. His new friends introduced him to it over fifteen years ago, when he moved to Berlin from a small West German town to study literature and to live in the vibrant capital. In 2008, when I met him in front of a falafel store, he declared himself a regular falafel consumer. His favorite place is called *Maroush*, which is located in the multicultural, alternative and trendy quarter of Berlin-Kreuzberg. Maroush is a typical falafel snack store in Berlin. The interior is composed of oriental-style tiles; old photos of Beirut hang from the dark rubbed-off walls, Arabic calligraphy decorates the menu, and as background music, an album of the famous Lebanese singer *Fairuz* runs around the clock.

Florian does not only like *Maroush* because of the food, but also because of its atmosphere, which mirrors his consumption style. In an interview, he states: "You know, I do not like these gentrification types of bars and cafés. Those hipster places in Prenzlauer Berg do not appeal to me at all. I prefer down-to-earth and traditional. Also when it comes to Arabic snack places, I prefer those where the atmosphere is traditional".[1]

Even though Florian perceives himself, with his taste for "authentic" falafel, as having nothing to do with gentrification, the Arabic (connoted) snack has become an integral part of Berlin's urban upgrading. During the last three decades, Arabic stores selling falafel, shawarma and halloumi have flourished in the gentrifying districts of Kreuzberg, Friedrichshain and Prenzlauer Berg in Berlin. This is far from accidental. Migrant entrepreneurs from Arab countries such as Lebanon, Palestine and Iraq promoted Berlin-style tastes of falafel and other dishes from the beginning as a European alternative to hipster middle class consumers' tastes.

One key to falafel's success lies precisely in branding an orientalized authenticity (see Said 2003) in the stores, which is mediated via – among other

1 Interview with Florian, 17th June 2009; translated from German. First names mentioned in the article are anonymized.

https://doi.org/10.1515/9781501508103-010

aspects – different deployments of Arabic linguistic symbols in decoration and atmosphere. This article attempts to analyze these deployments and consumptions of Arabic and other linguistic symbols in Berlin's falafel economies and examines their role in constructing authenticity in consumption places. I will show that consumers in Berlin's gentrification process favor representations understood as "authentic" of Arabic, not only because it meets their own Orientalist imaginations, but also because it allows them to perform and reify their own distinction vis-à-vis other social groups within and beyond the city. Authenticity here is understood not as a real origin, but as a cultural construct embedded in different socio-historical contexts (see Zukin 2010).

In the first section of this article, I will discuss the interrelations between (commercial) gentrification, taste and distinction and highlight why consuming authenticity can be understood as a key factor in this process. The section then discusses the commodification of ethnicities and language which form an important aspect of authentication. The second section moves to Berlin's falafel economies and provides some background on their rise and spread in Berlin's gentrification process and the role of Arab migrant entrepreneurs in this. In the third section, I will look more closely into different means of deploying Arabic and other languages in falafel stores, such as spoken language, decor and background music, and how these are recognized and evaluated by European consumers. Finally, I will introduce different representations of the döner snack, which consumers in my study, in the context of Berlin's gentrification process, mark as completely inauthentic because of its McDonaldized appeal, and from which they distinguish themselves quite strongly, conceiving of their tastes as superior in relation to what is regarded as "lower class". Here, taste for authenticity plays out as "a tool of power" (Zukin 2010: 3), since those inauthentic stores are marginalized in gentrified neighborhoods.

This article draws on ethnographic research on falafel stores in Berlin that was conducted between 2008 and 2010. The research was funded by the University Viadrina in Frankfurt Oder with a PhD-scholarship in the program "transnational spaces". The ethnographic research consisted of participant observation in the eateries, the collection of data in restaurant guides and internet forums, a mapping process as well as interviews with nineteen falafel store owners and nineteen falafel consumers (all conducted in German). Owners were all migrants to Berlin with Arab origins (Lebanese, Iraqi, Palestinian, Tunisian), who opened or took over their eateries in Berlin's inner-city quarters between 1987 and 2008. In the semi-structured interviews, they were asked about their entrepreneurial practices, strategies and motivations as well as observations about consumers and the neighborhoods. Consumers were between 18 and 42 years old, resided in different gentrifying neighborhoods (Kreuzberg, Prenzlauer Berg,

Mitte, etc.), were students or young professionals (social workers, journalists, film makers), spent parts of their daily routines in these neighborhoods and were regular falafel eaters. The majority of them moved to Berlin from other German regions in order to study or work, and others came from The Netherlands, Switzerland and England. Only two interviewees were of Berlin origin. The consumers' interview guide consisted of questions about personal backgrounds, eating-out habits, daily eating routines in Berlin's inner-city neighborhoods, as well as perceptions of falafel and other eateries. To detect consumers' taste preferences, interview partners were confronted with eight different photos of falafel stores and one döner store in Berlin. By evaluating eateries, consumers referred to different Arabic and other linguistic symbols. In this sense, what has been described as the social indexicality of language is what interviewees discuss here. Due to the more cultural anthropological orientation of this contribution, and for the sake of brevity, this theoretical strand will not be discussed further in this chapter (for a discussion, see Schulte, this volume).

2 Commercial gentrification, authenticity and ethnic commodification

Berlin has been strongly shaped by processes of gentrification in the last forty years (Lang 1998; Dörfler 2010; Holm 2010a). This was in part due to the city's particular local history as a divided city until 1989, which opened up neglected residential areas to investment and upgrading. However, gentrification should not only be traced to housing renovations, rising rents, and a subsequent change of the local population from an underclass to a wealthier middle and upper class. It also has a "commercial" side, which can be observed in the changing and gentrifying commercial landscapes, consisting of a wide gastronomization (Zukin 1995: 182) with new bars, pubs, restaurants, snack bars and small retail stores. This "commercial gentrification" has often been neglected in research,[2] yet it is central to the process of urban upgrading, since new infrastructure paves the way for middle class consumers and legitimates their presence in the quarter, while marginalizing and finally displacing other residential groups (Zukin 1990: 41).

2 In the widely read sociology/geography textbook "Gentrification", for example, one only finds a small paragraph regarding commercial gentrification (Lees, Slater, and Wyly 2008: 131).

What is at stake here is that marginalization already happens in early phases of gentrification, when big economic investment is not yet at play. As members of "the new middle class" (Butler 1997; Ley 1996), the early gentrifiers (typically students, artists and young creative professionals) attracted to old inner-city quarters possess only modest economic capital, yet they possess a large amount of cultural capital with regards to education, their habitus and a self-ascribed hegemonic taste. They use this in everyday consumption to distinguish themselves from more economically affluent groups, but also from an urban underclass (Stock 2014). Following a Bourdieusian (1984) approach, this cultural capital is reflected in their taste for consumer items loaded with cultural symbols, rather than with mass commercial ones. Gentrification can also be understood as a process where this initial cultural capital is transformed into economic surplus (Holm 2010b: 31).

Following this analysis, it is not surprising that (early) gentrifiers seek authenticity in their consumption practices, since it mirrors their longing for commodified culture. As Sharon Zukin (2010) has outlined in her book *Naked City. The Death and Life of Authentic Urban Places*, branded versions of authenticities shape contemporary urban gentrifying landscapes, be it in the consumption of old stock houses, the consumption of "authentic" regional eco food products, or in ethnic cuisines such as falafel stores. By consuming something "authentic", (early) gentrifiers claim to be authentic residents themselves, yet at the same time they displace and marginalize others. Zukin (2010: 3) writes: "Any group that insists on the authenticity of its own tastes in contrast to others' can claim moral superiority. But a group that imposes its own tastes on urban spaces – on the look of a street, say, or the feeling of a neighborhood – can make a claim to that space."

Consequently, ethnic businesses promoting a commodified ethnicity play a crucial role in constructing and selling authenticity in urban gentrified commercial landscapes, since they invoke a sense of exoticism for consumers (Stock 2017a: 9–10). The commodification of ethnicities has become a key aspect of contemporary consumer cultures (Comaroff and Comaroff 2009). John and Jean L. Comaroff point out the interrelation of ethno-commodities and authentication. Authentication for them is a two-sided process involving producers and consumers. It could be argued that producers also, to a certain extent, consume ethno-commodities. And consumers become producers, since they are complicit in the enactment of ethno-commodities and thus in their authentication (Comaroff and Comaroff 2009: 25–27). These aspects can be well observed in the promotion and consumption of ethnic cuisines in Germany, where ethnic foods and snacks have become widely spread diversified in terms of eating-out cultures, as can be observed for the development of Italian restaurants (Thoms 2010; see also Pichler this volume), döner food stalls (Seidel-Pielen 1996), and different Asian cuisines (Bui 2003; Byun and Reiher 2014). These cuisines are often linked to migration histories, positions in society as well as their re-negotiation (Möhring 2007). When it comes to food offerings, ethnic cuisines are usually adapted to local contexts and tastes, thus turning the category of "original food" obsolete. However, owners of shops are quite conscious in branding local versions of authenticities as a marketing tool, as, for example, You-Kyung Byun and Cornelia Reiher (2014) analyze in their article on Sushi restaurants in Berlin. The study about Arabic snack food presented in this chapter draws on the above-mentioned research conducted in the field of ethnic commodification while linking it more closely to distinction processes in gentrification.

This said, it is important to refer to another aspect in regards to ethnic commodification. Brandings and consumptions of ethnic food are embedded in wider discourses and stereotypes on ethnicities and thus shaped by power relations in societies (hooks 1992). One example is Anja Michaelsen's article "Asian Food Porn" (2006), in which she deconstructs how posters of Asians in Vietnamese restaurants are embedded in wider exotic discourses thus leading to a persisting "Othering". Ethnic food entrepreneurs often have to comply with demands of dominant social groups for exotic "othering" stereotypes in order to be economically successful (Niedermüller 1998, 293). Emerging from postcolonial literature (Said 2003; Spivak 1985), "Othering" refers to the ongoing discursive differentiation, exclusion and subordination of non-white societies and groups by dominant societies. One of the most pertinent and dominant othering-discourses is "Orientalism" (Said 2003), the portrayal of an imagined "Orient" by European and North-Amerian societies that is constructed as exotic, backward and uncivilized and patriarchal. Orientalism persists until today in Germany, and contemporarily mainly refers to representations of Arab and Turkish migrants (Dietze 2009, 26–27). This article will thus also ask how branding and consuming an orientalized authenticity leads to an ongoing othering of certain migration groups and thus a symbolic subordination in gentrification.

In ethnic cuisines, branded authenticity moreover particularly unfolds around different deployments of foreign language (Leeman and Modan 2010). Monica Heller (2010) states that while language has always been commodified, the economic value of language grew in importance in the symbolic economy of late modernity, as it is visible in tourism or niche branding such as ethnic commodities. Consuming language in commodified spaces is thereby closely linked to certain ideologies or discourses, like the link between English and modernity, as, for example, Elizabeth Lanza and Hirut Woldemariam (2014) show in their analysis of commercial advertisements in Addis Adaba. Language moreover is closely interlinked with late urban consumer landscapes, thus being both the outcome and a vehicle for a commodified space (Leeman and Modan 2010). In another article about gentrified Chinatown in Washingon D.C., Jennifer Leeman and Gabriella Modan (2009) analyze this interlinkage by using a qualitative approach (of observation, mapping and photography) that looks closer into the socio-historical and geographical embedding of language signs as well as their use. In particular, they analyze how new commercial establishment (that are non-Chinese owned) in this rapidly gentrifying area use Chinese-language signs as décor targeted towards consumers with no ties nor knowledge of Chinese.

This approach will be followed and extended here by analyzing how consumers distinction practices in different gentrifying neighborhoods of Berlin are linked to the consumption of Arabic linguistic symbols and language in falafel stores. First, however, I will provide some background on the rise and spread of falafel economies in Berlin.

3 Unnoticed gentrifiers – Arabic snack food and urban upgrading in Berlin

One of the first entrepreneurs who sold falafel in Berlin was the German-Iraqi owner of "Baharat", an Arabic and Turkish word that means "herbs". He knew falafel well from his childhood in Bagdad, where it was mainly served by Palestinian migrants. He himself started to sell falafel during the 1980s in bars in Kreuzberg, then in weekly alternative street markets and finally, he opened his own falafel shop at the Winterfeldtplatz in Berlin-Schöneberg in 1988 (Stock 2013: 72). Many other German-Arab migrants followed his example. Today, there are around one hundred Arab snack places in Berlin's inner-city quarters (Stock 2013: 82). In these shops, falafel, shawarma (the Arabic version of döner) and fried halloumi are served either in a sandwich or as a plate, together with tabboule, hummus and salad. A falafel (the common term in Germany for a sandwich filled with falafel and potentially other things) currently costs about three euros, the same price as a shawarma (a sandwich that holds shawarma).

The rise of falafel is first of all a consequence of Arab migration to West Berlin, which increased from the 1970s onwards. Lebanese and Palestinians (living in Lebanon as refugees at the time) took the chance to migrate to West Berlin during the Lebanese Civil War (1975–1990) by using a gateway through East Berlin, for which they received a transit-visa. From East Berlin, they continued their way to West Berlin, where they settled; however, they maintained a precarious legal status, since they were never accepted as refugees. Together with this migration from Lebanon, many Iraqis moved to Berlin as students or refugees from the Saddam regime. Overall, Berlin hosted about 30,000 people with citizenship from Arab countries in 2011 (Stock 2013: 60–67), even before large numbers of Arab migrants from Syria and Iraq arrived, starting in 2011. Today, Berlin hosts around 130,000 migrants with Arab citizenship (see Amt für Statistik Berlin-Brandenburg 2016). Many of the earlier Arab migrants faced exclusion from the wider job market and decided to open up their own businesses, an aspect often discussed in the literature on migration entrepreneurial businesses (Hillmann 2001; Light and Gold 2000).

However, this is only one side of the coin. Even though it is widely believed in Berlin, Arab snack entrepreneurs never targeted an Arab migrant community as their primary consumer group; they promoted their food from the beginning to an alternative and young German and European middle class in Berlin's gentrifying areas. This can be also concluded from numbers. One of the districts that hosts most of the falafel eateries in Berlin is the East Berlin quarter of Prenzlauer Berg. In 2010, a mapping exercise found seventeen Arabic-style falafel stores there, yet only 348 people with Arab citizenship lived in this area. In contrast, Berlin-Neukölln, the quarter with the highest number of Arab migrants (7,935 people with Arab citizenship), had only eleven falafel stores (Stock 2013: 82).

As outlined elsewhere more in detail (Stock 2013: 82–97), falafel stores have been an integral part of the gentrification that started in West Berlin's quarters along the border, such as Kreuzberg and Schöneberg. With the fall of the wall in 1989, the *Aufwertungskarawane* [gentrification caravan] (Holm 2010a: 89) moved to the East Berlin quarters of Mitte, Prenzlauer Berg and Friedrichshain. Since the early 2000s, gentrification returned to West Berlin, bringing a second wave to Kreuzberg. In recent years, the long-time working class district of Neukölln has been the focus of upgrading.

Arabic snack owners not only followed this "caravan" by opening their shops, but they were often at the forefront of early gentrification. The *Dada* Snack for example already opened in the central district of Mitte in 1998, located close to the famous arthouse of *Tacheles*. According to the owner, at that time the quarter was a shabby red-light-district: "We have brought life to this neighbourhood."[3] And the German-Palestinian owner of *Sanabel*, who opened up his snack store in 1998 at the Boxhagener Platz in Friedrichshain, a place that is now overly famous for its many bars and restaurants, states: "I was here alone for three or four years. The other shops all came after me. The shop owners came to eat at my place when they constructed and renovated

3 Interview with the owner of *Dada*, 8th May 2009, translated from German.

their shops and restaurants."[4] Thus, falafel vendors have shaped gentrification from the early stages onwards.

Falafel owners consistently describe their customers as typical early gentrifiers, defining them as 90–99% percent German/European,[5] young and educated, being artists, students or creative professionals (see Stock 2013: 98–105). Besides, they describe the taste of their patrons as "superior", as the owner of *Taebs Bistro* states: "Those are not the people eating currywurst or döner. Those are people with tastes."[6] In these descriptions, owners thus refer to the high cultural capital of their consumers, not only with regards to education and profession, but also incorporated in their consumption habitus. Consumers are thus part of the typical new middle classes of gentrification processes (Ley 1996).

It is not unusual for Arabic fast food entrepreneurs to have social backgrounds and lifestyles similar to their customers. For example, the owner of the *Zweistrom* [The Two Rivers] in East Berlin's Prenzlauer Berg studied art in Baghdad before he came to Berlin as a refugee and opened up a falafel snack bar in his neighborhood, where he had moved to as a resident. In menu and decor, he wants to express his educational background and his affinity for the arts. Regarding the decor, the owner of *Zweistrom* designed the interior of his shop with a computer program, decorated his walls with black and white portrait photos of Iraqis and used the Babylonian god *Maduk* as a branding logo. He moreover created different compositions of sauces and pastes for his sandwiches, such as sesame, garlic, humus, mango and hot sauce.[7] As it is the case for many ethnic cuisines in globalization, the Berlin-based entrepreneurs thus transform the recipes for serving falafel and shawarma to suit the tastes of their Berlin middle class customers, by using large-sized pitas, a substantial portion of different vegetables and salads and a mix of dressings, as well as branding their food as "vegetarian" or even "vegan". In Lebanon in contrast, falafel is only served with tahini, a bit of tomatoes and radishes (Stock 2017a: 9–10).

Looking at their entrepreneurial practices and motives, one could identify the owner of *Zweistrom* as well as other falafel owners as "culturepreneurs" (Lange 2007) in the districts, promoting new tastes to the gentrification milieu. Nonetheless, Arab migrant entrepreneurs are oftentimes not perceived in this way in public discourse as well as in everyday life. Instead, they are first and foremost perceived as "Arabs", who do not run a creative gastronomy, but only sell their tradition. Their cultural capital is thus neglected and they are

4 Interview with the owner of *Sanabel*, 18th May 2009, translated from German.

5 Some owners referred to them as "German", some as "European".

6 Interview with the owner of *Taebs-Bistro*, 15th August 2009, translated from German.

7 Interview with the owner of *Zweistrom*, 21st May 2009, translated from German.

symbolically subordinated to the cultural capital of other creative entrepreneurs. The owner of *Zweistrom* mentions reluctantly that while people acknowledged him as an artist in his early years, this has recently changed due to his entrepreneurial practice. Once, he heard a young woman entering his shop denoting him as the "Arab falafel man" while talking on the phone to a friend.[8] Thus one can state that while Arab migrant entrepreneurs are active actors and mediators of new tastes in gentrification, they yet remain unnoticed because they are culturalized as uneducated "Arabs" (Stock 2013: 116–120).

4 Consuming Arabic – Oriental stereotypes as a mirror of gentrification

Paradoxically, it is this culturalization that renders falafel stores successful in Berlin's gentrification process, since they invoke a sense of authenticity in their customers. In the following sections, I want to look more closely at consumer perceptions of falafel stores that reveal these taste preferences for staged authenticity. Consumers I interviewed in 2009 all belong to the above-mentioned new middle class with high cultural capital, yet low economic capital (Ley 1996), since they studied or had university degrees, partly work in creative professions (as writers, journalists) and consciously moved to gentrifying neighborhoods. What is striking is that they often refer to different uses of Arabic in the stores while talking about their everyday experience or evaluating photos of falafel stores during interviews.

It seems that Arabic linguistic symbols and use of language function as criteria to determine whether a store is evaluated as authentic and thus of good quality. To highlight this argument, I will look closer into the following deployments of Arabic: first in spoken language, second in decor, third in the naming of stores and, finally, in their background music.

4.1 Spoken language as authentication

Consumers often mention the presence of Arab visitors during interviews. Stefanie for example, a 31-year-old resident of Prenzlauer Berg, says the following: "What I like about falafel stores is that there are other Arab people sitting, talking and eating. And I think if the taste is good for them, the taste must be

8 Interview with the owner of *Zweistrom*, 21st May 2009, translated from German.

original."[9] For Stefanie as well as for others, listening to Arab people talking in their language becomes an index of quality, since for them it ensures that the falafel store sells authentic food. This of course is an illusion since most falafel owners state that the vast majority of their customers are of non-Arab origin. Many people with Arab origin who I spoke to in Berlin would not go to one of these falafel eateries, since they neither like the way falafel and shawarma is served in Berlin, nor do they believe in their good quality – particularly regarding the freshness of the deep-frying oil. However, from time to time employees would get visits from friends or family. Stefanie and other consumers portray these visitors as being the "original" customers, even though the latter would hardly ever eat in the shops.

For the interviewed consumers, the presence of Arab visitors invokes a laidback atmosphere which they are happy to observe and participate in. Anton, another 37-year-old resident of Prenzlauer Berg, states the following about his favorite restaurant *Daye* in his neighborhood: "There is always a group of men who run the store. And then friends or relatives would come by, sit on a chair in front of the door and drink a tea. And then they start chatting with each other. This is almost like a family reunion".[10] And Annika, a young Kreuzberg resident, talks about "family and kin clans"[11] being present in the shop.

Consumers perceive and experience those visits and everyday practices through an oriental lens, as Michael Haldrup, Lasse Koefoed and Kirsten Simonsen (2006) describe it in their article on "practical orientalism" in Denmark. Notions such as *clans, groups of men, laidback atmosphere*, and *having a tea and chatting* refer to wider notions that are related to oriental stereotypes such as down-to-earth, patriarchal, family-oriented and traditional (see also Said 2003). For consumers, perceiving these habits and listening to foreign chatting is a way to live an exotic experience in Berlin that lifts them out of their normal life-routines. For the falafel shop owners, however, this means a continuous form of othering, i.e., being perceived as the "oriental Other" (Haldrup, Koefoed, and Simonsen 2006: 80).

At the same time, falafel owners are quite conscious of branding this exotic otherness towards their consumers. This is one of the reasons why they would hire exclusively Arab employees in their businesses. The owner of *Zweistrom*, for example, states that he also met non-Arab people who would have been interested in working in his eatery. However, he poses the question: "What would

9 Interview with Stefanie, 15th June 2009, translated from German.
10 Interview with Anton, 22nd July 2009, translated from German.
11 Interview with Annika, 14th July 2009, translated from German.

you think, if there is a non-Arab person working behind the counter? Would it be problematic to you?"[12] And indeed, Monika, a 20-year-old filmmaker living in Prenzlauer Berg mentions this, when she talks about choosing a falafel place. In order to be certain that the place is "authentic", she says: "And what I pay attention to is if they talk Arabic to each other behind the counter."[13] Thus, the sound of spoken Arabic together with an Arabic appearance and alleged practices are an important branding factor for authenticity, even though none of the interviewed consumers understands any Arabic.

4.2 *Rissani* – oriental decor

The above-mentioned orientalization is even more prevalent with regards to decor in the falafel stores. During interviews, consumers were confronted with different photos of the interior of falafel stores. The old falafel restaurant *Rissani* is among those falafel stores that consumers cherish the most. *Rissani* was established in 1990 at Spreewaldplatz in the middle of Kreuzberg. The exterior of the store is quite unremarkable; it advertises itself as a venue with "oriental specialties" and has some tables and benches for people to sit and eat on during the summer season. Inside however, *Rissani* opens up in two large rooms that are painted in different colors and decorated with large paintings with Arabic calligraphies.

For Michael, a 30-year-old journalist living in Kreuzberg, *Rissani* is one of his favorite stores. He states: "*Rissani* is one of the falafel stores that stage this typical atmosphere, with carpets hanging from the wall and Arabic calligraphies."[14] He even brings his parents visiting from another German city to *Rissani*, since for him this is a typical, yet exotic experience in Berlin. Moreover, Ben, who had not been in this shop before, states: "This is very Arabic with the calligraphies and other linguistic symbols. This one gives you the feeling of being somewhere else. I like this shop very much."[15] And finally, Anton says about the photo: "This is nice. Very traditional. Really authentic."[16]

Indeed, many of Berlin's falafel stores would stage authenticity by inserting poetic calligraphies or religious Koran surahs into their shops, while at the same time using warm, dark colors. Consumers perceive these decorations through the

12 Interview with Zweistrom, 21nd May 2009, translated from German.
13 Interview with Monika, 18th July 2009, translated from German.
14 Interview with Michael, 7th August 2009, translated from German.
15 Interview with Ben, 17th July 2009, translated from German.
16 Interview with Anton, 22nd July 2009, translated from German.

Figure 1: Decor of *Rissani*, Berlin Kreuzberg, © Miriam Stock 2009.

lens of Orientalism as traditional, laidback and down-to-earth, and at the same time as exotic, giving them the feeling of being somewhere else (see Stock 2013: 172–180). However, it would be shorthanded to restrict consumers' perceptions to a wider embedded Orientalism in society since installations in falafel stores also mirror the consumers' taste. Stefanie, for example, says that she would prefer "shabby" places, because she does not identify herself as classy.[17] And Florian states, as mentioned in the beginning, that he would prefer "laid-back" and "traditional" falafel stores such as *Rissani* in Kreuzberg, in contrast to the "hipster gentrification bars" in Prenzlauer Berg, because it meets his own lifestyle and identity.[18] The interviewed consumers thus employ their taste for those authenticity-invoking decors and atmospheres to position themselves as authentic consumers, in the sense of not being part of gentrification, since they perceive gentrification as synonymous with money-affluent and chic.

At the same time, they are an integral part of this gentrification with their taste for authenticity, thus playing out their cultural capital. And falafel stores such as *Rissani* brand this authenticity, while at the same time replicating decor items of other bars and restaurants in Berlin's gentrification. One can

17 Interview with Stefanie, 15th July 2009, translated from German.
18 Interview with Florian, 17th July 2009, translated from German.

observe that falafel stores and other bars use similar decor items such as warm colors, rubbed-off walls, old furniture and dark lights, a retro postmodernist style that Frederic Jameson (1991) has identified as being typical of late capitalism, and a style that can be found in many bars and cafés in Berlin's gentrifying neighborhoods. The perceived oriental decor is thus less of a copy of an authentic version of falafel stores in the Middle East, than it is a mirror of Berlin's gentrifying style.[19]

4.3 *Zweistrom* – a name that is too German

There are falafel stores that choose a divergent strategy for their decor and presentation. The falafel store *Zweistrom* [The Two Rivers] in Prenzlauer Berg is one of these stores. *Zweistrom* opened in 2005 at the end of Kollwitzstraße; the owner was already introduced above. *Zweistrom* is quite a small store, consisting of only four tiny tables inside. In summer, people can also sit outside on the sidewalk under large parasols. In contrast to *Rissani*, when I show them the photo (2) below, consumers are more reserved when evaluating the falafel store of *Zweistrom*.

This is first and foremost due to the naming and branding of the store. Ben, a Swiss student doing Erasmus in Berlin and living in Friedrichshain, for example, says: "*Zweistrom*, this is a strange name. This name is too German. Ok, I understand because of Two-Stream-Land [The Two Rivers]. But it is too German. With an Arabic snack place, I associate more tradition and old culture. Also in regards to décor, this is too modern and rigorous."[20] Indeed, *Zweistrom* is one of the few snack places that chose a non-Arabic name, while still playing with its alleged origin. Most of the other places, however, sounded Arabic, such as *Baharat* (a blend of spices), *Rissani* (a town in Morocco), *Salsabil* (ginger) or the famous *Habibi* (my darling). For Ben and other interviewed consumers, a German name such as *Zweistrom* raises suspicions on that a falafel space would not be authentic since it did not fulfill their expectations of an oriental food place.

The naming of *Zweistrom* resonates with the overall perception of the store. Sarah, a 22-year-old student from The Netherlands living in Berlin, states: "It

19 See, for example, Lebanon. Falafel as well as other national snack eateries here actually followed a modernized appearance after the civil war, often consisting of franchised enterprises (see Kassan and Halwani 2004).
20 Interview with Ben, 17th July 2009, translated from German.

Figure 2: Presentation of *Zweistrom*, Prenzlauer Berg, © Miriam Stock 2009.

looks overall very chic. Those tables and chairs. I don't know, why I do not like something chic. But I think it does not fit the food that is served. If you could buy sushi there for example, this would fit. And this sign looks so hipster."[21] Sarah's expectations of Arab food culture intermingle with her own taste preferences. By consuming something not chic, she and other early gentrifiers distinguish themselves from more economically affluent groups in Berlin's gentrification process such as the ones present in Prenzlauer Berg.

On this basis, one could think that *Zweistrom* would have turned out to be one of the less successful falafel stores in Berlin's gentrifying neighborhoods. However, this is not necessarily the case; *Zweistrom* is a business that runs quite well from morning to evening. This might be due to its location in Prenzlauer Berg, an East Berlin, mainly German and European neighborhood that is known for its fast and vast upgrading in the 2000s (Dörfler 2010).

As a matter of fact, different constructions and positionings of Berlin's neighborhoods are reflected in the perceptions of different styles of falafel stores. During interviews, I asked consumers to locate falafel stores such as *Rissani* and *Zweistrom*. When asked about the location of the eateries, most consumers immediately state after seeing the photo (1) of *Rissani* that this restaurant must be situated in Kreuzberg, a neighborhood often portrayed as multi-cultural because

21 Interview with Sarah, 3rd August 2009, translated from German.

of its migrant population, as a hub for subcultures because of the high presence of artists and other creative entrepreneurs, and finally as not-yet-as-gentrified (Lanz 2007: 245–251; note that this evaluation probably would be different today). Lisa, a 35-year-old editor for example notes about the photo (1) of *Rissani*: "The interior is spicy. This is the typical Kreuzberg style".[22] With regards to *Zweistrom*, as portrayed in photo 2, Marion, a bar-owner, says: "It looks like a typical hipster coffeeshop in Prenzlauer Berg."[23] And Stephanie, who herself lives in the neighborhood and often goes to *Zweistrom*, even if she does not cherish the design, argues: "This store has adapted to the neighborhood of Prenzlauer Berg."[24]

This seems to suggest that different presentation styles of falafel stores mirror different images of Berlin's quarters in Berlin's gentrification process. As analyzed elsewhere in more detail, Kreuzberg is perceived by interviewed consumers as "authentic", "cosmopolitan" and "exciting". Prenzlauer Berg, in contrast, is evaluated as more German and bourgeois (Stock 2013: 193–198). For owners, including the one of *Zweistrom*, the latter constructions of an upgraded Prenzlauer Berg open up possibilities for presenting themselves in a divergent way that would not necessarily convey folkloristic orientalist stereotypes. And this is exactly what the owner says when talking about his design: "I wanted to do something modern with a hint of Iraqi."[25]

4.4 Arabic background music versus radio

Interviewed consumers also mention the background music that they would listen to while they consume a falafel sandwich or other dishes in the restaurants. Michael states about his favorite place *Rissani*: "And what I like about *Rissani* is the music. These strange sounds, strange voices, it feels like entering a different world."[26] Arabic music thus completes the authentic and exotic experience for consumers regarding the atmosphere. Many falafel stores would play different kinds of Arabic music, often in a non-stop loop, such as classical Arabic music at *Rissani*, different Arabic pop-music at *Habibi*, or one of the famous Lebanese singers such as *Fairouz* at *Maroush*.

22 Interview with Lisa, 21st July 2009, translated from German.

23 Interview with Marion, 6th July 2009, translated from German.

24 Interview with Stefanie, 15th July 2009, translated from German.

25 Interview with the owner of *Zweistrom*, 15th August 2009, translated from German.

26 Interview with Michael, 7th August 2009, translated from German.

Again, music becomes a factor in considering whether a store would count as authentic. Anton, for example, states about one falafel store close to his house in Prenzlauer Berg: "What I don't like in the Ali Baba snack bar in Prenzlauer Berg is that they play Kiss FM. But there are only tourists anyway."[27] Thus, his taste for authentic falafel stores functions as a tool of distinction against the increased tourism in Berlin's neighborhoods. Tourists, as portrayed by consumers during interviews, do not possess the local knowledge (Stock 2013: 291), which would allow them to distinguish a "good authentic" falafel store from a more commercialized one, at least from the perspective of the interviewed local falafel consumers. The latter group thus not only distinguish themselves from more economically affluent groups in Berlin's gentrification, but also from the growing presence of tourists, which are portrayed as non-legitimate and uninformed in the neighborhoods.

Owners and employees may become limited in their everyday practices by the consumer expectations of Oriental and Arabic music. For example, the owner of *Phönizier* in Prenzlauer Berg, who is staging an oriental atmosphere by using oriental pillows and low tables, says that once his CD player was broken, he decided to play radio music in his shop instead. Quite often, consumers would point to this fact and ask him if he could play oriental music. He reluctantly concludes: "The customers don't want anything else. We would like to play western music sometimes, but they don't want it."[28] In this case, the owner of *Phönizier* is limited in his choices of expression in order to comply with consumers' taste preferences for something authentic. As an intermediate conclusion to this section, it can be said that falafel owners are active mediators of new tastes in (early) gentrification, yet precisely because of their ongoing ethnicization, they continue to be subordinated to other catering entrepreneurs in gentrification (see Lange 2007).

In the final section, I want to introduce döner as a type of snack that is not (anymore) a part of the taste of Berlin's (early) gentrifiers. Even though döner places are almost identical to falafel snack bars, consumers mention different criteria that would make them avoid these places – criteria that are related to their distinction from lower classes with limited economic and cultural capital.

---

27 Interview with Anton, 22nd July 2009, translated from German.

28 Interview with the owner of *Phönizier*, 6th May 2009, translated from German.

5 Döner versus falafel – distinction from lower classes

Even before showing them the photo of the döner, interviewed consumers often referred to the Turkish döner snack to contextualize their tastes preferences for falafel and shawarma. This may be obvious, since Arabic and Turkish snack stores are quite similar in Berlin, the first type selling döner, the second shawarma, the Arabic version of it. Döner kebap stores often even include falafel on their menus, yet in a prefabricated version.

While my interview partners favor Arabic falafel snack bars, most of them agree that döner would not meet their taste at all. Michael for example states: "I never eat döner",[29] and Stefanie says: "The döner time is definitely over. We just don't eat döner anymore. Shawarma has outdone döner."[30]

Consumers list different reasons for coming up with these opinions. Michael identifies döner as being of bad quality because it was not handmade like shawarma, but often mass-produced in industries.[31] And Stefanie denounces the quality of döner more generally: "Those selling döner, they don't care if the taste is good. It is always the same idea."[32] Interviewed consumers thus have reservations about the quality, which may be fueled by past scandals regarding the döner industry. Overall, the interviewed consumers are quite disparaging and generalize in their statements about döner kebap stores.

This evaluation of döner is also repeated in comments about the following photo (3) of one of the döner kebap stores in Neukölln, with which interviewed consumers were confronted.

After seeing this photo, 34-year-old Annika declares why she would not enter the shop, even if it would have vegetarian options: "If this is first and foremost a döner place, and it smells like döner, and people are kind of döner people, then I would not like this place."[33] And Stefanie says: "I don't want to say that someone is stupid because he eats döner. But somehow you have the feeling that people who eat at falafel stores have a wider horizon with regards to their tastes."[34] Monika finally declares: "And those döner sellers, sometimes they stand there sweating behind the counter. And I think that is disgusting.

29 Interview with Michael, 7th August 2009, translated from German.
30 Interview with Stefanie, 15th July 2009, translated from German.
31 Interview with Michael, 7th August 2009, translated from German.
32 Interview with Stefanie, 15th July 2009, translated from German.
33 Interview with Annika, 14th July 2009, translated from German.
34 Interview with Stefanie, 15th July 2009, translated from German.

Figure 3: Döner Kebap Store, Neukölln, © Miriam Stock 2009.

But I don't mean this against Turks. I also think that the German currywurst is disgusting."[35] The last quote in particular hints at the symbolic location of döner stores. The interviewed falafel consumers in Berlin's gentrified neighborhoods would portray döner and its visitors as having limited tastes, being not that clean, meat-centered and similar to the original consumers of German currywurst. These connotations, taken together, all hint at an image of lower classes in a Bourdieusian sense, namely with both low economic and cultural capital, from which falafel consumers distinguish themselves through their allegedly superior, healthier tastes, implying and indexing their cultural capital (see Stock 2013: 271–293).

What is even more surprising is that Berlin's falafel consumers could already state on the basis of advertising on the streets if they would visit this store or not. When they are confronted with the photo of the döner eatery during interviews (photo 3), consumers refer to the photo billboards portraying the dishes, similar to the ones you would find above the counter at McDonalds. Most of the interviewed falafel consumers detest these photo billboards. Tom, another journalist from Berlin, states: "And then those ugly illuminated billboards, which are so abhorrent, that you ask yourself why they use it."[36] Michael comments: "Using

35 Interview with Monika, 18th July 2009, translated from German.
36 Interview with Tom, 17th August 2009, translated from German.

photos of dishes is cheap. This looks like they are very desperate."[37] And even the owner of *Habibi* says: "This is commercial at döner places. There is no art."[38]

In fact, within Berlin's gentrification process, falafel stores quite rarely make use of those photo billboards and instead use handwritten menus, wall paintings and calligraphy, as described above. Thus, while falafel stores in Berlin's gentrification process brand themselves as culturally authentic, döner stores choose a more commercial way of branding (Caglar 1995).

Ayse Caglar (1995) analyzes this commercial branding with regards to döner kebap. In her article *Mc Döner*, she shows that while from the 1970s to the early 1990s, döner kebap used more folkloristic presentations, in the 1990s they shifted to McDonaldized styles. This may be due to the rise and success of American fast food chains in Germany starting in the 1970s. But Ayse Caglar understands this transformation in a different way. While German-Turkish entrepreneurs established a very successful new food sector and were economically very successful as well, döner would still be portrayed as folkloristic in the media. To confront this ethnicization, döner entrepreneurs decided to transform their presentation to a McDonaldized version. One of the store owners in Berlin said, for example: "But in the midst of Europe [...] I want to realize something close to McDonald's. I want to show that Turks are also capable of setting up a good business and running it. The problem is to change the atmosphere, to offer a Turkish specialty without our atmosphere, to present it in a modern way. I want döner to go further" (Caglar 1995: 222–223). For him, commercial branding is a way to portray his good, modern taste and not something he would do out of despair. And other food entrepreneurs followed his example. One is the Arabic *City Chicken* restaurant in Berlin-Neukölln, that sells mainly half chickens (but no falafel) and uses an English sounding name as well as photo billboards. One of the owners declares in an interview about this decoration: "We also pay attention to modernization. Modernization is progress."[39] The deployment of the English language goes together with the overall McDonaldized presentation and branding of a catering businesses referring to a modernization discourse.

However, consumers in Berlin's gentrification process devalue this taste for commercial, McDonaldized brandings, which they perceive as subordinate to their own culturally affluent, authentic tastes. They thus indirectly deny döner kebap stores and other commercialized infrastructure a legitimate presence in these quarters. And indeed, while falafel stores flourish in Berlin's gentrification

37 Interview with Michael, 7th August 2009, translated from German.

38 Interview with the owner of *Habibi* at Südstern, 7th June 2010, translated from German.

39 Interview with one of the owners of *City Chicken*, 20th October 2010, translated from German.

process, with handwritten menus and oriental decor, döner stores become fewer in these quarters, especially in the non-Turkish neighborhoods of Prenzlauer Berg. In Kastanienallee, a famous street in Prenzlauer Berg, in 2012 there were five falafel eateries, but not a single döner (Stock 2013: 286). The cultural capital of gentrifiers may thus play a role in restructuring commercial landscapes in Berlin's gentrification process, even before economic capital is dominant. The taste for authenticity of this group can be seen as a "tool of power" (Zukin 2010: 3) to slowly but steadily appropriate central urban quarters, while marginalizing others groups and their tastes.

6 Conclusion

This article started by highlighting how gentrification is not only a process that is economically driven, but also a process in which the cultural capital of the new middle class plays an important role by restructuring urban commercial landscapes. In this way, selling and consuming authenticity become key aspects of gentrification and shape gentrifying landscapes of tastes that are branded, e.g., in ethnic food businesses, which have become widespread in gentrification but neglected in research. In these ethnic food businesses, language and linguistic symbols function as important tools of authentication.

As an example, this article has dug deeper to analyze the central role of Arab-German food entrepreneurs in Berlin's gentrification process, who opened falafel stores in the early phases of the process, promoted new tastes to their customers in gentrification and, thus, were part of transforming the quarter. However, even if those entrepreneurs could be identified as typical creative entrepreneurs of early gentrification, since they possess a lot of cultural capital, they are not portrayed as such; neither in the media nor in everyday life. This is due to their ethnicization as "Arabs", since their cultural capital was mainly understood through the lens of "ethnicity" and thus subordinated to that of other creative entrepreneurs.

Paradoxically it is precisely this ethnicization that renders falafel stores so successful in Berlin's gentrification process since they invoke authenticity – and this via different deployments of (foreign) language and linguistic symbols. Entrepreneurs are quite consciously staging authenticity in their stores by hiring Arab employees (speaking Arabic), by playing Arabic background music and by installing Arabic calligraphies in their stores. Yet, for them, this ongoing culturalization turns out to be a limitation, since they have to persist in the container of an "oriental Other". Ironically, ongoing gentrification and upgrading could open up a way for German-Arab entrepreneurs to portray themselves in a divergent way, as was discussed in the case of the owner of *Zweistrom* in Prenzlauer Berg, who uses a German name.

For falafel consumers in gentrification, consuming orientalized authenticity in falafel stores is not only an aspect that meets with their own orientalist stereotypes, but also an aspect that reflects their tastes for authenticated commodities. They then use these tastes not only to distinguish themselves from more economically affluent groups in gentrification, as well as from tourists coming from abroad, but also to demarcate themselves from lower classes (with limited cultural and economic capital). With their own cultural capital and taste for authenticity, falafel consumers in gentrification thus take part in restructuring urban inner-city quarters with their everyday practices – as much as the falafel food entrepreneurs who mediate these new tastes.

Finally, this article has shown that brandings of language and linguistic symbols should be studied more closely with regards to their effects on urban landscapes of tastes as well as restructuring of urban societies (see also Hüwelmeier, this volume). Language in ethnic eateries in cities such as Berlin may be less a hint of the "true origin" of different migrant groups prevalent in the cities, but rather a tool for branding authenticity and distinction.

Since 2015, many new Syrian restaurants and snack eateries have opened up in Sonnenallee, a commercial street in Neukölln serving new tastes of Arabic food in Berlin[40] and at the same time using new forms of styles, decors and commodified language that are mainly targeted towards newly migrated Syrian customers. These Syrian restaurants have led to an inner-ethnic gentrification of Neukölln and at the same time challenge the branding of conventional orientalized falafel snack in Berlin, for example, by using signs and language referring to a cosmopolitan Damascus (Stock 2017b: 53). Analyzing the different deployments of language in these new eateries would be an interesting new field of study to grasp the ongoing sociolinguistic economy of Berlin.

References

Amt für Statistik Berlin-Brandenburg (ed.). 2016. *Statistischer Bericht. Einwohnerinnen und Einwohner in Berlin am 30. Juni 2016.*https://www.statistik-berlin-brandenburg.de/.../2016/SB_A01-05-00_2016h01_BE.pdf *(accessed: 10 April 2018).*

Bourdieu, Pierre. 1984. *Distinction: A Social Critique of the Judgment of Taste.* Cambridge: Harvard University Press.

40 *Shawarma* for example is served as chicken meat with garlic sauce in a toasted sandwich with no salads and extras.

Bui, Pipo. 2003. *Envisioning Vietnamese Migrants in Germany. Ethnic stigma, immigrant origin narrative and partial masking*. Münster: Lit Verlag.

Butler, Tim. 1997. *Gentrification and the Middle Classes*. Hants: Ashgate.

Byun, You-Kyung & Cornelia Reiher. 2014. Kulinarische Globalisierung: Koreanische Restaurants in Berlin zwischen Authentizität und Hybridisierung. In Cornelia Reiher & Sarah Ruth Sippel (eds.), *Umkämpftes Essen. Produktion, Handel und Konsum von Lebensmitteln in globalen Kontexten*, 271–291. Göttingen: Vandenhoeck & Ruprecht.

Caglar, Ayse. 1995. McDöner: Döner Kebap and the Social Positioning Struggle of German Turks. In Janeen Arnold Costa & Gary J. Bamossy (eds.), *Marketing in a Multicultural World: Ethnicity, Nationalism and Cultural Identity*, 209–230. Thousands Oaks: Sage Publications.

Comaroff, John L. & Jean Comaroff. 2009. *Ethnicity, Inc.* Chicago and London: The Chicago University Press.

Dietze, Gabriele. 2009. Okzidentalismuskritik. Möglichkeiten und Grenzen einer Forschungsperspektivierung. In Claudia Brunner, Gabriele Dietze & Edith Wenzel (eds.), *Kritik des Okzidentalismus. Transdisziplinäre Beiträge zu (Neo-)Orientalismus und Geschlecht*, 23–54. Bielefeld: transcript.

Dörfler, Thomas. 2010. *Gentrification in Prenzlauer Berg? Milieuwandel eines Berliner Sozialraums seit 1989*. Bielefeld: transcript.

Haldrup, Michael, Lasse Koefoed & Kirsten Simonsen. 2006. Practical Orientalism – Bodies, Every Day Life and the Construction of Otherness. *Geografiska Annaler: Series B. Human Geography* 88(2). 173–184.

Heller, Monica. 2010. The Commodification of Language. *Annual Review of Anthropology* 39. 101–114.

Hillmann, Felicitas. 2001. Ethnische Ökonomien: eine Chance für die Städteund *ihre* Migrant (inn)en? In Norbert Gestring, Herbert Glasauer, Christine Hannemann, Werner Petrowsky & Jörg Pohlan (eds.), *Jahrbuch StadtRegion*, 35–56. Opladen: Budrich.

Holm, Andrej. 2010a: Die Karawane zieht weiter – Stationen der Aufwertung in der Berliner Innenstadt. In Mario Pschera, Cagla Ilk & Cicek Bacik (eds.), *Intercity Istanbul-Berlin*, 89–101. Berlin: Dagyeli.

Holm, Andrej. 2010b. *Wir bleiben Alle! Gentrifizierung – Städtische Konflikte um Aufwertung und Verdrängung*. Münster: Unrast.

hooks, bell. 1992. Eating the Other: Desire and Resistance. In bell hooks (ed.), *Black Looks. Race and Representation*, 21–39. New York: South End Press.

Jameson, Fredric. 1991. *Postmodernism, or, the Cultural Logic of Late Capitalism*. Durham: Duke University Press.

Kassan, Maher & Ziad Halwani. 2004: My Lebanese Sandwich. In Malu Halasa & Roseanne Saad Khalaf (eds.), *Transit Beirut. New Writing and Images*, 10–23. London: Saqi Books.

Lang, Barbara. 1998. *Mythos Kreuzberg: Ethnographie eines Stadtteils 1961–1995*. Frankfurt am Main: Campus.

Lange, Bastian. 2007. *Die Räume der Kreativszenen: Culturepreneurs und ihre Orte in Berlin*. Bielefeld: transcript.

Lanz, Stephan. 2007. *Berlin aufgemischt: Abendländisch – multikulturell – kosmopolitisch? Die politische Konstruktion einer Einwanderungsstadt*. Bielefeld: transcript.

Lanza, Elizabeth & Hirut Woldemariam. 2014. Indexing modernity: English and branding in the linguistic landscapes of Addis Ababa. *International Journal of Bilingualism* 18(5). 491–506.

Leeman, Jennifer & Gabriella Modan. 2010: Selling the City: Language, Ethnicity and Commodified space. In Elana Shohamy, Eliezer Ben-Rafael & Monica Barni (eds.), *Linguistic Landscape in the City*, 182–198. Clevedon: Multilingual Matters.
Leeman, Jennifer & Gabriella Modan. 2009. Commodified language in Chinatown: A contextualized approach to linguistic landscape. *Journal of Sociolinguistics* 13(3). 332–362.
Lees, Loretta, Tom Slater & Elvin Wyly. 2008. *Gentrification*. London: Routledge.
Ley, David. 1996. *The New Middle Class and the Remaking of the Central City*. Oxford & New York: Oxford University Press.
Light, Ivan & Steven J. Gold. 2000. *Ethnic Economies*. San Diego: Emerald Group.
Michaelsen, Anja. 2006. Asian Food Porn. Fremdheit, Geschlecht und Visualität in Metaphern der Einverleibung zeitgenössischer Populärkultur. *ZTG Bulletin* 32. 240–259.
Möhring, Maren. 2007. Gastronomie in Bewegung. Migration, kulinarischer Transfer und die Internationalisierung der Ernährung in der Bundesrepublik Deutschland. *Comparativ. Zeitschrift für Globalgeschichte und vergleichende Gesellschaftsforschung* 3. 68–85.
Niedermüller, Peter. 1998. Stadt, Kultur(en) und Macht. Zu einigen Aspekten »spätmoderner« Stadtethnologie. *Österreichische Zeitschrift für Volkskunde* LII/101. 279–301.
Said, Edward. 2003 [1978]. *Orientalism*, 5th edn. London et al.: Penguin.
Seidel-Pielen, Eberhard. 1996. *Aufgespießt! Wie der Döner über die Deutschen kam*. Berlin: Rotbuch.
Spivak, Gayatari C. 1985: The Rani of Simur. In: Francis Barker et al (eds.): Europe and its Others. Vol. 1. Colchester: University of Sussex. 247–272.
Stock, Miriam. 2013. *Der Geschmack der Gentrifizierung. Arabische Imbisse in Berlin*. Bielefeld: transcript.
Stock, Miriam. 2014. "Wer das allgegenwärtige Dönersandwich über hat". Arabische Imbissgastronomie und neubürgerliche Distinktion in Berlins Gentrifizierung. In Kasper Haase, Brigitte Frizzoni, Christoph Bareither & Mirjam Nast (eds.), *Macher – Medien – Publika: Beiträge der Europäischen Ethnologie zu Geschmack und Vergnügen*, 85–98.
Stock, Miriam. 2017a. Falafel gentrified. Neue "authentische" Geschmackslandschaften in Berlin und Beirut. *Dérive: Zeitschrift für Stadtforschung* 67. 6–12.
Stock, Miriam. 2017b. Falafeltrend – Männercafés – Willkommenskultur? Berliner arabische Gastronomien im Wandel. *Kuckuck, Notizen der Alltagskultur* 1. 50–54.
Thoms, Ulrike. 2010. Von der Migranten- zur Lifestyleküche: Die Karriere der italienischen Küche in Europa. *Europäische Geschichte Online (EGO)* http://www.ieg-ego.eu/thomsu-2010-de (accessed 16 April 2018).
Zukin, Sharon. 1990. Socio-Spatial Prototypes of a New Organization of Consumption: The Role of Real Cultural Capital. *Sociology* 24(1). 37–56.
Zukin, Sharon. 1995. *The Cultures of Cities*. Cambridge: John Wiley & Sons.
Zukin, Sharon. 2010. *Naked City: The Death and Life of Authentic Urban Places*. New York: Oxford University Press.

Philipp Krämer

11 Spanish in Berlin – potentials and perspectives in teaching and tourism

1 Introduction: Spanish on the rise

Among the many languages spoken in Berlin, Spanish may count as a peculiar one. On the one hand, it is not typically associated with immigration: In the representation of present-day Berliners or Germans, languages like Turkish, Kurdish or Arabic, but also Italian or the languages of former Yugoslavia are much more intimately linked to the history of post-war migration than Spanish. On the other hand, for a long time, Spanish has not been one of the canonical languages that are widely taught at school. Nevertheless, Spanish is very much present in Berlin, not least due to the fact that it is a "global language, albeit in a considerably less dominant position to that of English" (Mar-Molinero 2008: 28). We have to note that "English is not the universal lingua franca as is often assumed" (Hogan-Brun 2017: 95). One of the reasons for this is that "the global fortunes of Spanish are rising quite rapidly" (Graddol 1997: 58). This "in between" status makes it all the more interesting to study the significance of Spanish in the city, especially its position as a foreign language on the multi-faceted linguistic market. The aim of this paper is to investigate the relevance of Spanish as an L2[1] in Berlin in the education system and in the tourism industry.

In addition to Spanish as an L2, native speakers of Spanish are very much present in Berlin. The population statistics for the end of 2016 show that about 23,600 permanent residents of Berlin held passports from Spanish-speaking countries (Amt für Statistik Berlin-Brandenburg 2017). The absolute majority of this group are citizens of Spain (more than 14,000 people). Obviously, these figures need to be interpreted with caution since a person's nationality does not determine their language use or skills. We cannot assume that all citizens of officially Spanish-speaking countries would necessarily be speakers of Spanish; some might have inherited citizenship from their parents but grew up speaking German. Conversely, there is probably an important number of German citizens

1 Henceforth, the terms *L1* and *L2* will be used for languages acquired during (L1) and after (L2) the critical phase in childhood. In order to avoid confusion, the terms *first, second* or *third (foreign) language* will exclusively refer to the succession of language learned in primary or secondary schools, i.e., the chronological sequence of languages chosen as school subjects.

https://doi.org/10.1515/9781501508103-011

that are native speakers of Spanish if they have a background from Spanish-speaking families but did not acquire their (grand)parents' nationality. Citizens of other countries (e.g., the United States) may also be native speakers of Spanish even though it is not an official language in the country. In sum, the number of native speakers is probably much higher than what the statistics may suggest.

In addition to permanent residents, another important group of Spanish speakers are visitors, e.g., tourists or business travellers. In terms of linguistic significance for the economy, this group is probably even more important than those staying here for a longer time, since most long-term residents eventually learn German and blend in. Short-term visitors are a much more natural target group for offers and services in their native languages. The quantitative basis for this assumption will be discussed further down in the section about the hospitality business.

The constant presence and numerousness of Spanish L1 speakers contributes to the visibility of the language in the city's multilingual setup and it can stimulate motivations of non-speakers to acquire the language. This makes Berlin an interesting case to study, even though it might not be a unique setting since cities like Hamburg or Munich show a similarly high share of residents or visitors from Spanish-speaking countries (Statistikamt Nord 2017, 2018; Bayerisches Landesamt für Statistik und Datenverarbeitung 2018; Statistisches Amt München 2018). A comparison of the position of Spanish in the language markets of the three major cities in Germany could therefore be a consequential next step, especially given the fact that the tourism profiles and the educational systems differ slightly from one city to another.

Besides "inbound" contact with speakers of Spanish coming to Berlin for a shorter stay or for permanent residence, another important motivation to learn Spanish is "outbound" contact, that is, the prospects to travel to Spanish-speaking areas, to do business in Spanish-speaking countries or to communicate with friends or relatives abroad who speak Spanish. Whatever the personal motivations may be, it is interesting to determine in greater detail where and to what extent Spanish is taught and learned as a foreign language in Berlin.

In what follows, I will try to assess the role of Spanish among the languages spoken in Berlin. The notion of a *linguistic market* is to be taken in a rather literal sense here. It connects to what has been called *economics of language* or, more recently, *linguanomics*, i.e., "the ways in which linguistic and economic processes influence one another" (Grin 2003: 1; see also Coulmas 1992; Grin 1996; Hogan-Brun 2017). In the first part, I will look at the market for language learning and teaching on different levels of education: To what extent is Spanish an educational option among the languages that can be studied in Berlin? What is its "market share" compared to other languages, especially in the light of the continuing popularity of Spanish among younger people?

In the second part, I will examine a specific sector of Berlin's economy. In the past years and decades, the city has experienced an unprecedented boom in tourism. As a major international tourist destination, Berlin needs to accommodate customers with the most diverse linguistic backgrounds. Tourism is one of the sectors where multilingualism is most crucial for economic success and quality service (Duchêne and Piller 2011; Leslie and Russell 2006). A survey among employees in the hospitality business will show which significance they attribute to foreign languages in general, and to Spanish in particular.

This article seeks to contribute to a broader understanding of the value that is attached to Spanish as an educational, economic or personal resource that is worth acquiring or expanding in the context of a multicultural metropolis like Berlin. After all, as Mar-Molinero (2008: 28) puts it, a "motivation for learning Spanish implies a recognition of the perceived usefulness and the attractiveness of Spanish." Motivations in language learning have been a subject of extensive research in sociolinguistics, didactics and language acquisition (Gardner and Lambert 1972; Dörnyei 1998; Dörnyei and Schmidt 2001; Dörnyei 2003). Assessing the position of Spanish among other languages and attitudes attached to it can help to achieve a better understanding of these motivations and to reshape teaching methods or the promotion of language learning according to the learner's needs and expectations.

In more general terms, these questions are linked to the discussion as to which extent languages can be evaluated as resources at all. The notion of languages as resources has been widely criticized for reducing language(s) to mere bearers of economic value or social capital, but the concept also contributed greatly to the revalorization of marginalized languages in e.g., minority contexts (Lo Bianco 2017; de Jong et al. 2016; Ruíz 1984). With these tensions in mind, we can establish the relation between the purely economic relevance of Spanish, taking into account neoliberal thought which assesses multilingualism in terms of profit maximizing potentials (Duchêne 2011), and the subtler, less materialistic values attached to it. Therefore, the term *resource* will be used in a rather general sense: Languages can have an economic value, but they can also be valuable in the way that they increase the communicative potentials of individuals who speak them and of those they speak with. Thus, the resources can materially or immaterially benefit the speakers themselves (as *internal resources*) or they can benefit others (as resources *external* to those who profit from them).

If Spanish is indeed deemed an important resource for L2 speakers in Berlin, this can have further implications for Berlin's educational policy if the language's perceived importance will be taken into account by schools and other educational institutions. At the same time, the status of Spanish as a valuable resource can influence the way employees in language-dependent branches such as the tourism industry position themselves on the work market with specific qualifications, or even the way employers show appreciation for their employees' language skills.

2 Spanish in education

In Berlin, Spanish is present on all levels of education, from kindergartens and pre-schools to adult training. The Berlin agency for business and commerce considers multilingual kindergartens as an important economic factor as they can help attract qualified workforce among non-German speaking parents who are willing to move to Berlin and who would like their children to receive day care in their family language. The agency's website currently lists 31 kindergartens that offer day care in English, with Spanish kindergartens occupying the second rank with 22 kindergartens (Table 1).

Table 1: Number of kindergartens offering day care in languages other than German in July 2017 (Berlin Business Location Center 2017).

English	31
Spanish	22
Turkish	18
Russian	17
French	14
Italian	7

In addition to the more widespread languages, a considerable number of other languages are offered by individual kindergartens, including e.g., Polish, Greek, Hebrew or Vietnamese. Typically, the kindergartens offer bilingual day care so that the children will receive input in both German and the other language(s) that the kindergarten specializes in.

If one is to take the number of kindergartens as an indicator, there seems to be a considerable demand for childcare in Spanish. In sum, the bilingual Spanish-German institutions offer more than 1,000 day care places. As many kindergartens are founded on the basis of private initiatives, often following a specific pedagogical concept, the number of institutions is subject to frequent changes.

The number of bilingual Spanish-German primary schools is much lower. Only two schools have such an offer, however, taken together, they teach a total of 1,000 pupils. This number is also stable on secondary level where bilingual programmes are offered in the network of *Europaschulen* ('European schools' offering multilingual education with immersion through the use of at least two languages in instruction). Consequently, the number of places for bilingual education in Spanish and German is constant throughout the whole pre-school and school system. After the 2016 election, the Senate of Berlin announced that two more schools will offer bilingual Spanish-German education in the future, one on primary level and one secondary school. It can be expected that the number of children receiving bilingual education will grow considerably since these offers have been established.

All of these bilingual institutions target a rather specific audience. An important share of pupils in these schools typically has a Spanish-speaking family background and therefore speaks Spanish as (one of) their L1. In addition, the offer is used by non-Spanish-speaking parents who wish for their children to acquire Spanish at an early stage in a surrounding where they will be intensely exposed to the language (see Pfaff et al. 2014 for more information about minority and foreign language instruction in Berlin and Brandenburg).

Apart from these specialized schools, Spanish is not taught as a regular foreign language subject in elementary schools. However, this is typically the case in secondary education where bilingual offers are an exception while Spanish as a foreign language for classes with few or no native speakers are abundant. If we consider L1 and L2 education as two different "products" on the linguistic market, we can observe that the offer of L1 remains constant throughout the education system, while Spanish as a L2 is offered much more frequently to teenagers or adults and only exceptionally to younger children who attend one of the bilingual schools without being native speakers themselves.[2]

In secondary schools in Berlin, Spanish is currently not available as a first foreign language. This place is usually reserved for English, and only a few schools offer French or Russian as a first foreign language. If Spanish is learned, it is typically the second or third, rarely the fourth foreign language.

Both as a second and as a third language, French is taught more frequently than Spanish (Table 2, cf. also Pfaff et al. 2014: 92). As a second language, more schools offer Spanish than Latin which is, in turn, the most frequently offered third language. These findings reflect the overall attitudes described in a study which the Institut für Deutsche Sprache carried out in 2008. Among roughly

2 In the latter case, it becomes obvious once again that categories such as *L1* and *L2* are blurry. It is hard to decide to what extent Spanish can be considered a L2 if a child acquires it in a bilingual kindergarten at an early age without having a Spanish-speaking family background.

Table 2: Number of secondary schools in Berlin offering the top 5 languages as 2nd and 3rd foreign languages.[3]

	French	Spanish	Russian	Latin	Italian
2nd foreign language	424	114	25	60	6
3rd foreign language	85	66	17	97	13

2,000 respondents from all over Germany, 95.5% said that English should be taught at school, 65.8% said the same about French and 39.3% about Spanish (Gärtig, Plewnia, and Rothe 2010: 250).

In tetiary education, Spanish is offered as a main subject and as a minor at both Freie Universität Berlin and at Humboldt Universität Berlin. The two universities consequently offer Spanish classes on all levels both for students of Spanish linguistics and literature and for students of other subjects. At Technische Universität Berlin, foreign language classes are offered by an autonomous structure (*Sprach- und Kulturbörse, SKB*) for a large range of languages among which Spanish is one of the most popular.

Much more than the public education system from kindergartens up until universities, adult education is a market in the narrow sense, i.e., an area in which education is offered according to the commercial logic of supply and demand determined by individual interests and needs. This is especially the case in the sector of private language schools. As a matter of fact, the adult education market in Germany, particularly the market for language training, is very much split between private schools and the public *Volkshochschulen* (VHS). These last institutions are usually run by the local administrations or, in Berlin's specific structure as a city state, by the district administrations. The classes they provide are not supposed to generate any profit, but they are nevertheless dependent on a certain level of effective demand in order to cover basic costs and to justify public funding.

The Berlin VHS statistics for 2014 show that English had by far the biggest number of learners (German as a foreign language not considered). Almost 19,000 persons were enrolled in English classes on all levels combined from absolute beginners to specialized language trainings for the job. Spanish is in a very clear second position before French and Italian (Figure 1).

Nation-wide, the statistics look similar (Figure 2). English is by far the most frequently learned foreign language in Volkshochschulen (German as a foreign

3 Berliner Schulwegweiser 2016/2017; Senatsverwaltung für Bildung, Jugend und Wissenschaft.

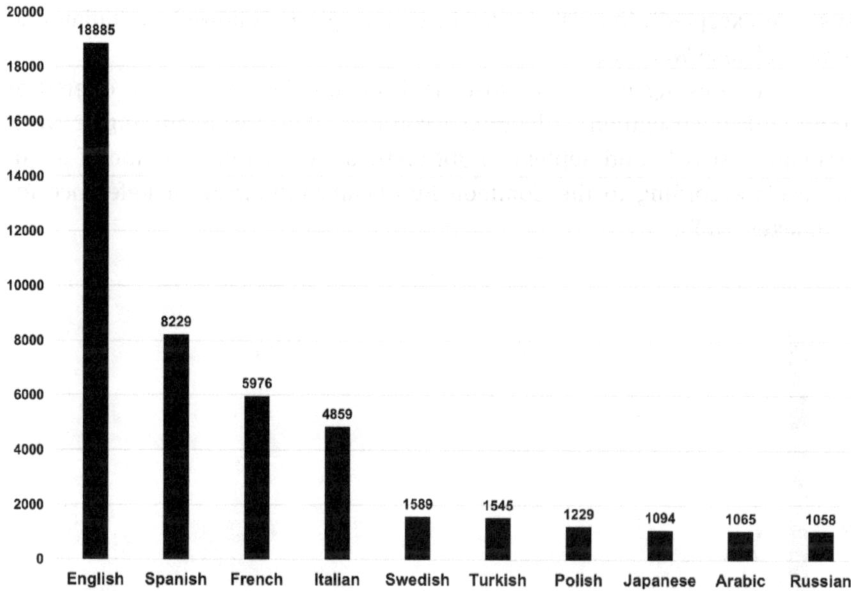

Figure 1: Number of persons enrolled in language classes at Berlin Volkshochschulen (Berliner Volkshochschulstatistik 2014).

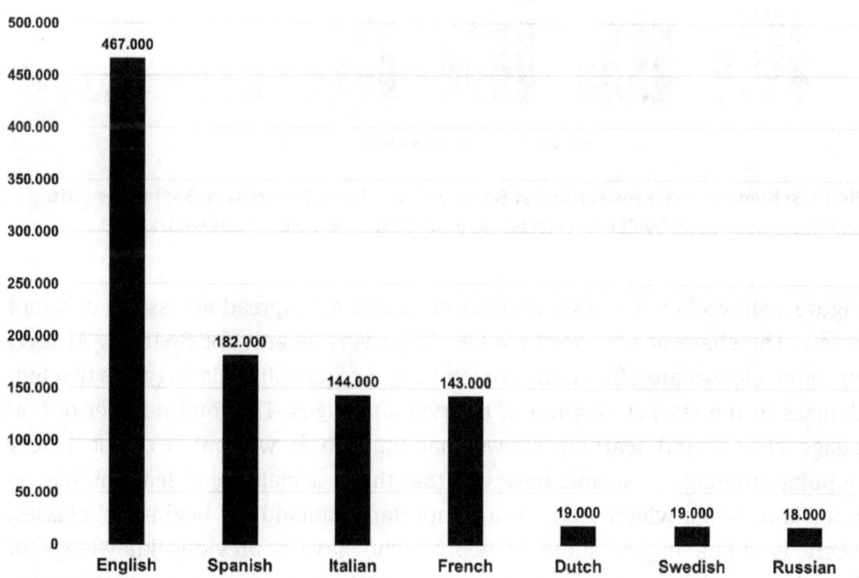

Figure 2: Number of persons enrolled in language classes offered at Volkshochschulen in Germany, 2015 (Huntemann and Reichart 2016: 31 / Deutsches Institut für Erwachsenenbildung).

language excepted). Spanish comes in second place, followed by Italian and French (cf. also Weiß 2009).

It is interesting to take a closer look at the classes that are offered at Berlin Volkshochschulen. A detailed account of all classes beginning between September 1st 2016 and September 30th 2017 shows the distribution of learning levels according to the Common European Framework of Reference for Languages (CEF).

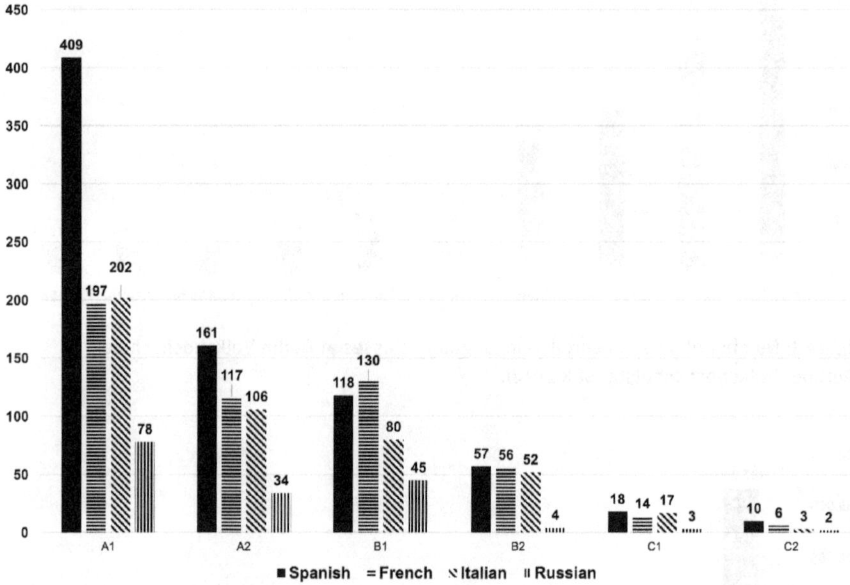

Figure 3: Number of classes starting at Berlin Volkshochschulen between September 2016 and September 2017, by CEF level (classes retrieved from www.berlin.de/vhs/kurse).

Figure 3 shows how the total number of classes was spread across the different levels. The share of advanced classes drops very steeply for Spanish. At level B1, more classes are offered for French than for Spanish. This suggests two tendencies in the market position of the two languages. The total number of language classes and learners shows that Spanish is without a doubt a very popular language. It seems, however, that the vast majority of learners has no prior knowledge which leads to an important demand for beginners' classes. There is still a higher share of people who have a previous knowledge of French, most likely because they learned it at school to some extent. In this case, the target group with a certain level of prior knowledge is relatively larger, so that making them an offer for B-level classes makes sense. Spanish is yet to grow into this position, i.e., the language has not yet achieved the critical mass where there are enough advanced L2 speakers that it would be economically attractive to offer more B or C level classes.

Seeing that French is still a much more widespread foreign language in secondary schools, we can observe how the adult education system connects to the classical education system and complements it. Classes at *Volkshochschulen* fill a demand which is not yet met (or maybe not even present to a larger extent) in secondary schools. One might assume that an important number of language learners decide at a later stage in life that knowing Spanish could be a useful skill, though their precise motivations can vary to a great degree. Specific data about the motivations of Spanish learners at *Volkshochschulen* are currently being gathered and results can be expected to be published soon.

In addition to *Volkshochschulen* as public institutions, a number of private language schools also offer Spanish classes. A few of them specialize in Spanish, including the *Instituto Cervantes* which is a public institution, but not funded by German authorities so that it may count as a private actor on the market.[4] According to a private-run and regularly updated database that pools information about private language schools in Berlin, a total of 29 private language schools offer Spanish courses (Figure 4). As these private institutions are reluctant to share figures and business information, it was impossible to gather reliable data about the exact number of learners or classes in different languages. An estimate would be very vague since there is a large variety of different forms of teaching ranging from individual tutoring via small groups to larger classes. The only quantitative data that is available at this point is the total number of language schools offering Spanish classes as compared to institutes offering other languages.

Again, Spanish is in second place after English. Together with French and Italian, Spanish is a very widely offered language. Since this type of data is very vague in nature, we can only speculate that the three Romance languages might have a similar market share in the private sector. It seems reasonable to assume that the number of language schools offering Spanish classes somehow reflects a very general demand since private schools would not be inclined to offer these classes if they didn't think this was economically beneficial.

To sum up, if we compare all levels of the education system and all types of offers for language training, Spanish and French are competing for the second rank after English. French is still in the lead in the classical public school

4 As Mar-Molinero (2008: 33) points out, the *Instituto Cervantes*, like comparable institutions from other countries, extensively cooperates with commercial actors and sponsors in order to promote language teaching abroad. The line between public and private offers, therefore, is not always completely clear.

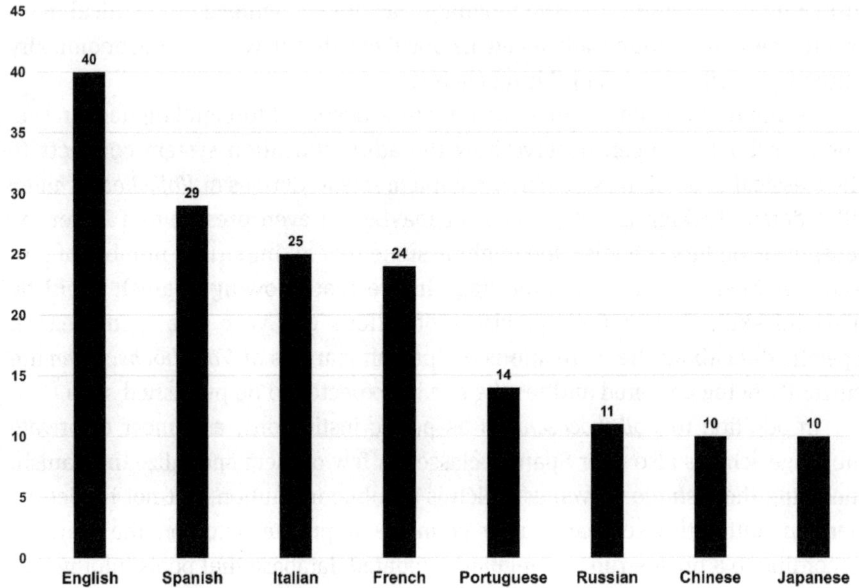

Figure 4: Number of private language schools by languages offered (June 2017). (Source: www.sprachschulen-berlin.info).[5]

system as *the* canonical second foreign language or in some special cases even as a first foreign language. In contrast, Spanish has a head start in adult education. This observation coincides with the general trends all over Germany where French is typically promoted much more intensely than Spanish in secondary education while Spanish is relatively popular in adult education (Grünewald and Küster 2017: 15–16). As a following step, it would be interesting to see whether Spanish learners frequently have some knowledge of French to begin with and expand their language portfolio with Spanish, or whether the two languages are independent of each other. If the first assumption is true, this would be another explanation for the importance of Spanish in the adult education market and the connection between the two parts of the education system. In this case, Spanish skills would be a qualification that adults add to their pre-existing language skills, typically consisting of English and French, sometimes also Latin, which they acquired during their school career. Seeing that Spanish is far from being marginal in secondary school, it is also possible that the current situation

5 Schools that offer several languages are counted once for each language. For schools that have several branches in the city, each branch was counted separately since they sometimes offer different languages in different branches.

attests to a transition which will continuously introduce Spanish as a canonical foreign language at school, either in addition to French or even in its place. Ultimately, this could change the economic character of Spanish as a product on the language market as it would be much more widely available as a regular qualification and much less as an exclusive skill.

The interest in Spanish in the education sector and its competition with French (and, to some extent, also with classical languages like Latin) also reflects a trend towards individualization and pluralization (Coste 2014: 18). What can be observed as a development due to the increasingly multilingual backgrounds and widely varying L1 repertoires of pupils in schools might also be true for the selection of foreign language subjects during the school career: individual motivations and attitudes shape different interests and, therefore, the need for a broader offer of different languages. Similarly, for minority family languages just as much as for canonical foreign languages, we have to take into account that prestige and instrumental value largely direct decisions in language education policy both by policy makers and by parents and pupils (Pfaff et al. 2014: 107). The next chapter will give one example of how Spanish as an L2 can indeed have an instrumental value for speakers and learners in Berlin.

3 Spanish in the hospitality business

3.1 Dataset and background

The presence of Spanish in Berlin's education market suggests that there is not only a considerable demand for learning the language but also a practical relevance for (future) L2 speakers. As mentioned in the introduction, an important part of native Spanish speakers that one can encounter in Berlin are visitors. In contrast to permanent residents, short-term visitors usually are not expected to speak German. The numerous services provided to visitors will often be offered in English as the global lingua franca, but it can nevertheless be attractive to also provide services in the visitors' first languages, especially the widespread ones.

In the tourism statistics for 2016, visitors from Spain were the 3rd largest group with over 310,000 visitors, after the United Kingdom and the USA, and largely before Italy, the Netherlands and France.[6] The number of overnight stays by visitors from Spain has been going up steadily in the past years as the economy of Spain picked up again after the crisis.

6 Tourismus-Statistik Berlin 2016 (Visit Berlin / Amt für Statistik Berlin-Brandenburg).

The visitor statistics for 2016 show that for a total of over 400,000 guests Spanish would most likely be an appropriate means of communication if their country of origin is to be taken as an indicator of their language background (Table 3). A similar deduction on the basis of countries of origin suggests that the number of visitors speaking Spanish, French, and Dutch might be roughly the same.

Table 3: Number of visitors from Spanish-speaking areas in 2015, Berlin tourism agency (Visit Berlin 2017).[7]

Spain	Central America	South America
310,683	30,074	76,401

In 2016, Berlin had a total of 5 million foreign visitors. Visitors from Spanish-speaking countries made up 8.3% of foreign visitors. English is the most important language not only because it is a lingua franca but also due to the number of visitors from the UK and the USA. The complex multilingualism in Berlin tourism makes it interesting to take a closer look at language practices and ideologies in the hospitality business: What do employees in the tourist sector in Berlin think about the role of Spanish in their work environment, in their interaction with guests and customers? What are their attitudes towards Spanish as a foreign language? What are their opinions about foreign languages in general, and about the position of Spanish in particular?

In order to address these questions, I designed an online questionnaire which I distributed with the help of the Berlin-Brandenburg branch of the trade union for the hospitality business (*Gewerkschaft Nahrung-Genuss-Gaststätten*, NGG). A total number of 137 participants completed the questionnaire. Not all of them were prepared to give the postal code of their work place in order to confirm that they did work in Berlin. With these datasets excluded, the sample contained a total of 118 questionnaires. In terms of basic biographical backgrounds, the sample turned out to be well balanced. Respondents aged 20 to 30 years were

7 Visitors from Brazil form an own category in the statistics and hence are not part of the zone called *South America*, leaving almost exclusively Spanish-speaking countries for this category (the number of visitors from Suriname and Guyana will probably be negligible). The zone *Central America* also includes the Caribbean and hence a (probably low) number of citizens from non-Spanish speaking countries such as Jamaica, Haiti or Trinidad and Tobago. Again, the reservations as to the correspondence between country of origin and language background apply.

overrepresented which was to be expected since jobs in hotels and restaurants are typical part-time opportunities for younger people such as students. Work experience of the respondents stretched out between a record of 55 years in the branch to absolute beginners, with an average of 15 years. Male respondents were overrepresented in the sample. Whether there are any gender-based effects in attitudes towards Spanish would be an interesting question for further analysis of the data.

Respondents were also asked to state in which types of business they worked. Again, the sample comprised a relatively well-balanced number of datasets from the two main types of businesses, i.e., accommodation businesses and restauration businesses. Within the category of accommodation businesses, about one half was from the budget segment (hostels, B&Bs, hotels with three stars or less) while the other half was in the advanced or luxury segment (hotels with four or five stars).

Most datasets were from employees working in the inner city districts of Berlin (Mitte, Friedrichshain-Kreuzberg, Charlottenburg-Wilmersdorf, Prenzlauer Berg) where the majority of the hotels or restaurants are located and where visitors typically stay.

3.2 Languages in the hospitality business

The vast majority of the respondents were native speakers of German, only a few were fluent but not native speakers. About one in three respondents had at least some basic knowledge of Spanish. Unsurprisingly, knowledge of English was very widespread. Almost all respondents were fluent in English or they had an advanced level. It is safe to say that English and German are indispensable for any job in the Berlin tourism sector that requires customer contact. This confirms the finding, established for large multinational corporations but valid also for smaller businesses, that “English now fulfils several functions as a business language in Germany” (Erling and Walton 2007: 32).

Knowledge of French was also widespread. More than 60% of the respondents had at least some basic knowledge, even though more advanced skills were rather rare. French has a comfortable head start over Spanish. This places Spanish in a similar category with Italian or Russian as a language which is not completely absent while it doesn’t reach the level of the two dominant foreign languages (Figure 5). Again, these languages coincide with those mentioned by respondents in multinational corporations as being important means of communication in addition to German and English (Erling and Walton 2007: 39).

Languages like Turkish or Arabic that are linked to post-war migration were almost absent from the sample. This was unexpected since the post-migrant

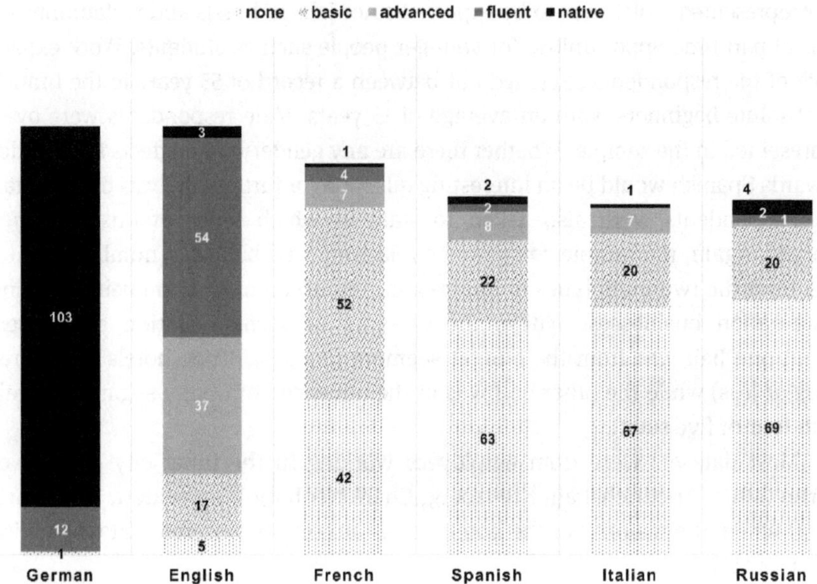

Figure 5: Language skills of the respondents (absolute numbers).

communities are well represented in the hospitality business. However, they were probably hard to reach via the communication channels in which the survey was distributed. Persons with a so-called "migration background" very often work in family owned businesses in the hospitality industry. Hence they were much less likely to receive the invitation to the survey because they usually are not members of the trade union I cooperated with.

Respondents were also able to fill in languages that were missing in the list. This yielded a number of very different languages on different skill levels. Polish, Dutch or Scandinavian languages but also Japanese and Korean were mentioned several times. Also some less widespread languages like Mandinka, Guaraní, Estonian and German Sign Language were mentioned.

3.3 Utility and necessity of Spanish

With their varied skills, employees in the tourist sector are able to communicate with speakers from many different backgrounds. In theory, at least, they fulfil a key requirement for rentable activities in a multilingual work environment with a highly diverse clientele (Duchêne 2011: 84–85). However, this doesn't automatically mean that they make use of their language skills. The object of the subsequent question set was the relevance of foreign languages in the employees' daily work routine. Respondents were asked to rate the utility of a number of languages for their professional activities. As was to be expected, the vast majority confirmed that they use languages other than German on a daily basis. Half of the respondents said that they were in contact with Spanish speakers in the work place at least once a week or even daily. While there was no doubt about the predominant utility of German and English, French and Spanish now received a similar score. Opinions about French seemed a little more divided so that the number of respondents who rated the usefulness of Spanish in the top two levels was even slightly higher than that for French (Figure 6). Compared to the level of actual competence in the two Romance languages, Spanish has already become more relevant in reality than the distribution of Spanish skills suggests.

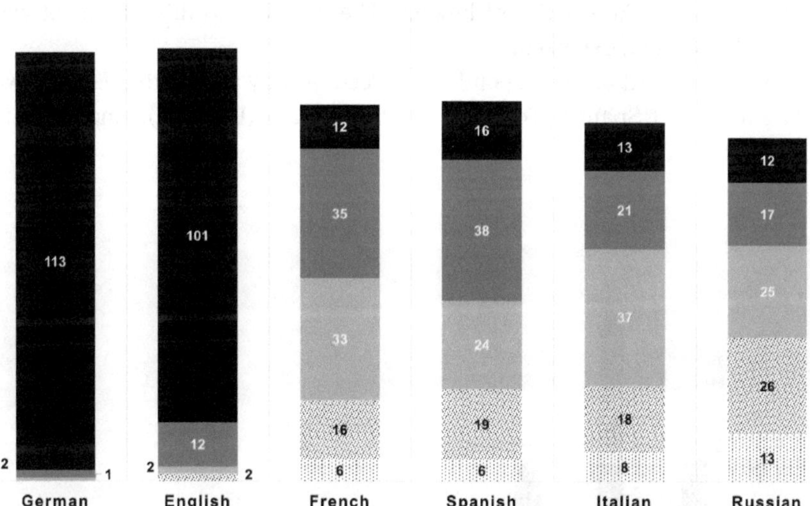

Figure 6: Respondents' utility ranking of languages in the hospitality business (absolute numbers).

Interestingly, the answers for Spanish and French show quite a considerable level of correlation with a high significance.[8] This correlation is much stronger than that between the rates for English and Spanish, or between English and

8 Kendall's rank correlation: $z = 8.0842$, $p = 6.259e^{-16}$, $tau = 0.6767247$.
Pearson's product moment correlation: $t = 11.233$, $df = 97$, p-value $< 2.2e^{-16}$, $cor = 0.7519247$.

French. It seems that those respondents who thought Spanish was useful also found French useful, or vice versa.

This points at two different mind-sets among staff in the hospitality business. There is one group of persons who think that English is sufficient to communicate with non-German speaking guests. Another group is convinced that additional languages are indeed useful, but it doesn't matter whether this is French, Spanish or both. What counts is the ability to communicate in the customers' or guests' own language. Consequently, the judgment about the utility of English for all other speakers is independent from this question.

This particular question – the utility of English and Spanish as compared to other languages – was part of another section of the survey consisting of a number of metalinguistic statements for which respondents were asked to give levels of agreement. Judgments were to be given on a five-step Likert scale marked "fully disagree" and "fully agree" on the extremes.

One such statement was the claim that Spanish was unnecessary as long as one had sufficient knowledge of English. The reactions to this statement were less conclusive than expected.

About one third of the respondents agreed or fully agreed that English was sufficient so that Spanish skills were not necessary (Figure 7). Another third

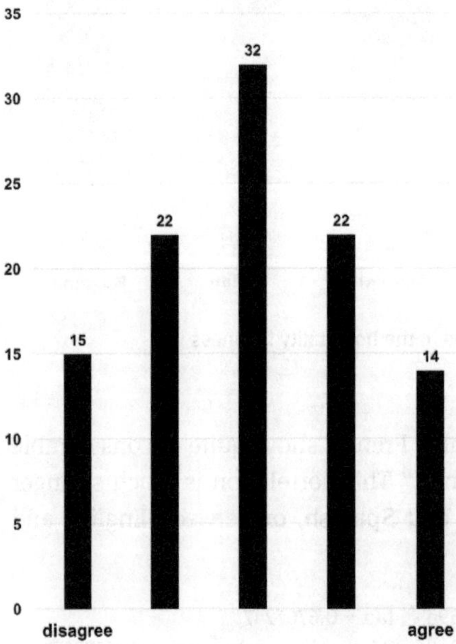

Figure 7: Answers to the statement "If you have good English skills, you don't need to speak Spanish to work in the hospitality business".

disagreed more or less strongly, while the third part was indifferent. In total, this question yielded almost a perfect distribution.

The difference of the reactions to this question as compared to the previous one can be explained with nuances in the phrasing. In the first case, respondents were asked to rank languages according to how *useful* they were. The second question was about whether or not Spanish was *necessary* for speakers of English. Even though the result for the second question might look inconclusive, the comparison of the two does tell us something about the attitudes towards Spanish. It seems that employees in Berlin's tourism sector indeed found it a useful skill to have although it is not immediately necessary since, as the overview of the respondents' language skills showed, they all have sufficient knowledge of English.

A language with this profile can be an asset on the work market. Employers will always expect their staff to have a skill that is indispensable. A skill which is useful but not expected might increase a candidate's career chances.

Ultimately, such rankings and comparisons show how speakers attribute a certain market value to each language and how they also assess these values through comparing one language to another. What exactly establishes this value and how speakers evaluate the utility of a language, then, needs to be explored in more detail. The judgement whether or not Spanish was useful at all didn't depend on a person's Spanish skills as such. One could expect that those who speak Spanish would tend to present their qualification as useful because it would seem odd to admit to having skills with no relevance. Conversely, non-speakers of Spanish might want to tone down the importance of Spanish skills as a face-saving strategy. Yet, no conclusive correlation could be found between the level of Spanish skills and the utility judgment. It seems that Spanish-speaking and non-Spanish-speaking employees assess the relevance of the language primarily on the basis of external criteria such as communicative or economic utility construed from observations independent of their own language skills (see below, parts 3.5 and 3.6).

In order to identify factors which further contribute to judgments about Spanish, respondents were asked to mark their agreement or disagreement with a number of further statements, again using Likert scales as described above. The statements addressed three dimensions of language attitudes: economic utility, communicative utility and an affective or intuitive component. These areas of reflection relate to established categories in sociolinguistic research which regularly operate with attitudes that are either connected to status or to solidarity (Dragojevic 2017: 9). The two categories of utility, then, lean towards the status dimension while the affective component is connected to the solidarity status that a language represents in the eyes of the speakers. Additionally, the two utility dimensions connect to what has been called “instrumental” and “integrative” orientations in L2 learning motivations (Noels 2001). The “instrumental” orientation mirrors the expectation of gaining material benefit from the qualification while the “integrative” orientation is supported by the expectation of gaining personal contacts and opportunities to communicate with more people.

However, it would be a simplification to assume that every element of reflection and hence each of the statements presented in the questionnaire corresponds directly to only one of the three dimensions that guide the analysis. They should rather be considered as a continuum from economic utility via communicative utility to the affective component. The affective judgement of a language is closely related to the perceived communicative value, especially when communication in informal settings with friends or family members is concerned. The communicative value attributed to a language, on the other hand, can also have implications for its economic utility.

3.4 Affective component

In order to assess the affective value of Spanish, respondents were asked whether they thought that Spanish was a difficult and a beautiful language, and whether they considered learning it a waste of time. This last item was supposed to test if respondents generally saw an abstract value in the language beyond mere material use while the two other items addressed widespread stereotypes attached to most languages of the world that are known to a larger number of non-speakers.

Interestingly, respondents did not qualify Spanish as a particularly difficult language (Figure 8, left). This is rather surprising given the structural distance between German and Romance languages, especially since speakers of German traditionally tend to see French as a rather difficult language to learn (Sigott 1993: 24). It would be interesting to explore in more detail what triggers this difference in judgments about these two closely related languages that share many structural properties.

In the particular context of the present study, there might be two possible explanations: A considerable number of respondents had previous knowledge of French, so they might consider Spanish rather easy to learn with this background which enables a transfer within the Romance language family. Additionally, many respondents stated that they were often confronted with speakers of East Asian languages like Korean and Japanese. In comparison with these languages which are considered more distant, Spanish maybe seemed much more accessible.

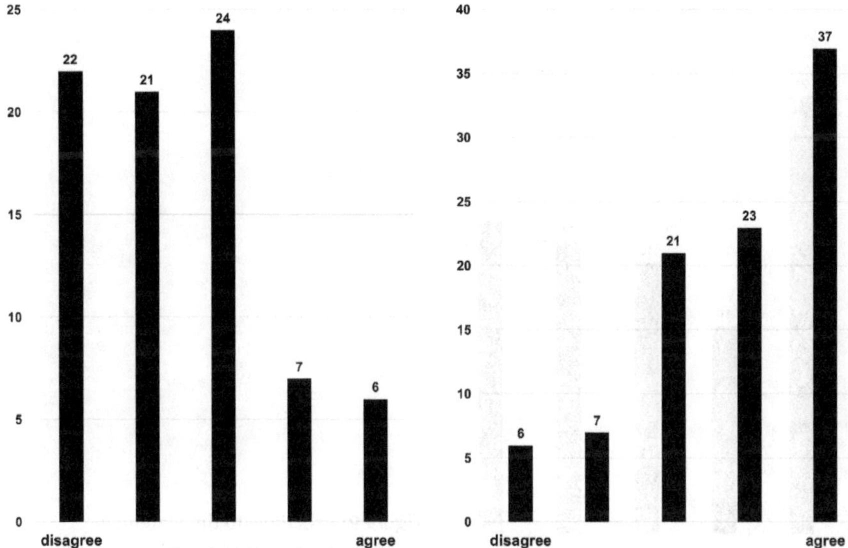

Figure 8: Reactions to the statement "Spanish is a difficult language" (left) and "Spanish is a beautiful language" (right).

As for the aesthetic judgment, a clear majority agreed with the statement that Spanish was a beautiful language (Figure 8, right). This result is in line with other studies in which Spanish was evaluated as a particularly likeable language (see e.g., Plewnia and Rothe 2011 who conducted a study among pupils in 9th and 10th grade).

Generally speaking, Spanish had a rather favourable position among employees in the tourist sector. One might expect that this would lead to an increased motivation to learn Spanish. This question was put before those respondents who stated that they didn't have any knowledge of Spanish. The result was surprisingly inconclusive (Figure 9).

The respondents were virtually divided between the options. It seems, then, that other factors must play a more decisive role. Even though Spanish benefits from a very positive image, the motivation to actually learn it doesn't depend exclusively on affective and intuitive attitudes. More rational arguments like utility most likely also play a role. It can't be excluded that this component was also influenced by the fact that the whole questionnaire was very much centred on languages in the workplace, so respondents might have put more weight on the utility component in this context than they would have done in a different setting.

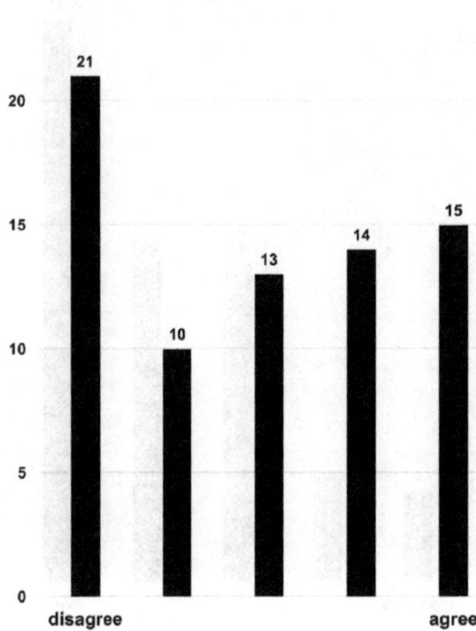

Figure 9: Reactions to the statement "I would like to learn Spanish in the future".

3.5 Communicative utility

As mentioned above, the question whether or not Spanish is useful or valuable can have two sides: On the one hand, speakers judge the utility of a language based on its communicative reach: Does it help me to talk to more people than if I didn't speak Spanish? Is it in any way helpful to connect with other people? Does it provide a communicative advantage even though it might not be strictly necessary, e.g., on a symbolic level to show respect or to accommodate others? It has been shown that positive attitudes – including affective values – increase the inclination to speak a language (Dragojevic 2017: 17). On the other hand, speakers can also judge a language on the basis of a material benefit it brings along.

In order to test the first of the two dimensions, respondents were asked whether they thought they should try to speak the languages of their guests whenever this is possible. This was intended to find out in greater detail what "communicative utility" meant to the respondents. It has been shown that the wish to interact with a specific speaker group can sustain learning motivations (Noels 2001: 128). However, a widespread view also holds that "communication and multilingualism are antitethical" (Lo Bianco 2017: 34). In the present context, this would mean that some respondents might consider it more useful to have a good command of English in order to communicate successfully with guests rather than speaking several languages "imperfectly" according to their self-perception. Communication can be efficient if both parties use a language that they speak well, and in many cases this will probably be English. However, in a business setting, language choice also has a service component so that speaking a particular language on a sufficient or even basic level can also be useful in the sense that an employee can accommodate customers with speaking their language. As Graddol (1997: 29) points out, "there is a rule of thumb that [. . .] selling must be carried out in the customer's language unless the commodity is in short supply or there is a monopoly provider." Since the hospitality business is a highly competitive market, the rule of thumb clearly applies, which frequently leads to a choice of language for the guest's benefit while the employee uses a language they are less familiar with.

Upon the statement that employees should preferably use the guest's language, respondents' opinions were split (Figure 10, left). There was only a slight tendency to agreement, but a relative majority was indifferent toward this question.

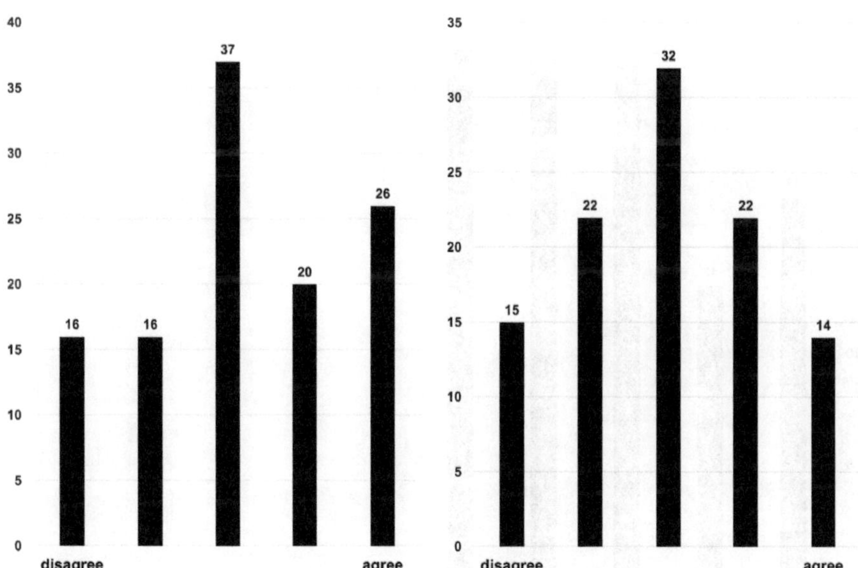

Figure 10: Reactions to the statement "In the hospitality business, you should speak the customer's language whenever possible" (left) and "If you have good English skills, you don't need to speak Spanish for a job in the hospitality industry".

The opposite scenario to accommodating customers in their first language would be an all-English policy for any non-German-speaking guest. Therefore I also asked whether respondents felt it was unnecessary to speak Spanish if they had a good command of English. If this was the case, the utility of Spanish would be more that of a symbolic gesture rather than a real communicative need. Again, the results were spread almost evenly across all possible opinions (Figure 10, right).

Once again, Spanish is in the in-between position. It can be a useful option, but it still is more of an individual choice than a basic requirement. Spanish seems to be neither indispensable nor superfluous. In a service situation, "necessity" is not the only or even the primary criterion for using a particular language. Choices are made in a space of possibilities which comprises language skills, preferences and symbolic values of all the languages that are potentially available. Symbolic value is especially important for customer relations in order to show consideration and courtesy.

As a matter of fact, a considerable majority of respondents agreed with the statement that Spanish skills help to provide a better service (Figure 11).

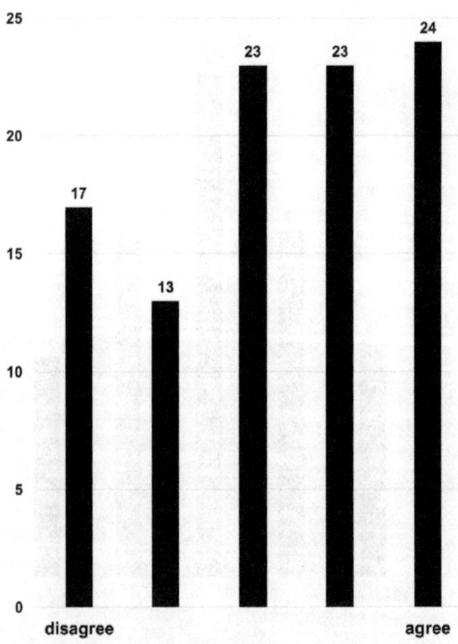

Figure 11: Reactions to the statement "With the help of Spanish skills, you can provide better service".

Among those respondents who didn't have any knowledge of Spanish, more than one in three reported that customers sometimes addressed them in Spanish even though they did not even know whether they spoke Spanish at all. On the other hand, the vast majority (78.9%) said that their customers were not surprised when they didn't receive service in Spanish.

As a general rule, speaking Spanish in the hospitality business might have a function similar to that of a free welcome drink: it is not something that customers expect to get or that is part of indispensable services, but it makes a good impression and can enhance customer loyalty or satisfaction. In a highly competitive market, this can be a very decisive factor. For Berlin's tourism business, then, Spanish is a soft factor that contributes to a differentiation of services and individualizes businesses in the sector.

3.6 Economic utility

As mentioned above, the third and last level of reflection about Spanish tested in the questionnaire is the economic significance of the language, especially that for the respondents themselves. The communicative utility described until now was mainly oriented towards guests or customers and the way they benefit from Spanish skills of employees because they receive better service or because they need to make less of an effort to communicate. The question whether the employees themselves benefit from their skills is independent from this external value.

One indicator for such a personal benefit is the hiring process. Only a small number of participants confirmed that language skills in general were explicitly considered when they applied for a job in the hospitality business or when they employed others (Figure 12, left). Two interpretations are possible for these findings. Either the owners or managers do not think that language skills are important after all – an assumption which seems implausible in this work context because most probably the opposite is true so that language skills are seen as a matter of course. Most likely the respondents took issue with the idea that language skills were to be considered "explicitly", as stated in the questionnaire, because they felt that this would suggest language skills were more important than other qualifications.

Since the clientele of most businesses is probably very heterogeneous, one can assume that most owners do not necessarily look for skills in particular languages other than English. Consequently, it was not to be expected that respondents would value Spanish as a major career asset, but still one in five (22%) agreed with the statement that Spanish skills increased career prospects in the hospitality business.

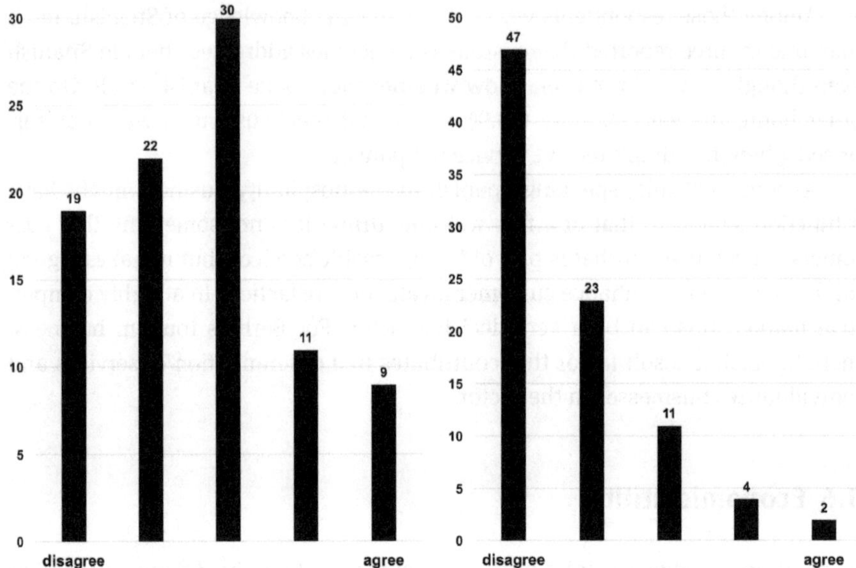

Figure 12: Reactions to the statements "Spanish skills improve career prospects in the hospitality business" (left) and "Spanish skills are a good argument to demand a higher wage" (right).

Given the rather low demand for Spanish on the work market in the hospitality business, it is no surprise that Spanish skills do not yield any immediate material benefits for the employees. Most respondents disagreed with the statement that knowing Spanish would be a factor which could allow them to ask for a higher wage (Figure 12, right).

We have to bear in mind, however, that the hospitality business is a low-wage sector, so it is probably quite difficult to negotiate better salaries on the basis of individual qualifications, especially if the given qualification is not felt to be indispensable. In more general terms, Spanish skills have not reached a level of relevance that would make them a primary qualification on the job market in the hospitality sector. A majority of respondents said that speaking Spanish would not increase their chances if they were looking for a new job.

It seems that the numerical importance of Spanish-speaking guests and customers in Berlin is not mirrored in the material value of Spanish skills in the hospitality business. There is no direct reflection of the language's presence in this branch and its recognition as a qualification on the work market in terms of career development or salary. As Duchêne (2011: 104) puts it, we can observe a certain level of "banalization" of multilingualism due to the lack of recognition and material remuneration of skills which, after all, are pivotal for the economic success of the businesses. In the United States, the "return on investment" for Spanish on the work market has been shown to be particularly low compared to other languages because there is a relatively high number of potential employees who speak Spanish (Hogan-Brun 2017: 85–86). In the tourist sector in Berlin, the purely material value of Spanish seems to be similarly low even though there is a substantial number of Spanish-speaking customers and the supply in workforce with this particular skill is not abundantly available. However, as Berlin is generally a very multilingual city, the tourism industry is in a fairly comfortable situation since employers will generally have no difficulty finding potential employees who speak other languages than English and German. In comparison to other places and countries, especially those where English is the dominant language or where foreign language learning is less widespread, this is certainly an advantage for Berlin (see e.g., Leslie and Russell 2006 for the limitations in the British tourism industry).

4 Conclusion: global Spanish as a resource and a product

In a broad perspective, Spanish has an ambivalent position in Berlin's "language market" and in the hospitality business as one of the key sectors where contact with speakers of Spanish is frequent.

On the market for foreign language learning, Spanish is offered in some particular sectors. It is present first and foremost in the adult education market, while the classical education system from kindergartens to secondary schools has not quite caught up with French. Spanish seems to be a typical skill that people add *after* they completed primary and secondary education. In this particular position, Spanish is an attractive "product" to sell because the adult education sector is much more open to private businesses and to commercial providers than regular education. While there might be competition between French and Spanish as foreign languages in the second rank behind English, French is still much more monopolized by public institutions of general education so that Spanish offers more opportunities for commercial providers. In addition, "global Spanish" profits from its world-wide image and the multiple positive connotations attached to it. The ideal of Spanish is stripped of negative political or historical references which might weaken its reputation such as the colonial past or a notion of present-day linguistic imperialism similar to that attached to English – provided that learners are or were familiar with this historical background at all (Mar-Molinero and Paffey 2011: 759–761; García 2011: 680–681; Schneider 2014). At the same time, the realities in Berlin and many other places in the world show how Spanish is more and more detached from commonplace associations with a specific nation or territory (Berthele 2008). Instead, it is increasingly becoming an abstract idea associated with cultural references, practices and attitudes.

Investigating the position of Spanish on the language market brings along another key question which ultimately also touches upon linguists' conceptions of languages. The way languages are taught and learned today still very much reflects the idea of discrete units (Makoni and Pennycook 2005). Booking a language class is a deliberate choice for one language over another, and the bookings themselves break down the immaterial and continuous acquisition of knowledge into small packages with a distinct price. This way, the position of a particular language within the confusing linguistic diversity of a modern metropolis can become more visible. Simultaneously, offering such "product units" perpetuates the image of languages as homogeneous entities which can be delimited, named (as such, they appear in catalogues, class schedules, invoices, pay slips etc.) and also connected to particular values, stereotypes and attitudes. Despite the ongoing "paradigm shift" in linguistics towards a conception of language as less clearly bounded and stable forms of speech and communication (Blommaert and Rampton 2011: 3), this way of treating named languages within the superdiverse setting of a city like Berlin needs to be reflected in research. Since the conception of languages – and specifically their standard forms – are deeply entrenched "ideas in the mind" of most speakers and learners (Milroy 2001: 543), linguistics needs to reflect this reality. As a consequence, we need to accept to some extent the fiction of languages as units which, in turn, also shapes the setup and practices of our research.

Teaching languages as "units", however, always remains a fictitious act. Both teachers and learners might think that they target a particular "standard" to acquire. Yet, learners often have a (conscious or unconscious) personal affinity for a specific regionally and socially bound form of language while the teacher or other learners may use different ones. The classroom itself, then, becomes a space where the "system" that we call Spanish is immanently variable and subject not only to influences from the learners' first languages but also from their preferences within the wide variational spectrum of Spanish. Such preferences need not necessarily be connected to particular countries or nations (Ricento 2017). Learning Spanish very often is more of a global trend or a lifestyle choice rather than a mere act of "buying a product *made in Spain*".

As far as the hospitality business is concerned, Spanish skills are not as widespread as French skills. Nevertheless, employees in this sector have very positive attitudes towards Spanish. They generally consider Spanish to be a useful language, one that can be an asset and that can help provide good services. Most respondents reported that they were frequently in contact with Spanish speakers, so those who speak Spanish have ample opportunity to use their skills. Nevertheless, Spanish is not (yet) deemed an indispensable skill. As of now, the position of Spanish in the hospitality sector is probably most aptly described with the formula *useful, but not necessary*. The positive judgments about Spanish and its use for the benefit of customers are in stark contrast to attitudes frequently expressed in the United States where Spanish is much more associated with a negative stereotypical image of "the immigrant", with low prestige and a weak socioeconomic value. Within the English-only ideology of the US, offering services in Spanish is seen by many as an unnecessary or even dishonourable gesture towards "the others" (Fuller 2013: 13–18). While this attitude targets permanent residents of the country and their linguistic rights, employees in the hospitality business in Berlin construct speakers of Spanish as short-time visitors or guests so that the language itself is seen as an entity exterior to the society they live in. This makes it easier to attach unreserved positive associations to the language since it is not seen as a threat to the constructed self-image of the surrounding society.

The benefits of Spanish skills are distributed unevenly. If employees in the tourism sector speak Spanish, this is most useful for those guests or customers who are speakers of Spanish and who may have difficulty communicating in English or German. Such a particular service may help increase customer satisfaction and loyalty which can yield direct or indirect profit for the business owners (see Duchêne 2011 for a similar account in another travel related setting viz. the airport of Zurich). The employees themselves rarely benefit materially from their Spanish skills since they are not valued in this particular dimension on the work market. It seems, though, that this is not the primary motivation to learn Spanish anyway. Instead, personal and immaterial motivations prevail. Second language speakers in Berlin do indeed benefit from their Spanish skills in that they gain better access to a cultural context they are interested in.

García (2011: 679) objects to the widespread notion that "although Spanish is demographically powerful, it is economically weak". On a global scale, the objection is certainly warranted. Nevertheless, as far as Berlin is concerned, economic considerations are not the predominant factors that make people choose to learn Spanish. As a matter of fact, the direct material value of Spanish in Berlin's hospitality business is limited. Affective factors, a positive image, trends and especially private motivations seem to be much more important motivations for learners of Spanish than work or business (see Schneider 2010: 650 for a similar scenario in the specific setting of Salsa communities).

This is true even for many employees in the hospitality sector who are in contact with the language on a regular basis in a professional setting.

These observations also have an impact on the way we can consider languages as resources. Thus far, the *language-as-resource* framework mainly looks at multilingual settings in which traditional or new minority languages are targeted by language policy and planning. However, also "big" languages and canonical second languages taught in education systems can be considered in the light of this framework. It can be noted, then, that Spanish, just as English, is a global language which is considered to have a high status as a resource. Yet, its status is more that of a cultural and social than an economic resource (Lo Bianco 2017: 42–45). It would be interesting to explore in what way this influences the L2 speakers' ambition to achieve a certain level of proficiency. Maybe the fact that an overwhelming majority of Spanish classes are offered at level A is not only a consequence of most adult learners having no previous knowledge of Spanish. It might just as well indicate that many of them don't necessarily feel the need to get to an advanced level if Spanish unfolds its value as a social and cultural resource already at a more basic level. In terms of a language's status as an economic resource, the concept might need further specification as to the beneficiary of the resource: As the example of Spanish in Berlin's hospitality industry shows, a language can be a an external rather than an internal resource, that is, a resource which is located with the speaker while others (who do not necessarily speak the language themselves) benefit from it.

References

Amt für Statistik Berlin-Brandenburg. 2017. *Statistischer Bericht. Einwohnerinnen und Einwohner im Land Berlin am 31. Dezember 2016.*

Bayerisches Landesamt für Statistik und Datenverarbeitung. 2018. *Beherbergungsstatistik Januar – Dezember 2017.* https://www.muenchen.de/rathaus/Stadtverwaltung/Referat-fuer-Arbeit-und-Wirtschaft/Tourismusamt/B2B/Statistik.html (accessed 16 March 2018).

Berlin Business Location Center. 2017. *Mehrsprachige Kitas in Berlin.*

Berthele, Raphael. 2008. A Nation is a Territory with one Culture and one Language. The Role of Metaphorical Folk Models in Language Policy Debates. In Gitte Kristiansen & René Dirven (eds.), *Cognitive Sociolinguistics: Language variation, cultural models, social systems*, 301–332. Berlin & New York: Mouton de Gruyter.

Blommaert, Jan & Ben Rampton. 2011. Language and superdiversity. *Diversities* 13(2). 1–21.

Coste, Daniel. 2014. Plurilingualism and the challenges of education. In Patrick Grommes & Adelheid Hu (eds.), *Plurilingual education. Policies – practices – language development*, 15–32. Amsterdam: Benjamins.

Coulmas, Florian. 1992. *Language and economy.* Oxford et al.: Blackwell.

de Jong, Esther J., Zhou Li, Aliya M. Zafar & Chiu-Hui Wu. 2016. Language policy in multilingual contexts: Revisiting Ruiz's "language-as-resource" orientation. *Bilingual Research Journal* 39. 200–212.

Dörnyei, Zoltán. 1998. Motivation in second and foreign language learning. *Language Teaching* 31. 117–135.

Dörnyei, Zoltán (ed.). 2003. *Attitudes, orientations, and motivations in language learning*. Malden & Oxford: Blackwell.

Dörnyei, Zoltán & Richard Schmidt (eds.). 2001. *Motivation and Second Language Acquisition*. Honolulu: National Foreign Language Resource Center.

Dragojevic, Marko. 2017. Language Attitudes. *Oxford Research Encyclopedia of Communication. Subject: Language and Social Interaction, Intergroup Communication* DOI: 10.1093/acrefore/9780190228613.013.437.

Duchêne, Alexandre. 2011. Néolibéralisme, inégalités sociales et plurilinguisme: l'exploitation des ressources langagières et des locuteurs. *Langage et société* 136. 81–108.

Duchêne, Alexandre & Ingrid Piller. 2011. Mehrsprachigkeit als Wirtschaftsgut: Sprachliche Ideologien und Praktiken in der Tourismusindustrie. In Georg Kreis (ed.), *Babylon Europa. Zur europäischen Sprachlandschaft*, 135–157. Basel: Schwabe.

Erling, Elizabeth J. & Alan Walton. 2007. English at work in Berlin. *English Today* 23(1). 32–40.

Fuller, Janet M. 2013. *Spanish speakers in the USA*. Bristol et al.: Multilingual Matters.

García, Ofelia. 2011. Planning Spanish: Nationalizing, Minoritizing and Globalizing Performances. In Manuel Díaz-Campos (ed.), *The Handbook of Hispanic Sociolinguistics*, 667–685. Malden et al.: Blackwell.

Gardner, Robert C. & Wallace E. Lambert. 1972. *Attitudes and Motivation in Second-Language Learning*. Rowley, MA: Newbury House.

Gärtig, Anne-Kathrin, Albrecht Plewnia & Astrid Rothe. 2010. *Wie Menschen in Deutschland über Sprache denken. Ergebnisse einer bundesweiten Repräsentativerhebung zu aktuellen Spracheinstellungen*. Mannheim: Institut für Deutsche Sprache.

Graddol, David. 1997. *The Future of English? A guide to forecasting the popularity of the English language in the 21st century*. London: British Council / The English Company.

Grin, François. 1996. Economic approaches to language and language planning: an introduction. *International Journal of the Sociology of Language* 121. 1–16.

Grin, François. 2003. Language planning and economics. In: *Current Issues in Language Planning* 4(1). 1–66.DOI: 10.1080/14664200308668048 (accessed 22 September 2017).

Grünewald, Andreas & Lutz Küster (eds.). 2017. *Fachdidaktik Spanisch. Handbuch für Theorie und Praxis*. Stuttgart: Klett.

Hogan-Brun, Gabrielle. 2017. *Linguanomics. What is the market potential of multilingualism?* London et al.: Bloomsbury.

Huntemann, Hella & Elisabeth Reichart. 2016. *Volkshochschul-Statistik: 54. Folge, Arbeitsjahr 2015*.

Leslie, David & Hilary Russell. 2006. The importance of foreign language skills in the tourism sector: A comparative study of student perceptions in the UK and continental Europe. *Tourism Management* 27(6). 1397–1407.

Lo Bianco, Joseph. 2017. Accent on the positive. Revisiting the "Language as Resource" orientation for bolstering multilingualism in contemporary urban Europe. In Hagen Peukert & Ingrid Gogolin (ed.), *Dynamics of Linguistic Diversity*, 31–48. Amsterdam: Benjamins.

Makoni, Sinfree & Alastair Pennycook. 2005. Disinventing and (Re)Constituting Languages. *Critical Inquiry in Language Studies* 2(3). 137–156.
Mar-Molinero, Clare. 2008. Subverting Cervantes. Language Authority in Global Spanish. *International Multilingual Research Journal* 2(1–2). 27–47.
Mar-Molinero, Clare & Darren Paffey. 2011. Linguistic Imperialism: Who Owns Global Spanish? In Manuel Díaz-Campos (ed.), *The Handbook of Hispanic Sociolinguistics*, 747–764. Malden et al.: Blackwell.
Milroy, James. 2001. Language ideologies and the consequences of standardization. *Journal of Sociolinguistics* 5(4). 530–555.
Noels, Kimberly A. 2001. Learning Spanish as a Second Language: Learners' Orientations and Perceptions of Their Teachers' Communication Style. *Language Learning* 51(1). 107–144.
Pfaff, Carol W., Jingfei Liang, Meral Dollnick, Marta Rusek & Lisa Heinzmann. 2014. Minority language instruction in Berlin and Brandenburg. Overview and case studies of Sorbian, Polish, Turkish and Chinese. In Patrick Grommes & Adelheid Hu (eds.), *Plurilingual education. Policies – practices – language development*. 87–110. Amsterdam: Benjamins.
Plewnia, Albrecht & Astrid Rothe. 2011. Spracheinstellungen und Mehrsprachigkeit. Wie Schüler über ihre und andere Sprachen denken. In Ludwig M. Eichinger, Albrecht Plewnia & Melanie Steinle (eds.), *Sprache und Integration. Über Mehrsprachigkeit und Migration*, 215–253. Tübingen: Narr.
Ricento, Thomas. 2017. Conzeptualizing language: linguistic theory and language policy. *Dynamics of Linguistic Diversity* 6. 13–29.
Ruíz, Richard. 1984. Orientations in Language Planning. *Bilingual Research Journal* 8(2). 15–34.
Schneider, Britta. 2010. Multilingual Cosmopolitanism and Monolingual Commodification: Language Ideologies in Transnational Salsa Communities. *Language in Society* 39(5). 647–668.
Schneider, Britta. 2014. *Salsa, language and transnationalism* .Bristol et al.: Multilingual Matters.
Sigott, Günther. 1993. *Zur Lernbarkeit von Englisch und Französisch für deutsche Muttersprachler: eine exploratorische Pilotstudie*. Tübingen: Narr.
Statistikamt Nord. 2017. *Statistische Berichte – Ausländische Bevölkerung in Hamburg am 31.12.2016*.
Statistikamt Nord. 2018. *Statistische Berichte – Beherbergung im Reiseverkehr in Hamburg. Dezember 2017*.
Statistisches Amt München. 2018. *Die ausländische Bevölkerung nach der Staatsangehörigkeit 2017*.
Visit Berlin. 2017. *Tourismus-Statistik 2016*. Amt für Statistik Berlin-Brandenburg.
Weiß, Christina. 2009. Fremdsprachen – Trendsprachen. Konjunkturen des Sprachenerwerbs Erwachsener am Beispiel des Volkshochschulangebots. *DIE Zeitschrift für Erwachsenenbildung* (2). 45–48.

Section 4: **Localities**

Janet M. Fuller

12 Linguistic landscapes and the making of an imagined community

1 Introduction

What does it mean to be "cosmopolitan" in Berlin? This study examines the construction of an imagined cosmopolitan community with a walk through the linguistic landscape of Berlin and an analysis of the underlying language ideologies. There are competing discourses of inclusion and exclusion reproduced through signs on businesses in the Berlin space, reflecting the complex positionings of different groups in society.

This analysis is embedded in ongoing ethnographic, sociolinguistic and discourse analytic research which examines issues of multilingualism, immigration, and national belonging in Berlin and Germany. The insights and interpretations are based on my previous linguistic ethnography in bilingual classrooms (2005–2006), my own experiences living in Berlin (most recently 2013–2014, with frequent research visits since that time), and consumption of German media (books, newspapers, TV and film), as well as more structured research activities such as interviews with young Berliners and media analyses of online discussion about immigration and integration. This is a qualitative analysis, firmly situated in an ethnographic tradition; while it clearly does not represent all perspectives on language ideologies in Berlin, it captures many social implications of language choice in the linguistic landscape of this city.

The study of linguistic landscapes has emerged as a way to study the use of language in the public sphere, including signs, business names, window displays, advertisements, and graffiti – in short, all visible use of language. As noted by Landry and Bourhis (1997), the issue in the linguistic landscape is the salience of particular codes. Such language use is significant because it does not merely reflect the patterns of use, social statuses and meanings of particular languages, but also shapes their perceived values and works to construct identities and identity categories (Shohamy, Ben-Rafael, and Barni 2010; Cenoz and Gorter 2006; Gorter 2013; Helôt et al 2012; Stroud and Mpendukana 2009). Linguistic landscapes do not represent populations of speakers in a straightfor-

https://doi.org/10.1515/9781501508103-012

ward way – that is, the language varieties which appear the most are not necessarily the vernaculars of the majority – but rather, these public linguistic presentations reproduce ideologies about language and particular codes. The linguistic landscape can thus perpetuate the dominance of a majority code or challenge hegemonic language ideologies, or, as is often the case, do both of these things.

The current study focuses on the language choices in signs used by commercial enterprises for store names, advertising slogans, and information about their goods and services. I address the process of cultural commodification, through which association with a culture becomes something you can buy. Leeman and Moden (2010: 191) note that language is a "readily identifiable index of ethnicity and cultural authenticity" and it is often commodified as such. The creators of particular signs thus make use of the symbolic dominance of a particular variety in order to attract customers, but may also employ minority languages to commodify diversity. The use of immigrant languages in the cityscape is part of the creation of their significance (Bogatto and Helôt 2010) but can also construct essentialist identities for immigrant groups.

There are two main trends in the commodification of language varieties in the Berlin linguistic landscape which I will discuss. First, English is often used to construct a global/modern identity for businesses and their customers; this has been noted in other studies in Berlin (Papen 2012), in other places in Germany (Piller 2001, 2003) and elsewhere (e.g., Kasanga 2010). Second, minority languages and dialects are used as an index to a particular cultural, ethnic, regional or national group; in the symbolic economy, such uses are often an attempt to sell authenticity (Heller 2003; Leeman and Modan 2009, 2010).

However, multilingual practices (passive and active) are also part of the construction of a cosmopolitan identity. As discussed in the introduction to this volume, the Berlin brand of cosmopolitanism is not (or not solely) about access to high culture (see also Mandel 2008). Berlin cosmopolitanism is also about familiarity with products and customs from many sources, what Pécoud (2002) describes as a kind of intercultural competence and diversity in everyday life. Such cosmopolitanism is often linked to consumer habits. Thus, language choices are used to target articular audiences, but also to sell the commodity of cosmopolitanism itself. In Berlin, this involves languages which are rooted in its complex history of immigration and integration. The linguistic landscapes discussed here illustrate how the transnational experiences of some blend into the cosmopolitan lives of others.

2 Social identities, language ideologies, and the construction of the imagined community

This research relies on a social constructivist perspective which holds that both the social identities of individuals and social categories (e.g., national or ethnic groups) are discursively produced and reproduced. That is, the identities of speakers (or writers) are not the source but the outcome of language use (Bucholtz and Hall 2005). Similarly, the boundaries of social categories, and their associated characteristics, are not fixed but are something that is reproduced and reconstructed through discourse.

There is also the construction of the imagined community, a term developed by Anderson ([1983] 1991, 2006). National communities are prime examples of imagined communities; although a member of a nation cannot possibly know all, or even most, of their fellow members, there is a sense of community: "It is imagined as a *community*, because, regardless of the actual inequality and exploitation that may prevail in each, the nation is always conceived as a deep, horizontal comradeship" (Anderson 1983: 1516; italics in original).

In this analysis, I focus not on the nation but on the city-state of Berlin as an imagined community, and examine how local identities based on putative linguistic proficiency are constructed through language choices on signs. These identities are part of the construction of the imagined community of Berlin; that is, the languages (or at least words) understood by the consumers in this community are linked to consumption preferences which are indicative of social and cultural traits and customs.

Ideologies about the value of different ways of speaking are inherent in the construction of language-based social categories. Those constructing the linguistic landscape draw on social meanings and associations of particular lexical items, phrases, and codes to create an image and identity for their businesses and the customers they serve.

A dominant language ideology in many countries is the ideology of normative monolingualism. This ideology mandates that the "natural" state of a political unit (e.g., nation) is monolingual, and that multilingualism is a threat to unity. Further, if individuals are multilingual, a strict separation of languages is desirable – thus, language mixing is stigmatized. In Germany, this ideology is present in the recognition of one official language (German) and discourses about immigration and integration which stress the importance of speaking German, often at the expense of immigrant languages

(Ehrkamp 2006; Fuller 2012). However, there are few discourses which stigmatize multilingualism per se in the Berlin context, and there are many indications of the value of multilingual repertoires. Thus, pluralist ideologies compete with, and often feel as if they are dominating, monoglossic ideologies in the linguistic landscape of Berlin. As we will see in the analysis below, in some cases the mixture of different languages is part of a playful engagement with multilingualism.

Essentialist connections between language and social groups have a particular profile in Germany, where I argue that diversity is most often discussed in terms of differences in nationality or national background (this contrasts with, for example, the U.S., where I would describe diversity as most often discussed in terms of "race"). Thus, a sign at a hairdresser's aimed at inclusivity in their customer base welcomes people of all nationalities: *Bei uns sind alle Nationalitäten Herzlich Willkommen, denn wir sind Alle manchmal Ausländer* [With us all nationalities are welcome, as we are all foreigners sometimes]. I suggest that what might be more relevant in this context would be linguistic diversity (can I request a pageboy cut in English or Spanish, as well as German?) or phenotypic differences (will you know how to cut, perm or style my kind of hair?). While conceptualizing diversity in terms of nationality is no better or worse than any other unidimensional view of diversity, it has some specific consequences relevant to this analysis. Essentialist understandings of national identity simplify the relationship between language and nationality, and make some languages only deemed appropriate for speakers of a particular background, or in particular contexts. In the linguistic landscape these connections are commodified to construct the authenticity of goods and services of international origin. In these instances, language choice is potently meaningful, and differences in which languages are used, and by whom, are part of the construction of an ideology about particular languages and their speakers.

The ideological distinction between immigrant bilingualism and elite bilingualism underlies the linguistic landscapes discussed, although, as I will discuss, this distinction is also blurred in these data. In many contexts, immigrant bilingualism is not valued because immigrant languages are associated with low social status groups of speakers and are seen as an impediment to integration and upward mobility. However, in the linguistic landscape immigrant languages become a way of commodifying diversity, and the use of an immigrant language may be based on the essentialist link between language and culture (or, often, cuisine). Elite bilingualism, on the other hand, promotes the proficiency of prestigious global languages, such as English. Thus, English usually serves a different function than immigrant languages in the linguistic landscape; it is rarely about a particular national identification, but instead part of global orientation. In this study of the Berlin linguistic landscape, I will show how both immigrant and global languages are used to construct an imagined community of cosmopolitan Berliners.

3 Globalization, glocalization and cosmopolitanism

In signs, slogans and advertisements produced by businesses, language is commodified to attract customers. There is a strong global trend toward the celebration and commodification of multilingualism. Pandey (2016) discusses this in the context of award-winning fiction, noting how English-language fiction contains what she calls linguistic exhibitionism, which both re-establishes the hegemony of English but also capitalizes on "multilingualism-lite" (Pandey 2016: 7). In fiction, as, I suggest, in linguistic landscapes, the use of a global or majority language makes sense in terms of wide appeal, but multilingualism in less widely understood languages also has market value. Emblematic and token uses of languages other than the dominant language carry a certain cultural cachet, and evoke modern, global identities. While particular languages (English, Turkish, Hindi, Italian) have meanings which are culturally embedded, there is also a wider, more general ideology which links multilingualism to global sophistication and the glamor of cultural awareness; in other words, to cosmopolitanism. The use of a particular language may thus be in part a bid for authenticity but simultaneously part of a claim to multicultural chic; an illustration of this can be found in Figure 1, a picture of the sign of a shop selling Indian gift items. There is explicit reference to the Indian origin of these products, and the business name, *Namaste*, is a word which is well known by people who do not speak any Indian languages. Further, the text in German makes the target audience of this signage not Indian-background immigrants but the general population of Berlin consumers.

The social meanings of English in this study reflect the processes of globalization and glocalization. In many examples, English is used for things which are also constructed as specific to Berlin; thus, the connection between Berlin identities and cosmopolitanism is created. Glocalization, the development of local norms of use for a global language, can also be seen in this context in the development of new meanings for English borrowings, which will be discussed below. These glocalizations, however, are less part of a specifically Berlin identity than a broader German or European adoption of English, reflecting that

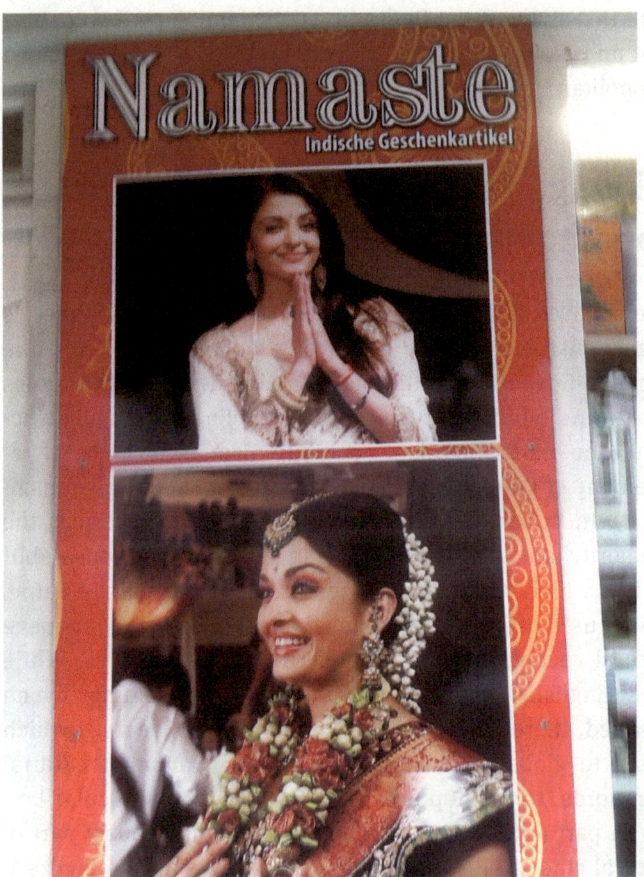

Figure 1: Namaste, Indische Geschenkartikel [Hindi: 'Greetings', German: 'Indian gift items']. Source: Janet M. Fuller.

Berlin linguistic norms are also embedded in wider national and international practices.

In the following analysis, I will examine how English and immigrant languages are used in particular neighborhoods of Berlin to create local identities for the cosmopolitan consumer. While the dominant themes are globalization and essentialist associations between ethnic or national origin groups and languages, there are challenges and developments which construct cosmopolitan identities for minority group members as well as mainstream consumers.

4 Methodology

The goal of this research is to analyze the language ideologies reproduced in linguistic landscapes with a particular focus on the construction of the imagined community of cosmopolitan Berlin. How does multilingualism, with its inherent association with faraway places, ultimately function to construct local Berlin identities?

The approach taken here is qualitative, not a statistical survey of how many signs can be found in each language, but an assessment of the visibility of these languages and how they interact in the linguistic landscape with the dominant language of German. The data were collected by taking walking tours along major thoroughfares in the areas discussed and photographing signs, window displays and advertisements in languages other than German. In addition to these systematic surveys of particular streets, I also documented signs that caught my attention as I went about my daily business in various districts of Berlin. Thus, this is a discourse analysis of a multi-authored text, and one which cannot ignore the positionality of the researcher. I am a native speaker of English and fluent speaker of German, with no competence in Turkish or Arabic, two languages that are prominent in the landscapes I observed. I have lived in Berlin for a total of almost ten years, but this is spread out over four decades; so while I feel at home in Berlin I am not a resident.

The linguistic landscape data was largely collected over a period of four years, beginning during the 2013–2014 academic year when I was living in Berlin, but is ongoing during my trips to Berlin several times a year. I began photographing signs as I came across them in my everyday life in Berlin; although I lived in Wilmersdorf in 2013–2014, my usual haunts included Kreuzberg, Schöneberg, Charlottenburg and Mitte, with occasional forays into Spandau, Dahlem and Prenzlauer Berg. I also took several research trips to Kreuzberg, Wedding and Neukölln and walked the main streets, systematically taking pictures of signs which included text that was not in (standard) German; I also made a trip to Mariendorff and one to Lichtenberg to collect linguistic landscape data. I also had multiple stays in Kreuzberg, with visits lasting between two weeks and two months, between December 2014 and November 2016, for a total of about five months.

Further, my analysis of the sociolinguistic meaning of these signs is based on my ongoing sociolinguistic and ethnographic research in Berlin, interviews with young adults, and media analyses (see Fuller 2012, forthcoming). That is, my understanding of the meanings of these different codes is based on my own everyday experiences with them as well as my investigation of the attitudes and experiences of a range of Berlin residents with global and immigrant languages and their speakers.

5 The Berlin dialect

Although one would imagine that the local dialect would be a resource for the construction of local identity, I have observed few examples of the Berlin dialect to construct businesses as locally owned and operated. When I began working on this analysis in 2016, I could find only two uses of the Berlin dialect in advertising local businesses, and neither of them presents particularly good evidence for the use of the dialect to construct contemporary Berliner identity. One of them is *Allet Schick* ('everything chic', with *allet* being a dialect form corresponding Standard German *alles*), a store which notes on its sign that it sells *Second Hand & Vintage* clothing. Although I would classify *second hand* and *vintage* as loanwords from, not switches into, English, the use of these English-origin terms nonetheless functions socially much like English slogans, i.e., to construct a modern identity. Perhaps to a lesser extent, *Schick*, as a borrowing from French *chic* similarly creates a connotation of international, well, chicness. Here, then, the use of the Berlin dialect, while clearly an important part of the image of the business as a local enterprise, is combined with the use of global languages which are equally part of the Berlin repertoire.

Another example of the use of the Berlin dialect in advertising which has stood the test of time is from a store founded in 1957 in Berlin-Lichterfelde, *Horst Lehmann Getränke GmBH* (http://www.ick-koof-bei-lehmann.com/). This is a beverage store, and it has long used the slogan *Ick koof bei Lehmann* 'I shop at Lehmann's', which contains the Berlin dialect variant *ick* of the pronoun *ich* 'I' and the verb form *koof* corresponding to Standard German *Ich kaufe* 'I buy'. Although I cannot find documentation of the date this slogan was introduced, I know from personal experience that it dates at least back to the 1980s, before English had become a salient part of the linguistic landscape of Berlin. While the dialect in this case is clearly a marker of local identity, it originated in a time when English was more clearly a foreign, rather than global or glocal, language, at least in terms of use in advertising. Thus, this is also not a good example of use of the local dialect as a robust part of the contemporary construction of local identity.

Of course, the linguistic landscape is always changing, and on a trip to Berlin in September 2017 (perhaps not incidentally on the weekend of the German election), I noted use of the Berlin dialect immediately upon arrival, in signs advertising the shopping opportunities in the main train station, and also in a billboard for the *Berliner Sparkasse* (a Berlin bank) which appeared in subway stations throughout the city. The former managed to incorporate every stereotype of the Berlin dialect in a single slogan: *Berlin, wa? Also, ick find mir scharmant!* [Berlin, right? Well, I think I'm charming!] – the tag question *wa* (shortened version of *nicht wahr?* literally 'not true?'), the Berliner dialect variant of *ich* with a stop instead of a fricative, the use of the dative pronoun *mir* instead of the standard *mich*. The bank sign limited itself to the spelling of the first person singular pronoun as *ick* in the slogan *Banking wie ick will!* [banking, how I want [it]]. Based on the appearance of these signs, it would clearly be inaccurate to say that the Berlin dialect is not part of the repertoire of codes used to construct local identities for businesses. However, compared to the use of English, these uses are still relatively rare, supporting the claim here the imagined community of Berlin is constructed with global linguistic repertoires.

6 English in Berlin

English is everywhere in Berlin – not just in all districts of the city, but also in all types of signs and in various functions. The focus of this analysis is the language choices made by businesses to advertise their products and services, but such language use is not done in a vacuum. Part of the linguistic landscape in Berlin includes English as a lingua franca in official contexts. In public transportation, in museums, and in other state-provided services, information is often presented in both German and English; in some cases (e.g., in the subway cars) French is also used. While institutions designed to deal with immigrants offer translations into other languages, aside from these locations there is very little translation into languages spoken by migrant populations, such as Turkish, Arabic, Italian, Vietnamese or Russian. The choices made by business owners about their signs and slogans are made with the backdrop of English as a lingua franca in Berlin, in Germany, and in all of Europe and beyond.

Given this status, it should come as no surprise that English is not usually used to reference a particular English-speaking population or nation; instead, it tends to be a more general index of modernity and a global orientation. An excellent example of this can be found in a sign for a children's clothing store in Berlin, which contains the text *667 The Baby of the Beast – Mode for Freche Kinder and Eltern mit Humor* [fashion for cheeky children and parents with a sense of humor] – *Don't Panic It's Organic – Made in Germany – Öffnungszeiten* [opening hours] .... Here, we see English being used emblematically to appeal to parents who are concerned about consuming organic products – a global concern – but these parents are also assumed to be German speakers, as the slogan and store information are presented in German. The argument I make here is that this global orientation has become a trait of the imagined Berlin community.

English names and slogans for hairdressers in Germany are well established as a site for the commodification of English (see Koll-Stobbe 2015). This does not just involve store names in English, but there are many of those: *Hairline, Streetcut, VIP Beauty Club, Beauty and Nails, Your Nails, Beauty Hair, Golden Hair Friseur, Hair Vision* (to name just a few). There are frequently slogans offered in English (*Pimp My Hair, For Natural Beauty, Enjoy Your Hair*) and also services – the ubiquitous *cut and go* or the use of the phrase *happy haircut* at one beauty shop, both meaning a haircut without blow drying and styling. We also see an example of bilingual word play in the name of a hairdresser's on Kotbusser Damm called *Cutbusser*.

The linguistic playfulness of *Cutbusser* is also found in signs for other types of businesses. Erling (2004) discusses an advertisement for the BSR (*Berliner Stadtreinigungsbetriebe*, the city streetcleaning service) using a bilingual pun *We kehr for you* – the German word *kehren* means 'sweep', and the root is pronounced similarly to English 'care'. Another example which relies on phonological similarity of English and German words is found in the name of a late-night shop, colloquially called a *Späti* (from German *spät* 'late'). This shop name, *SpäTea & Coffee*, blends German and English to create a clever name for an after-hours shop (see Figure 2).

Figure 2: SpäTea & Coffee. Source: Janet M. Fuller.

More common, however, are completely English slogans for businesses, such as the above-mentioned *Pimp My Hair*; others include *small moments in big city life* in a home furnishings shop, *to the loo* for the bathroom at an upscale mall, and *Panini – nice to eat you* at a shop selling Italian sandwiches.

As in this last example, there is some tendency for food which is associated with cultures and countries outside of Germany to use English to market their products, sometimes in combination with other (non-German) languages; English can be used to indicate Otherness in cuisine more generally. So we have both *Asia Box* and *King Box* for Asian fast food restaurants, a Japanese restaurant that advertises *Sushi and Hot Dishes* and a pizzeria that sells *Italian Food.*

Fitness centers also frequently have English names: *Fitness First, Women Fitness, Fitness & Friends.* In this case, there may be an association with U.S. culture – made explicit in the case of *American Fitness* – as it is commonly believed that fitness trends originate in the U.S.

The language ideologies that underlie these uses of English include an openness to the use of English as part of a way of appealing to customers who are not from any one particular subset of Berlin society but represent the general population – people who eat, get their hair cut, drink coffee and go to fitness centers. In some cases, there may be some connotation of connection to a particular Anglophone culture (e.g., a connection between the U.S. and fitness centers), and of course there are also shops which specialize in Anglophone or Anglophile products which use English to emphasize that (e.g., *Another Country* bookstore in Kreuzberg which sells English language literature, and around the corner *Broken English*, a shop which sells imported British consumables and household items). But for the most part, English, alongside German, is simply part of the repertoire of the members of the imagined community of Berlin and does not belong to a particular national identity.

The bleaching of national meaning is perhaps most readily observable when English is used to advertise things that are quintessentially German – for instance, a German airline named *Germanwings*. There are also usages which are specifically rooted in Berlin – for example, a store selling science fiction and fantasy games has the name *Battlefield Berlin,* locating it in the Berlin space but also linking it to global gaming communities. On an even more local level, the English phrase *Out of Berlin* is used to advertise a travel agency which describes itself as *Das Kiez Reisebüro* [the neighborhood travel agency] – the neighborhood in this case being the *Gräfekiez,* a Kreuzberg neighborhood.

The process of glocalization is also at work with some English loanwords. Glocalization is the use of global resources in ways that have developed in the local context. One such development is the use of the phrase *to go* in Berlin, and in Germany more generally. What is interesting about the process of borrowing here is that the meaning of the term has shifted away from a literal interpretation to a meaning I would gloss as 'convenience'. Initially this phrase was used in the way it is used in English, for a product that can be consumed on site or taken away; this exactly parallels the use of German *zum Mitnehmen* 'to take away'. One of the products that was first offered 'to go' was coffee, and it was possible to see various combinations of English and German – *Coffee to go, Kaffee to go, Kaffee zum Mitnehmen.* This was easily extended to food as well – e.g., *snack to go*, with exactly the same meaning – the product can be bought and taken away to be consumed.

However, in 2005 I first noted that the meaning of *to go* had changed somewhat, as evidenced by a sign advertising the newspaper *Welt Kompakt* [World Compact] using the slogan *die erste Zeitung to go* [the first newspaper for take away]. This is at first glance nonsensical, as all newspapers can be taken away after they have been bought. However, what is different about this particular newspaper is that it is smaller in size and therefore more practical to take with you and read in the confined space of a bus or subway car, for instance. So, *to go* in this case does not mean simply that you can take it with you, but that it is convenient to do so. It is now common to see food shops at train stations advertising that their products are 'to go'. This usage encompasses the literal meaning, but since that literal meaning is obviously always the case with food bought from a grocery store, the real message here is not that you can take it with you but that it will be convenient for you to do so.

This meaning of convenience becomes further extended in the use of *to go* for a massage which I saw on a sign in Berlin Schöneberg: *Jade Massage – "to go"*. I initially found this uninterpretable – how can a massage be 'to go'? I discovered that what this means is that you do not need an appointment; because the massage is done not by human hand but by an automated massage bed (jade balls which roll up and down the spine), you can just walk in and if a bed is free, have a massage. Thus here *to go* has lost all literal meaning but instead the aspect of convenience (i.e., no need to make an appointment) has become the entire glocalized meaning.

Given that some of these phenomena – in particular the glocalization of *to go* – are used in businesses outside of Berlin, what makes the use of English part of Berlin cosmopolitanism in particular? In part, of course, is the use of English to advertise businesses that present themselves as locally rooted (e.g., *Out of Berlin* as the slogan for *Das Kiez Reisebüro*). But also, as will be discussed in the next section, the linguistic landscape contains more than simply German and English – many immigrant languages are also part of the cosmopolitan flair of the city streets.

7 Immigrant languages in Berlin

If we accept the idea that Berlin cosmopolitanism relies heavily on international awareness, it is no surprise that English is frequently used alongside other foreign languages, thus coupling a global identity with the construction of authenticity through text in languages specifically related to the good and services advertised. This text is often in languages which are recognizable but largely unintelligible to the average Berliner. For example, there is a restaurant named *King's Chicken* with the name also written in Arabic, a Korean Fried Chicken restaurant called *Angry Chicken* with the English slogan *so so angry* as well as text in Korean, and a Taiwanese restaurant which gives its names as *Beef House* in English and Mandarin, with the German description of *Taiwanesische Küche* [Taiwanese cuisine]. There is also a restaurant name *Come 2 Eat* which advertises both *helal* food (i.e., food prepared according to Islamic dietary laws), with the term repeated in Arabic, and *Hausgemachte Burger* [homemade burgers]. In all of these cases, most of the target clientele will be unable to read the Arabic, Korean or Chinese orthography. While of course also those proficient in these languages are also potential customers, they are unlikely to be the majority.

Of course, the situation with Arabic has changed since the influx of refugees beginning in 2015. My linguistic landscape research in Neukölln prior to that showed use of Arabic both in translation and emblematically, especially to sell food. A return trip to the same blocks along Karl-Marx-Allee showed an increase in Arabic to sell an even wider range of products and services – international phone cards, healthcare, German courses, job search consultation, and travel deals, along with untranslated usages of Arabic that had not been previously salient. The target audience for much of this appears to be new Arabic-speaking arrivals, but it cannot always be clearly distinguished from the commodification of Arabic to sell *helal* foods or other commodities, thus complicating the linguistic landscape and a simplistic analysis of the meanings of codes. In some cases, Arabic appears to be used to appeal only to Arabic speakers, in other cases it is used to construct authenticity of products associated with the Arabic-speaking world, but other usages may combine these functions.

An important focus in the study of immigrant languages in the linguistic landscape of Berlin is the use of Turkish, which contrasts sharply with the use of English. First, Turkish is noticeable primarily in neighborhoods which have historically been home to large numbers of Turkish-background residents. Three such districts – Kreuzberg, neighboring Neukölln, and Wedding – were the target of my research. In my forays into other districts, both central and outlying, I found far less use of Turkish in these areas than in Kreuzberg, Neukölln and Wedding, and it was primarily found in grocery and gastronomy establishments.

This contrasts with English, which is found frequently in all districts (although much more in the central districts which cater more to tourists, indicative of its role as a lingua franca).

Turkish is important in the linguistic landscape because Turkish-background residents continue to be the largest group of migration-background inhabitants of Germany, and in Berlin. Immigrants from Turkey began coming to Germany in large numbers as *Gastarbeiter* [guest workers] in the 1950s, and many stayed and have made Germany their home. There are now four generations of people of Turkish background in Germany, and many of them have German citizenship and are monolingual in German. The Turkish-background population is very diverse, and the use of Turkish in the linguistic landscape reflects this. There is a societal discourse about Turks being unintegrated into German society (Ehrkamp 2006; Korteweg and Yurdakul 2009; Fuller forthcoming), but simultaneously some aspects of Turkish culture – in particular, food – are well integrated into German society.

In the linguistic landscape, much of what is seen in Turkish is a translation of information also provided in German. For example, a chain discount store *Pfennigland* has a sign saying “welcome” in both German and Turkish over the door in its stores in Wedding and Neukölln, and a driving school in Neukölln advertises its services in both German and Turkish. In these cases, these German businesses are catering to an imagined Turkish-speaking customer base. Token uses such as “welcome” do not assume a monolingual Turkish-speaking population, but do assume an identification with the language even for those Turkish speakers who also speak German. This practice is inclusive in portraying Turkish speakers as part of the Berlin population, but it also quite literally welcomes them only in certain districts.

However, in other cases the translation is from Turkish to German – for instance, a shop selling formalwear lists their offerings in Turkish, *Gelinlik, Kinalik, Damalik,* with the translations into German as *Hochzeitskleid, Verlobungskleid, Bräutigam Anzug* [wedding dress, engagement dress, groom’s suit]. However, *Kinalik* is actually a dress for a henna party (a pre-wedding gathering at which the bride and the female guests decorate their hands with henna); there is no exact translation for this into German, as henna parties (although not unique to Turkey) are not part of the usual German wedding culture. In this case, the Turkish text constructs the customers as part of a sub-group which maintains cultural traditions linked to Turkey.

Turkish is most commonly used to label food, and this seems to serve the dual purpose of constructing authenticity for the cuisine, and also catering to a Turkish-speaking customer base. This is illustrated in a sign for a grocery store, *Nasib Gilda*, in which on one side of the door, the Turkish sign proclaims that it is a *helal* market; on the other side of the door is a sign repeating the store name accompanied by the German phrase *Türkische Küche auf Ihren Herd* [Turkish cuisine on your stove]. In this case, the signage constructs the identities of the customers as including both Turkish speakers, who are framed as consumers of *helal* meat, but also more generally those who like Turkish food (but are not concerned about the process used to prepare the meat). The connection between the Turkish language and *helal* meat – a clear construction of Turkish speakers as Muslim – is further seen on a sign at a butcher shop: in German the text merely advertises the meat as 'fresh', but in Turkish it is said to be *helal*. Thus, the same information is not deemed relevant to speakers of the two languages, constructing speakers of Turkish as culturally distinct from German speakers.

Which services and products are advertised in Turkish is also part of the construction of the social category of Turks in Berlin through the linguistic landscape. On the one hand, Turkish is used to advertise things that are seen as connected to Turkish culture; as discussed above, this is primarily food but also formalwear for culturally specific events. On the other hand, Turkish is also used to sell mainstream goods or services (such as at the driving school and discount stores mentioned above). The difference between these two is that in the former, what is written in Turkish is at times not the same as what is written in German, and the Turkish speaking customers are constructed as looking for culturally specific things that are not relevant to German speakers. For the mainstream products and services, the Turkish is a translation of the German text, so Turkish speakers are constructed as wanting the same products and services as the German-speaking mainstream, but distinct in their linguistic repertoire.

However, we can also see signs of competing discourses which construct Turks as integrated and Turkish as part of the Berlin cosmopolitan code. For example, a chain grocery store, *Bolu*, is connected to the Turkish population through labelling itself in large letters as *Helâl et Pazarı* [*helal* meat market], but also uses a picture of the Brandenburg Gate – a common symbol of Berlin – on its sign. Another Berlin grocery store chain is called *Eurogida*, the word *gida* in Turkish meaning 'grocery store' (see Figure 3). The name of the store clearly marks this grocery store chain as being part of Europe more generally, but also Turkish. The message appears to be that Turkish grocery stores are part of what makes Berliners sophisticated Europeans, who have international tastes. Supporting this interpretation is the message on the Facebook page for *Eurogida*, where they describe their store with the following: *Unser Team verfügt bereits über eine zwanzigjährige Erfahrung und setzt im deutsch-türkischen Einzelhandel auf Modernität und Innovation* [Our team already has 20 years of experience and puts modernity and innovation in German-Turkish retail].

Figure 3: Eurogida. Source: Janet M. Fuller.

As can be seen in the upper right corner of Figure 3, part of what makes *Eurogida* "Turkish" is that they sell *helal* products. Here and elsewhere in the Berlin landscape, there is the implication that words connected to cuisine, such as the term *helal*, or names for popular dishes such as *Köfte* or *Döner*, will be understood by the majority population; and if not understood, words such as *merkez* 'center' or *gida* 'store' will be recognized as Turkish and establish authenticity for establishments selling Turkish food. This is central to the construction of the imagined cosmopolitan community of Berlin.

These practices present a challenge to a language ideology which distinguishes between elite and immigrant bilingualism, as in these cases immigrant languages are also part of the cosmopolitan identity being constructed through multilingualism. Several examples have been given above including Arabic, Korean and Chinese, used alongside English and German; there are also many examples of the use of Turkish, English and German. One example is the Turkish-named clothing store *Rida*, which uses only Turkish on the sign for the store name, *Rida Hayallerin Ötesinde* [Turkish: 'Rida [name of the store] beyond dreams'], but features an English sign proclaiming a "big sale" in the window. Another example, a store selling formal wear for children, has been either renamed or replaced by a store with a Turkish name and signage only in Turkish. It was previously named *Kids Elegance* and also had the German name *Elegante*

Kindermode [elegant children's fashion] on the awning, as well as a sign entirely in Turkish which advertised gifts for special events. But while this change may (or may not) indicate a move toward a less global orientation for this particular business, there is no dearth of other businesses that continue to use German, Turkish and English to sell their products. For instance, a sign in the heart of Kreuzberg advertises a breakfast café with a mixture of Turkish (*merkez simit evi* 'center sesame ring' [a Turkish breakfast food house]), German (*Frühstücken auf Türkische Art, direkt hier im Hof* [breakfast in the Turkish way, right here in the courtyard]) and the English (*Turkish-Breakfast*). A Neukölln eatery boasts that they are the *King of Cigköfte* [King of Turkish meat balls] and *King of Waffel* (note the German spelling of 'waffle'), saying that their food is *Einfach Lecker* [German, simply delicious].

In many ways, the use of English to describe things explicitly labelled as Turkish in Berlin should come as no surprise: Turks in Berlin, like everyone else in Berlin, and Turks in Turkey, learn and use English in ways which construct them as part of the modern, global world. What is notable is that such uses of English which align Turkish speakers with the rest of the inhabitants of Berlin challenge the discourse of Turks as unintegrated (see Fuller 2019). Instead, they contribute to the construction of Berliners – including those of migrant background – as multicultural. This linguistic landscape speaks eloquently about the imagined community of Berlin: its residents are not just bilingual but multilingual, part of a global economy and modern society that uses the national language, immigrant languages, and the global language of English.

8 Conclusion

English, as a global language, is commodified to construct cosmopolitan identities for businesses and consumers, but at the same time is undergoing glocalization – thus, the imagined community of Berlin is multilingual not because it is less German, but because being German includes the use of English, at least in token and emblematic ways.

Immigrant languages are sometimes used to construct essentialist imagined communities of unintegrated immigrants who need information about goods and services in their language. But these same languages are also used emblematically, to show transnational identities for businesses, and to appeal to the cosmopolitan imagined communities who associate foreign language use by a business with the authenticity of the foreign goods and services provided. A cosmopolitan Berliner gets a massage as well as coffee *to go*, and also does not need a translation of *helal* or *Namaste*.

These linguistic landscapes attest to an imagined community in which migration-background and cosmopolitan identities overlap and intertwine. Immigrant languages may be commodified to sell authenticity, but the speakers of these languages also use English and German, and use them to appeal to everyone in the Berlin community.

The cosmopolitanism of Berlin relies not only on the cultural cachet of English as a global language, but also familiarity with immigrant and international foods, cultural practices and languages. Yet there are competing discourses in the linguistic landscape; it is superficially inclusive, but also constructs the imagined community as consisting of German and Other as distinct social categories. Indeed, it is this very construction of difference which is necessary for the multiculturalism of the imagined Berlin community.

Acknowledgements: Thanks to the following people for help with translations of signs: Aslihan Akkaya, Meral Dollnick, Jason Hsieh, Ali Aljohani, and Yooju Jeon.

References

Anderson, Benedict. 1983. *Imagined communities: Reflections on the origin and spread of nationalism*. (subsequent editions in 1991 and 2006). London: Verso.

Bogatto, François & Christine Helôt. 2010. Linguistic landscape and language diversity in Strasbourg: the 'quartier gare'. In Elana Shohamy, Eliezer Ben-Rafael & Monica Barni (eds.), *Linguistic landscape in the city*, 275–291. Bristol: Multilingual Matters.

Bucholtz, Mary & Kira Hall. 2005. Identity and interaction: A sociocultural linguistic approach. *Discourse Studies* 7(4–5). 585–614.

Cenoz, Jasone & Durk Gorter. 2006. Linguistic landscape and minority languages. *International Journal of Multilingualism* 3(1). 67–80.

Ehrkamp, Patricia. 2006. "We Turks are no Germans": assimilation discourses and the dialectical construction of identities in Germany. *Environment and Planning* 38(9). 1673–1692.

Erling, Elizabeth J. 2004. *Globalization, English and the German university classroom: a sociolinguistic profile of students of English at the Freie Universität Berlin*. Edinburgh: University of Edinburgh dissertation.

Erling, Elizabeth J. 2007. Local identities, global connections: Affinities to English among students at the Freie Universität Berlin. *World Englishes* 26(2). 111–130.

Fuller, Janet M. 2012. *Bilingual pre-teens: Competing ideologies and multiple identities in the US and Germany*. Oxford: Routledge.

Fuller, Janet M. 2019. Discourses of Immigration and Integration in German Newspaper Comments. In Andreas Musloff & Lorella Viola (eds), *Migration and media: Crisis communication about immigration in Europe and the world*, 317–338. Amsterdam: John Benjamins.

Gorter, Durk. 2013. Linguistic landscapes in a multilingual world. *Annual Review of Applied Linguistics* 33. 190–212.

Gramling, David. 2009. The New Cosmopolitan Monolingualism: On Linguistic Citizenship in Twenty-First Century Germany. *Die Unterrichtspraxis/Teaching German* 42(2). 130–140.

Heller, Monica. 2003. Globalization, the new economy, and the commodification of language and identity. *Journal of Sociolinguistics* 7(4). 473–492.

Helôt, Christine, Monica Barni, Rudi Janssens & Carla Bagna. 2012. Introduction. In Christine Helôt, Monica Barni, Rudi Janssens & Carla Bagna (eds.), *Linguistic landscapes, multilingualism and social change*, 17–26. Frankfurt am Main: Peter Lang.

Kasanga, Luanga A. 2010. Streetwise English and French advertising in multilingual DR Congo: Symbolism, modernity, and cosmopolitan identity. *International Journal of the Sociology of Language* 206. 181–205.

Koll-Stobbe, Amei. 2015. Ideofiers in the commercial city: a discursive linguistic landscape analysis of hairdressers' shop names. In Mikko Laitinen & Anastassia Zabrodskaja (eds.), *Dimensions of Sociolinguistic Landscapes in Europe. Materials and Methodological Solutions*, 53–76. Frankfurt am Main: Peter Lang.

Korteweg, Anna & Gökçe Yurdakul. 2009. Islam, gender, and immigrant integration: Boundary drawing in discourses on honour killing in the Netherlands and Germany. *Ethnic and Racial Studies* 32(2). 218–238.

Landry, Rodrigue & Richard Y. Bourhis. 1997. Linguistic Landscape and Ethnolinguistic Vitality: An Empirical Study. *Journal of Language and Social Psychology* 16(1). 23–49.

Leeman, Jennifer & Gabriella Modan. 2009. Commodified language in Chinatown: A contextualized approach to linguistic landscape. *Journal of Sociolinguistics* 13(3). 332–362.

Leeman, Jennifer & Gabriella Modan. 2010. Selling the City: Language, Ethnicity and commodified space. In Elana Shohamy, Eliezer Ben-Rafael and Monica Barni (eds.), *Linguistic landscape in the city*, 182–198. Bristol: Multilingual Matters.

Mandel, Ruth. 2008. *Cosmopolitan anxieties: Turkish challenges to citizenship and belonging in Germany*. Durham & London: Duke University Press.

Pandey, Anjali. 2016. *Monolingualism and linguistic exhibitionism in fiction*. New York: Palgrave Macmillan.

Papen, Uta. 2012. Commercial discourses, gentrification and citizens' protest: The linguistic landscape of Prenzlauer Berg, Berlin. *Journal of Sociolinguistics* 16(1). 56–80.

Pécoud, Antoine. 2002. Cosmopolitanism and business among German-Turks in Berlin. *Journal of the Society for the Anthropology of Europe* 2(1). 2–12.

Piller, Ingrid. 2001. Identity constructions in multilingual advertising. *Language in society* 30(2). 153–186.

Piller, Ingird. 2003. Advertising as a site of language contact. *Annual Review of Applied Linguistics* 23. 170–183.

Shohamy, Elana, Eliezer Ben-Rafael & Monica Barni. 2010. Introduction: An approach to an "ordered disorder". In Elana Shohamy, Eliezer Ben-Rafael and Monica Barni (eds.), *Linguistic landscape in the city*, xi–xxvii. Bristol: Multilingual Matters.

Stroud, Christopher & Sibonile Mpendukana. 2009. Towards a material ethnography of linguistic landscape: Multilingualism, mobility and space in a South African township. *Journal of Sociolinguistics* 13(3). 363–386.

Mehmet Fatih Özcan

13 The linguistic landscapes of Kreuzberg and Neukölln: a comparative analysis of two neighborhoods

1 Introduction

The city has repeatedly been a place of constructed desires and hopes of various social groups. However, urbanization processes and their allocations do not kindle only positive images and experiences by dwellers of this particular residential and working area. Collateral and spasmodic agglomerations of single or multiple urban area(s) trigger manifold societal, architectural, and infrastructural problems, which are the object of scientific analyses of various disciplines and their intersections (see Fuchs, Moltmann and Prigge 1995: 15). So far, such analyses consider urban development and gentrification processes; processes that are significant challenges for (or chances of positive) social structural processions. The metropolis and the myths it creates unlock additional semantic levels for the city as a socially constructed and spatially generated entity.

Like other globally well-known metropolises, Berlin solicits attention as a fast growing, developing conglomeration of diverse societal currents of domestic and foreign incomers. Its European and international urban atmosphere is also accompanied by its function as a node for global political decision making and the young innovative and dynamic digital economy. The latter piles the pressure on the social space-related textures of (inner) urban space(s).[1] Thus, linguistic diversity and its comparability in particular areas within the city has become the multidirectional focus of sociolinguistic analyses.

Essentially, the study of *Linguistic Landscapes* (LL) is devoted to these highly diverse perspectives on the interrelation of urbanism, languages and society. The interconnectedness of social structural changes and urban development is assumed to affect various language communities. Consequently, it causes far-reaching changes in the composition of the LL – including changes

1 The distinction provides a basis for understanding urban neighborhoods and how linguistic particularities of such areas influence inner and outer perception. Due to page limitations, this aspect will not be discussed.

https://doi.org/10.1515/9781501508103-013

such as gentrification. In this sense, gentrification within the metropolis does not necessarily affect all urban areas uniformly and directly: it characterizes distinctive developments in the areas concerned. Notwithstanding, processes of change and transformation in adjacent neighborhoods are unevenly distributed but nevertheless may be mutually dependent and interconnected.

Following up on this assumption, this paper compares two adjacent boroughs in the south of the centre of Berlin, Kreuzberg and Neukölln. The comparison includes detailed analyses of the Linguistic Landscapes of the targeted neighborhoods, Graefekiez and Reuterkiez. This study investigates the question whether advanced gentrification results in lower linguistic diversity in the Graefekiez than in the Reuterkiez. In this context, a secondary research question entails whether the effects of gentrification in the Graefekiez indicate higher proportions of prestigious European languages than minority languages. The study is divided into four thematic sections, beginning with the theoretical implications of LL research.

The first section provides a theoretical perspective on the materialization of public space. The social actor becomes an evident element in the theoretical *Gestalt* of the urban linguistic landscape. The approaches by Ben-Rafael (2009) and Reblin (2012) complement the linguistic analyses of space as a framework for linguistic production – from a communicative perspective to a linguistic utterance. Secondly, the areas of interest are described in terms of social structural developments and the characteristics of both neighborhoods, based on selected results of social space analyses by TOPOS, are introduced (2008, 2011). The findings are interpreted and evaluated with social statistical data, highlighting population and *demolinguistic* developments, describing demographic compositions of selected language communities.[2] The third section presents the methods and the results of the Linguistic Landscape analyses. As a structuralist approach, LL is informed by the work of Landry and Bourhis (1997); some of these structuring effects of public signage in urban space are taken up in this section. Parts two and three are sub-divided by the thematic foci in the theoretical section. The conclusion summarizes the results of this study.

2 This is an interdisciplinary approach combining demography and linguistics, which expands and stimulates further theoretical considerations. According to Barni and Bagna (2009: 127), such processes are known as demolinguistics or on a larger scale also geolinguistics (see also Barni and Extra 2008; De Vries 1990; Lachapelle and Henripin 1980; and Van der Merwe 1989).

2 Perspectives on public space: social interaction and linguistic *Gestalt*

The theoretical framework for LL research demands a terminological clarifications of space. For this study, the sociological perspective provides an important perspective since LL research concentrates on linguistic objects marking public space (see Ben-Rafael 2009: 40).[3] The latter is of vital significance for holistic sociolinguistic analyses as it influences the recognition of social facts surrounding the environment of human beings (see Durkheim [1895] 1964). This "permeable", open, shared, accessible and viewable environment is a dynamic concept, which is also dependent on "social actors" and their intention, interaction and meaning construction in the dialectic of public and private usability (see Goffman 1963, 1981).[4]

The idea of public space is a derivative of Habermas's public sphere; an area established between the state and the private sphere. Social actors, civil society, organizations and service providers do not only present but also shape public discourse (see Habermas [1962] 1989). Public space represents "[...] every space in the community or the society that is not private property [...]" (Ben-Rafael 2009: 41). Geographically, it is understood as a "centre" with a clear "set of streets and one or two squares, in small localities, and of several large areas in metropolitan cities" (Ben-Rafael 2009: 41). Additionally, public space is not just accessed by inhabitants but also by those actors visiting or passing by. The latter group discerns this space mostly holistically, highlighting the idea of linguistic Gestalt: instead of varieties, as pieces of the entirety of the symbolic construction, public space is rather perceived as a landscape-like picture (see Ben-Rafael 2009: 43).

---

3 "Generally Linguistic Landscape refers to the visibility and salience of languages on public and commercials signs in a given territory or region" (Landry and Bourhis 1997: 23). The concept derives initially from language planning. Landry and Bourhis' work re-issues the term in an empirical study about ethnolinguistic vitality in a bilingual setting. The aspect of bilingualism in Canada only exists through institutionally legitimatized acknowledgement of its multilingual society and the social relevance of the languages in the public everyday life (see Harwood, Giles and Bourhis 1994; see Leclerc 1989). They discuss the relation between ethnolinguistic vitality perception and language behavior of French Canadian minorities.

4 "Social" is put in quotes because institutions, organizations as well as governmental structures are also defined as actors although they cannot be personified as social actors in the strict sense. In fact, their scope of interaction is limited due to the absence of social exchange between two more equal social actors. Nevertheless, social exchange can be performed only due to representation.

Due to the fact that LL mainly focuses on urban areas, specifically cities, it is important to standardize the definitional terminologies and to draw boundaries between city and street as well as urban, public and private space. For this reason, the next paragraph covers the essentials of urban public spaces and their semiotic properties.

3 Perspectives on urban public space: city, street and sign

In this study, the function of the city and particularly the function and form of streets are essential – without intersections and parallel streets, cities would not exist (see Reblin 2012: 11). City streets connect functionally (in-)different locations, or adjacent boroughs and neighborhoods with each other and enable communication and (social) interaction between actors including the materialized elements in their environment (see Reblin 2012: 13). Thus, "the city [represents] an intense focal point [. . .] of social relations in time and space" characterizing a unique social construction (Massey 1999: 102).

In this context, publicly accessible "polyfunctional" urban spaces manifested in streets – shopping streets or "big city streets" in particular – combine various characteristics. They serve as channels of transportation and movement as well as spaces of transaction, interaction and habitation (see Reblin 2012: 13). Zukin argues:

> Shopping streets affirm both difference and sameness, a tendency to identify either *with* or *against* the Other [. . .] Shopping spaces are a valuable prism for viewing public culture. The types of goods that are sold, at what prices, and in what forms – these are the everyday experiences in which physical spaces are "conceived" in the light of social structure. (Zukin 1995: 257).

However, various impulses and characteristics of quarters or urban areas influence the structure of the street as well (see Reblin 2012: 13). Thus, cities have a mirroring effect implying that "streets and the streetscapes are particularly important in defining the character of urban areas" (Nasar 1989: 32).

Semiotics of materialized space are an essential component of LL research. The complex physical configuration demands an interdisciplinary approach. "The city [may be] seen as a collection of objects", but the organization of these objects involves environmental factors or scope of action of its inhabitants (Krampen 1979: 6, quoted in Reblin 2012: 14). Since there are infinite possible interpretations of the complex texture of signs and writings, there are always manifold ways of codification, as Reblin (2012: 14) underlines. Reblin's (2012: 14) example of a shop highlights this complexity. A shop inscription can be categorized as the shop name, the history of use, the negligence of the façade or even all three. Thus, it is a valuable aspect to keep track of a so-called "code of the street" instead of focusing on the isolated categorization of the objects observed.

Finally, the relationship between the code and the constructed image of the street creates a complex cognitive perception and representation of the street by the actors involved (see Reblin 2012: 15). This notion of the urban space is a prime element in the analysis of the LL but also in structuring the linguistic objects in the urban landscape.

4 Area of interest: the neighboring boroughs Friedrichshain-Kreuzberg and Neukölln

The area of analysis is located in the centre of Berlin – at the southern border of the district Friedrichshain-Kreuzberg and at the northern border of Neukölln. Friedrichshain-Kreuzberg is the union of the formerly independently administrated eastern district Friedrichshain and the western district Kreuzberg. Figure 1 displays the neighboring districts of both bordering areas that are investigated. Figure 2 shows the neighborhoods of the bordering boroughs, as well as the selected data collection sites.

The social structure of Kreuzberg is of particular interest for further analyses because it is diverse in many ways. Besides a high proportion of cultural and social diversity, the district is also known to be one of the most popular residential areas within the so-called *S-Bahn Ring*.[5] However, gentrification and relatively high demands for housing compared to other districts have triggered displacement of low social status residents to outer regions of the district (see Blasius 1993). Neukölln is also one of the concerned areas of new settlement due to relative low living costs and its immediate proximity to the Kreuzberg Graefekiez neighborhood (TOPOS 2012: 49).

The second district is located in the south eastern part of Berlin between the districts Friedrichshain-Kreuzberg in the north, Tempelhof-Schönberg in the west and Treptow-Köpenick in the east. Neukölln is relevant for our study because the here studied Reuterkiez is embedded in this district. The following

5 The *S-Bahn Ring* is a circle line of the metropolitan train system (*S-Bahn*) which is conceived of as marking the boundary between inner-city districts and the suburban areas of Berlin.

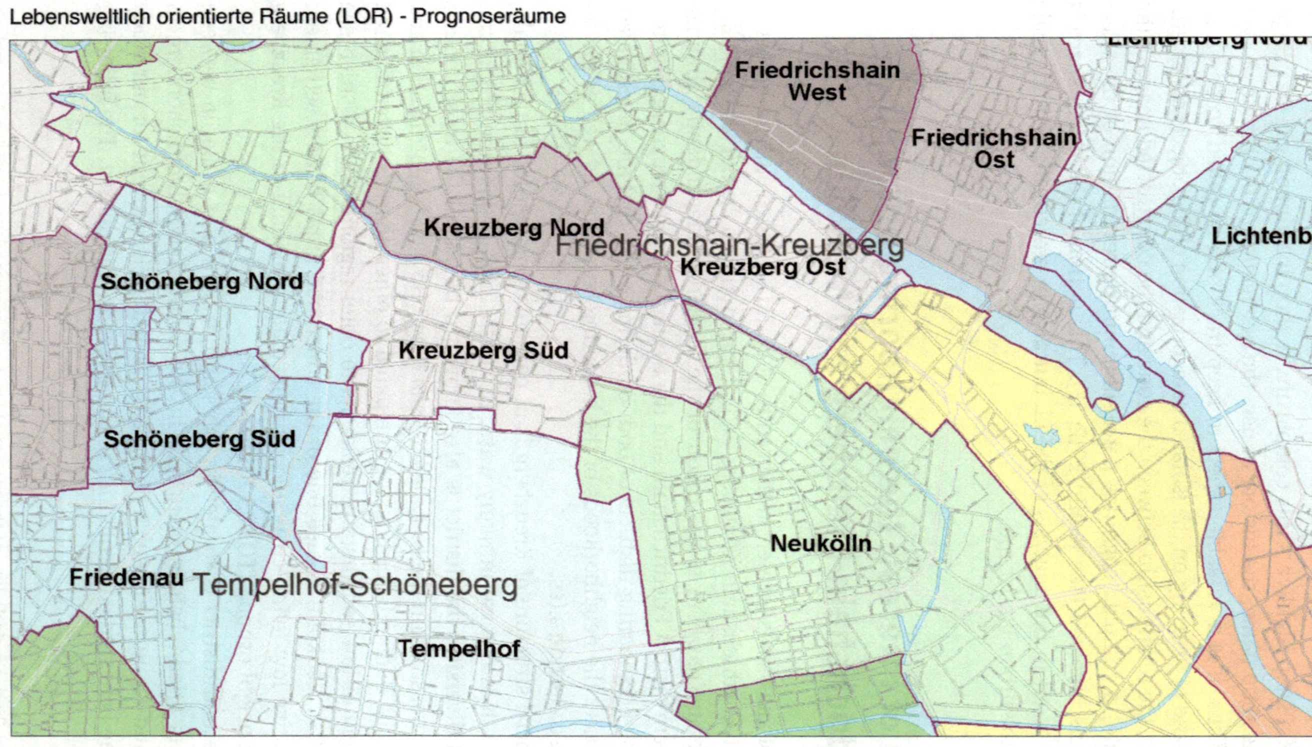

Figure 1: Area of the district border between Friedrichshain-Kreuzberg and Neukölln (trend space level) (Senatsverwaltung für Stadtentwicklung und Umwelt 2013a).

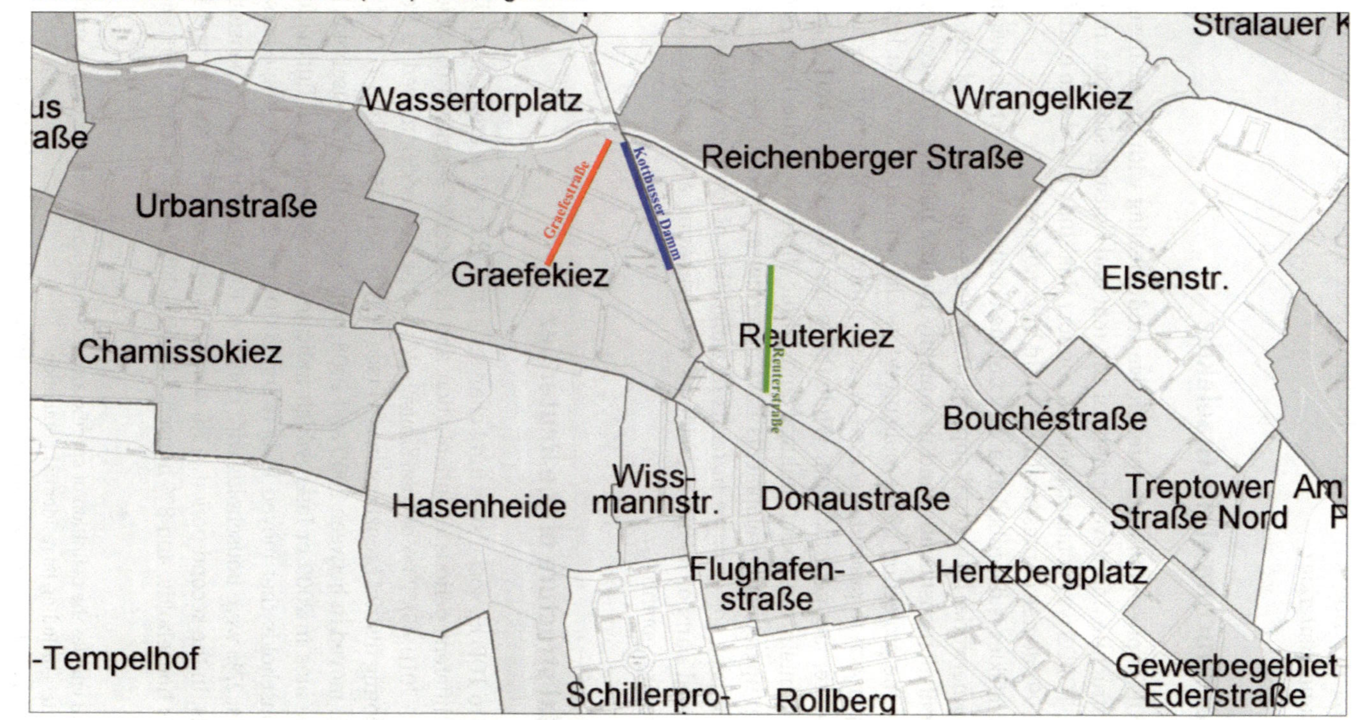

Figure 2: Area of Graefe- and Reuterkiez at Friedrichshain-Kreuzberg and Neukölln border (planning space level) – Data collection areas (Senatsverwaltung für Stadtentwicklung und Umwelt 2013b).

two sections describe key aspects in the social structural development of Graefekiez and Reuterkiez.

4.1 Social structure of the Graefekiez

In 2008, TOPOS presented a comprehensive study dealing with the analysis of the social structure and development of the rent and housing situation in the Graefekiez. TOPOS was commissioned to conduct this study in order to examine whether a 1995 decree of preservation should be continued.[6]

The Graefekiez is described as a very unique housing area in which civic initiatives and networks for mutual support affect the social structure of the residential population sustainably and in a mainly positive manner. This concerns particularly the protection of the milieu and its characteristics due to a legally effective approach to prevent processes of segregation as well as negative developments concerning gentrification. While this aspect turns out to be a specific desire to maintain the social, cultural and ethnic diversity in the Graefekiez, many urban upgrading developments have nevertheless affected the area negatively in the past, for example in terms of emigration of lower-income and socially deprived parts of its initial residents to neighboring areas with relatively lower upgrading potentials.

4.2 Social structure of the Reuterkiez

According to TOPOS, social structural changes in the Reuterkiez are highly influenced by different periods of inhabitation and by specific segments of society (see TOPOS 2011: 45). 23% of total households in the Reuterkiez moved in from the neighboring district Kreuzberg in 2011 (see TOPOS 2011: 25).[7] While 47% of all households moved in between 2000 and 2008, only 20% of those households inhabited the area in 2009 or later, which indicates a high degree of fluctuation. 38% of households that moved in between 2000 and 2008 were single-person households, 27% were households with children, 10% student and 2% pensioner households. In the second period, 45% were single-person, 26% student and 1% pensioner's households, and 8% households with children (see TOPOS 2011: 46).

6 §172 BauGB enables the definition of specific areas to be preserved in terms of their specific urban characters including its residential population.

7 In comparison, only 10% of total households in the Graefekiez moved in from Neukölln in 2008 (TOPOS 2011: 25).

The proportion of migrant households dropped from 42% in the first period to 33% in the second. While 25% of the area's population are "pioneers" and 26% "gentrifiers" in the first period, the values change in the second period to 41% pioneers and 33% gentrifiers (TOPOS 2011: 46). The terms "pioneers" and "gentrifiers" are labels for particular segments of society.[8]

By comparing the net income of total households in the Reuterkiez in 2011 with those data of the Graefekiez in 2008, it is noticeable that there are remarkable differences between the neighborhoods. In the Graefekiez, 20% of total households have a low net income (500 EUR to 900 EUR), while there are 23% of total households with a high net income (2,600 EUR and more). In comparison to the Graefekiez, only 10% of total households have a low and 18% a high net income in the Reuterkiez. However, 20% of total households in the Reuterkiez have a net income of 1,500 EUR to 2,000 EUR (see TOPOS 2011: 18).

This implies that the social structural differences between both neighborhoods depend on the net income of the households. In addition, the income level is comparably higher in Reuterstraße than in Graefestraße. This results in a more socially significant gentrification in the Reuterkiez than in the Graefekiez.[9] Thus, social structural changes are not exclusively triggered by a large group of gentrifiers but also through processes of selection: the affected groups of low-income households and people with migrant backgrounds are (involuntarily) displaced from the Reuterkiez (TOPOS 2011: 23).

Against the backdrop of the TOPOS results, the following chapter deals with the evaluation of statistical data describing the social structure of the Graefekiez and Reuterkiez.

---

8 A pioneer is someone born after 1970 with an A level or a higher degree, a monthly income below 1,350€, one child in the household at most and with an academic or artistic profession (Blasius 1993; TOPOS 2011: 8). On the contrary, a gentrifier shares almost the same features as a pioneer but is born after 1960 and has an equivalent income above 1,750€ (Blasius 1993; TOPOS 2011: 8). Such categorization helps clarify the effects on urban development processes by specific segments of society. However, it is doubtable that the definitions of social structural criteria 20 years ago meet the requirements of current social developments.

9 In a presentation of the release of the TOPOS 2011 document on 12 March 2012, Sigmar Gude concludes that the development of the Reuterkiez resembles that in the Graefekiez (TOPOS 2012: 22). The social development of the Reuterkiez is especially attributed to households moving in since the period of 2000 and 2008 (TOPOS 2011: 46). Furthermore, the increase of gentrifiers and pioneers in 2009 influences the increase in rent levels up to 15% above the average district level. Both groups have an above average income whereas the pioneers have an approximately 10% higher income than the reference groups in other neighborhoods of Neukölln. The pioneers in the Reuterkiez do not have a positive relationship with their neighborhood and one third intends to leave the area (TOPOS 2011: 47).

5 Population statistics

Table 1 to 4 highlight the demographic structure of Berlin, the boroughs Friedrichshain-Kreuzberg and Neukölln and the neighborhoods Graefekiez and Reuterkiez between 2008 and 2012. Additionally, the statistical series presents a selected number of variables to allow for an overview. Some criteria are primarily set by standard definitions of the statistical office (see Amt für Statistik Berlin-Brandenburg 2013a, 2013b, 2013c for the definition of migrant background (MB) and region of origin). Further political criteria such as membership in the League of Arab States or linguistic criteria such as the (recognition of) minority language status and lingua franca (that is, Turkish, Arabic and English) are also considered in the data evaluation and are categorized into and indicated by the abbreviation *ext.* in the tables (Crystal [1986] 2010: 368, 371). Population statistics are an important indicator for social structural transformations in the observed areas and yield information about the changing distribution of possible language communities. However, it is important to note that this statistical representation of possible language communities is based only on demographic representations of nationalities.

The overall results of the Turkish language user statistics indicate sinking population and potential Turkish speaker values; however, the negative development occurs less drastically in the Graefekiez than in the Reuterkiez. Particularly, the number of Turkish-speaking individuals who are classified as “foreigners” are decreasing across the observed time frame (note, however, that individuals classified as ‘German’ who use Turkish are not decreasing).

By considering the population of potential Arabic speakers, the developments are similar to those of potential Turkish users, although the total amounts differ by the factor of two to three. There are potentially more Turkish users than Arabic speakers. Looking at the factors for the Graefekiez, we notice that there is an even development in demographics. However, in the Reuterkiez we see a faster decrease in the foreigner population than in the increase of the corresponding German population. Thus, this highlights the different rates of demographic developments in the neighborhoods concerning Arabic-speaking residents.

Finally, looking at potential English speaker data, it is noticeable that the shift in proportions of potential language users occurs first in the Reuterkiez in 2009, where the foreign population of potential English users with a migration background outweighs the foreign population of potential Arabic users with a migration background. In the Graefekiez, this shift starts first in 2010. Since that time, the ratio between both potential language user groups further drifts apart. Initially, these particular progressions in sociolinguistic demographics

Table 1: Population statistics with selected values (Amt für Statistik Berlin-Brandenburg 2013d).

Region	Borough	Neighborhood	Group / Country	2008	2009	2010	2011	2012
Berlin	Friedrichshain-Kreuzberg	Graefekiez	**German with migrant background**					
			FRA*	52	67	63	54	87
			LBN	275	334	351	345	359
			NGA	493	463	500	523	557
			PSE	79	56	63	66	0
			POL	185	209	185	170	195
			SRB	24	28	38	24	27
			TUR	735	702	742	768	789
			Total	2,690	2,722	2,934	3,022	3,180
			Foreigner					
			FRA	175	162	191	202	217
			ITA	182	188	207	214	280
			LBN	191	174	150	148	142
			PSE	216	205	185	168	0
			POL	275	216	180	190	216
			SRB	174	144	121	134	120
			TUR	1,675	1,555	1,453	1,394	1,342
			USA	198	182	169	181	209
			Total	5,203	4,792	4,666	4,728	4,858
		Total		18,099	17,806	18,017	18,318	18,748
	Total			**262,257**	**259,967**	**261,090**	**265,361**	**269,471**

(continued)

Table 1 (continued)

Region	Borough	Neighborhood	Group / Country	2008	2009	2010	2011	2012
	Neukölln	Reuterkiez	**German with migrant background**					
			FRA	53	70	66	80	71
			LBN	322	323	313	315	325
			NGA	933	920	895	913	944
			PSE	59	36	47	34	0
			POL	346	320	277	302	295
			SRB	120	140	126	126	115
			TUR	1,267	1,234	1,278	1,272	1,264
			Total	4,281	4,254	4,307	4,441	4,547
			Foreigner					
			FRA	251	265	243	302	337
			ITA	295	352	356	402	420
			LBN	198	160	155	141	132
			PSE	398	389	348	308	0
			POL	712	622	470	504	488
			SRB	536	498	401	358	316
			TUR	2,627	2,441	2,191	2,089	1,982
			USA	203	231	199	217	271
			Total	8,555	8,198	7,381	7,649	7,933
		Total		27,088	26,914	26,408	26,939	27,427
	Total			**305,519**	**307,650**	**307,204**	**313,245**	**318,356**
Total				**3,362,842**	**3,369,672**	**3,387,562**	**3,427,114**	**3,469,621**

* FRA = France, ITA = Italy, LBN = Lebanon, NGA = Nigeria, PSE = Palestinian Territory, POL = Poland, SRB = Serbia, TUR = Turkey.

Table 2: Population statistics with selected value "Turkish" (Amt für Statistik Berlin-Brandenburg 2013d).

Region	Borough	Neighborhood	Turkish	2008	2009	2010	2011	2012
Berlin	Friedrichshain-Kreuzberg	Graefekiez	**German with migrant background**					
			Total	735	702	742	768	789
			ext. Total	772	735	781	818	838
		Total		2,690	2,722	2,934	3,022	3,180
	Total			35,586	36,873	38,254	39,447	40,896
			Foreigner					
			Total	1,675	1,555	1,453	1,394	1,342
			ext. Total	1,793	1,689	1,665	1,598	1,604
			Pooled					
			Total	2,410	2,257	2,195	2,162	2,131
			ext. Total	2,565	2,424	2,446	2,416	2,442
		Total		5,203	4,792	4,666	4,728	4,858
	Total			60,420	56,480	55,446	57,433	60,464
	Neukölln	Reuterkiez	**German with migrant background**					
			Total	1,267	1,234	1,278	1,272	1,264
			ext. Total	1,328	1,302	1,368	1,372	1,379
		Total		4,281	4,254	4,307	4,441	4,547
	Total			51,123	53,165	55,369	57,760	59,989
			Foreigner					
			Total	2,627	2,441	2,191	2,089	1,982
			ext. Total	3,040	2,870	2,589	2,506	2,454
			Pooled					
			Total	3,894	3,675	3,469	3,361	3,246
			ext. Total	4,368	4,172	3,957	3,878	3,833
		Total		8,555	8,198	7,381	7,649	7,933
	Total			69,329	68,752	65,315	68,109	70,933

Table 3: Population statistics with selected values "Arabic" (Amt für Statistik Berlin-Brandenburg 2013d).

Region	Borough	Neighborhood	Arabic	2008	2009	2010	2011	2012
Berlin	Friedrichshain-Kreuzberg	Graefekiez	**German with migrant background**					
			Total	515	515	563	577	557
			ext. Total	563	546	601	631	609
		Total		2,690	2,722	2,934	3,022	3,180
	Total			35,586	36,873	38,254	39,447	40,896
			Foreigner					
			Total	532	493	440	402	377
			ext. Total	595	537	497	454	438
			Pooled					
			Total	1,047	1,008	1,003	979	934
			ext. Total	1,158	1,083	1,098	1,085	1,047
		Total		5,203	4,792	4,666	4,728	4,858
	Total			60,420	56,480	55,446	57,433	60,464
	Neukölln	Reuterkiez	**German with migrant background**					
			Total	548	532	529	538	597
			ext. Total	627	639	648	662	724
		Total		4,281	4,254	4,307	4,441	4,547
	Total			51,123	53,165	55,369	57,760	59,989
			Foreigner					
			Total	755	726	632	573	521
			ext. Total	872	838	722	679	639
			Pooled					
			Total	1,303	1,258	1,161	1,111	1,118
			ext. Total	1,499	1,477	1,370	1,341	1,363
		Total		8,555	8,198	7,381	7,649	7,933
	Total			69,329	68,752	65,315	68,109	70,933

Table 4: Population statistics with selected values "English" (Amt für Statistik Berlin-Brandenburg 2013d).

Region	Borough	Neighborhood	English	2008	2009	2010	2011	2012
Berlin	Friedrichshain-Kreuzberg	Graefekiez	**German with migrant background**					
			Total	113	173	197	196	227
			ext. Total	143	179	206	213	245
		Total		2,690	2,722	2,934	3,022	3,180
	Total			35,586	36,873	38,254	39,447	40,896
			Foreigner					
			Total	534	463	484	528	580
			ext. Total	555	492	502	559	619
			Pooled					
			Total	647	636	681	724	807
			ext. Total	698	671	708	772	864
		Total		5,203	4,792	4,666	4,728	4,858
	Total			60,420	56,480	55,446	57,433	60,464
	Neukölln	Reuterkiez	**German with migrant background**					
			Total	183	210	166	205	237
			ext. Total	186	222	183	232	262
		Total		4,281	4,254	4,307	4,441	4,547
	Total			51,123	53,165	55,369	57,760	59,989
			Foreigner					
			Total	684	729	717	772	964
			ext. Total	726	769	761	824	1,031
			Pooled					
			Total	867	939	883	977	1,201
			ext. Total	912	991	944	1,056	1,293
		Total		8,555	8,198	7,381	7,649	7,933
	Total			69,329	68,752	65,315	68,109	70,933

were less effective for the Reuterkiez than the Graefekiez due to the size of potential Arabic users in 2010 and 2011. After this period, potential English users decisively outnumbered the group of potential Arabic users in the Reuterkiez.

5.1 Population results and expectations for the LL of the neighborhoods

The social structural data hints at aspects of sociolinguistic developments in the respective neighborhoods. While there is a specific focus on the prevention of the loss of ethnic and cultural networks due to gentrifying displacement in the Graefekiez, the demographic progressions in the Reuterkiez point towards an intensive shift in ethnolinguistic vitality of particular language communities. In this context, it is crucial to analyze the changes in the social and cultural structure as well as how linguistic demographics correlate with the diversity of the LLs in the respective neighborhoods.

The following hypotheses will be tested: linguistic diversity is comparably higher in the Graefekiez because of the protection of the social structure due to the milieu protection act. Thus, the Reuterkiez is less linguistically diverse and socially weaker since it is not protected. Furthermore, this negatively affects the total amount of linguistic items in the public space, leading to a less diverse LL.

In contrast, the Graefekiez has a diverse LL including more speakers of prestigious languages such as English, French and Italian whereas less prestigious languages such as Turkish and Arabic occur more often in the Reuterkiez. In addition, initial pioneering of the Reuterkiez and first signs of gentrification point at a growing number of prestigious language representations.

In order to test these hypotheses, it was necessary to create methodological categories to collect, evaluate and analyze linguistic data of the LL in the Graefekiez and Reuterkiez.

6 Methods

A substantial part of the methodology of this study derives from Barni and Bagna's approach to digitally mapping linguistic data (Barni and Bagna 2009: 131). The general purpose of the methodology is to visualize and categorize linguistic traces and their stratification in a predefined public space.

Field data was collected in the neighborhoods' eponymous roads, *Graefestraße* (GS) and *Reuterstraße* (RS). An additional field data site is the large three-lane two-way A-road *Kottbusser Damm* (KD), dividing the districts Friedrichshain-Kreuzberg and Neukölln, and connecting the neighborhoods Graefekiez and Reuterkiez. The KD approximately follows cardinal directions north to south-south east.

The choice of these roads is derived from the assumption that the eponymous roads fulfil a specific representative function for the areas. Such representative function includes a distinctive character with particular political, social, cultural, and commercial infrastructure for the neighborhood. Additionally, the roads also exert a symbolic value to all residents as well as those people passing by. The KD acts as an "invisible border" between the two areas; this is also presented as an individual data collection site and in the results of the data evaluation.

A DSLR camera was used to document the LL data. Photographs were taken of all written items in the corresponding areas. The images mainly depict a single item or multiple items on a specific background. Some items were photographed multiple times; they either do not fit on a single photograph or they are presented in three dimensions (e.g., poster around a light post).

Secondly, field data was categorized with spreadsheet software. The total length of the observed GS is approximately 557.94 meters, while the total length of the RS is approximately 523.2 meters. Thus, to grant the highest possible comparability, only 537.89 meters of the KD (from north to south) were considered in the data evaluation. Most importantly, only data that indicates a reference to the data collection site is considered. Graffiti, stickers, and posters without a specific variety and illegal bill-sticking were excluded. A test run resulted in a disproportionately large number of items with an unknown type of language or without any context-related meaning for the proximate vicinity.

Social-space analysis includes sets of categories describing the (background) material, size and position within public space. Such an analysis provides insights about the physical configuration and semiotic effects of each item. Due to the polyfunctionality of the urban space, this analysis indicates sensory impressions of the "code of the street". The category "height" for example enables the description of different semiotic functions such as the degree of visibility.[10] It also includes the type of text implementation – differentiation between handwritten, printed, constructed, or carved letters. The results provide essential information about the type of contact between item producer and reader;

10 Everything above eye-level was valued as "high", while below the eye-level was labelled as "low". The value "medium" describes the area between eye-level and reachable heights.

hand-written items or items written in chalk signify a conscious handling of language whereas flashing LEDs or fluorescent lamps attract attention or intend to address readers at specific times of the day.

Sociolinguistic analysis covers the category "context", specifying centers of interest within communicative interaction (Barni and Bagna 2009: 134). The values range from "advertisement" up to "warning". The category "place" shows a direct real-world reference. In this context, "level" describes the item creator – either top-down or bottom-up (Shohamy 2006: 111). All items that are private property are labelled as bottom-up.

Finally, three additional categories are included in macro-linguistic analysis that classify the collected data according to semantic importance. Although some scholars argue that the occurrence of the English language in non-English speaking societies is mainly a prestige phenomenon, this study does not follow this assumption (see Ross 1997; Shohamy 2006). All language data indicating multilingual items is categorized in "relevance", "dominance", and "function of other languages" (Barni and Bagna 2009: 135).

Relevance describes which variety is primarily visible, signaling a greater semiotic importance than another variety – influencing factors are size of letters or the style of font. *Dominance* defines which variety occupies the semantic prerogative of interpretation. This classification demonstrates the symbolic value and function of the semantically dominant language. *Function of other language* describes the function of the less dominant language. Less dominant languages operate as translation, explanation, or informative purposes. However, it can also serve as an accessory language or a language that adopts words of the dominant language to own a grammatical function (see Barni and Bagna 2009: 135). The ideas of arrangement of information on multilingual items are also included (see Reh 2004).

7 General results

Looking at Table 5, a total number of 3,455 LL items were collected in three data collection sites on both sides of the GS and RS and on the KD. A total amount of 1,981 items were collected in the Graefekiez – 1,186 items in the GS and 795 items in the KD. In comparison, a total sum of 1,474 items was gathered in the Reuterkiez – 646 items in the RS and 828 items on the Reuterkiez's side of the KD. Thus, comparably high amounts of LL items on the KD side of the Reuterkiez indicates the street's LL quantitative impact on the overall Reuterkiez area's LL.

Table 5: Social space-related Linguistic Landscape data.

Category	Class	Graefekiez			Reuterkiez			Grand Total
		Total	GS	KD	KD	RS	Total	
Amount	count	1981	1186	795	828	646	1474	3455
	item/m	1,81	2,13	1,48	1,54	1,23	1,39	1,6
Size	small	825	542	283	290	316	606	1431
	medium	771	407	364	413	210	623	1394
	large	385	237	148	125	120	245	630
Height	high	840	522	318	375	279	654	1494
	medium	612	363	249	242	235	477	1089
	low	529	301	228	211	132	343	872
Material	blackboard	32	26	6	3	14	17	49
	cardboard	64	35	29	41	36	77	141
	glass	32	29	3	2	2	4	36
	metal	216	148	68	84	87	171	387
	paper	562	375	187	209	182	391	953
	plastic	986	497	489	471	275	746	1732
	wood	42	42	–	–	19	19	61
Textual genre	leaflet	7	7	–	–	60	60	67
	movable sign	138	62	76	16	14	30	168
	paper	261	185	76	89	67	156	417
	poster	123	87	36	105	57	162	285
	sign	936	564	372	433	298	731	1667
	sticker	413	218	195	154	120	274	667
External position	bin	74	38	36	37	15	52	126
	door	113	58	55	39	21	60	173
	ground	153	73	80	24	15	39	192
	light post	47	16	31	62	33	95	142
	sign post	110	60	50	78	63	141	251
	wall	601	387	214	277	176	453	1054
	window	451	264	187	176	150	326	777
Type of writing	carved	16	9	7	4	5	9	25
	chalk	25	23	2	–	8	8	33
	constructed	176	122	54	57	76	133	309
	glued	241	190	51	35	140	175	416
	printed	1407	744	663	710	370	1080	2487
	written	85	78	7	9	38	47	132

Since all three roads have a different total length, the average ratio of item per meter provides a better comparison. There are 2.13 items per meter in the GS and only 1.23 items per meter in the RS. Table 5 shows that the combination of the GS and KD lowers the average item per meter value to 1.81 in the Graefekiez, while on the other side of the road, a combination raises the value to 1.39 in the Reuterkiez. In summary, the KD's 3.02 items per meter value has a considerable effect on the neighborhood's LL item constellation.

The distribution of item sizes in the GS and RS as well as between both sides of the KD is nearly similar while the total distribution in the corresponding neighborhoods differs. There are more small than medium sized items in Graefekiez, while in the Reuterkiez it is nearly balanced. There are more items placed up high than at medium or low heights in the GS and in the KD; moreover, the amount of medium height items in the RS is higher compared to those items in a different height.

When it comes to the material character of LL items, plastic is the most frequently occurring material in all three streets. However, there are some minor differences. While there are 26 instances of blackboard material in the GS, there are only 14 instances of this in the RS. There is also more wooden material in the GS than in the RS. The occurrence of glass is similarly distributed. Interestingly, there is also a lot of cardboard in both neighborhoods. This is a result of the 2013 federal election canvassing in both areas.

Looking at the textual genre, meaning the type of frame on which the text is embedded, the relatively high number (62) of movable and paper signs in the GS stands out compared to the RS (14). The most visible aspects in this category are the considerably high amount of signs in the GS (564) but also the nearly same ratio between signs and stickers on the Graefekiez' side of the KD and the RS. In addition, the external position indicates differences in the LL of the neighborhoods. While there are more items positioned on the ground and on doors in the Graefekiez than in the Reuterkiez, there are comparably more items on light posts in the Reuterkiez. Similar values in both neighborhoods can be found with sign posts and bins.

The analysis of the type of writing on items shows some interesting results. While there are similar values on both sides of the KD in terms of printed and handwritten writing, there are nearly twice as many handwritten items in the GS than in the RS. Glued items are much more common in the RS than in the GS. Furthermore, it can be assumed that handwritten items address the reader directly, while fluorescent lamps and LED technology indicate an attraction-related function. However, many shop signs placed up high may serve to illuminate the street.

7.1 Sociolinguistic results

Particularly the data in Table 6 provides some important insights about the sociolinguistic features of the areas. While the total amount of advertisements in the KD predominates, there is a relatively high number of service-related items in the GS. Political LL items are more apparent visually in the Reuterkiez compared to the Graefekiez. Thus, this suggests that there is more frequent canvassing in the Reuterkiez than in the Graefekiez.

The distribution of the context variables denotes some marked differences between the two neighborhoods. In the Graefekiez, local development initiatives and social services are the most common social contexts. In the Reuterkiez, youth coaching and social awareness are the most frequent elements; the number of magazines with a local society related theme depicts an exception in the Reuterkiez. There is a specific sense of responsibility in local self-governance when it comes to social coexistence within the Graefekiez. Furthermore, there is a significant demand for social support and youth coaching initiatives in the Reuterkiez.

There are significant differences in the neighborhoods concerning political topics. A high number of political figures campaign in the Graefekiez (39) while in the Reuterkiez political parties make more political demands (64). Furthermore, specific political discourses are present in the Reuterkiez public space including antiracism, demands for refugee rights, and anti-refugee residential obligations. These are common issues in the Reuterkiez affecting the residential population. Therefore, political contexts in the Graefekiez are guided by political figures – particularly linked to names other than German (namely Turkish). In the Reuterkiez, political topics define the context of LL items. This implies that an already politically enlightened residential population in the Graefekiez does not have to be encouraged for political engagement while a socially marginalized residential population in the Reuterkiez is being motivated to participate politically.[11]

The distribution of bottom-up and top-down levels shows more bottom-up than top-down items in all data collection sites. There are relatively more top-

11 Political canvassing has a huge impact on data evaluation. Predominantly the Left and the *Piraten* canvas in the RS, and *Bündnis '89/Die Grünen* (Green Party) and the Social Democrats (SPD) canvas in the GS. The latter also use languages other than German such as Turkish names or slogans. Furthermore, political campaigns also differ according to the neighborhood. While the Greens solicit votes from potential voters with a direct candidate more often in the Graefe neighborhood's side of the KD, its political topics are more often presented on the Reuter neighborhood's side of the KD. Objects from the Christian Democrats (CDU), according to the results, are only marginally found in the KD.

Table 6: Sociolinguistic-related Linguistic Landscape data.

Category	Class	Graefekiez			Reuterkiez			Grand Total
		Total	GS	KD	KD	RS	Total	
Domain	public	1971	1181	790	821	646	1467	3438
	work-related	10	5	5	7	–	7	17
Context	advertisement	328	140	188	151	60	211	539
	culture	53	51	2	4	69	73	126
	information	1046	649	397	416	261	677	1723
	notice	68	18	50	59	23	82	150
	politics	52	36	16	41	46	87	139
	service	331	331	123	132	120	252	583
Social context	awareness	1	1	–	2	2	4	5
	local development initiative	8	8	–	–	–	–	8
	magazine	–	–	–	–	16	16	16
	social service	9	9	–	–	–	–	9
	support	6	6	–	–	6	6	12
	youth coaching	–	–	–	–	4	4	4
Political context	activism	3	3	–	–	–	–	3
	anti residential obligation	–	–	–	–	1	1	1
	antiracism	–	–	–	–	1	1	1
	demand	8	4	4	28	36	64	72
	refugee rights	–	–	–	–	1	1	1
	environment	1	–	1	–	–	–	1
	naturalization	–	–	–	–	2	2	2
	notice	1	1	–	2	–	2	3
	political figure	39	28	11	11	–	11	50
	rent	–	–	–	–	5	5	5
Neighborhood context	commerce	38	34	4	6	8	14	52
	culture	53	51	2	4	69	73	126
	education	1	1	–	–	18	18	19
	health	9	2	7	–	–	–	9
	job offer	7	2	5	7	–	7	14
	local	2	2	–	–	–	–	2
	political	52	36	16	41	41	82	134
	religion	1	–	1	2	2	4	5
	social	24	24	–	2	28	30	54
Level of information	bottom-up	1530	932	598	649	485	1134	2664
	top-down	451	254	197	179	161	340	791

down items in the RS but also in the Graefekiez. In each road, isolated from its neighborhood position, more items in both categories can be found in the KD. Thus, governmental influence on LL items remains generally low, while the scope of privately set items differs when looked at from a neighborhood's perspective.

Finally, social and political circumstances of the neighborhoods strongly influence the context of LL items. In addition, the analysis of different contextual relationship between LL items and the neighborhoods shows that there are complex distinguishing characteristics.

7.2 Linguistic results

There are up to sixteen languages on a single LL item. One to three languages on a single LL item is the most common occurrence (Table 7). There are more monolingual than multilingual signs in all data collection sites. The number of monolingual items in the GS and in the Graefekiez outnumbers the results in the RS and Reuterkiez.

In the GS, French and Italian monolingual items outnumber Turkish and Arabic monolingual objects. In the RS, the results are reversed; Turkish is nearly equally present as English. Overall, English monolingual items are the most frequent in both neighborhoods, with less items occurring in the Reuterkiez. Surprisingly, there is a high occurrence of French monolingual items in the Reuterkiez's side of the KD.[12] The Turkish language is one of the most prominent languages on monolingual items besides English. However, the results show that there are additional languages challenging its dominant position in the LL; particularly in the context of socio-structural changes or due to current changing proportions in language communities.

While Turkish appears beside German on many multilingual items, other languages occur on multilingual items as well. In the Graefekiez, the linguistic diversity is vibrant. Chinese, French, Greek, Italian, Portuguese, Spanish, Swedish, and Arabic appear in considerable amounts. Thus, more language communities are addressed, although sparingly. The average Turkish word count has the highest value in the RS. It is even twice as high as the total average Turkish word count. While looking at the developments from the GS via KD to the RS, the average Turkish word count is subject to fluctuations. Thus, the data potentially indicates a complex landscape structure for Turkish in the areas.

12 All of these French monolingual items occur around a single shop.

Table 7: Language-related Linguistic Landscape data.

Category	Class	Sub-Class	Graefekiez			Reuterkiez			Grand Total
			Total	GS	KD	KD	RS	Total	
Amount of languages	1		1647	996	651	673	551	1224	2871
	2		546	298	248	276	172	448	994
	3		138	87	51	45	18	63	201
	4		8	4	4	–	–	–	8
	7		7	–	–	–	–	–	7
	8		–	–	–	–	8	8	8
	11		11	–	11	11	–	11	22
	16		16	16	–	–	–	–	16
Language on monolingual sign	Arabic		3	1	2	2	5	7	10
	English		176	105	71	78	43	121	297
	French		12	12	–	13	2	15	27
	German		1399	854	545	553	455	1008	2407
	Italian		14	12	2	–	2	2	16
	Turkish		37	8	29	23	39	62	99
Language on bilingual sign	English	Italian	3	–	3	–	1	1	4
		Turkish	4	1	3	3	–	3	7
	German	Arabic	9	9	–	4	1	5	14
		Chinese	2	2	0	–	–	–	2
		English	164	93	71	93	48	141	305
		French	8	3	5	2	–	2	10
		Greek	4	–	4	–	–	–	4
		Hebrew	–	–	–	–	1	1	1
		Italian	20	17	3	–	–	–	20
		Persian	–	–	–	–	1	–	1
		Portuguese	5	5	–	–	–	–	5
		Spanish	5	5	–	–	–	–	5
		Swedish	1	–	1	–	–	–	1
		Turkish	37	11	26	32	30	62	99
		Vietnamese	–	–	–	–	1	–	1
	Turkish	Arabic	2	–	2	–	–	–	2
Ø Word count L2	Arabic		6,0	8,0	4,0	2,5	4,0	3,3	4,7
	English		4,3	5,5	3,1	3,1	3,6	3,4	3,9
	French		3,3	4,0	2,6	1,7	–	0,9	2,1
	Italian		8,8	15,5	2,0	–	13,0	6,5	7,7
	Turkish		3,0	3,2	2,7	4,2	9,8	7,0	5,0

The results of the linguistic analysis highlight a complex relation between aspects of neighborhoods' social spaces and the LL data. The combination of analytic categories reveals additional readings that go beyond the interpretation of monocausal relations. However, the linguistic function of LL items does not only provide results for further sociolinguistic interpretations; it also emphasizes the unique proportions of different languages to each other and in the context of the neighborhood.

7.3 Semantic and semiotic results

Looking at Table 8, the most relevant language on multilingual LL items is clearly German. English is not only the second most relevant language in all areas, but its value in the GS equals the total of all other data collection sites. In the RS, Turkish exceeds English. Italian is only a significant language in the RS. A similar relevance occurs nearly equally in all areas, slightly more often in the Reuterkiez.

Semantic significance of languages on multilingual LL items indicates that German appears in all areas. Numerically, it appears more often in the Graefekiez but occurrences are relatively equal in both neighborhoods. English, however, appears more often in the Graefekiez. In the RS, there is a high amount of semantically equal items whereas on the Reuterkiez's side of the KD, the proportion between English and semantically equal items is balanced. Turkish occurrences outnumber English in the RS. In all areas, the semantically subordinate language specifies the content of the dominant language. In the Reuterkiez, the subordinate language appears to clarify content more often than in the Graefekiez. In the KD, the subordinate language is used for advertising purposes. In addition, the presentation of political demands as well as additional information and descriptions are functions that emerge solely in the Graefekiez.

Most interestingly, the presentation of political demands expands the interpretation of political contexts. While political demands are predominantly presented in the German language in the Reuterkiez, the subordinate language in the Graefekiez addresses potential voters from alternative language communities. Subsequently, political situations are not solely personified in the Graefekiez, they are expressed in different languages. The arrangement of information on multilingual LL items shows that information in different languages predominantly complement each other in all areas. However, signs that have information in different languages complementing each other are relatively more often present in the Graefe- are than in the Reuterkiez. There are comparably high amounts

Table 8: Semantics- and semiotics-related Linguistic Landscape data.

Category	Class	Graefekiez			Reuterkiez			Grand Total
		Total	GS	KD	KD	RS	Total	
Relevance	English	84	60	24	21	15	36	120
	Equal	18	15	3	5	5	10	28
	German	275	165	110	161	89	250	525
	Italian	14	14	–	–	1	1	15
	Turkish	37	20	17	11	21	32	69
Dominance	English	27	13	14	10	3	13	40
	Equal	14	6	8	10	22	32	46
	German	377	238	139	180	97	277	654
	Italian	1	1	–	–	–	–	1
	Turkish	2	–	2	1	8	9	11
Function of semantic subordinate language	abbreviation	–	–	–	–	4	4	4
	additional info.	9	9	–	–	–	–	9
	advertisement	5	–	5	6	–	6	11
	clarification	9	6	3	30	10	40	49
	description	2	2	–	–	–	–	2
	neologism	2	–	2	1	1	2	4
	political demand	10	8	2	–	–	–	10
	specification	294	171	123	113	64	177	471
Arrangement of information	complementary	259	147	112	121	39	160	419
	duplicating	21	10	11	23	17	40	61
	fragmentary	18	10	8	5	12	17	35
	multiple monolingual	24	23	1	–	9	9	33
	overlapping	5	4	1	–	1	1	6

of items with multiple monolingualisms in the GS followed by the RS. On the one side, there are more items with duplicated content in the Reuterkiez. On the other side, there are more items with fragmentary multilingualism in the Graefekiez.

8 Conclusion

There is not only a verifiable difference between both neighborhoods in terms of social organization but also in their social statistical development. While advancing gentrification hits the Reuterkiez in distinct dimensions, developments appear less dramatic in the Graefekiez. Statistical data also reveal the influx of English users outnumbering other language communities.

Thus, it can be concluded that an advanced gentrification does not necessarily result in further negative progression of the social structure of an urban area. Graefekiez demonstrates that it can potentially be slowed by protective measures. The developments in both areas indicate a distinctive change in the societal proportions of particular language communities.

Additionally, both neighborhoods have unique linguistic landscapes with distinctive sociolinguistic features. In this sense, the border road Kottbusser Damm fulfils a specific function and has a decisive effect on the LL of the areas. It divides both neighborhoods not only in geographical but also in linguistic terms. This is clearly the case with regards to linguistic diversity.

The Graefekiez has an extensive and more complex landscape. While local self-governing initiatives focus on attempting to politically include language groups, they visually address language groups with multilingual affinities. In addition, the Turkish language community has a considerable political power in the neighborhood. Nevertheless, there is a salient competition between prestigious languages and migrant languages for linguistic visibility in the public space. Although the Graefekiez is more linguistically diverse, there is a threat of linguistic displacement linked to negative social structural developments.

The LL of the Reuterkiez reveals a striking difference to its counterpart. Social precariousness is reflected in high proportions of political demands and social service initiatives. Beside a limited linguistic diversity in the LL, there is a significant appearance of the Turkish language, indicating an exclusively dominant language community. However, in terms of semantic relevance, the Reuterkiez provides more often equal semantic complexity of languages present on multilingual signs. Advanced gentrification of the Graefekiez does not result in a lower linguistic diversity of its LL. However, the amount of prestigious languages is comparably higher than that of migrant languages in the Graefekiez compared to the Reuterkiez.

Finally, this paper has provided a comprehensive picture of the relationship between social structure, urban development and linguistic diversity in public spaces. All three elements sustainably influence the composition and progression of the LL of urban neighborhoods. Additionally, current geographical and social considerations no longer provide an extensive perspective on the development of urban life. While the social space-related boundaries within the city are increasingly dissolving, it is the sociolinguistic perspective /analysis that provides essential insights about urban areas and their social, cultural and political conditions. The study of LL enables to look at the concrete forms of language representation in public spaces. Capturing this holistic picture of a dynamic and vivid linguistic world represents one of the ongoing projects of sociolinguistics.

References

Amt für Statistik Berlin-Brandenburg. 2013a. *Herkunftsgebiet*. https://www.statistik-berlin-brandenburg.de/suweb/metadata/EWRBEE/Herkunft.html (accessed 06 September 2017).

Amt für Statistik Berlin-Brandenburg. 2013b. *Migrationshintergrund*. https://www.statistik-berlin-brandenburg.de/suweb/metadata/EWRBEE/Migration.html (accessed 06 September 2017).

Amt für Statistik Berlin-Brandenburg. 2013c. *Palästinenser*. https://www.statistik-berlin-brandenburg.de/suweb/metadata/EWRBEE/Palaestinenser.html (accessed 06 September 2017).

Amt für Statistik Berlin-Brandenburg. 2013d. *Einwohnerstatistikregister Berlin. Migrationshintergrund*. https://www.statistik-berlin-brandenburg.de/statis/login.do?guest=guest (accessed 06 September 2017).

Barni, Monica & Carla Bagna. 2009. A mapping technique and the linguistic landscape. In Elana Shohamy & Durk Gorter (eds.), *Linguistic Landscape. Expanding the Scenery*, 126–140. London: Routledge.

Barni, Monica & Guus Extra. 2008. Mapping linguistic diversity in multicultural contexts. Cross-national and cross-linguistic perspectives. In Monica Barni & Guus Extra (eds.), *Mapping linguistic diversity in multicultural contexts*, 3–42. Berlin: Mouton de Gruyter.

Ben-Rafael, Eliezer. 2009. A sociological approach to the study of linguistic landscapes. In Elana Shohamy & Durk Gorter (eds.), *Linguistic Landscape. Expanding the Scenery*, 40–54. London: Routledge.

Blasius, Jörg. 1993. *Gentrification und Lebensstile. Eine empirische Untersuchung*. Wiesbaden: Deutscher Universitätsverlag.

Crystal, David (ed.). 2010 [1986]. *The Cambridge Encyclopedia of Language*, 3rd edn. Cambridge: Cambridge University Press.

De Vries, John. 1990. On coming to our census. A layman's guide to demolinguistics. *Journal of Multilingual and Multicultural Development* 11(1–2). 57–76.

Durkheim, Emile. 1964 [1895]. *The rules of sociological method*. New York: The Free Press of Glencoe.

Fuchs, Gotthard, Bernhard Moltmann & Walter Prigge (eds.). 1995. *Mythos Metropole*. Frankfurt am Main: Suhrkamp.

Goffman, Erving. 1963. *Behavior in public places*. New York: Free Press.

Goffman, Erving. 1981. *Forms of talk*. Philadelphia: University of Pennsylvania Press.

Habermas, Jürgen. 1989 [1962]. *The structural transformation of the public sphere. An inquiry into a category of Bourgeois society*. Cambridge: Polity Press.

Harwood, Jake, Howard Giles & Richard Y. Bourhis. 1994. The genesis of vitality theory. Historical patterns and discoursal dimensions. *International Journal of the Sociology of Language* 108(1). 167–206.

Krampen, Martin. 1979. *Meaning in the urban environment*. London: Pion.

Lachapelle, Réjean & Jacques Henripin. 1980. *La situation démolinguistique au Canada. Évolution passée et prospective*. Montréal: Institut de recherches politiques.

Landry, Rodrigue & Richard Y. Bourhis. 1997. Linguistic landscape and ethnolinguistic vitality. An empirical study. *Journal of Language and Social Psychology* 16(1). 23–49.

Leclerc, Jacques. 1989. *La guerre des langues dans l'affichage*. Montréal: VLB éditeur.

Massey, Doreen. 1999. Cities in the world. In: Doreen Massey, John Allen & Steve Pile (eds.), *City worlds*, 93–150. London & New York: Routledge

Nasar, Jack L. 1989. Perception, cognition, and evaluation of urban places. In: Irwin Altman & Ervin H. Zube (eds.), *Human behavior and environment. Public places and spaces*, 31–56. New York: Plenum Press.

Reblin, Eva. 2012. *Die Straße, die Dinge und die Zeichen. Zur Semiotik des materiellen Stadtraums*. Bielefeld: transcript Verlag.

Reh, Mechthild. 2004. Multilingual writing. A reader-oriented typology. With examples from Lira Municipality (Uganda). *Journal of the Sociology of Language* 170. 1–41.

Ross, Nigel J. 1997. Signs of International English. *English Today* 13(2). 29–33.

Senatsverwaltung für Stadtentwicklung und Umwelt. 2013a. *FIS-Broker Sachdatenanzeige. Lebensweltlich orientierte Räume (LOR) – Planungsräume*. http://fbinter.stadt-berlin.de/fb/index.jsp (accessed 06 September 2017).

Senatsverwaltung für Stadtentwicklung und Umwelt. 2013b. Lebensweltlich orientierte Räume (LOR) in Berlin. http://www.stadtentwicklung.berlin.de/planen/basisdaten_stadtentwicklung/lor/ (accessed 06 September 2017).

Shohamy, Elana. 2006. *Language policy. Hidden agendas and new approaches*. London: Routledge.

TOPOS. 2008. *Sozialstruktur und Mietentwicklung im Erhaltungsgebiet Graefestraße*. http://www.berlin.de/imperia/md/content/bafriedrichshain-kreuzberg/abtstadtpg/amtstaplverm_baa/stapl/stadterneuerung/graefe_endbericht.pdf (accessed 06 September 2017).

TOPOS. 2011. *Sozialstrukturentwicklung in Nord-Neukölln*. http://www.schillerpromenade-quartier.de/uploads/media/NNK_TOPOS_End.pdf (accessed 06 September 2017).

TOPOS. 2012. *Sozialstrukturentwicklung in Nord-Neukölln*. http://www.quartiersmanagement-berlin.de/fileadmin/content-media/Nachrichten/Neukoelln/2011/SozStrukNNK_120312.pdf (accessed 06 September, 2017).

Van der Merwe, Izak J.1989. Geolinguistics of Afrikaans in metropolitan Cape Town. *South African Journal of Linguistics* 7(2). 92–96.

Zukin, Sharon. 1995. *The cultures of cities*. Cambridge, Mass.: Blackwell.

Gertrud Hüwelmeier

14 Bazaarlingualism in Berlin's *Đồng Xuân Center*: anthropological perspectives

1 Introduction

Berlin is a city with a unique history as a divided place, which resulted in a specific history of migration. West Berlin experienced different waves of migrant groups, most of them came from the 1950s onwards as 'guest workers' *(Gastarbeiter)* from other European countries, while a smaller number arrived as boat refugees from Vietnam in the late 1970s and early 1980s. In East Berlin, tens of thousands of contract workers from socialist countries all around the world arrived throughout the 1980s. New groups of migrants have been coming to the reunified city since the fall of the Berlin Wall and due to the recent movement of refugees from various parts of the world to Germany. The *Đồng Xuân Center,* a multi-ethnic bazaar in the eastern part of Germany's capital, is a site where Turks, Indians, Vietnamese and members of other immigrant groups encounter each other. Called the "Vietnamese Market" or "Little Hanoi" by some outsiders, the locality is frequently visited by people from a variety of ethnic and religious backgrounds. In light of this diversity, the *Đồng Xuân Center* needs to be conceived not only as a venue for economic exchange, but also as a place for encounter and conviviality, as a site of multilingualism and therefore a cosmopolitan space.

Over the past ten years, I conducted ethnographic fieldwork among Vietnamese in the eastern and western part of Berlin, in the eastern and western part of Germany and in North and South Vietnam, while participating in the everyday life in people's homes and in religious rituals in various contexts. As many Vietnamese are engaged in trading, I carried out fieldwork in marketplaces in Berlin as well.[1] It is exactly in these localities that diasporic Vietnamese

1 I conducted ethnographic fieldwork with migrant groups in the Berlin and in the *Đồng Xuân* Center since 2005 (DFG funded Research Project HU 1019/ 2-1 and 2-2) "Transnational networks, religion and new migration" based on participant observation and interviews. I proceeded fieldwork in a subsequent research project "The Global Bazaar," funded by the German Research Foundation (2012–2015; HU 1019/3-1). In this project, multi-sited ethnographic fieldwork was carried out in various migrant run marketplaces in Berlin, Warsaw and Prague. Throughout the years I visited the *Đồng Xuân Center* intermittently, while main periods of fieldwork took place for 12 months from 2005 to 2006, for 6 months in 2010 and 2011 and two months in 2012.

My research project "Religion, Media, and Materiality. Spiritual Economies in Southeast Asia", funded by the German Research Foundation (2015–2018; HU 1019/4-1), is based on

https://doi.org/10.1515/9781501508103-014

encounter Muslims, Hindus, Sikhs and other people with diverse religious and ethnic backgrounds, who are also trading in these places. Practicing various forms of communication notwithstanding, the aim of this contribution is to explore the written language uses on notice boards in a multi-ethnic marketplace in Berlin.

As people from various parts of the world, particularly from Asia, come together in the Berlin bazaar, they engage in practices of translanguaging. In trying to make themselves understood by others, they use various languages to create and maintain economic and social relations. I investigate how people communicate when they bring different life histories, migration narratives, and trajectories to interactions in this particular locality. In the *Đồng Xuân Center*, people communicate multimodally, using the spoken word and ritual interactions as well as gesture and signing. This paper focuses on written signs, but these notices, however, are not the only way of communication within the market. Some traders, not knowing the language of other distributors, interact with salespersons from different backgrounds ritually, for example by inviting them to taste the food they brought from home with a recipe from their country of origin, or share a cup of tea with a different flavour. Traders speak their national languages while communicating with co-ethnics, and use German or learner repertoires of German while chatting with traders from other countries or with clients from various backgrounds.

By focussing on noticeboards in the bazaar and analysing the ads placed there by predominantly Vietnamese migrants, such as job posts or lonely hearts ads, I take a close look at the language mix, contents, and addressees of written messages. The notices indicate the needs and anxieties of migrants in Berlin, in particular with regard to residence permits and economic activities, but also referring to political and religious affiliations as well as gender issues within and beyond the market. Due to the massive insecurities in migrants' lives, the advertisements speak their own language about the uncertainties of life far away from home, but closely connected with a migrant's country of origin. Thus, by taking into account recent critiques of methodological nationalism, this paper argues for an anthropological perspective in analysing the diversifying linguistic and socio-economic landscape in the eastern part of Berlin. The ethnographic exploration of small advertisements in multi-ethnic and multi-religious places aims to contribute to a better understanding of migrants' everyday lives

ethnographic fieldwork in Hanoi, including popular religious practices in various marketplaces. I would like to thank the editors of this volume and the anonymous reviewers for valuable comments and suggestions on an earlier draft.

in a superdiverse city, on the one hand, and points to the creation and maintenance of their transnational ties on the other hand.

2 Linguistic diversity in a superdiverse bazaar

Like many other cities, the city of Berlin, not least due to the fall of the Berlin Wall and the diffuse nature of migration flows to the capital since the early 1990s, has experienced an increase of new groups of people who bring along various competences and practices from a variety of countries. There is a growing awareness that over the past two decades, globalisation and transnational migration have altered the face of ethnic, religious and linguistic diversity in societies all over the world. As a result, the multiculturalism of an earlier era, conceptualized broadly as an ethnic minority paradigm, has been replaced by what Steven Vertovec (2007) calls "super-diversity", characterized by an increase of different categories of migrants, nationalities, languages and religions. Taking this research perspective into account, I will focus on migrant-run marketplaces in the eastern part of Germany's capital which have been established since 2005. By exploring a variety of language practices in these multi-ethnic localities, I suggest that the bazaar is not only a place for economic exchange, but also a site where linguistic diversification contributes to new and hybrid ways of communicative practices. However, without referring to experiences of migration, date of arrival, and to transnational social and cultural ties, including language, we cannot fully grasp the impact and significance of the varieties of diversity in the host country. In the following I consider the dynamic interplay of an increasing number of "new, small and scattered, multiple origin, transnationally connected, socio-economically differentiated and legally stratified immigrants" (Vertovec 2007: 1024), who have arrived in Germany in recent decades, both prior to and after the fall of the Berlin Wall. However, it was not until many years after the reunification of the country and the city that German authorities slowly began to realize that Germany has become a country of immigration. Only recently, at the end of 2015, when hundreds of thousands of refugees were arriving from Syria and other regions, did the authorities concede that German society will dramatically change over the next few years, becoming much more diverse than ever before in terms of ethnic, religious and linguistic diversity (Hüwelmeier 2016: 10).

As bazaars are perfect places of encounter, my contribution zooms in on a particular locality, namely Berlin's *Đồng Xuân Center* – which shares its name with the most famous market in Hanoi, meaning "spring meadow" – a migrant-run trading site located in the eastern part of the city. In exploring language practices in this multi-ethnic location, I draw on ideas about the increasing complexity of variables in view of the everyday lives of people in places characterized by high levels of transnational migration in conjunction with social scientists' recent thoughts on diversity in the marketplace (Hiebert et al 2015). Looking at linguistic practices in the bazaar not only broadens the perception of the marketplace beyond its function as a purely economic locality, but also reminds sociolinguistics of the complex dynamics of diversity, which challenge established identities, categories, standards, registers and styles "from below" (Arnaut 2012).

Taking a closer look at notices on bulletin boards and migrants' ads on these boards, enables us to learn more about the needs and anxieties of migrants in Berlin, in particular with regard to residence permits, religious issues and economic activities. In addition, we gain a better understanding about the social life in this multi-ethnic place and peoples' transnational connections. Critics of methodological nationalism (Wimmer and Glick Schiller 2002) have contributed to awareness about the significance of the nation-state as a container model for research. Yet, despite the broadening of the research lens to include cross-border ties, the nation-state still matters, in particular with regard to language issues, as I have discussed in relation to migrants' religious gatherings (Hüwelmeier 2011). The concept of "national languages" as a salient element of a nation-state's identity is very strong (Jørgenson et al. 2011: 35), as demonstrated by the use of the naturalisation test in Germany as part of the citizenship application (see also Tanager, this volume). The languages found on the marketplace noticeboards reveal much about the lives lived across borders, simultaneously rooted in different places.

3 Berlin's most famous asia market

The *Đồng Xuân Center* was established in 2005, and was initially dominated by Vietnamese traders who had formerly been contract workers in East Germany. However, from the very beginning, vendors from other parts of the world, mainly from Asia, also established businesses within the market. As the group of traders diversified in recent years, the number of clients and visitors increased. Thousands of Vietnamese in the eastern part of Berlin reside in the pre-fabricated apartment buildings (*Plattenbauten*) in the area around the market, living side by side with other migrant groups, such as people from Russia, and with Germans. In this paper I will mainly focus on Vietnamese, as this group plays a significant role in the social life of the market. As previously noted, the date of arrival of different migrant groups and their region of origin are important variables in understanding the hierarchies, tensions, and political sensibilities among migrants in a given place. In exploring what makes Berlin a unique place for the encounter of both boat people from South Vietnam and contract workers, a majority coming from North Vietnam, I will briefly focus on the different histories of Vietnamese immigration to the two Germanies, which has certain impacts on the different groups' political affiliations in the now reunified host country.

Thousands of students and apprentices from the northern part of Vietnam, which was a communist country since 1954, came to the GDR in the late 1960s and early 1970s. After they finished their studies they returned to Vietnam. In West Germany, a small number of Vietnamese students travelling to the Federal Republic of Germany (FRG) in the 1950s was trained as engineers or doctors at the universities there. After the political split of North and South Vietnam in 1954, many of them decided to stay in West Germany, and others came from South Vietnam some years later. A number of Vietnamese from this first group of migrants married West Germans, and they are considered to be integrated into German society, with some achieving professional success.

While different groups of Vietnamese were already living and working in the two Germanies prior to the 1970s, it was not until the end of the American War in Vietnam that large numbers of Vietnamese migrated to West and East Germany. About 40,000 boat refugees fled South Vietnam on small, leaky boats and arrived in the western part of Germany in the late 1970s. They comprised the largest migrant group from East Asia at the time and their arrival transformed the multicultural landscape in West Germany. As a result of generous support programs from the federal government such as language courses and family reunification policies in the early 1980s (Beuchling 2003), boat refugees have become incorporated into German society, in contrast to other migrant groups that did not receive the same level of federal support.

Based on a bilateral agreement between the Socialist Republic of Vietnam and the GDR, signed in 1980 and renewed in 1987, tens of thousands of Vietnamese entered East Germany in the 1980s. Many former Vietnamese students returned to the GDR as well, to support the contract workers in translations services. Most of the contract workers came from the northern part of Vietnam and went to work in GDR state-owned companies. They remained in the GDR for four to five years, living in special housing under the control of the East German state authorities and the Vietnamese embassy. When the Berlin Wall fell in 1989 and Germany was reunited in 1990, the fate of the Vietnamese contract workers still living in eastern Germany was up in the air. During this time of great insecurity, the government of the newly reunited Germany sought political solutions for the migrants, including financial incentives for returning to Vietnam and temporary legal guidelines for those who did not wish to return to their home country.

The political division of Germany into West and East therefore affected the destinations of migrants from different parts of Vietnam: while boat people, mainly from southern Vietnam, sought refuge in West Germany, other Vietnamese migrants, mainly from northern Vietnam, arrived in East Germany as contract workers. After the fall of the Berlin Wall, other groups of migrants, namely Vietnamese asylum seekers who had been contract workers in other former socialist countries, entered reunited Germany as well. Due to violence including murders among rival gangs of Vietnamese cigarette sellers on the black market in Berlin and eastern Germany in 1996, former contract workers were widely represented as a "cigarette mafia" in the German press (Bui 2003). Although a small number of boat people and contract workers built up social relations such as marriages and economic ties with each other after 1990, in general members of the two groups kept apart from each other. Internal differences among Vietnamese in Germany are mainly based on pre-migration political differences, and continue to shape the interactions among Vietnamese communities in Germany and in Berlin today (on still-felt effects of political divisions based on capitalism and communism in Berlin, see also the introduction to this volume). Post-1990 immigration from various regions in Vietnam and recent migration from rural localities highlight the increasing complexity of diversification such as date of arrival, city and rural background, legal status and gender. A number of Vietnamese encounter each other in the new Asian marketplaces in Berlin, Warsaw and Prague. Political sensitivities among different groups of Vietnamese still exist in the German diasporas, with different perspectives on colonial and post-colonial history in their country of origin, on revolution, war and reunification under a communist regime after 1975, on mass migration from South Vietnam to "the West" and on *global socialist networks* and *socialist cosmopolitanism* (Hüwelmeier 2017a), created and maintained by those who are, to this day, loyal to the communist regime in their home country. Transnational economic networks strengthen certain ties to the home country, thereby connecting people and places across borders. According to statistics, in 2017, 16 652 Vietnamese[2] citizens were living in Berlin, compared to 13 959 Vietnamese citizens in 2012.[3] However, these numbers do not tell us anything about numbers of Vietnamese who became German citizens and do not inform us about the amount of undocumented Vietnamese.

---

2 https://www.statistik-berlin-brandenburg.de/publikationen/stat_berichte/2017/SB_A01-05-00_2017h01_BE.pdf. Access 15.12. 2107.

3 https://www.statistik-berlin-brandenburg.de/publikationen/stat_berichte/2013/SB_A01-05-00_2012h02_BE.pdf. Access 15.12.2017.

Prior to the fall of the Berlin Wall, the locality of the Asia market was considered the property of the Socialist government of the GDR. It was not until 2005 that a migrant investor purchased the former industrial site in Berlin-Lichtenberg and built a new market under the name *Đồng Xuân Center*. The market was newly constructed in an environment whose architecture is characterized by hundreds of pre-fabricated apartment blocks from the socialist period. Today these buildings are home to about 4,000 Vietnamese, Russians, and people from other places, many of whom are clients and visit the bazaar on a regular basis. Meanwhile, traders from China, Pakistan, India, Kuwait, Vietnam, and other countries sell their products in the *Đồng Xuân Center*. With its cheap products, its restaurants, and Asian supermarkets, the bazaar is a perfect place for meeting other people. Many customers, a number of whom are retailers, are non-Vietnamese, and come from different parts of Germany and Europe, such as Poland and the Czech Republic, to buy low-cost commodities in large quantity. Customers also include non-trading Vietnamese, who prefer to visit the *Đồng Xuân Center* to buy fresh vegetables and other items in the Asia supermarkets located in the bazaar. Apart from this group, people from the local neighbourhood, that is to say low-income Germans, Russians, and Vietnamese, come to the market on a regular basis in order to find bargains (*Schnäppchen*) such as toys for their children or cheap textiles. Others, such as young people, visit the tattoo shop, the cheap hair dresser, or one of the Vietnamese restaurants. Africans buy plantains and other food and Muslim women, partly with headscarf and long dress, are rubbing along. Another group of visitors includes tourists, as city guides promote the bazaar as an "exotic" place. The locality, however, which is not a neighbourhood, but a bazaar, has never been "Little Hanoi", as described by the press. At the opening of the market in 2005, more than half of the traders were of Vietnamese background, but nowadays Vietnamese wholesalers form a minority among the group of traders, most of them coming from Asia. In light of the growing ethnic diversity in the *Đồng Xuân Center*, the manager has considered changing the name of the market into *Asiatown* (Hüwelmeier 2016: 13), but did not realize the renaming until today.

4 Communication in a multi-ethnic space

The multi-ethnic composition of the market leads to the question of how communication is conducted within it. As Arjun Appadurai (1996) has suggested, the cultural flow of people, goods and ideas has resulted in new mobilities and the mixing of groups in various places. In response to demographic and social changes, ideas about languages, language groups and speakers, and communication have shifted, seemingly at a faster rate than science has been able to keep up with. Already some decades ago, anthropologist Johannes Fabian, renowned for his anticolonial writings, noted in regard to sociolinguistics and its difficulty in dealing with situations in which foreigners or strangers settle in a new surrounding:

> As it seems now, sociolinguistics is at odds with the 'changing', processual, creative and emergent characteristics of communication because its rules only catch established features and, perhaps, some variation within established features. It has, therefore, considerable difficulties with communicative exchanges between speakers who are not members of the same community, who do not share systems of rules, at least not fully, and whose interaction is such that in all probability they will never share the rules. This is the case of the foreigner or stranger who settles in another society and whom sociolinguists, tellingly enough, tend to view as an irritating deviant, not as a person who creatively transcends confin, 18, quoted in Arnaut 2012: 11).

Over the past decades, in particular due to accelerated processes of globalisation and the migration of millions of people, much has changed in anthropology as well as in sociolinguistics. As Arnaut suggested (2012: 11), a critical sociolinguistics of diversity should discard the concept of multiculturalism and its affirmation of established differences and hierarchies. By suggesting this, he refers to linguistic anthropologists Blommaert and Rampton, who emphasize that, "rather than working with homogeneity, stability and boundedness as the starting assumption, mobility, mixing, political dynamics and historical embedding are now central concerns in the study of languages, language groups and communication" (Blommaert and Rampton 2011: 3). Inspired by the work of Jan Blommaert (2014) who analyzed advertisements in a multi-ethnic neighbourhood in Antwerp in Belgium, I focus on traces hidden in notices that were displayed in the marketplace, traces which point to transnational migration flows and their social and cultural dynamics. Drawing on different notices in the *Đồng Xuân Center*, I highlight the multilayeredness of the messages: First, they point to a gradual change in the diaspora, which means that they emphasize the will to stay in the host country. Second, they point to transnational connections and political loyalty to the home country. Third, they indicate a number of difficulties migrants face in the host country. The topics of the advertisements span job offers, lonely hearts, political announcements, religious gatherings, and translation services. Even though the *Đồng Xuân Center* is a multi-ethnic locality in which people communicate in many languages, the addressees of the notice board are predominantly Vietnamese. One reason for this is the fact that a majority of customers in the market are Vietnamese who live close to the bazaar. Therefore, I will focus on this group of migrants, while keeping in mind that there are diverse groups communicating in the market.

4.1 Job ads

A number of advertisements refer to job offers, ranging from work in a bistro or restaurant to baby sitting or domestic service. Most of the notices on the notice boards are written in Vietnamese, sometimes with German mixed in. The following job ad, written in Vietnamese, and translated into English in this contribution, illustrates tensions among people from different parts in Vietnam. "I come from the North. I look for work as a babysitter. Please contact in case of interest." In analysing this notice, one has to take into account political sensibilities among various regions in Vietnam. The addressees of the ad are Vietnamese from the northern part of Vietnam, probably people from urban Hanoi, as they form a majority among the former contract workers in the eastern part of Germany. The sender of the message is from the north[4] and knows that northerners will generally not look for a babysitter from another region, as they consider people from other parts of Vietnam "backward" and "from the countryside". Vietnamese middle class households "from the North", which means predominantly from Hanoi, do not want their children to be looked after by a babysitter from Central Vietnam, as they want their children to speak "proper" Vietnamese, not the repertoires from Central Vietnam or any other place they consider "underdeveloped". Recently arrived migrants from Central Vietnam, in many cases undocumented, are classified as "others" by people from urban Hanoi, as new migrants are mostly poor and from a rural background. Vietnamese from the northern part of Vietnam, a region historically and politically distinct from other regions, and considered to be the first region that became communist, would be reluctant to make close contacts with Vietnamese from Central Vietnam, not to mention Vietnamese from South Vietnam, the former political other of the communist North until 1975 (Hüwelmeier 2008; 2017a). As this example illustrates, political sensitivities, including cultural differences, must be taken into account in order to properly understand the messages within the ads in the *Đồng Xuân Center*.

Another job ad points to the importance of residence permits and official documents, called 'papers' (*Papiere*) in colloquial German, a term generally

4 The ad reads: "tôi người Bắc muốn tìm việc trông trẻ. Ai có nhu cầu xin LH". In this case, gender is not displayed.

used by migrants referring to visa and other legitimating documents, identifying someone as a legal or undocumented migrant. The following notice, written in Vietnamese, advertizes a job as a kitchen helper and highlights the requirement of documents. "Looking for a male kitchen helper in Asia Buffet. Please with documents. If you are interested, please contact." Vietnamese in the *Đồng Xuân Center* sometimes engage with the Pakistani and Indian traders to ask about their experiences in obtaining residence documents. In these conversations, they will use the colloquial German term *Papier* (they use the singular form, as some have difficulties in pronouncing [r] and the [əe] at the end of *Papiere*, which means 'documents' in this context). In the spoken Vietnamese language as well as on the written ads, Vietnamese use the colloquial German term *Papier* ('documents'). *Không có papier*, for example, means 'do not have documents' and is a phrase with a mix of Vietnamese and German. Traders from different migration backgrounds will understand the term *Papier*, as it is linked to everyday difficulties and experiences in the host country, such as gaining residence permits. If a Vietnamese asks a Pakistani *Hast du Papier?*, which should be re-translated or re-read as 'Do you have documents?', the Pakistani will immediately know what is meant by the question, as traders in the bazaar are constantly talking about documented and undocumented people. This is a hot topic, as a number of the new migrants from Vietnam arriving in recent years have come without documents. Some of them are working in the market or are looking for jobs there. The *Đồng Xuân Center* is a desirable place for new migrants to work because co-ethnics will understand their language. In addition, newcomers feel safe in this locality compared to other places in Berlin, where nobody will take care of them. In the case of police raids, which happened several times while I was doing fieldwork in the market, undocumented migrants were able to escape due to a particular system of information.

4.2 Lonely hearts

The importance of documents is particularly relevant to those who have recently arrived in Berlin as illegal migrants and who need to find ways for obtaining a residence permit. In the case of female migrants from Vietnam, one of the ways to acquire such documents is by getting to know German men, possibly with the prospect of marriage. Some lonely hearts ads in the *Đồng Xuân Center* highlight the needs of undocumented female Vietnamese and the desires of male Germans. It is too dangerous for the women to put a lonely hearts ad with their phone number on the board, due to police raids in the market, but one does find ads written by German men looking for a female Vietnamese partner. While some Germans might be seriously interested in finding a woman from Vietnam, others know about the difficult situation of female undocumented Vietnamese quite well and take advantage of the desperate situation of migrant women. „Ich suche eine vietnamesische Frau von 18–35 Jahren (freundlich, nett) für Familie. Ich bin ein deutscher Mann, schlank, gutaussehend, freundlich (Anfang 40 Jahre)." Translated into English, it reads as follows: "I am looking for a Vietnamese woman, 18–35 years old, (friendly, nice) for family. I am a German man, slim, handsome, friendly (in my early 40ies)." This notice was written only in German and addresses Vietnamese women with some chance for starting a family. The following ad was written in German and Vietnamese, with some obviously important words underlined by the author of the ad. "Ich, über 50, 1,71, ca 75 kg, Handwerker, hilfsbereit, sehr kinderlieb, eigene Wohnung und schönen Garten, suche keine Asiatin (wie Thai) nur für Sex, sondern endlich wieder eine Vietnamesin zum glücklichen Zusammenleben, auch ohne Papier (dann ab 30), da ich helfen will." The Vietnamese version was translated into English in this contribution: "I, over 50, 1,71, about 75 kg, handyman, helpful, love children, own apartment and nice garden, not looking for an Asian woman (like Thai) only for sex, but finally again a Vietnamese for a happy relationship, even without documents (in this case only above 30), because I want to help." Note that *wie Thai* 'like Thai' was added later, probably by someone else, pointing to the stereotype that German men prefer women from Thailand for sex only. Several words have been underlined and therefore seem to be important for the reader of the ad, namely the words: *keine Asiatin* 'no Asian woman', *endlich wieder* 'finally again', *auch ohne Papier* 'even without documents', *da ich helfen will* 'because I want to help'.

An interpretation and analysis of the underlined words and phrases in this ad highlights the fact that the term *ohne Papier* ('without documents') plays a crucial role here as well. It may also be possible that the ad was written by a Vietnamese as a German probably would have written the grammatically correct term *ohne Papiere*. While this ad does not talk about marriage but about a happy relationship (whatever that may mean), in other cases a marriage relationship with a German husband is the only way for some recently arrived Vietnamese migrant women to be granted the right to remain in Germany (*Bleiberecht*). However, the most "popular" way of obtaining a residence permit is to become pregnant, as the term "for family" in the first ad signals. There is a growing number of cases in which Vietnamese women (and women with other backgrounds as well) have become pregnant with the biological father identified as a German (however only in the document), in order to obtain a residence permit (*Bleiberecht*). As is well known among German authorities, this method for securing documents for female asylum seekers is a big business for some people. In response, the German government recently changed the law to put a stop to this way of obtaining a right to stay "by fraud".[5] As pregnant asylum seekers want their children to become German citizens, they need, according to German law, a male German biological father. Feigned paternity (*Scheinvaterschaft*), seems to be not only of benefit for some German men as well as notaries and lawyers, but also for migrant women and mothers, who then have the right to remain in Germany. Unfortunately, however, many of these women end up in prostitution, as they have to pay huge sums of money to various people in Germany as well as to those in Vietnam who financed the trip to go abroad (personal communication).

4.3 Political loyalties

Some ads on the notice board in the *Đồng Xuân Center* point to hometown associations. Vietnamese are invited to join these groups in order to strengthen social and political ties between home and host country, and between home and host region. Identification with the politics of the country of origin is, in the case of the Socialist Republic of Vietnam, experienced in joining hometown associations. These groups serve not only to demonstrate political solidarity with the country of origin, but also to organize "cultural" events in the host country, such as the New Year Festival or regional festivities. Vietnamese from all over Germany will gather at a certain date in Berlin or in another part of Germany to celebrate important national or local rituals known from Vietnam.

Part of the political engagement of Vietnamese in Germany relates to the death of important heroes and military leaders in Vietnam. An obituary, depicted on the wall of the *Đồng Xuân Center* during my fieldwork in 2013 and a subsequent memorial service performed on the grounds of the market for the deceased military leader Võ Nguyên Giáp highlights transnational political affects. General Võ Nguyên Giáp, a close friend of Hồ Chí Minh, was famous for having organized and fought the battle of *Điện Biên Phủ* in 1954, where the *Việt Minh* surrounded and besieged the French. A number of male participants in the public memorial service in the bazaar cried, as a Vietnamese woman told me later. While showing

5 https://www.welt.de/vermischtes/article165267259/Asylbetrug-mit-deutschen-Scheinvaterschaften.html (accessed 12 August 2017). http://www.stuttgarter-zeitung.de/inhalt.schein-vaterschaft-asylbewerberinnen-mit-kind-erschleichen-sich-bleiberecht.154d8389-cfd7-480f-a4ab-1f8f4de5625a.html (accessed 12 August 2017).

emotions in public is not what is expected from Vietnamese men, in this situation, deep feelings, connected with the anticolonial war and with the war against America, were commemorated. The obituary and the photograph of the deceased on the walls of the *Đồng Xuân Center* remind Vietnamese to fulfil religious obligations in the case of death. Second, displaying the obituary of a political hero indicates the influence of the Socialist Republic of Vietnam in the *Đồng Xuân Center* and highlights close ties between the market and the Vietnamese Embassy in Berlin. Its representatives join political and cultural events in the *Đồng Xuân Center*, such as the celebration of the Women's Day in Vietnam. Due to the Vietnamese background of the market manager and the many Vietnamese visiting the market, of whom a considerable number has known each other since GDR times, political loyalty to the home country is performed on the territory of the bazaar. Political loyalty includes patriotism and respect towards the Socialist Government, which enabled tens of thousands of Vietnamese contract workers to live and work in the GDR in the 1980s. Simultaneously, being selected for study or work in socialist fraternal countries was a gratification for parents' and grandparents' support in fighting against French colonialism and later against the Americans in Vietnam. Referring to "international socialist solidarity and friendship", strong transnational ties were created and maintained between Berlin and Hanoi, and still continue.

4.4 Religious practices

Participation in mourning rituals, as discussed in the previous section, is a moral obligation for most Vietnamese. However, there is a variety of transnational religious ties that are created and performed in the *Đồng Xuân Center*. Ads written in Vietnamese with invitations to participate in many kinds of religious gatherings are depicted on the notice boards in the marketplace. Language plays a significant role in performing religious practices. Vietnamese, convening in a Vietnamese Buddhist bazaar pagoda on the grounds of the *Asia Pacific Center*, another wholesale market in the eastern part of Berlin, speak in Vietnamese to the Buddhist nun, and the Vietnamese Buddhist nun, who has been living in Germany for more than 20 years, is not able to talk to a German audience (Hüwelmeier 2013b). Language is not the only reason why migrants sometimes stick in their own groups. It is also the invisibility of migrants' religious places which makes it difficult to even find the localities of religious assembling (Burchard and Becci 2016; Hüwelmeier 2016). This was recently highlighted by Blommaert (2013), who focused on 16 places of worship in a multiethnic neighbourhood in Antwerp, including several mosques and a number of evangelical churches located in ordinary residential buildings or former retail spaces. Only small signs of identification written in the native language of migrants refer to the existence of these spaces.

In the *Đồng Xuân Center*, visitors will notice a number of small shrines established at the entrance of Vietnamese shops. These religious objects are transferred from Vietnam and every morning, the shop owner will offer fresh fruit, cigarettes and sometimes alcohol, burn incense and pray for good business to gods and spirits (Hüwelmeier 2008). Buddhist ceremonies are performed on the grounds of the bazaar on special occasions, and only recently, a mosque was established in a former office close to the bazaar.

On a wall in the bazaar, I noticed an invitation for participating in a religious gathering at a mosque, written in Arabic and in German. This is another indication, that not only Vietnamese display advertisements in the market. Furthermore, this points to the fact, that the *Đồng Xuân Center* is a multireligious and multi-ethnic site and not a "Vietnamese market". Another ad on the notice board, written in Vietnamese, indicated an invitation to a religious gathering in the International Gospel Center in the eastern part of Berlin. Language matters in religious settings, and evangelical and Pentecostal Vietnamese, even if they sense themselves to be part of a global Christian charismatic movement, will have difficulties to proselytize non-Vietnamese: First-generation migrants speak Vietnamese and, depending on age and date of arrival, hardly speak German. In contrast to African Pentecostal churches in Berlin, where most of the Pentecostal "crusades" or evangelisation campaigns are performed in English or French, the former colonial languages (Hüwelmeier and Krause 2010), the language of singing and preaching in Vietnamese prayer sessions is Vietnamese (Hüwelmeier 2011: 448). However, if any Germans join the service, as some did during a "crusade" in a Vietnamese trade center in which I participated some years ago, the preaching will be translated into German by second-generation Vietnamese church followers. Second-generation Vietnamese speak German fluently and help their parents with business matters, tax issues, and government bureaucracy.

4.5 Translation services

While second-generation Vietnamese support their parents in finding their way through the German bureaucratic maze, there are many situations in which migrants require translation services. Notices from lawyers on the bulletin boards of the *Đồng Xuân Center* point to crucial issues for Vietnamese, namely the translation and certification of various kinds of documents. One ad offering services included both a German and a Vietnamese flag. Displaying different national flags in the same context appears to suggest a way of signalling transnational awareness and mutual understanding. A sign on the car of a driving school on the grounds of the market displays a steering wheel with colours of the German flag, the Vietnamese flag, and the stars from the EU flag. In the case of the translation service, the ad was written in Vietnamese and offered services such as support in all bureaucratic matters, for example in obtaining certificates for marriage documents. Services included accompanying clients to government offices, consultation and conversation in these places, contacts to lawyers and teachers, and interpretation services at the job centre and in hospitals. The latter service was offered by a male Vietnamese with a PhD "from the Freie Universität Berlin, living in Germany for 30 years, speaking German fluently".

It was striking that the ads promoting legal services listed many of the delinquencies that seem to be associated with "deviant behaviour" of migrants, such as living in Germany without documents, burglary, theft, driving without licence. Some of the German lawyers target the market for potential clients, as the ads were written in both Vietnamese and German and promised clients support from a translation service for legal advice and in the case of a trial.

5 Gender in the marketplace

An intriguing aspect of diversity is the mix of languages in the marketplace, as well as the wide range of advertisements, from lonely hearts ads to looking for a marriage partner or a job, offers of translation and interpretation services, obituaries, and religious advertising, among others. Interestingly, nearly all ads were written by Vietnamese, with only a few written by German men, such as the lonely hearts ads. I rarely came across ads written by or addressed to Indian, Pakistani, Turkish, or Chinese people. In other words, the target group of the ads are Vietnamese. One reason for the dominance of Vietnamese in the *Đồng Xuân Center* is, as already mentioned, the high density of people with Vietnamese background living in the neighbourhood. Another reason for the predominance of ads written by Vietnamese is the gender-based division of labour in the multi-ethnic bazaar (Hüwelmeier 2017b). No Indian, Pakistani or Turkish women work in the marketplace. However, a considerable number of traders are Vietnamese women, visible in the public space of the market. As in Vietnam, where numerous women are engaged in trading (Leshkowich 2014; Hüwelmeier 2018), retailing and wholesaling became quite an important source of income for many Vietnamese families after the fall of the Berlin Wall. This is true for other migrant-run markets such as in Warsaw, Budapest and Prague, where women form the dominant group of traders (Hüwelmeier 2013a). As Vietnamese women are absent from home for long hours, they need babysitters and domestic helpers. For this reason, female traders hire other personnel such as shop assistants and therefore, most of the ads on the notice boards are addressed to women. Vietnamese women, as they represent a majority of female vendors in the *Đồng Xuân Center*, are communicative and maintain networks with co-traders of any background. Like other salespeople, they request their stall neighbour to keep an eye on their shop or salesroom if they meet with clients for lunch, and ask them to call by mobile phone if another client is approaching or looking for the stall owner. Support, solidarity and conviviality are performed in the bazaar, as this is a place where traders spend most part of the day with their "market family". Vietnamese Women play an important role in the production of a friendly-minded superdiverse setting.

6 Conclusion

Besides communication via spoken language and ritual, non-verbal signs such as notices are important indications for encounter and exchange among various groups of people in Berlin's most famous bazaar, the *Đồng Xuân Center*, named "Little Hanoi" by the press or labelled *Asiatown* by others. Advertisements are visual displays and should be therefore considered as part of visual anthropology and media studies in general (Askew & Wilk 2002; Ginsburg et al. 2002, consider also Özcan, this volume and Fuller, this volume). They are material objects, mediating between different worlds and diverse actors. The analysis of notices in multi-ethnic places challenges scholars to look deeper into the content of displays, which refer to certain desires, needs, and transnational ties of migrants living in a superdiverse city such as Berlin. Bazaarlingualism, therefore, is a way of communication in multi-ethnic marketplaces, where people from various countries encounter each other on an everyday basis, performing everyday cosmopolitanism by trading, bargaining, and chatting in many languages.

In a century of accelerated migrations, cosmopolitan cities are made visible in the increasing number of restaurants with food from around the world (see also Stock, this volume), events such as street festivals celebrating the culture of specific parts of the population (Werbner 2015: 569) and, with regard to Berlin, in the establishment of venues such as the *Đồng Xuân Center*. Though, despite their heterogeneity, multicultural cities are characterized as much by separations as mixing. This is also true with respect to particular places such as post-socialist bazaars in eastern European countries (Hüwelmeier 2013a). In the *Đồng Xuân Center* in the eastern part of Berlin, reference to the own ethnic group exists side by side with mingling and mixing. The exoticization of *Asiatown* notwithstanding, the bazaar, with its ethnic restaurants, tattoo shops, and cheap textiles made in China, India and Vietnam, attracts clients from many countries, and is therefore a particular location in the post-socialist city. It is a site where creativity and solidarity transcend classes, hierarchies, ethnic groups, and languages. Regardless of tensions in the marketplace, such as poaching clients from competitors, a multitude of migrants live and work side by side in the multi-ethnic bazaar, where culturally creative encounters and sociality are performed on a daily basis. It is exactly this what makes the *Đồng Xuân Center* a cosmopolitan space *in situ*.

References

Appadurai, Arjun. 1996. *Modernity at large: Cultural dimensions of globalization*. Minneapolis: University of Minnesota Press.

Arnaut, Karel. 2012. Super-diversity: elements of an emerging perspective. *Diversities* 14(2). 1–16.

Askew, Kelly & Richard R. Wilk. 2002. *The anthropology of media: A reader*. Malden: Blackwell Publishers.

Beuchling, Olaf 2003. *Vom Bootsflüchtling zum Bundesbürger*. Münster: Waxmann Verlag.
Blommaert, Jan & Ben Rampton. 2011. Language and superdiversity. *Diversities* 13(2). 1–21.

Blommaert, Jan. 2013. *Ethnography, superdiversity and linguistic landscapes: Chronicles of complexity*. Bristol: Multilingual Matters.

Blommaert, Jan. 2014. Infrastructures of superdiversity: Conviviality and language in an Antwerp neighborhood. *European Journal of Cultural Studies* 17(4). 431–451.

Burchardt, Marian and Irene Becci. 2016. Religion and Superdiversity: An Introduction. *New Diversities*, Vol. 18, No. 1. 1–7.

Bui, Pipo. 2003. *Envisioning Vietnamese Migrants in Germany*. Münster: LIT-Verlag.

Fabian, Johannes. 1979. Rule and process: Thoughts on ethnography as communication. In: *Philosophy of the Social Sciences*. Vol. 9, No. 1. 1–26.

Ginsburg, Faye, Lila Abu-Lughod & Brian Larkin (eds.). 2002. *Media worlds: Anthropology on new terrain*. Berkeley, CA: University of California Press.

Hiebert, Daniel, Jan Rath & Steven Vertovec. 2015. Urban markets and diversity: Towards a research agenda. *Ethnic and Racial Studies* 38(1). 5–21.

Hüwelmeier, Gertrud. 2008. Spirits in the market place. Transnational networks of Vietnamese migrants in Berlin. In Michael Peter Smith & John Eade (eds.), *Transnational ties: Cities, identities, and migrations*, CUCR book series, Vol. 9, 131–144. New Brunswick, NJ: Transaction Publishers.

Hüwelmeier, Gertrud. 2011. Socialist cosmopolitanism meets global Pentecostalism: Charismatic Christianity among Vietnamese migrants after the fall of the Berlin Wall. *Ethnic and Racial Studies*, Special Issue 34(3). 436–453.

Hüwelmeier, Gertrud. 2013a. Post-socialist bazaars. Diversity, solidarity and conflict in the marketplace. *Laboratorium* 5 (1),Special Issue: *The social Lives of postsocialism*, Caterina Borelli & Fabio Mattioli (eds.), 52–72.

Hüwelmeier, Gertrud. 2013b. Bazaar pagodas. Transnational religion, postsocialist marketplaces and Vietnamese migrant women in Berlin. *Religion and Gender* 3(1). 76–89.

Hüwelmeier, Gertrud. 2016. Enhancing spiritual security in Berlin's Asian bazaars. *New Diversities*, Special Issue: *Religion and Superdiversity* 18(1). 9–22.

Hüwelmeier, Gertrud. 2017a. Socialist cosmopolitans in postsocialist Europe. Transnational ties among Vietnamese across Eastern Europe in the Cold War period and thereafter. *Journal of Vietnamese Studies* 12(1). 130–158.

Hüwelmeier, Gertrud. 2017b. From contract workers to entrepreneurs. Gender and work among transnational Vietnamese in East and reunited Germany. In Joanne Miyang Cho & Douglas T. McGetchin (eds.), *Gendered Encounters between Germany and Asia. Transnational Perspectives since 1800*, 275–290. Cham, Switzerland: Palgrave MacMillan.

Hüwelmeier, Gertrud. 2018. Ghost markets and moving bazaars in Hanoi's urban space. In Kirsten Endres & Ann Marie Leshkowich (eds.), *Traders in motion*, 69–80. Ithaca, NY: Cornell University Press.

Hüwelmeier, Gertrud & Kristine Krause. 2010. Der Heilige Geist im Gewerbegebiet. Transformationen der religiösen Landschaft Berlins am Beispiel pentekostaler Netzwerke. *Berliner Blätter* 53. 83–95.

Jørgenson, Jan Norman, M.S. Karrebaek, L.M. Madsen & J.S. Moller. 2011. Polylanguaging in superdiversity. *Diversities* 13(2). 23–37.

Leshkowich, Ann Marie. 2014. *Essential trade. Vietnamese women in a changing marketplace.* Honolulu, HI: University of Hawai'i Press.

Vertovec, Steven. 2007. Super-diversity and its implications. *Ethnic and Racial Studies* 29(6). 1024–1054.

Werbner, Pnina. 2015. The dialectics of urban cosmopolitanism: Between tolerance and intolerance in cities of strangers. *Identities: Global Studies in Culture and Power* 22 (5), Special Issue: *Mobility and Cosmopolitanism*. 569–587.

Wimmer, Andreas & Nina Glick Schiller. 2002. Methodological nationalism and beyond. Nation-state building, migration and the social sciences. *Global Networks* 2 (4).301–334.

Patrick Stevenson

15 Moving stories: writing Berlin lives

1 Introduction

Like other global cities, Berlin has a long history of inward migration, absorbing incomers as diverse as Huguenot and Bohemian refugees in the 17th and 18th centuries on the one hand and post-1945 migrant workers from the Mediterranean rim and socialist states such as Cuba, Mozambique and Vietnam on the other (see, for example, Read and Fisher 1994; Weiss and Dennis 2005). All of these earlier migrations have left their traces in every aspect of social and cultural life, from cuisine to vernacular speech, enduring markers of influences that in many cases are no longer evident synchronically. However, the social and demographic composition of Berlin today is so heterogeneous and fluid that it almost seems to be defined by the confluence of strangers from all corners of the earth. Furthermore, contemporary migration flows are now often more particularized, more random, than the organized patterns of religious flight or labor recruitment in the past (Gogolin 2010; Vertovec 2007, 2010).

As the other chapters in this volume have shown, recent research on the increasing complexity of urban societies such as Berlin, arising from increased transnational mobility over the last 25 years, has highlighted different dimensions of diversity in terms of language knowledge and linguistic practices (see also Blommaert 2010, 2013; Rindler Schjerve and Vetter 2012). As a result, we are developing a deeper awareness and understanding of the scope and complexity of linguistic diversity in contemporary cities and we have gained many insights into the creative practices which have arisen as a result of intense and sometimes fleeting language contacts. In particular, we have acquired a more sophisticated appreciation of the possibilities afforded by multilingualism that offset the obstacles it is often considered to present and a more refined feel for what Gogolin and Meyer (2010: 525) call the "linguistic texture of migration societies".

In this concluding chapter I want to propose the addition of a biographical dimension to the study of the sociolinguistic economy of Berlin, taking an approach that is sensitive to individual responses to particular historical conditions and social circumstances, in order to try to understand the complexity of the migration experience in migrants' own terms. The focus here, then, is on the users, rather than the uses, of language and my aim is to explore – through one extended example – ways in which individuals with personal histories of

https://doi.org/10.1515/9781501508103-015

migration reflect on how their "lived experience of language" (Busch 2010, 2015) has shaped their transnational life worlds and ways in which they structure their life stories around these experiences, both in the present and in the past. The title of the chapter is consciously ambiguous: such stories are about their narrators' experiences of moving from one place to another and they are also often moving in their emotional impact on their tellers (and, indeed, their audiences).

I adopt here a particular orientation on what Busch (2010: 58) calls *Spracherleben*, by which she means

> how people living in multilingual contexts perceive and evaluate the particularity of their linguistic knowledge and what experiences, feelings or ideas they associate with it. Or to put it another way: how they – in relation to others or to themselves – experience, position and represent themselves as multilingual. What we're concerned with is the relationship between the lived experience of language and individual life stories on the one hand, and historical-social configurations with their constraints, power structures, discourse formations and language ideologies on the other. [my translation]

This approach entails a speaker-centred perspective that tracks ways in which linguistic resources are compiled, enhanced or discarded in the course of an individual's life (Blommaert and Backus 2011). Applied to the experience of contemporary migrants in Berlin and other metropolitan cities, it means exploring how experiences with language shape transnational life worlds or, more figuratively still, what Brizić (2006) calls "the secret life of languages".

My discussion here draws on a larger ethnographically oriented study of "Berlin lives". Inspired by research in sociolinguistics (e.g. Block 2006; Burck 2005) and social anthropology (e.g. Bahloul 1996; Bezirksamt Neukölln 1996a, b; Miller 2008), as well as the documentary journalism of Irina Liebmann (2002), the project explores the concept of *Spracherleben* through the language biographies (Franceschini 2010; Franceschini and Miecznikowski 2004; Nekvapil 2000, 2003; Stevenson and Carl 2010) of inhabitants of a single apartment block in an inner-city district of Berlin. The building is the domicile of a random collection of "intimate strangers" (Mac Giolla Chríost 2007: 15), almost all of whom have a migration background, and in its changing ethnic and linguistic composition it reflects the shifting ethnolinguistic mosaic of the city. The ultimate aim of the study is to compose a kind of biography of the house, but I will concentrate here on developing the idea of life (hi)stories as language stories. Focusing on one inhabitant of the building, I want to show what doing "biographical work" means in this context and how narrating experiences with language involves creating stories of biographical transformation (Treichel and Bethge 2010: 113).

2 Life stories as language stories

Language biographies are a particular kind of life story, normally constructed by individuals in collaboration with a researcher, in which the narrators reflect on their experiences with language in the course of their lifetimes and use this reflection as a focused way of organising their personal history. They are therefore also a special kind of discourse on language in two senses. First, as a personal travelogue through space and time they create a diachronic dimension of language use by drawing on individual and collective resources of memory and projecting past experiences onto present circumstances (and in some cases into the future). They give voice to individuals affected by social change and allow them to transform their experience into stories that build "story worlds", or "storied worlds" (Schiffrin 1996, 2002), within which they can assemble disparate fragments of memory into a more or less coherent and continuous account or version of their lives and construct a sense of self. Such "memory narratives" are therefore an opportunity to reinterpret the past from the perspective of the present, but they may also, as I shall try to show, offer an opportunity to revisit the past in order to recreate or reclaim something that has been lost or removed. A life story is thus "more than a recital of events" (Rosenwald and Ochberg 1992: 8–9), a simple chronicle, for although temporal ordering is an essential element of composing a story (De Fina 2003: 11) achieving coherence and continuity entails a substantial editorial process in which "events are selected, compressed, shaped, recreated and reconstructed for the occasion of the telling" (Cortazzi 2001: 388–389), so that every story is an interpretation of experience.

Secondly, it follows from this first point that language biographies are a "privileged locus for the negotiation of identities" (De Fina, Schiffrin, and Bamberg 2006: 16), and a form of "situated discursive practice" (De Fina 2003: 5) which gives individuals an opportunity to process and develop personal identities "online" (Georgakopoulou 2007), from a contemporary perspective in which the relationships between different language forms – in the case to be discussed here, Turkish, (varieties of) Kurdish and German – have been recontextualized in relation to changed social, political and economic conditions. Telling these stories is, then, a form of writing history "from below" (Finnegan 1997: 74–5); they are reflective accounts of how people choose to make language relevant in their construction of their place in the world.

In the present context, I am interpreting narrative as what De Fina and Tseng (2017: 382) call a "mode of understanding", deployed here as a means of "building knowledge about processes of displacement and relocation as lived by narrators and their stories' protagonists", using stories "both as objects and as tools" of research. More specifically, I see language biographies as a particular kind of narrative in which individuals with first-hand experience of migration articulate this experience in terms of ways in which it is conditioned and shaped by the translocation from one "(socio)linguistic regime" (Gal and Woolard 2001) to another and by their (often changing) relationships with language in general as well as with particular linguistic varieties.

3 Researching language in the city

First, however, I want to explain my approach to the challenge of researching language in the city. A key issue for the present volume is the relationship between the two concepts "language" and "city". Linguists tirelessly problematize their principal object of study, deconstructing "language" in one breath only to rehabilitate it in the next (Makoni and Pennycook 2007), but with relatively few exceptions (most notably perhaps Mac Giolla Chríost 2007; Block 2006) rarely allow their research to be inhibited by similar misgivings over their understanding of the urban location in which much of it takes place. In sociolinguistics, "the city" is typically no more than a setting or venue in which linguistic (inter) actions occur (see also introduction to this volume). A second fundamental issue is the question of scale: beyond the broad brush of statistical analyses, how can we seriously construct an account of language knowledge, practices or perceptions in an entire city that can lay claim to any kind of representativeness?

Complicating both of these perspectives, the particularity and the scope of the contemporary city in which language is observed, is the process by which the gradual accretion of physical, social and cultural features of the urban environment is erased in our consciousness, so that cumulative and constantly changing versions of the city collapse into a single "synchronized" image in the here and now. The city that we perceive is thus a kind of palimpsest, in which historical layers are obscured. Blommaert (2013: 11–13) argues that we do the same thing with our language resources: words, expressions, styles, manners of speaking that have "different historicities" and therefore different "indexical loads". They co-exist in what he calls "layered simultaneity" but are elided in everyday practice through what he refers to as "synchronization": "an act of interpretation in which the different historical layers of meaning are folded into one 'synchronic' set of meanings".

Urban sociolinguistics should therefore foreground the tight and complex layering of relationships between language, time and place, and the tensions arising from these relationships motivated much of the research on the indexicality of different varieties of German in Berlin before and after 1989 (Stevenson 2002, consider also Schlobinski this volume). In the decades following the *Wende*, however, the linguistic profile of the emerging city has been characterized less by intralinguistic variation than by burgeoning multilingualism, the result of rapidly increasing and diversifying social movements. Yet, the much-vaunted cosmopolitanism of today's Berlin is not new: as indicated above, phases of migration into Berlin can be traced back across its eight centuries. We can lose sight of these earlier migrations if we restrict our gaze to the post-1945 context, dominated initially by labor migration in both East and West, which has now been overlaid by multiple new and intersecting forms of mobility: from all corners of the world, permanent and temporary, voluntary and enforced, in search of work or learning, leisure or refuge.

So the social stratigraphy of the city is deep and complex, and the diversity of the present is an inflection of the diversities of the past. From my perspective, seeking to understand the nuanced ways in which confrontations with unfamiliar language regimes shape the experience of migration, the challenge was how to represent this diversity as normality and how to capture the randomness of urban co-existence without sacrificing coherence in the narrative. Film director Volker Heise confronted a similar issue when he sought to capture what he saw as the essence of urban life: "maximale Verschiedenheit auf engstem Raum" [maximum diversity in the most limited space] (programme notes, *24h Berlin*). How, he asked himself, do we narrate a city today? His solution, realized first in Berlin and later in Jerusalem, was to recruit multiple local film teams to record simple events of everyday life across the city in a single 24-hour period, edit them into a single documentary lasting exactly 24 hours and then broadcast it in real time. In this way, he aims to narrate the city through its people, but "we tell stories not about but of people ... we don't present them, we try to understand them through the way they construct their own lives" [my translation] (programme notes, *24h Berlin*).

Heise's Berlin film is a creative intervention into the life of a city through the lives of its inhabitants: he is telling a story about their stories by knitting them together into a single fabric and allowing patterns to emerge. On a much less ambitious scale, I have attempted in a recent project (Stevenson 2017) to do something similar with the language biographies of a small group of five individuals who had nothing in common other than the first-hand experience of migration – and a shared address, an apartment block (*Mietshaus*) in Neukölln, which I refer to as Mareschstraße 74. The aim was to compose an integrated account of their stories about language in the city.

The appeal of a single bounded location such as this is that it gives a localized context for studying diversity, access to the detail beneath the banality of generalization. Apartment buildings, in particular, are attractive as research sites as they embody some of the fundamental characteristics of the city:

- they combine order and disorder (through communal rules and individual behaviours);
- they embody the urban paradox of stability and change (with long-term residents on the one hand and irregular flows of occupants on the other);
- and their random assemblage of inhabitants exemplifies the archetypal "intimate strangers", living "in close physical proximity and distant social propinquity" (Mac Giolla Chríost 2007: 9).

The Berlin *Mietshaus* is a hyperlocal environment that may or may not constitute a place-based "community" or a "neighborhood under one roof"; the older social complexity of 19th century courtyards (*Hinterhöfe*), with dwellings, businesses and workshops, services and leisure opportunities, is now rare since these different functions and activities have been dispersed within and across locations. But for today's inhabitants of Mareschstraße 74 both physical and virtual translocal ties abound, articulated and instrumentalized in their stories: for example, the reclusive Marek's frequent cross-border journeys to the small Polish town where he adopts an alternative, gregarious persona; Ludmila's nostalgic yearning for the conviviality of her home in the Caucasus; or Hoa's repeated invocations of her native Hanoi as it figured in her life at various times between the mid-1950s and the present (see Stevenson 2017 for detailed discussion of their stories). Gathered by chance in one building, perhaps only provisionally the end point of their travels, these story-tellers tell tales that restore a sense of movement and dynamism to their circumstances by regenerating the transitional trajectories of their lives.

The cosmopolitan milieu of Mareschstraße 74 today presents a radically different world of experience from the apartment block investigated 40 years earlier by Irina Liebmann, but her study provided an important methodological orientation for my own project (Liebmann 2002).[1] She interviewed 32 inhabitants of a *Mietshaus* in Prenzlauer Berg, today a super-trendy, gentrifying tourist hotspot, but at that time (in 1980) an unrenovated district in East Berlin popular with artists and intellectuals. The building was chosen at random and Liebmann engagingly describes what happens when you ring one doorbell after another and begin chatting to the inhabitants in a way that I think concisely captures the essence of the exercise and, for me, its appeal. What you get, she says is (2002: 7 [all translations my own]):

1 Liebmann's book was first published by the Mitteldeutscher Verlag in the GDR in 1982 but the references here are to the edition published by the Berlin Verlag in 2002.

> a montage of [such] life episodes, refracted from the unique to the infinite, combined by a shared living space, a frame which, like the accounts themselves, is coincidental and inevitable.

The conversations she conducted were unprepared – either by her or her participants – and consisted of a spontaneous "combination of biography, recollection and commentary". She is at pains to stress that she took her participants seriously and made no attempt to "check" their stories:

> The narrator could make his [sic] own choice, I took seriously the version he had found for me at the moment we met: his presentation of his own space and its occasional contact with world history/events, **both** in the everyday aroma of roast potatoes.

However, while her participants were demographically broadly homogeneous (ethnically German tenants), the residents of many Berlin apartment blocks today are diverse in different ways from their original occupants: now there may be a mixture of owner-occupiers, individual renters and communal groups, and they are likely (in some areas at least) to come from many parts of the world. So the Berlin *Mietshaus* is rich with potential as both a research site and a metaphor for contemporary urban life. Like Liebmann, I chose my particular site because of its ordinariness: it is like the Berlin street in a story by Günter Kunert, which is "rich in promise, the same as a hundred others and quite unique" (Kunert 1968; translation from Marven and Constantine 2009: 44). The house was "rich in promise" for me as its inhabitants had very different backgrounds. The five individuals I chose to write about are not "representative" of any social category other than, perhaps, "new Berliners"; their stories are offered as exemplary not of "the migration experience" itself but of ways of reconstructing the process of transition.

I see each of the participants from the perspective of what Busch (2015) calls the "experiencing" or "speaking subject", who is "formed through and in language" and in this way becomes – or makes themselves – a historical figure, a person in history. The speaking/experiencing subject is not only relating a small piece of their personal history but also, in doing so, they are locating or inserting themselves in(to) a wider and deeper social history. To illustrate this narrative process, here is the language biography of one of the participants: Ferhat's story.[2]

---

2 Ferhat's story is an extract from Stevenson (2017), reproduced in edited form here by kind permission of the publisher, Palgrave Macmillan. The original German interview transcripts can also be found there.

4 Ferhat's story

Ferhat "assumes" his first language was Kurdish. He's not sure, as he was born and grew up in Istanbul speaking Turkish – his father insisted all the children should learn "proper" Turkish – but his mother could only speak Kurdish, the language she had brought with her from their village in the east of the country. So his earliest recollections of home communication are of a pattern common to many bilingual families: his mother spoke to him in Kurdish, he replied in Turkish. Why, then, has he brought up his own son speaking Kurdish – in Berlin?

To understand this, we need to unpack some of these key words in Ferhat's story – Turkish, Kurdish, even Berlin perhaps – and assemble both the chronology and the topography of his life (for discussion of these terms, see Stevenson 2017: 99). What complexities are condensed into simple naming terms and what effects does this have on our interpretation of Ferhat's experience? What is the relationship between languages, times and places in Ferhat's biography and how are these features woven together to form the fabric of his life?

Ferhat's use of these linguistic, ethnic and geographical terms in his story reveals a complex set of interlacing sensitivities. But there was a time when even these labels were not available to him, a time before he became fully aware of the political motivation for naming "languages", of the implications of "knowing" a particular "language" or of the potential consequences of declaring yourself a speaker of it. His parents and older siblings had moved to Istanbul shortly before he was born in 1963, and through them and the social environment in which he grew up he was exposed in particular ways to two different languages (or "linguistic varieties"). How far was he aware of this? How did he conceive of them?

Ferhat 1

> Ferhat: So I had two languages but not consciously, I mean I had this awareness through the discrimination of being a Kurd, sort of concealed, I didn't say in public that I know er [that] language, and I knew nothing at all about Kurds, Kurdistan. In my mind I thought, in our village we speak like this, I mean this language is ours, particular to us and nowhere else. What are we, which language do we speak? I knew, I was never informed: are there Kurds? What *is* that? I knew that my mother only spoke Kurd-, I mean only spoke a language that er we actually called it Kurmanci, amongst ourselves, that's what the language is called, Kurmanci, I thought, in our village they speak this language, I mean area around the village, and that was that.
>
> Patrick: So you didn't have a name for this language?
>
> Ferhat: The local language, I mean not Kurdish but we said Kurmanci, a dialect of Kurdish language, Kurmanci, *that's* what I heard.

Recounting his early experience of language in Istanbul now, in his late 40s, Ferhat the narrator brings both specialist knowledge about language and an ability to rationalize thought processes to his explanation of how young Ferhat, the protagonist in his story, responded to what he heard around him. Turkish is not mentioned at all at this point, its presence is only implicit in the claim that he didn't openly reveal his knowledge of Kurdish. In fact, he may not even have used the name 'Kurdish'. For the child, there was simply "a way of speaking" that was particular to the people in and around the village that his family came from: "in our village we speak like this"; and we have a name for the way we speak there, we call it *Kurmanci*.

Now, in retrospect, Ferhat can apply the concept of "a language", that may be seen as incorporating different varieties or "dialects", to bring this individual perception of speech practices into a wider analytical framework. And the narrator attributes to himself-as-protagonist a strong sense of linguistic ownership that is associated, exclusively, with his family and its place in the world: "In my mind I thought, in our village we speak like this, I mean this language is ours, particular to us and nowhere else … I thought, in our village they speak this language, I mean area around the village, and that was that." Narrator and protagonist momentarily trip over each other when Ferhat corrects himself as he is about to use, anachronistically in the context of his story, the term "the Kurdish language" to refer to his awareness as a child of the extent of his mother's linguistic repertoire. He replaces this with "a language that we actually called Kurmanci" and then confers legitimacy on this naming practice by asserting "[and] that is what the language is called".

Ferhat had, he says, *two* languages, "but not consciously". What can he mean by this? It seems clear from what he goes on to say that alongside the taken-for-granted Turkish language of his native city he was aware of the quite distinct Kurmanci that is, from the child's perspective, confined to the family's home village. But there is a nascent sense that languages or "ways of speaking" have to do with something more than place. "Kurdishness" and "being Kurdish" are portrayed as emergent concepts, perhaps present in his lexicon but not yet defined. What does seem to have been evident to the young Ferhat is a sense of peril attached to identifying with these concepts and that knowing what he can now call Kurdish would indicate a dangerous affiliation, exposing him to risk. His elder siblings had spoken Kurdish in the village but abandoned it on moving to Istanbul: "you were afraid you'd be laughed at if you spoke differently". The fear of "speaking differently", of not conforming to a strongly dominant norm, of making yourself conspicuous, was compelling.

So in the course of his socialization Kurdish acquired for Ferhat three associations: it was a localized "village language", a private "domestic language" and an emblematic "political language". It came to represent intersecting spatial, social and political worlds. He also became aware of another dimension, an extension of the others, as his father had to learn Turkish when he was called up for military service:

Ferhat 2

> Ferhat: The [Turkish] language was a man's language and the women's language was Kurdish. When men achieved something, for example, only then was Turkish spoken. It's, I mean women, the language was, in that sense too had a female status, in a negative sense, the language. And if you had a job you always spoke Turkish.

What he had thought of as his mother's language appeared, then, to be generalized as "the women's language", and Turkish was "a man's language". But more than that: the "gendering" of the two languages was part of an ideology that attributed inferior social value to women and reserved the possibility of individual achievement to men. Women were trapped inside the social position allocated to them and confined to – or perhaps by? – the language associated with that position. Men had the opportunity to "improve" their social standing through gaining employment and then publicly confirming, or ratifying, their personal advancement and change of status by adopting (however imperfectly) the more highly valued, non-local language.

However, the subsequent subversion of this language ideology by the political activism of women in the Kurdish movement is one of the ways in which Ferhat charts the revaluation of the Kurdish language. It is re-contextualized in his story precisely by the actions of "very open, strong women", who become engaged in the political process:

Ferhat 3

> Patrick: Did women's social status change?
>
> Ferhat: Yes. And especially in Kurdistan because the movement, Kurdish movement, because the women were very active. There were these military conflicts, that's to say it was mainly men who were involved in them, Kurdish men too, but then Kurdish women came too, they have their own army, I mean entirely women, they took on a lot of responsibility. That was on the one hand, and secondly on the legal level too, because the men weren't there, they took on a lot of active responsibility. For example, I can remember, about 15 years or so ago, the demos [political demonstrations], it was overwhelmingly women and children, because the police, Turkish police, of course if there are men there, then they take them away at once, to prison, torture, killing, everything. And so the women said of their own accord, we'll do it. I think, the movement, there are a lot of active women there.

He invokes "Kurdistan" here not primarily as a geographical location but as a site of struggle and radical social re-alignment, in opposition to the Turkish state, which figures – here and elsewhere in his narrative – in the guise of authority ("the police", emphatically "the Turkish police") associated with extreme political violence. And yet Ferhat doesn't represent himself in his story as unequivocally committed to a radical Kurdish identity and, as we'll see, Kurdistan for him is variously a space for political action, a physical space to visit as an outsider-insider and a virtual space, an idea.

I have dwelt on Ferhat's experiences in Turkey, before he moved to Berlin, because this is where the development of what he repeatedly calls his consciousness of linguistic and ethnic difference begins or, to be precise, where Ferhat the narrator situates it in his story. He began to wonder why his mother should have to struggle with another language to manage her shopping and now he rationalizes his tentative efforts to start speaking Kurdish with her in Istanbul as being motivated by a growing political awareness. Not only that, he also historicizes his actions and their motivations more broadly by placing them in the context of comparable political movements in western Europe that I, as his audience, would be more familiar with:

Ferhat 4

> Ferhat: I think my Kurdish was a bit political, it developed for political reasons. I mean, I can remember when I was in Istanbul, before I came [here], I had started, tried, to talk Kurdish with my mother, but that was really purely political, because I think at that time, I mean the 70s, '68 movements [Patrick: Mhmm], exactly, you had that in Turkey too, there was, exactly, this leftist movement and then also Kurdish, and this leftist movement was pro-Kurdish. They made an issue of it, I mean this taboo.

Gaining knowledge about discrimination, oppression and political violence changed Ferhat's understanding of language knowledge as a form of social capital, replete with potential risks and benefits. He came to realize that knowing what it meant to "be Kurdish" in Turkey bestowed a certain value on "speaking Kurdish" in Turkey. He began to speak his mother's tongue, the "village language", as an adolescent in the city of Istanbul, but his move as an adult to the metropolis Berlin was decisive not only in his personal development but also in the emergence of Kurdish as an active element in his linguistic repertoire. He came to Berlin as a student in the early 1990s, first studying electronics and computer science, but this was interrupted by a period of illness and he "fell into" work with the Red Cross, supporting Kurdish refugees. He subsequently trained as a social worker and now manages educational projects for young refugees from many parts of the world.

Here, in Berlin, he learned German, which he unquestioningly accepts as normal and as necessary:

Ferhat 5

> Ferhat: There are automatically languages that you speak. If you've grown up here, you speak German ... We live in Germany, the German language must be perfect, that's clear.

But it was here, too, that he found the right conditions to develop greater fluency in Kurdish, which in terms of the requirements of daily life he didn't strictly need. On the one hand, both as a student and in his subsequent working life, German was the dominant "public" language and, on the other hand, most of his friends were "Turkish". The drive to revive his dormant knowledge of Kurdish seems to fulfil some other, perhaps emotional, need. Although he says the lingering fear of personal sanctions against Kurdish-speakers was hard to shake off, his early experience in Berlin was liberating:

Ferhat 6

> Ferhat: Then I came here, then again I think more through political, I developed a bit. I started listening to Kurdish music, and then I went quite often to Kurdish cultural clubs, we played Kurdish music, came into contact like that, for a long time.

The contact with cultural traditions, uprooted from their geographical origins but also liberated from political constraints on practising them, created new opportunities for Ferhat to encounter the language associated with them. He also gradually learns to *read* Kurdish, a skill previously precluded by the fear of surveillance but one that becomes possible in the "free space" of Berlin and that will become important to him in bringing up his children:

Ferhat 7

> Patrick: You hadn't read Kurdish before that?
>
> Ferhat: No, because it was forbidden. Kurdish literature, perhaps there were a few but if there were then we were afraid to buy, I mean, we were afraid, secret police, if I buy that at a stall then it's noted straight away. So that's why I never had that in Turkey ... Here of course there was a free space for Kurdish and Kurds, and here my language developed.

Since Kurds of all nationalities come together in the diaspora in Berlin, he finds that Kurmanci is a lingua franca he shares, for example, with Syrian Kurds, so that communicating with them is easier than with Turkish speakers of other

Kurdish varieties such as Zaza or Sorani. And the "free space" he now inhabits allows him to explore political territory into which he had previously lacked the linguistic means and the confidence to venture in Kurdish:

Ferhat 8

> Ferhat: You can have a conversation, but beyond that, I mean if you're talking about politics for example, that came very very late with me. Whether you know the words, mentally I wasn't so prepared to talk about political things in Kurdish, in a serious way, I mean on an intellectual level. It wasn't, you know, switch over straight away, even if he's er a Kurd we still switched automatically into Turkish, although we're Kurds. And so in that sense the language became higher because it has a different value in Turkey now, I mean estimation, through the movement, parties and so on the language became more legitimate. It's not just a village language. On Turkish television now there are Kurdish speakers right up to professors, you know, speaking Kurdish, they say academic things in Kurdish, and at first I had to laugh.

What he perceives as the new legitimacy of Kurdish, no longer "just a village language" but a broadcastable idiom for serious scientific discourse, conjures the prospect of a new option, a new form of identification. Speaking Kurdish in Berlin is not a communicative necessity, it's a creative act that enables, or facilitates, the construction of a more complex self. But why should this matter to Ferhat? Developing and sustaining a third language alongside the languages of local belonging requires a considerable investment of time and energy. He talks a number of times about the "political motivation" for his language learning, so does this imply a growing attachment to some form of Kurdish identity?

Perhaps. But the indications in his narrative are ambivalent in this respect. In the passage above he says that switching into Turkish to discuss political issues had been an automatic procedure "even if we are Kurds"; in the context, though, this could be shorthand for "even though we are Kurdish-speakers". On another occasion, when explaining to me the relationship between the different varieties of Kurdish, Ferhat says, apparently distancing himself from "the Kurds": "There are, well, the Kurds say dialect, I say language, the Kurds don't want to call it that". And this impression is reinforced when he seeks to position himself more explicitly:

Ferhat 9

> Ferhat: In terms of mentality, I'm still an Istanbuler, I mean, I don't call myself a Kurd but an Istanbuler, so in terms of mentality I'm from the city. And I always made friends in that way, overwhelmingly Turkish friends. But once I was here we often discussed Kurds and Kurdistan. But I didn't leave, there are people who leave and really move into the Kurdish milieu. I stayed here, for a long time I had almost only Turkish friends, but still acknowledged.

Here, "Kurds" and "Kurdistan" are objects of discussion, not of identification, and there is a "Kurdish milieu" – a looser concept than "community" and one that doesn't seem to imply or require membership – to which he could have access and in which he could immerse himself, but he chose not to do so. And he is, categorically, "not a Kurd" but "an Istanbuler", a city person. So, I asked in another conversation later, just to be clear about this, he would call himself an "Istanbuler"?

Ferhat 10

> Ferhat: Not really, Istanbul Kurd, I mean, not Kurdistani … My town, the way the migrants live here, you know, in Berlin, they say I'm a Berliner of Turkish descent, you know, you can put it like that, Istanbul mentality and so on, because in Istanbul many people congregated there, Istanbul Lasa [people from the southern Caucasus, mostly now living in north-eastern Turkey], ethnic, or Arabs, you can also say Istanbul Arabs, that's how I label myself. But not from Kurdistan, saying I come from Kurdistan, I can't, I don't say that.
>
> Patrick: You wouldn't say that?
>
> Ferhat: No no, I'm not from Kurdistan, I'm from Istanbul. I'm a Kurd from Istanbul.

On reflection, then, he prefers the more complex, composite category of "Istanbul Kurd" or, on further consideration and with a slight shift of emphasis, "Kurd from Istanbul". At all events, he is insistent in his rejection of Kurdistan as his place of origin or a place to which he owes allegiance. However, this is not to say that Kurdistan has no place in his life. It recurs in his story as what I would like to call a "locus of orientation", a point around which he assembles formative experiences that give meaning and coherence to the disparate components of his sense of self. We have already seen how Kurdistan became an object of discussion for him amongst his social circle in Berlin and how he refers to it more concretely, if still not in a clearly defined way, in the context of political conflict and social change in Turkey. It assumes additional significance when he talks about his travels with his children, visiting parts of Turkey and northern Iraq, as – this is my formulation – a "Kurd from Istanbul living in Berlin".

If the move to Berlin opened up the "free space" for Ferhat to develop his active use of Kurdish, a visit from his new Berlin home to "Turkish Kurdistan" revealed to him previously unsuspected possibilities with the Kurdish language:

Ferhat 11

> Ferhat: I went on a trip to Kurdistan once with my friends, for the first time a trip to Kurdistan back home in Turkey, and I noticed "Oh, the language is being used very well" [for example, in local elections].

This direct exposure to increased use of Kurdish in the region, complemented by its growing media presence, seems to have encouraged his personal project, but he realized that the lack of institutional support – in Turkey, let alone in Berlin – meant that sustaining this language required substantial individual motivation and determination: "You have to make a conscious decision, because there is no school, no institutions to give automatic support, you have to decide, I want to maintain this language, you know?". German and Turkish can apparently take care of themselves, but Kurdish needs to be nurtured. For Ferhat, the turning point, he says, came with the birth of his children: the Kurdish language project on which he had tentatively embarked himself years earlier was converted into a policy for the next generation. But if Kurdish was – in practical terms – a superfluous linguistic resource for Ferhat, in which he had chosen to invest for his own purposes, why would he impose this burden on his Berlin-born children?

The plan was ambitious and would demand commitment and consistency of application, not least since Ferhat was still in some sense a "learner" himself and opportunities for his children to use Kurdish in Berlin were relatively limited. Nevertheless, he used exclusively Kurdish (which was "very hard work") with his first child, his son Zoran, and his wife spoke only German, her first language. He was confident that Zoran would learn Turkish "one way or another", as it was a "dominant language" in the neighborhood, and when the time came Zoran attended a German-Turkish bilingual primary school. At first, Ferhat was apprehensive about the school's attitude towards his language practices, but: "So far I've had no negative experiences, I still speak Kurdish with him, even when I'm picking him up from school, everyone knows it's my language". "It's my language": speaking Kurdish openly with his son in the institutional context of a school privileging Turkish alongside German, and acknowledging or even claiming it as his own, is a declaration of loyalty to the language that shows how far his confidence and conviction have risen since leaving Istanbul.

This "one parent, one language" model is, of course, widely used in bilingual families. But here there is a twist:

Ferhat 12

> Ferhat: Then my daughter was born and then, this time, that was a bit of a test for me. I sort of felt my Turkish was under pressure, my Turkish. But this, Turkish was of course an important language for me.

Having “banned himself”, as he puts it, from speaking Turkish or German to his son, he now felt himself pulled in another direction: “And after that I said to myself it’s a bit hard but I must bring the language into the family somehow, the Turkish language, you know?”. In his determination to promote Kurdish as a family language, he had inadvertently relegated his other legacy language, Turkish, out of the home into the street and the classroom. His solution was to complicate his policy further by speaking only Turkish with his daughter, resulting in trilingual conversations around the breakfast table and both children developing partially overlapping repertoires, speaking German to each other and acquiring a passive knowledge of each other’s “father language”.

When I first spoke with Ferhat, his son and daughter were 7 and 5 years old respectively. Three years later, I was curious to know how his plan was working out. His son has now moved to a *Gymnasium* (a secondary school leading to the *Abitur*, the university entrance qualification), where all the teaching is delivered in German, but Ferhat is pleased with his son’s progress:

Ferhat 13

> Ferhat: My son speaks Kurdish now and can also understand Turkish. That’s achieved what I wanted. He has Turkish friends, neighbors, so the Turkish language isn’t completely lost to him. He can even say a few things, but he can certainly understand.

The perhaps surprising development is that he is now also speaking some Kurdish with his daughter, a change that he negotiated with her:

Ferhat 14

> Patrick: She always heard Kurdish.
>
> Ferhat: Yes yes, she understands when someone speaks Kurdish, then she definitely understands. I said, at school you’re learning Turkish very well [she is now at the bilingual primary school], she also speaks Turkish, and then I said, so that you also get to be strong in Kurdish I’ll speak Kurdish to you, ok? She says yes, she was pleased.

But he takes a cautious approach in this respect, because Turkish is still “more dominant” in Berlin, and he wants to leave language choices to the children themselves: “they have a free choice, so the pressure is on me really; I made the offer, I’ll speak Kurdish, you can answer in German”.

The real measure of the success of Ferhat’s language policy, in his terms, becomes apparent when he talks about his travels with his son to Turkey and Iraq. Ferhat’s double experience of migration – the indirect experience of his family's internal migration from the rural east to cosmopolitan Istanbul, then his own move to Berlin – recontextualized his knowledge of Turkish and Kurdish twice. In Istanbul, Turkish was unchallenged as the default language of the public sphere; the family language Kurdish/Kurmanci was stigmatized and marked as rural, backward and politically suspect, and so it became confined to the domestic domain. Ferhat then found that Turkish retained a dominant status in his Berlin social world, alongside the state language German, but here Kurdish was liberated from the denigration to which it was subjected in Istanbul and he felt able to embrace it more confidently. The displacement of the language made it possible for him, for the first time, to own it. For Zoran, however, whose experience of migration is entirely second-hand, Kurdish has always been simultaneously a domestic language – through his father's choice, as an act of affirmation rather than as an act of protective seclusion – and a language out of place. For him, therefore, Kurdish needed to be "emplaced"[3] in order for it to achieve something meaningful in his life.

Creating what for me was an unexpected symmetry in his story world, Ferhat enacts this emplacement or relocation of Kurdish by narrating not only (unsurprisingly) his visits with his son to the family village but also several trips to Iraqi Kurdistan:

Ferhat 15

> Ferhat: I've often gone to Kurdistan with him. Iraq had a big influence on him. I mean, I'm fine with the language, you know, but I've never had a Kurdish flag and so on, I mean, I'm not like that, flags and so on, but children have a different perspective. When we were there: "Kurdish flag, what *is* that?" For him that was sort of another world. I always offered him theoretical, language and so on, but he couldn't picture how it functioned like that, that society. And then of course they saw: "Soldiers!", you know, Peshmerga, "Kurdish, they're Kurds, wow". They'd seen Turkish things, and German, but never Kurdish. Then they spoke Kurdish with them, amazing, you can't imagine, and of course they were nice, you know, played with the children and so on, so it was a pretty good experience, that Kurdish is spoken everywhere.

The endorsement of Kurdish that Ferhat had experienced on his travels with his friends in parts of Turkey where the language was becoming more widely used in public life had allowed him to recalibrate the language in relation to others. Here he lets Zoran voice his sense of wonder, curiosity and excitement at hearing his

3 The concept of emplacement is used by Scollon and Scollon (2003) to refer to an aspect of geosemiotic theory that deals with the location of linguistic signs in the physical world. I am using it here in an extended sense to refer to the social and geographical location or "situatedness" of linguistic varieties.

private, family language transported from the banality of domestic discourse to a wholly new world of public experience. Suddenly, "Kurdishness" is translated from the abstract "theoretical" domain to a physical realm replete with the powerful symbolism of flags and soldiers' uniforms, offering an entirely new source of identification – "so *they* are Kurds" – and they are speaking his language.

What was the impact of this experience, I wondered, and I asked: "Until then he'd only spoken Kurdish with *you*?".

Ferhat 16

> Ferhat: With me or within a small group ... And when we came back I noticed that his interest in Kurdish was higher. He started to answer in Kurdish, that was a step up. Until then he'd said very little, just words, not sentences, but since then he's started to speak Kurdish.

Both father and son had encountered Kurdish through parental input, in the one case by necessity, in the other as a matter of policy. Both father and son developed their fluency and proficiency in the parent's language only when it acquired a political dimension – in the broadest sense of the term – and in both cases this metaphorical journey required a physical journey, but in opposite directions.

In Istanbul, Ferhat stumbled awkwardly onto his mother's linguistic territory, but he found his feet when he discovered that Kurdish was a Berlin language, one of many, one that allowed him to bridge the geographical distance separating him from the Kurdish homeland by using it to explore the previously suppressed part of his family's life remotely, from afar. Zoran's visits with his father to Iraqi Kurdistan ignited his Kurdish consciousness and aligned the language with other symbolic representations of Kurdishness. These different experiences appear in Ferhat's narrative as similarly transformative moments that gave him and his son a licence to speak in a new way.

These episodes and these experiences ultimately lead both father and son "back" to "our village", the village where neither of them was born and that neither has lived in but which Ferhat's family left to move to Istanbul and where he and his siblings are now building a shared house. Here, Zoran discovers that his knowledge of Kurdish constitutes a form of local social capital:

Ferhat 17

> Ferhat: It's good that he had very little Turkish, he's still only got a little, because he can express himself very well in Kurdish but not in Turkish, and that's good because in our village they also speak Turkish but they can speak Kurdish too, and through my son they're *forced* to speak Kurdish ... And I think he influenced the others.

Many other families have followed the same route that Ferhat's had taken, migrating to Turkish-speaking cities and leaving Kurdish behind. And when they return with their children in the summer, they bring Turkish with them. But Zoran's relative lack of proficiency in Turkish is – from his father's perspective at least – an opportunity to exploit his knowledge of Kurdish and even to encourage others to do so too. So at the end of Ferhat's story, Kurdish/ Kurmanci has become, again, but now in a positive way, a "village language". And it concludes, poignantly, with an image of the young Berliner Zoran breezily chatting to his grandmother in their shared local language in a way that Ferhat had not managed with her in *his* childhood:

Ferhat 18

> Ferhat: My aim was that they should enjoy the language, now they enjoy the language. And with my mother for example [he] has a very good relationship. I always listen to them talking in the kitchen, in the house in the village, he tells her Kurdish things. If it wasn't for this language, he would never have got to know my mother, I mean not really got to know her intimately.

There are apparent inconsistencies, perhaps even contradictions, in Ferhat's narrative and the tensions between "then and now" and "there and here" in his life story are not fully resolved. His migration from Turkey to Germany appears to be permanent and he feels "at home" in Berlin, and yet he is building a house in "our village". The life he constructs in his story moves between three locations – the family village, Istanbul and Berlin – and the three languages / language varieties in his repertoire jostle with each other for significance in relation to the places and relationships that matter to him. Maintaining his complex linguistic repertoire, and transferring it in a different configuration to his children, has imposed a substantial burden on him. But his multilingual project and his efforts to sustain it provide a common strand through his narrative and create a sense of coherence across the disparate elements of his experience.

5 Conclusions

Language figures in Ferhat's narrative not so much in terms of linguistic knowledge or skills, although these have their role to play, and the same applies to the narratives of the other inhabitants of Mareschstraße 74. These stories deal more with moments or phases in their narrators' lives (times that psychotherapist Charlotte Burck (2005) refers to as "languaged periods", similar in turn to

Pujolar and Puigdevall's *mudes* or "biographical junctures" (2015))[4]when linguistic actions have had (potentially) transformative effects or when certain kinds of language knowledge have created or obstructed opportunities. And they deal with ways in which the narrators have developed their own "(socio) linguistic regime" as a means to find their own place in the social worlds they move into.

The German term *Selbstverortung* – self-emplacement, or "locating your self yourself" – captures very well this active process of accommodation or "becoming at home": of *Beheimatung*, as psychologist Beate Mitzscherlich (2000) calls it, understanding *Heimat* not as a place but as a condition, a state of mind. So the "story about stories about language" is ultimately about different ways in which individuals "find a place for themselves" in the diverse and cosmopolitan environment of the city and how they knit together some of the "languaged moments" in their lives.

What I hope has emerged from the project as a whole is a set of different "Berlin lives", versions of how 5 people from different parts of the world (Turkey, Poland, Russia and Vietnam) with very different backgrounds and trajectories each, in their own way, used their experience with language to construct an account of how they negotiated their transition from one "life world" to another. Of course, my version is just one of many ways of representing these "lives" and I have deliberately left open the possibilities of further interpretation. But however partial and provisional they may be, their purpose is to reach out beyond the particular curiosity of individual experience to indicate ways of understanding and engaging with the lived experience of language in transnational contexts: through one extended vignette I have tried in this chapter to show how reflections on language use can help us peel away some of the historicized layers of experience with language that might otherwise remain submerged inside the homogenizing synchronic wrapping of the "multilingual migrant". More generally, I suggest that adopting a speaker-centred biographical approach to complement sociolinguistic analyses of language distribution and use may allow us to gain more nuanced insights into the complexity and creative potential of language in the city.

Acknowledgements: I would like to thank the two anonymous reviewers of the first draft of this chapter for their close critical engagement with my text and for their constructive comments.

4 I am grateful to an anonymous reviewer for drawing my attention to the concept of *mudes*.

References

24h Berlin – Ein Tag im Leben. 2009. Film directed by Volker Heise, co-produced by zero one film, rbb and ARTE.

Bahloul, Joelle. 1996. *The Architecture of Memory: A Jewish-Muslim household in colonial Algeria, 1937–1962*. Cambridge: CUP.

Bezirksamt Neukölln (ed.). 1996a. *Schillerpromenade 27, 12049 Berlin: Ein Haus in Europa*. Opladen: Leske & Budrich.

Bezirksamt Neukölln (ed.). 1996b. *Ein Haus in Europa: Stadtkultur im Museum*. Opladen: Leske & Budrich.

Block, David. 2006. *Multilingual Identities in a Global City*. Basingstoke: Palgrave.

Blommaert, Jan. 2010. *The Sociolinguistics of Globalization*. Cambridge: CUP.

Blommaert, Jan. 2013. *Ethnography, Superdiversity and Linguistic Landscapes*. Bristol: Multilingual Matters.

Blommaert, Jan & Ad Backus. 2011. Repertoires revisited: "knowing languages" in superdiversity. *Working Papers in Urban Language and Literacies* 67.

Brizić, Katharina. 2006. The secret life of languages. Origin-specific differences in L1/L2 acquisition by immigrant children. *International Journal of Applied Linguistics* 16(3). 339–362.

Burck, Charlotte. 2005. *Multilingual Living*. Basingstoke: Palgrave.

Busch, Brigitta. 2010. Die Macht präbabylonischer Phantasien. Ressourcenorientiertes sprachbiographisches Arbeiten. *Zeitschift für Literaturwissenschaft und Linguistik* 160. 58–82.

Busch, Brigitta. 2015. Linguistic repertoire and *Spracherleben*, the lived experience of language. *Working Papers in Urban Language and Literacies* 148.

Cortazzi, Martin. 2001. Narrative analysis in ethnography. In Paul Atkinson, Sara Delamont, Amanda Coffey, John Lofland & Lyn Lofland (eds.), *Handbook of Ethnography*, 384–394. London: Sage.

De Fina, Anna. 2003. *Identity in Narrative: A study of immigrant discourse*. Amsterdam: John Benjamins.

De Fina, Anna, Deborah Schiffrin & Michael Bamberg (eds.). 2006. *Discourse and Identity*. Cambridge: Cambridge University Press.

De Fina, Anna & Amelia Tseng. 2017. Narrative in the study of migrants. In Suresh Canagarajah (ed.), *The Routledge Handbook of Migration and Language*. 381–396. London: Routledge.

Finnegan, Ruth. 1997. Storying the self: personal narratives and identity. In Hugh Mackay (ed.), *Consumption and Everyday Life*. 65–111. London: Sage.

Franceschini, Rita (ed.). 2010. Sprache und Biographie. [Special issue]. *Zeitschrift für Literaturwissenschaft und Linguistik* 160.

Franceschini, Rita & Johanna Miecznikowski (eds.). 2004. *Leben mit mehreren Sprachen / Sprachbiographien*. Bern: Peter Lang.

Gal, Susan & Kathryn Woolard. 2001. Constructing languages and publics: authority and representation. In Susan Gal & Kathryn Woolard (eds.), *Languages and Publics: The making of authority*. 1–12. Manchester: St Jerome.

Georgakopoulou, Alexandra. 2007. *Small Stories, Interaction and Identities*. Amsterdam, Philadelphia: John Benjamins.

Gogolin, Ingrid. 2010. Stichwort: Mehrsprachigkeit. *Zeitschrift für Erziehungswissenschaft* 13(4). 529–547.

Gogolin, Ingrid & Meinert A. Meyer. 2010. Editorial. *Zeitschrift für Erziehungswissenschaft* 13(4). 525–528.

Kunert, Günter. 1968. Alltägliche Geschichte einer Berliner Straße. In Günter Kunert, *Die Beerdigung findet in aller Stille statt*, 24–28. Munich: Carl Hanser.

Liebmann, Irina. 2002. *Berliner Mietshaus*. Berlin: Berlin Verlag.

Mac Giolla Chríost, Diarmait. 2007. *Language and the City*. Basingstoke: Palgrave Macmillan.

Makoni, Sinfree & Alastair Pennycook (eds.). 2007. *Disinventing and Reconstituting Languages*. Clevedon: Multilingual Matters.

Marven, Lyn & Helen Constantine (eds.). 2009. *Berlin Tales*. Oxford: Oxford University Press.

Miller, Daniel. 2008. *The Comfort of Things*. Cambridge: Polity.

Mitzscherlich, Beate. 2000. *"Heimat ist etwas, was ich mache." Eine psychologische Untersuchung zum individuellen Prozess von Beheimatung*. Herbolzheim: Centaurus Verlag.

Nekvapil, Jiří. 2000. On non-self-evident relationships between language and ethnicity: how Germans do not speak German, and Czechs do not speak Czech. *Multilingua* 19(1–2). 37–53.

Nekvapil, Jiří. 2003. Language biographies and the analysis of language situations: on the life of the German community in the Czech Republic. *International Journal of the Sociology of Language* 162. 63–83.

Pujolar, Joan & Maite Puigdevall. 2015. Linguistic mudes: how to become a new speaker in Catalonia. *International Journal of the Sociology of Language* 231. 167–187.

Read, Anthony & David Fisher. 1994. *Berlin: Biography of a city*. London: Hutchinson.

Rindler Schjerve, Rosita & Eva Vetter (eds.). 2012. *European Multilingualism: Current perspectives and challenges*. Bristol: Multilingual Matters.

Rosenwald, George C. & Richard L. Ochberg. 1992. *Storied Lives: The cultural politics of self-understanding*. New Haven, London: Yale University Press.

Schiffrin, Deborah. 1996. Narrative as self-portrait: sociolinguistic constructions of identity. *Language in Society* 25(2). 167–204.

Schiffrin, Deborah. 2002. Mother and friends in a Holocaust survivor oral history. *Language in Society* 31(3). 309–354.

Scollon, Ron & Suzanne Scollon. 2003. *Discourses in Place: Language in the material world*. London: Routledge.

Stevenson, Patrick. 2002. *Language and German Disunity: A sociolinguistic history of East and West in Germany, 1945–2000*. Oxford: OUP.

Stevenson, Patrick. 2017. *Language and Migration in a Multilingual Metropolis: Berlin lives*. London: Palgrave Macmillan.

Stevenson, Patrick & Jenny Carl. 2010. *Language and Social Change in Central Europe: Discourses on policy, identity and the German language*. Edinburgh: EUP.

Treichel, Bärbel & Katrin Bethge. 2010. Neue europäische Mehrsprachigkeit. Zum Zusammenhang von Sprache und Biographie in europäischen Lebensgeschichten. *Zeitschrift für Literaturwissenschaft und Linguistik* 160. 107–128.

Vertovec, Steven. 2007. Super-diversity and its implications. *Ethnic and Racial Studies* 30(6). 1024–1054.

Vertovec, Steven. 2010. Towards post-multiculturalism? Changing communities, conditions and contexts of diversity. *International Journal of Social Science* 61(199). 83–95.

Weiss, Karin & Mike Dennis (eds.). 2005. *Erfolg in der Nische? Die Vietnamesen in der DDR und Ostdeutschland*. Berlin: Lit Verlag.

Index

https://doi.org/10.1515/9781501508103-016